VISUAL QUICKSTART GUIDE

MACROMEDIA FREEHAND MX

FOR WINDOWS AND MACINTOSH

Sandee Cohen

Peachpit Press

macromedia®
PRESS

Visual QuickStart Guide
Macromedia FreeHand MX for Windows and Macintosh
Copyright © 2003 by Sandee Cohen

Peachpit Press

1249 Eighth Street
Berkeley, CA 94710
800 283-9444 • 510 524 2178
fax 510 524 2221
Find us on the Web at http://www.peachpit.com
To report errors, please send a note to errata@peachpit.com

Published by Peachpit Press in association with Macromedia Press
Peachpit Press is a division of Pearson Education

Notice of Rights

Notice of Liability

Trademarks

Editor: Cary Norsworthy
Production Coordinator: Lisa Brazieal
Compositor & Interior Design: Sandee Cohen
Cover Design: The Visual Group
Copy Editors: Pamela Pfiffner and Dave Awl
Indexer: Steve Rath
ISBN 0-321-18650-8

0 9 8 7 6 5 4 3 2

Printed and bound in the United States of America

THANKS TO

Pam Pfiffner, my copy editor. At this point we are a well-oiled machine.

Dave Awl, copy editor from Peachpit. Not only did you do a great job on catching errors, but your dry wit made it a joy to make corrections.

Cary Norsworthy, my witty and eagle-eyed Peachpit editor. Thanks for all the support and terrific advice.

Toby Malina, who did a great technical edit.

Nancy Ruenzel, publisher of Peachpit Press.

Lisa Brazieal, production coordinator.

Steve Rath, who creates the best index in the business.

Ian Kelleigh, creator of freehandsource.com, for his help describing how the Flash action scripting works. His Web site is one of the best resources for FreeHand tips, techniques, history, and bug reports.

Diana Smedley of Macromedia. Thanks for the press briefing over breakfast.

Dave Halpin, FreeHand engineer. Any time you want to get together for coffee to discuss the future of computer graphics, I'm ready.

Olav Martin Kvern, who may have gone on to other programs, but still is a FreeHander at heart.

Michael Randazzo and the staff of the New School Computer Instruction Center.

Pixel, my cat. She did absolutely nothing to help me with this book. However, she gets very snippy if she isn't mentioned.

David Lerner and the brilliant technicians at **Tekserve.** You guys bailed me out when kernel panics threatened to derail my computer.

Colophon

This book was created using Macromedia FreeHand MX and Adobe Photoshop 7 for illustrations; Adobe InDesign 2 for layout; and Ambrosia SW Snapz Pro for screen shots. The computers used were a 450 MHz G4 Power Macintosh and a G4 PowerBook running Mac OS X.

FreeHand 10 for Windows ran on Virtual PC from Connectix. (No Intel inside.)
The fonts used were Minion and Futura from Adobe and two specialty fonts that I created myself.
A single cable modem Web connection was shared between computers using the miraculous Xsense XRouter Pro.

TABLE OF CONTENTS

INTRODUCTION

Welcome to learning Macromedia FreeHand. If you are like most people who are just starting out with the program, you may find it a little overwhelming. This Visual QuickStart Guide has been written to help you sort out the many different features.

FreeHand is one of the most versatile graphics programs for the computer. At its simplest, FreeHand is a vector drawing program. It allows you to create varied artwork such as drawings, logos, and illustrations.

FreeHand also lets you add scanned artwork from programs such as Macromedia Fireworks or Adobe Photoshop. This makes it an excellent layout program to create ads, book covers, posters, and so on. FreeHand has a multiple-page feature that allows you to create newsletters and flyers, as well as multi-page presentations with differently sized pages.

Finally, FreeHand uses the newest Flash technology to turn FreeHand artwork into animations. FreeHand also lets you save your files in formats that can be posted directly onto the World Wide Web.

Using This Book

The first few chapters provide overviews of the program. You may find that you do not create any artwork in those chapters. Do not skip them. They contain information that will help you later.

The middle chapters of the book contain the most artistic information. This is where you can see how easy it is to create sophisticated artwork using FreeHand.

The final chapters are about printing, preferences, and using your artwork with other applications and the Web. Some of this information refers to technical printing terms. If you are not familiar with these terms, speak to the print shop that will be printing your artwork.

Using the Exercises

If you have used any of the Visual QuickStart Guides, you will find this book very similar. Each of the chapters consists of numbered exercises that deal with a specific technique or feature of the program. As you work through each exercise, you gain an understanding of the technique or feature. The illustrations for each of the exercises help you judge if you are following the steps correctly.

Instructions

Working with a book such as this, it is vital that you understand the terms I am using. This is especially important since some books use terms somewhat incorrectly. Therefore, here are the terms I use in the book and explanations of what they mean.

Click refers to pressing down and releasing the mouse button on the Macintosh, and the left mouse button on Windows. You must release the mouse button or it is not a click.

Press means to hold down the mouse button, or the keyboard key.

Press and drag means to hold the mouse button down and then move the mouse. In later chapters, I use the shorthand term *drag*; just remember that you have to press and hold as you drag the mouse.

Menu commands

FreeHand has menu commands that you follow to open dialog boxes, change artwork, and invoke certain commands. These menu commands are listed in bold type. The typical direction to choose a menu command might be written as **Window > Panels > Style**. This means that you should first choose the Window menu, then choose the Panels submenu, and then choose the Style command.

Keyboard shortcuts

Most of the menu commands for FreeHand have keyboard shortcuts that help you work faster. For instance, instead of choosing New from the File menu, it is faster and easier to press the keys on the keyboard. On the Macintosh, the keys are Cmd-N. On Windows, the keys are Ctrl-N.

Keyboard shortcuts are sometimes listed in different orders by different software companies or authors. For example, I always list the Command or Ctrl keys first, then the Option or Alt key, and then the Shift key. Other people may list the Shift key first. The order that you press those modifier keys is not important. However, it is very important that you always add the last key (the letter or number key) after you are holding the other keys.

Learning keyboard shortcuts

While keyboard shortcuts help you work faster, you really do not have to start using them right away. In fact, you will most likely learn more about FreeHand by using the menus. As you look for one command, you may see others that you would like to explore.

Once you feel comfortable working with FreeHand, you can start adding keyboard shortcuts to your repertoire. My suggestion is to look at which menu commands you use a lot. Then each day choose one of those shortcuts.

For instance, if you do a lot of blends, you might decide to learn the shortcut for the Blend command. For the rest of that day use the Blend shortcut every time you need to make a blend. Even if you have to look at the menu to refresh your memory, still use the keyboard shortcut to actually apply the blend. By the end of the day you will have memorized the Blend shortcut. The next day you can learn a new one.

Onscreen element appearances

Some of the onscreen elements, such as the toolbars, may look different in this book from your settings. That's because I changed those panels to make them easier to read. For more information on customizing the toolbars, see Chapter 29.

Cross-platform issues

One of the great strengths of FreeHand is that it is almost identical on both the Macintosh and Windows platforms. In fact, at first glance it is hard to tell which platform you are working on. However, because there are some differences between the platforms, there are some things you should keep in mind.

Modifier keys

Modifier keys are always listed with the Macintosh key first and then the Windows key second. So a direction to hold the Command/Ctrl key as you drag means to hold the Command key on the Macintosh platform or the Ctrl key on the Windows platform. When the key is the same on both computers, such as the Shift key, only one key is listed.

Generally the Command key on the Macintosh (sometimes called the Apple key) corresponds to the Ctrl key on Windows. The Option key on the Macintosh corresponds to the Alt key on Windows. The Control key on the Macintosh platform does not have an equivalent on the Windows platform. Notice that the Control key for the Macintosh is always spelled out while the Ctrl key for Windows is not.

Platform-specific features

A few times in the book, I have written separate exercises for the Macintosh and Windows platforms. These exercises are indicated by (Mac) and (Win).

Most of the time this is because the procedures are so different that they need to be written separately. Sometimes features exist only on one platform. Those features are then labeled as to their platform.

Learning FreeHand

With a program as extensive as FreeHand, there will be many features that you never use. For instance, if you are a graphic artist or illustrator, you may never need any of FreeHand's text or layout features. Or you may never need to create charts or graphs. And if you are strictly a print person, you may never need to do any exporting as Web animations. Do not worry. It may be hard to believe but even the experts don't use all of FreeHand's features.

Find the areas you want to master, then follow the exercises. If you are patient, you will find yourself creating your own work in no time.

And don't forget to have fun!

Sandee Cohen (SandeeC@vectorbabe.com)
April 2003

FREEHAND BASICS 1

E ver wonder why houses are built from the ground up? After all, the basement is so dull, so basic. Why not start with something more flashy like the windows, the front door, or the roof? The reason is that if you don't have a firm foundation as you start building, your house won't stand very long.

The same is true when you learn a computer graphics program. As excited as you must be to learn Macromedia FreeHand, there are a few basics that we need to cover before we can go on to the fun stuff.

This chapter covers those basics: the onscreen panels and toolbars. So although you may be tempted to skip ahead to the fun stuff in the other chapters, please take a moment to look at what's here.

Think of this chapter asyour set of blueprints that will help you navigate through the rest of FreeHand.

Launching FreeHand

You open or launch the FreeHand application the same as most other computer programs.

To launch FreeHand:

◆ Double-click the FreeHand MX application icon ❶.

or

(Win) Choose **Start** > **Programs** > **Macromedia** > **FreeHand MX** ❷.

or

Double-click the icon for a previously saved FreeHand document ❸. This launches FreeHand and brings you directly to that document.

Onscreen Elements

When you launch FreeHand, you see the various onscreen elements that control the different aspects of the program ❹. These elements, called panels and toolbars, can be closed, opened, resized, or moved around the screen to suit your own work habits.

TIP FreeHand remembers the layout of the onscreen elements when you quit the program. The next time you open FreeHand, the panels and toolbars will be arranged in the same position.

❶ *You can launch FreeHand by double-clicking the* **FreeHand application icon.**

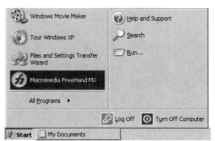

❷ *You can also launch FreeHand from the* **Windows Start menu.**

❸ *You can launch FreeHand by double-clicking the* **icon for a FreeHand document.**

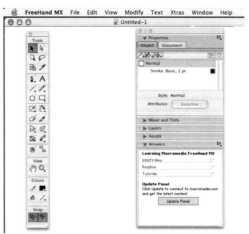

❹ *The* **default arrangement** *for the Tools panel and other panels.*

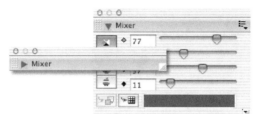

⑤ *The difference between a* **minimized panel** *(left) and a* **maximized panel** *(right).*

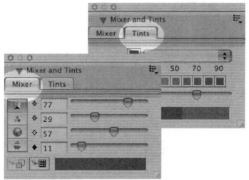

⑥ *Click the* **panel tab** *to switch from one panel to another in a panel group.*

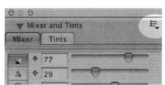

⑦ *Click the* **panel menu icon** *to open the menu for the active panel.*

⑧ *Use the* **Group [panel name] with** *submenu to move a panel from one group to another.*

Working with Panels

When you first install FreeHand, the panels are grouped into an arrangement that the Macromedia engineers thought you would like to work with. You can close and open the panels so they take up space on the screen only when needed.

To minimize and maximize panels:

◆ Click the triangle in the title bar of a panel **⑤**. When the triangle points down, all the elements in the panel are displayed. When the triangle points to the right, only the title bar of the panel is displayed.

Panels can be arranged into groups that are displayed under a single panel title bar with tabs for each panel in the group. You can then select each individual panel in the group.

To select a panel in a group:

◆ Click the tab for a panel **⑥**. That panel will become the active panel and will be displayed in front of the other panels in the group.

You can also move panels from one group to another.

To move panels between groups:

1. Click the panel menu icon for a panel **⑦**.

2. Choose one of the other panel groups from the Group [panel name] with submenu **⑧**.

   or

   Choose New Panel Group to separate the panel into its own group.

If you combine panels into a group, you can rename the group into a more general name for the group. For instance, the Color Mixer and Tints panels could be grouped under the name Color Controls.

To rename panels:

1. Choose Rename Panel Group from the panel menu. The title of the panel is replaced by a field.

2. Type the new name of the panel in the field **❾**.

3. Press the Return or Enter key to apply the new name to the panel.

You can combine panels or panel groups together with other panels or groups into an onscreen element called a *dock*. When panels are docked it makes it easier to move the panels around the screen.

To combine panels into a dock:

1. Drag a panel group by the gripper dots on the left side of the panel title bar **❿**.

2. Move the panel onto the area of another panel. A highlight appears **⓫**.

3. Release the mouse button. The panel is now docked with the other panels.

To move a panel out of a dock:

1. Drag the panel by the gripper dots away from the dock. A rectangle appears indicating the panel is outside the dock area **⓬**.

2. Release the mouse button. The panel appears as its own onscreen element.

❾ *You can* **rename a panel group** *by typing a new name in the title bar field.*

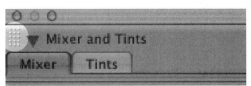

❿ *The* **gripper dots in a panel group** *let you move the panel in and out of a dock.*

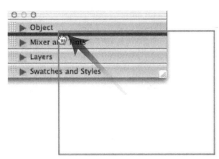

⓫ *The* **dock highlight** *shows you where a panel group will be added to the docked panels.*

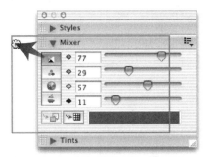

⓬ *Drag a panel to* **remove it from a dock.**

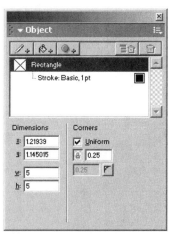

⓭ *The* **Object panel** *changes its display depending on the object that is selected.*

⓮ *The* **Document panel** *controls the document's pages and printer resolution.*

⓯ *The* **Answers panel** *provides links to information about FreeHand.*

Panel Descriptions

Each of the panels has a different function. Here is a brief description of what each panel does. This will help you decide which panels you need to have open as you work. *Note: The panels in these illustrations have been separated from their original panel groups to make it easier to see just the individual panels.*

Object panel

The Object panel (**Window > Object**) lets you set the fill, stroke, and effects for objects **⓭**. You can also set the text attributes for text blocks. The Object panel also sets the position and size attributes for objects. The Object panel changes its display depending on the type of object selected. The Object panel is one of the most important panels for styling objects in FreeHand.

Document panel

The Document panel (**Window > Document**) controls various attributes of the FreeHand document including creating and modifying pages **⓮**.

Answers panel

The Answers panel (**Window > Answers**) gives you quick links to what's new in FreeHand, tutorials, and other information about the program **⓯**.

Panel Descriptions

Layers panel

The Layers panel (**Window > Layers**) allows you to control the order in which objects appear onscreen 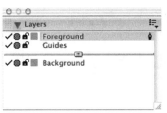. The Layers panel also lets you control the non-printing elements in the document. Layers can also be used as part of creating animations.

Swatches panel

The Swatches panel (**Window > Swatches**) lets you store colors and apply them as the strokes and fills for objects 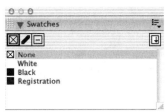.

Styles panel

The Styles panel (**Window > Styles**) lets you store the appearance of graphics and text as styles that can be easily reapplied to other objects .

Library panel

The Library panel (**Window > Library**) stores the graphic symbols that are used to help automate working with FreeHand 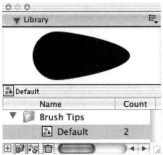. They are also used for working with brushes, master pages, and creating the symbols used when exporting as Flash (SWF) animations.

⑯ *The* **Layers panel** *controls the order in which objects appear.*

⑰ *The* **Swatches panel** *stores the colors used in your documents.*

⑱ *The* **Styles panel** *lets you store graphic and text styles.*

⑲ *The* **Library** *stores symbols for creating brushes, master pages, and Flash (SWF) animations.*

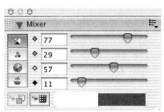

㉕ *The* **Mixer panel** *lets you define specific colors.*

㉑ *The* **Tints panel** *makes tints of colors.*

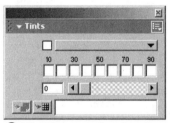

㉒ *The* **Halftones panel** *controls custom screens.*

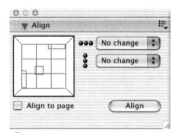

㉓ *The* **Align panel** *lets you align or distribute objects.*

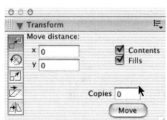

㉔ *The* **Transform panel** *lets you numerically move, rotate, scale, skew, or reflect objects.*

Mixer panel

The Mixer panel (**Window > Color Mixer**) allows you to define colors according to four different modes: CMYK, RGB, HLS, and the Macintosh or Windows color pickers **㉕**. These colors can be applied directly to objects or stored in the Swatches panel.

Tints panel

The Tints panel (**Window > Tints**) lets you create tints or screens of colors. You can apply the tints directly to objects or store them in the Swatches panel **㉑**.

Halftones panel

The Halftones panel (**Window > Halftones**) is used to set custom screens for objects such as tints, gradients, blends, and scanned images **㉒**. Custom screens are visible when artwork is printed.

Align panel

The Align panel (**Window > Align**) is used to align or distribute selected objects on their sides, tops, bottoms, and centers **㉓**. This ensures your layouts are neat and tidy.

Transform panel

The Transform panel (**Window > Transform**) allows you to move, rotate, scale, skew, or reflect objects by numerical controls **㉔**.

Panel Descriptions

Navigation panel

The Navigation panel (**Window** > **Navigation**) is used to add navigational elements and Flash commands to FreeHand documents .

Find & Replace Graphics panel

The Find & Replace Graphics panel (**Edit** > **Find & Replace** > **Graphics**) is used to make changes to many objects in a document 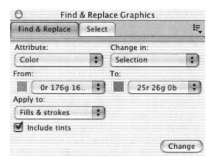 at the same time. For instance, you can search for all objects that contain a specific color and replace that color with another. You can also use the Select tab in the Find & Replace Graphics panel to select objects that have a specific attribute.

Find Text panel

The Find Text panel (**Edit** > **Find & Replace** > **Text**) is used to make changes to all the text in a document 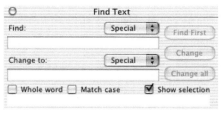. For instance, you can change all instances of one word into another.

The **Navigation panel** *is used to add navigational elements that are part of HTML, SWF, and PDF files.*

The **Find and Replace Graphics panel** *lets you make global changes to graphics in your documents.*

The **Find Text panel** *lets you make global changes to text in your documents.*

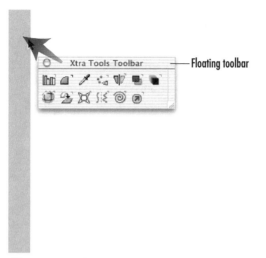

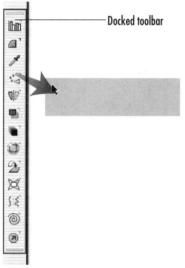

Drag a toolbar to dock it to the top, bottom, or left side of the work area.

Drag a toolbar to undock it from the sides of the work area.

Working with Toolbars

Toolbars are another type of onscreen element that contains tools and commands for working with FreeHand. Toolbars cannot be docked or grouped with panels. Toolbars can float anywhere onscreen or they can be positioned so they stick to the top, bottom, or left side of your work area. All the toolbars, except the Tools panel, are found under the **Window > Toolbars** submenu.

To dock a toolbar to the work areas:

1. Drag the title bar of the toolbar towards the edge of the work area.

2. When you see the gray box or outline of the toolbar, release the mouse ㉘. The toolbar appears inside a gray area that is part of the work area.

To released a docked toolbar:

1. Drag the toolbar out from the gray docking area.

2. When you see the gray box or outline of the toolbar, release the mouse button ㉙. The docked toolbar is converted into a floating toolbar.

TIP You can also customize toolbars so they display the exact commands and tools that you want. For instance, you can move the tools from the Xtra Tools toolbar over to the Tools panel.

Working with Toolbars

Toolbar Descriptions

FreeHand ships with seven toolbars arranged according to their functions. However, you can customize the toolbars so they contain your own sets of tools and commands.

Main toolbar

The Main toolbar (**Window** > **Toolbars** > **Main**) contains icons that let you apply the most commonly used commands in FreeHand such as Save, Copy, Paste, Undo, and so on ❸⓿.

Text toolbar

The Text toolbar (**Window** > **Toolbars** > **Text**) contains some of the most commonly used attributes for working with text ❸❶. This makes the Text toolbar a quick alternative to using the five different text modes of the Object panel.

Xtra Tools toolbar

The Xtra Tools toolbar (**Window** > **Toolbars** > **Xtra Tools**) contains specialized tools ❸❷. These tools may not appear in the Tools panel. The Xtra tools include the Arc, Smudge, and Graphic Hose tools.

❸⓿ *The* **Main toolbar** *contains icons for commands such as New, Open, and Save.*

❸❶ *The* **Text toolbar** *lets you apply text attributes such as font, point size, and alignment.*

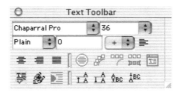

❸❷ *The* **Xtra Tools toolbar** *contains added tools that are not in the Tools panel.*

33 *The* **Xtra Operations toolbar** *contains commands for working with objects.*

34 *The* **Controller toolbar** *is used when previewing Flash (SWF) movies.*

35 *The* **Envelope toolbar** *lets you control shape modifications for objects and text.*

36 *The* **Info toolbar** *is displays information about selected objects.*

Xtra Operations toolbar

The Xtra Operations toolbar (**Window > Toolbars > Xtra Operations**) contains icons that let you apply Xtra Operations such as Emboss **33**.

Controller toolbar

The Controller toolbar (**Window > Toolbars > Controller**) is used to work with the preview of Flash (SWF) movies **34**.

Envelope toolbar

The Envelope toolbar (**Window > Toolbars > Envelope**) lets you assign the features of FreeHand's envelopes to distort text **35**.

Info toolbar

The Info toolbar (**Window > Toolbars > Info**) shows the size, position, and other attributes of objects as they are created and manipulated **36**.

Status toolbar

The Status toolbar (**Window > Toolbars > Status**) controls various attributes of the document such as the preview mode and magnification **37**. The Status toolbar is only available as a floating toolbar in Windows. On the Macintosh it is permanently fixed to the bottom of the document window.

37 *The* **Status toolbar** *displays properties of a document. The Windows version can be moved around the screen. The Macintosh version is fixed to the bottom of the document window.*

Toolbar Descriptions

Tools Panel

The most vital part of FreeHand is the Tools panel (**Window > Tools**) which contains the program's primary tools. The Tools panel also contains the controls for the fill and stroke colors for objects ㊳.

Strictly speaking the Tools panel is a toolbar, not a panel. It doesn't group with the panels and it adheres to the sides of the work area like a toolbar. Perhaps since Tools toolbar sounds silly, Macromedia calls it the Tools panel.

To use a tool:

1. Click the tool you want to use.

2. Move your cursor to the page and use the tool.

TIP The corner symbol indicates that there are additional controls you can set to change how the tool works ㊴. Double-click the corner symbol to access the dialog box for the tool.

The triangle next to a tool indicates that the tool is part of a toolset that contains additional tools.

To open a toolset:

1. Press the toolset triangle next to the visible tool ㊵.

2. Choose the tool from the toolset ㊶.

㊳ *The* **Tools panel** *in its default setting.*

㊴ *The* **corner symbol** *next to a tool indicates that a dialog box controls the setting for the tool.*

㊵ *The* **triangle symbol** *next to a tool indicates there are additional tools in the toolset.*

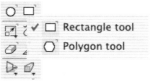

Rectangle tool
Polygon tool

㊶ *A* **toolset** *contains additional tools you can choose.*

DOCUMENT BASICS 2

When I first started teaching computer graphics, my students didn't come in to learn just Macromedia FreeHand. For many of them it was their first time using a computer. So not only did they need to learn how to create artwork, they had to grasp the concepts of opening documents, saving files, creating new versions of those files, and so on.

These days I doubt that you're sitting down to learn FreeHand without ever having used a computer before. Even if you've only used a word processing program and surfed the Internet, you'll find many of the basic commands the same from one program to the next. (That's why they call them "basics.")

But there are some features that are unique to FreeHand—not even other Macromedia applications have them. So even if you feel comfortable with graphics applications, don't skip this chapter completely.

Basic Menu Commands

The basic menu commands are used to start new documents, open existing documents, and save your work. You can also use a basic command to go back to the last saved version of a file. There are also commands that undo your most recent actions. Finally, the basic commands are also used when you want to quit working with FreeHand.

To create a new document:

◆ Choose **File** > **New**.

or

Click the New icon in the Main toolbar (**Window** > **Toolbars** > **Main**). This creates a new untitled document.

TIP If you have trouble deciphering the icons, move your cursor over the icon and pause for a moment. A tool tip with the name of the command appears **❶**.

TIP Each new untitled document has the temporary name *Untitled* followed by a number.

To open an existing document:

1. Choose **File** > **Open**.

or

Click the Open icon in the Main toolbar.

2. Use the operating system navigation controls to find the document you want to open.

3. Click Open. The document opens in a new window.

❶ *The* **tool tips** *tell you which commands are controlled by which icons in the toolbars.*

Menus, Icons or Keyboard Commands?

FreeHand offers you different ways to activate commands. For instance, to open a new document you can choose the command from the menu bar (**File** > **New**), use a keyboard command (Cmd/Ctrl-N), or click the icon for the command on a toolbar.

So which is the best way to work? It depends.

If my fingers are already on my keyboard, I use a keyboard command.

If I'm working with the mouse, I usually go to the menu command.

Finally, I find it's easiest to click the icon on a toolbar when I use a stylus and pressure-sensitive tablet.

As you work, you will discover the way that's best for you.

Basic Menu Commands

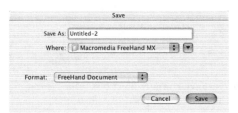

2 *The* **Save** *dialog box lets you name a file, choose a format, and choose the place where the file is saved.*

3 *You can save your work as a FreeHand Document, FreeHand Template, or Editable EPS.*

Save or Save As?

If you are working on an untitled document, there is no difference between the Save or Save As commands. Both open the Save dialog box where you can name the file.

However, once you have named and saved a document, there is a difference between the two commands:

File > **Save** saves the changes to the file without opening the Save dialog box.

File > **Save As** re-opens the Save dialog box so you can save the document under a new name. The original file is left unchanged. This lets you save various versions of your file.

Once you have named a document, the Save command saves the changes without opening the Save dialog box.

As you work in a new document, the current state of your document only exists in the computer's RAM. This means that if your computer crashes you will lose that work. So, you need to save your work as a file that exists on a disk.

To save an untitled document:

1. Choose **File** > **Save** or **File** > **Save As**. The Save dialog box appears **2**.

2. From the Format (Mac) or Save as Type (Win) pop-up menu, choose the type of document **3**:
   - **FreeHand Document** is the native file format for FreeHand files.
   - **FreeHand Template** is used to protect the file from inadvertent changes. If you save the file as a template, it will always open as an untitled file.
   - Choose **Editable EPS** if you want to place the file in a layout program such as QuarkXPress, Adobe InDesign, or Adobe PageMaker.

3. Enter a name for the document.

4. Use the operating system navigation controls to find the location where the file should be saved.

5. Click Save to save the file.

TIP To make changes to a template, open it and make the changes. Use the Save As command to save the document with the same name as the original template.

Basic Menu Commands

As you work, any additional changes you make to the document also need to be saved.

To save additional work:

◆ Choose **File** > **Save**. The previous version of the file is replaced by the current version.

You can also save a document under a new name. This allows you to make incremental versions of each change of the document.

To save a document under a new name:

◆ Choose **File** > **Save As**. This opens the Save dialog box. *Follow the steps on page 15 to rename and save the file.*

To close a document:

1. Choose **File** > **Close**.

   or

   Click the Close box.

2. If you have not saved the document, an alert box asks if you want to save the document **❹**.

   • Click **Save/Yes** to save your changes.
   • Click **Don't Save/No** to close the document in the last saved version.
   • Click **Cancel** to leave the document open.

As you work on a document, the Undo command makes it easy to step back through the actions you have taken.

To undo previous actions:

◆ Choose **Edit** > **Undo**.

To redo an action you have undone:

◆ Choose **Edit** > **Redo**.

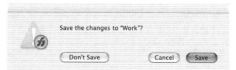

❹ *The* **Save changes alert box** *reminds you to save any changes applied to a document.*

The Price of Undos

The number of actions you can undo is set in the General Preferences.

The default setting is 10, which I think is a little low. However, don't go crazy and set a huge number. The higher the number you set, the greater the amount of RAM that is needed to run FreeHand.

I like a setting of 30. If I need more than that, I can use the **File** > **Revert** command.

Memorize the undo/redo shortcuts!

Ordinarily I don't list the keyboard shortcuts for the commands I mention here in the book. I figure you can easily look them up to learn them yourself.

However, it is probably a good idea to memorize the shortcut for Undo (Cmd/Ctrl-Z) and Redo (Cmd/Ctrl-Y) for Redo.

With those two shortcuts you can quickly go back and forth as you work.

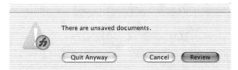

There are unsaved documents.

Quit Anyway   Cancel   Review

❺ *The* **Review dialog box** *prompts you to save or discard any changes you have made in your documents before quitting/exiting FreeHand.*

Closing or Quitting?

There's a difference between closing a FreeHand document and quitting the FreeHand program. When you close a document, the application is still available to open other files. When you quit the program, the application is no longer active.

In the early days of working with computers, it was important to quit an application in order to free memory to launch other applications.

With Windows and Macintosh OS X, you don't have to quit programs to free up memory.

To revert to the last saved version:

1. Choose **File > Revert**. An alert box appears asking you to confirm your command.

2. Click the Revert button to restore your document to the last saved version.

TIP You can also revert to the last saved version by closing the document without saving any changes and then reopening it.

To quit FreeHand:

1. Choose **FreeHand MX > Quit FreeHand MX** (Mac OS X) or **File > Exit** (Win). If there are no unsaved documents, the application closes.

2. If there are unsaved documents, the Review dialog box opens **❺**.

   • Click **Review** to see each of the open documents along with the Save Changes dialog box.
   • Click **Quit Anyway** (Mac) or **Exit** (Win) to close all documents, discarding any unsaved work.
   • Click **Cancel** to remain in the application.

TIP You can turn the Review feature on or off by changing the Preferences settings.

Using the Windows Wizards

FreeHand for Windows has Wizards that make it easy to create new documents with particular settings.

To use the Wizards:

1. Choose **Help** > **Wizards**. The Choose a Wizard screen appears **6**.

2. Click the icon for the Wizard you want to use.

   - **Welcome** opens the Welcome to FreeHand MX Wizard.
   - **Setup** helps you arrange the document with a specific unit of measurement, page size, orientation, and colors.
   - **Screen-based** helps you set up a document for publication on the Internet or in multimedia projects.
   - **Stationery** sets up a document for use as a letterhead, business card, and envelope.
   - **Publication** sets up a document with one or more pages.

3. Follow the instructions for the Wizard.

To use the Welcome to FreeHand MX Wizard:

1. Launch FreeHand. The Welcome to FreeHand MX Wizard appears **7**.

   or

   Click Welcome in the Choose a Wizard screen.

2. Click the icon for what you want to do.

   - **New** opens a new document.
   - **Previous File** opens the last file you worked on.
   - **Open** opens the dialog box that lets you open a previously saved document.
   - **Template** opens one of the templates that ship with FreeHand.
   - **FreeHand Help** opens the FreeHand online Help information.

   TIP Deselect the checkbox if you do not want to see the Wizard again.

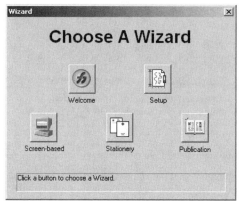

6 *The* **Choose a Wizard screen** *takes you through the steps to create different types of documents.*

7 *The* **Welcome to FreeHand MX Wizard** *makes it easy to perform various tasks when you first launch the program.*

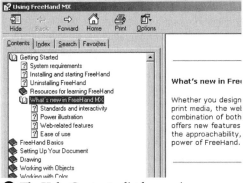

❽ *The* **Help Contents** *displays various FreeHand topics.*

Getting Help

In my dreams, this book is all you need to understand FreeHand's features. However, the reality is that there may be times when the electronic help files can explain an esoteric feature that is beyond the scope of this book. The help files also offer electronic searches that make it easy to find specific features.

To use the Using FreeHand Help system:

1. (Win) Choose **Help** > **Using FreeHand.** This launches your Internet browser and opens the opening screen of the Using FreeHand files.

    or

    (Mac) Choose **Help** > **FreeHand MX Help.** This launches the Apple Help Center.

2. Click the navigation buttons on the left side to access the help files **❽**.

    -   **Contents** displays a list of topics on the left side of the screen.
    -   **Index** lets you choose topics alphabetically.
    -   **Search** opens an Applet window that lets you enter a specific search term.

Getting Help

DISPLAY OPTIONS 3

Billions of years ago, people used to create artwork on stiff boards called *mechanicals*. If they wanted to see tiny details, they moved their head closer to the mechanical. If they wanted to see the whole picture, they held the mechanical farther away.

Creating computer artwork is different. Although you may want to sit closer or press your nose against the monitor screen, it is actually easier to use the magnification controls to zoom in or out.

However, unlike the primitive board mechanicals, Macromedia FreeHand offers many more features for how your artwork is displayed. You can create guides and grids that make it easy to align objects. You can display the onscreen rulers to help you judge the size of objects. And you can control how colors and images appear on the screen.

Athough these features do not affect the final output or printing of your artwork, they are important in how quickly and efficiently you work.

Setting the Artwork View Modes

You don't have to view your files exactly as they will finally print. FreeHand offers different options for how artwork is displayed onscreen. Some options show more details of the artwork, but take longer to be displayed. Other options display faster, but show less detail.

The Preview mode shows the best representation possible of how your artwork will print ❶. However, very complicated artwork may take a long time to display in the Preview mode.

To view artwork in the Preview mode:

◆ Choose Preview from the menu at the bottom of the document window ❷. The menu shows the mode you are currently working in.

In the Fast Preview mode, you see basic colors but blends and gradients are shown with less detail ❸. This makes the screen redraw faster than the Preview mode.

To view artwork in the Fast Preview mode:

◆ Choose View > Fast Mode. If you are in the Preview mode you switch to the Fast Preview mode.

or

Choose Fast Preview from the pop-up menu at the bottom of the document window.

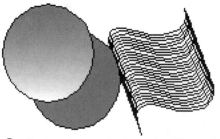

❶ *The* **Preview mode** *shows the fills, strokes, and other elements that will print.*

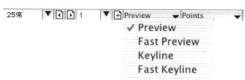

❷ *The* **View mode menu** *switches between the view modes.*

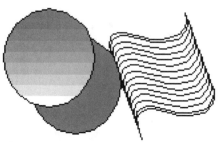

❸ *The* **Fast Preview mode** *shows the elements without smooth blends and gradients.*

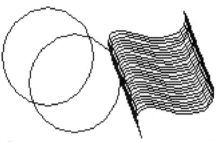

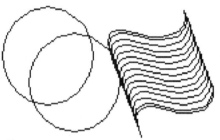

❹ *The* **Keyline mode** *shows only the outlines that define the shape of objects.*

❺ *The* **Fast Keyline mode** *shows fewer steps between blends.*

In Keyline mode, you see only the outlines that define the shapes of paths **❹**. The keyline mode makes it easier to select objects and speeds up the screen redraw.

To view artwork in the Keyline mode:

◆ If there is no checkmark next to the Keyline command, choose **View > Keyline**. This changes the setting from the Preview to the Keyline mode.

TIP If there is a checkmark, you are already in the Keyline mode and choosing the command switches to the Preview mode.

or

Choose Keyline from the pop-up menu at the bottom of the document window.

In the Fast Keyline mode, you see fewer steps between blends **❺**.

To view artwork in the Fast Keyline mode:

◆ Choose **View > Fast Mode**. If you are in the Keyline mode you switch to the Fast Keyline mode.

or

Choose Fast Keyline from the pop-up menu at the bottom of the document window.

Screen Redraw Obsession

Why so many different settings for displaying objects? Well, part of the reason has to do with the the speed of the screen redraw.

When you move around the screen to see new parts of your artwork, FreeHand has to redraw what is on the screen. If you have many objects or complicated gradients and blends, that redraw can take time.

If you're just starting out creating simple graphics, you most likely will not need to use the Fast Mode to improve screen redraw. However, as your artwork becomes more sophisticated, you may want to take advantage of the improved screen redraw.

Also, you can use layers to hide complicated artwork to help you improve the screen redraw.

Setting the Artwork View Modes

Working with Rulers

Just as in real life, you can use FreeHand's rulers to see how big things are. FreeHand has two rulers that extend along the top and left sides of your document window **6**.

To see the page rulers:

◆ To make the rulers visible, choose **View > Page Rulers > Show**. If Page Rulers is checked the rulers are visible. If you choose Page Rulers when it is checked, you turn off the rulers.

FreeHand's electronic rulers are much more flexible than the ones in real life. You can easily change the unit of measurement in FreeHand's electronic rulers. Changing the units of measurement also changes the units in dialog boxes and panels.

To change the unit of measurement:

◆ Choose one of the eight units of measurement from the menu at the bottom of the document window **7**.

TIP Although your document may be in one unit of measurement, you can still enter sizes in other units and FreeHand will convert them into the chosen units.

- For **picas**, type **p** after the number.
- For **inches**, type **i** after the number.
- For **millimeters**, type **m** after the number.
- For **kyus**, type **k** after the number.
- For **centimeters**, type **c** after the number.
- For **pixels**, type **x** after the number.
- Type **p** before the number for **points**.
  or
- Type **pt** after the number for **points**.

6 *The **page rulers** run along the left and top sides of the document window.*

7 *Use the **Units of Measurement** menu to change the measurements for the document.*

What is a kyu?

Besides being a terrific word for playing Scrabble®, according to Russ Rowlett (www.unc. edu/~rowlett/ units/index.html) a kyu is a metric unit of distance used in typography and graphic design. The kyu, originally written and pronounced as Q, is equal to exactly 0.25 millimeter, about 0.71 point. The spelling "kyu" seems to have been introduced by Macromedia.

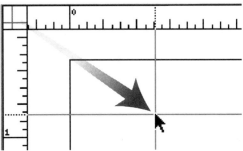

❽ *Drag the* **zero point crosshairs** *to change the position of the zero point on the rulers.*

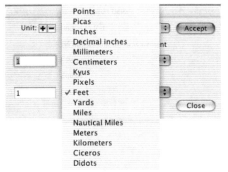

❾ *Use the* **Edit Units** *dialog box to create your own custom units of measurement.*

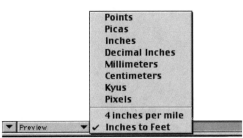

❿ *The* **custom units pop-up menu.**

⓫ **Custom units** *appear in the units of measurement pop-up menu.*

The zero point of the rulers is usually located at the upper-left corner of the page. However, you can change that position to help measure objects on your page.

To change the zero-point position:

◆ Drag the zero point crosshairs out from the top-left corner of the rulers **❽**.

TIP Double-click the zero point crosshairs in the rulers to reset the zero point to the upper-left corner of the page.

In addition to the basic units of measurement, you can create custom units. For instance, you can create a custom unit where one inch equals six feet. This is helpful if you create large-scale artwork such as blueprints.

To define custom ruler units:

1. Choose **View** > **Page Rulers** > **Edit**. This opens the Edit Units dialog box **❾**.

2. Enter a descriptive name for the custom unit in the Unit field.

3. Use the first pop-up menu to choose one of FreeHand's basic units of measurement **❿**.

4. Enter a number in the field for how many of these units will be used.

5. Use the second pop-up menu to choose what the amount should equal. In addition to the basic units you can choose feet, yards, miles, nautical miles, meters, kilometers, ciceros, and didots.

6. Enter a number in the field for how many of these units will be used.

7. Click Accept to accept this custom unit.

8. Select Add as unit of measurement to add this custom unit to the pop-up menu at the bottom of the document window **⓫**.

9. Click the Close button to close the Edit Units dialog box.

TIP Click the plus or minus buttons to add or delete the custom units.

Working with Guides

Once the rulers are visible, you can use them to create guides on your page. Guides can be used to divide pages into different areas as well as to help you align objects.

TIP In addition to creating guides using the rulers, you can create and work with guides using the Layers panel. *(See Chapter 12, "Layers and Layering.")*

To create guides by dragging:

1. Choose **View** > **Guides** > **Show**. (If Show is checked, the command is selected.)

2. Move your pointer so that it touches either the top (horizontal) ruler or the left (vertical) ruler.

3. For a horizontal guide, press and drag the cursor from the top ruler down into the page **⑫**.

   or

   For a vertical guide, press and drag the cursor from the left ruler onto the page **⑬**.

TIP Drag your arrow from the ruler onto the page, not the pasteboard.

TIP As you drag from the rulers a line appears that shows where your guide will be when you release the mouse.

4. Release the mouse to set the guide.

TIP To turn a path into a guide, you need to place the path on the Guides layer.

To move a guide to a new position:

♦ Use the Pointer or Subselect tool to drag the guide into the new position.

To delete a single guide:

♦ Use the Pointer or Subselect tool to drag the guide off the page onto the pasteboard.

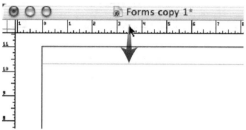

⑫ *To create a **horizontal guide**, place your pointer on the top ruler and drag down into the page area.*

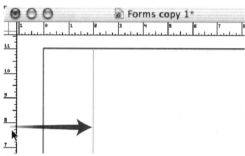

⑬ *To make a **vertical guide**, place your pointer on the left ruler and drag to the right.*

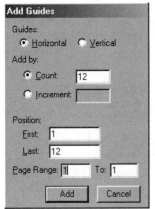

⑭ *The **Guides dialog box** lists all the guides on each of the pages as well as their positions.*

⑮ *The **Add Guides dialog box** allows you to create multiple guides at regular intervals.*

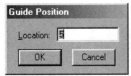

⑯ *The **Guide Position dialog box** allows you to relocate guides precisely.*

If you want to work with many guides at once, you should use the Guides dialog box.

To add guides at numerical positions:

1. Double-click any guide or choose **View** > **Guides** > **Edit**. The Guides dialog box appears **⑭**.

2. Click Add to open the Add Guides dialog box **⑮**.

3. Choose Horizontal or Vertical.

4. To set a specific number of equally spaced guides, click Count and enter the number.

5. To set a specific distance between guides, click Increment and enter the spacing.

6. Use the First and Last fields to specify where the guides should start and end.

7. Use the Page range to set the pages on which the guides should appear.

8. Click Add to return to the Guides dialog box.

9. Click OK in the Guides dialog box. The new guides are listed in the Guides dialog box and inserted on the page.

TIP If you want the guides in front of the artwork, you need to change the order of the Guides layer.

To reposition guides using the Guides dialog box:

1. Double-click the guide or choose **View** > **Guides** > **Edit** to open the Guides dialog box.

2. Select the guide from the list.

3. Click Edit. This opens the Guide Position dialog box **⑯**.

4. Enter a new location in the field and click OK to return to the Guides dialog box.

5. Click OK to close the Guides dialog box and institute the changes.

Working with Guides

To delete guides using the Guides dialog box:

1. Double-click the guide or choose **View** > **Guides** > **Edit** to open the Guides dialog box.

2. Select the guide or guides from the list.

3. Click Delete/Remove.

4. When you have finished, click OK.

TIP Hold Cmd/Ctrl to select multiple non-contiguous guides or hold Shift to select contiguous guides in the Guides dialog box.

TIP Any path can be turned into a guide by selecting it and then double-clicking the Guides layer in the Layers panel.

TIP The Release button in the Guides dialog box turns the selected guide into a regular path.

You can lock guides to prevent them from being moved.

To lock the guides:

◆ Choose **View** > **Guides** > **Lock**. If you choose Lock when it is checked, you unlock the guides.

TIP You can also lock guides using the Layers panel.

As you move objects, you may want them to jump so that they align with guides. This is called *snapping to guides*. The Snap To Guide cursor indicates that the object has jumped into alignment with a guide 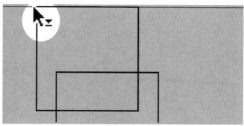.

To turn on Snap To Guides:

◆ Choose **View** > **Snap To Guides**. If Snap To Guides is checked, the feature is already on.

TIP The Preferences let you control the snap to distance—how close the object has to be before it will jump to the guide.

⑰ *The* **Snap To Guide cursor** *indicates that the object being moved will jump into place along a guide.*

Don't Cover Your Page With Guides

You may be tempted to cover your page with many guides. Try to avoid that. Each guide you create adds to the size of the file. You may also find it distracting to work with all those guides.

Any time you find yourself about to create many guides, think about using FreeHand's automatic grids.

Unlike guides, grids don't add to the file size, and they can be automatically changed to new increments.

Working with Guides

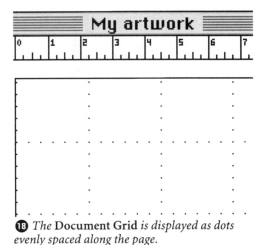

⑱ *The* **Document Grid** *is displayed as dots evenly spaced along the page.*

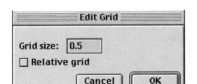

⑲ *The* **actual grid** *is a series of lines that connect the dots of the visible document grid.*

⑳ *The* **Edit Grid dialog box** *lets you change the increments of the document grid.*

Working with Grids

I grew up using guides, but then I discovered FreeHand's grids. Grids are much more powerful and versatile than guides. If you change your design, grids are much easier to modify than guides. You can also use one object to be the starting point of the grid for other objects.

To view the document grid:

◆ Choose **View** > **Grid** > **Show**. If you choose Show when it is checked, you turn off the grid.

TIP Although the grid is displayed as dots **⑱**, the actual grid is created from lines that intersect those dots. So the grid is active along the lines that connect the dots **⑲**.

To change the document grid intervals:

1. Choose **View** > **Grid** > **Edit**. The Edit Grid dialog box appears **⑳**.

2. In the Grid size field, type the distance you want between the imaginary lines of your grid.

TIP The Relative grid checkbox is described on the next page.

3. Click OK or press Return/Enter.

TIP You can change the size of the grid at any time.

Working with Grids

You can work with objects so that their edges always fall on the grid. This is called setting an object to *snap to* the grid .

To turn on Snap To Grid:

◆ Choose **View** > **Grid** > **Snap To Grid**. If you choose Snap To Grid when it is checked, you turn off the feature.

TIP The grid does not have to be visible for objects to snap to it.

TIP If Snap To Grid is on, you cannot draw objects between the grid intervals.

You can also work with a relative grid. Instead of the grid starting at the edge of the page, a relative grid uses the selected object as the start of the document grid. When the relative grid is turned on, if you copy one object, the copy is aligned to the original 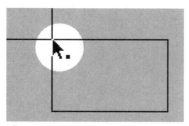.

To work with a Relative Grid:

◆ Check Relative Grid in the Edit Grid dialog box.

FreeHand also lets you snap to points 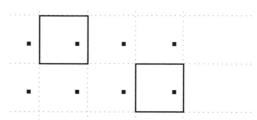. This lets you use the points of one object as a type of grid so you can align other objects.

To turn on Snap To Point:

◆ Choose **View** > **Snap To Point**. If Snap To Point is already checked, you turn off the feature when you select the command.

TIP Snap To Point overrides Snap to Guides, which in turn overrides Snap to Grid.

TIP FreeHand (Mac) offers sounds that play when the object snaps to a guide, the grid, or a point. The sounds are set in the Preferences.

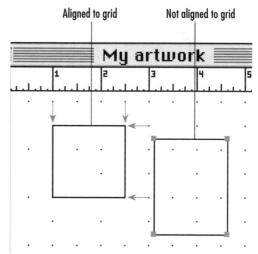

21 *When an object is drawn with* **Snap To Grid** *on, its sides stay on the grid. When Snap To Grid is off, the sides fall between the intervals.*

22 *Turning on the* **Relative grid** *means that when the object is duplicated, it stays aligned to the object's relative grid (dotted lines) rather than the document grid square dots.*

23 *The* **Snap to Point dot** *next to the pointer indicates that the object being moved will snap to a point on the other object.*

24 *The* **Fit All command** *changes the magnification so you can see all the pages in the document.*

Setting the Magnification Options

When working in your document, you may find that you need to see different magnifications. There are many ways to zoom in and out of your document.

To zoom using the View menu:

- ◆ You can use one of the View menu commands to change the magnification of your document.

  - **View > Fit All** adjusts the magnification so you can see all the pages in your document **24**.
  - Choose **View > Fit to Page** to adjust the magnification so you can see the entire page you are working on **25**.
  - **View > Fit Selection** adjusts the magnification so that the selected item fills the window **26**.
  - **View > Magnification** lets you choose one of the magnification settings in the submenu. These are the same as the settings in the Magnification pop-up menu.

25 *The* **Fit To Page command** *changes the magnification so you can see all the items on the current page.*

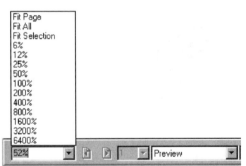

26 *The* **Fit Selection command** *changes the magnification to zoom in on the selected item.*

27 *The* **Magnification menu** *lets you choose one of the preset magnifications.*

To use the Magnification pop-up menu:

- ◆ Choose one of the preset magnification settings from the Magnification menu at the bottom of the document window **27**.

To enter exact magnification amounts:

1. Double-click or drag across the number in the Magnification menu **28**.
2. Type in the percentage at which you would like to view your page. (You don't need to type the % character.)
3. Press the Return/Enter key.

28 *Use the* **Magnification menu** field *to enter an exact magnification.*

183

To use the Zoom tool:

1. Click the Zoom tool in the Tools panel .

2. Click the Zoom tool on the object you want to zoom in on. Click as many times as you need to get as close as necessary to the objects you are working on.

   or

   Click and drag the Zoom tool diagonally across the area you want to zoom in on. When you release the mouse button, you zoom in on the area 30.

TIP Press the Cmd/Ctrl key and Spacebar to get the Zoom tool without leaving the tool that is currently selected in the Tools panel.

TIP Hold the Opt/Alt key while in the Zoom tool to zoom out from objects. The icon changes from a plus sign (+) to a minus sign (–) 31.

29 *The* **Zoom tool** *in the Tools panel.*

30 *Use the Zoom tool to increase the magnification of a specific object by* **dragging a marquee** *around that object. The dashed-line marquee shows the area being selected.*

31 *Hold the* **Opt/Alt key** *while in the Zoom tool to zoom out from an object.*

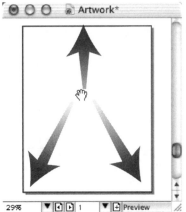

32 *The **Hand tool** in the Tools panel.*

33 *The **Hand tool** lets you drag any which way you want to move around the page.*

Moving Around

One of the easiest ways to spot a novice computer user is to watch them use the document window scroll bars to move up and down or from side to side on the page. While they will eventually get to where they want to be, most experienced users use the Hand tool which lets you move up, down, left, right, and diagonally—all without ever touching the sides of your window.

To use the Hand tool:

1. Click the Hand tool in the Tools panel **32**.
2. Press and drag the Hand tool inside the document window **33**.

TIP Press the Spacebar to temporarily use the Hand tool without leaving the tool that is currently selected in the Tools panel.

TIP Do not press the Spacebar to access the Hand tool while you are within a text block or you will insert many spaces into your text.

Use the Zoom Tool and Hand Tool Shortcuts!

I haven't chosen the Zoom or Hand tools in the Tools panel in years. So how do I zoom in and out on my artwork? I use the Zoom and Hand tool keyboard shortcuts. And the sooner you learn them the better your FreeHand experience will be.

While you are using any tool, hold the Spacebar. This gives you the Hand tool that lets you move around the screen.

Then add the Cmd/Ctrl key to access the Zoom tool. You can now click or drag to zoom in on objects.

Now add the Opt/Alt key to zoom out from objects.

This is why the really efficient designers always have their fingers moving up and down on those three keys. (Sharon Steuer, author of *The Illustrator Wow! Book,* calls this a "Finger Dance.")

Moving Around

Setting Custom Views

This is, in my opinion, one of the most overlooked features in FreeHand. Instead of relying on the preset magnifications and view commands, you can set your own custom views. A custom view remembers the magnification and the position of the screen. Custom views are very helpful anytime you find yourself zooming and moving into the same area over and over.

To create a custom view:

1. Choose the magnification and page position you want for the view.

2. Choose View > Custom > New. The New View dialog box appears ➌➍.

3. Type a name for the view.

4. Click OK to close the dialog box.

To use a custom view:

◆ Choose View > Custom and choose one of the custom views listed at the bottom of the submenu.

   or

   Choose the custom view listed at the bottom of the magnification pop-up menu at the bottom of the document window.

To edit a custom view:

1. Change your magnification and position to the way you want your new view to appear.

2. Choose View > Custom > Edit. The Edit Views dialog box appears ➌➎.

3. Select the view you want to change and click Redefine.

4. Click OK. This closes the dialog box and sets the new view.

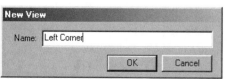

➌➍ *The* **New View dialog box** *is where you can name a custom view.*

➌➎ *The* **Edit Views dialog box** *is where you can redefine or delete custom views.*

WORKING WITH PAGES 4

What is the size of a page? In most word processing programs, a page usually corresponds to the size of the paper in the printer.

But in programs such as Macromedia FreeHand, a page can be used to designate the size of the paper in the printer, or the size of the Web page, or the size of the Flash movie.

FreeHand offers more flexibility than many page layout and vector drawing programs. Not only can you have multiple pages, but each page can have its own size. This makes FreeHand an excellent choice for creating a wide variety of layouts such as envelopes, business cards, and letterheads.

Some people work with FreeHand for years, and never use anything more than one page for each document. Others could not work at all without FreeHand's multiple pages to create booklets and other small documents.

Adjusting Page Size and Orientation

Inside the document window is the page on which you create your work. An area called the *pasteboard* surrounds the page ❶. You use the Document panel to adjust the size and orientation of the page.

To display the Document panel:

◆ To open the Document panel, choose **Window > Document**.

As you create documents, you may need to change your page to a different size.

To set a page size in the Document panel:

◆ Use the page size pop-up menu in the Document panel ❷.

If none of the preset sizes is right for your job, you need to create a page with custom measurements. For instance, if you create business cards, you would want your page to match the trim size of the cards.

To create a custom-size page:

1. Choose Custom from the Page Size pop-up menu of the Document panel.

2. Enter the horizontal measurement in the x field ❸.

3. Enter the vertical measurement in the y field ❸.

4. Press Return/Enter on the keyboard to apply the sizes to the page.

❶ *The* **page** *sits inside the* **pasteboard** *area.*

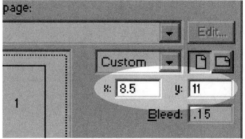

❷ *There are* **nine preset page sizes** *in the Document panel which lets you enter the exact measurements for any size page.*

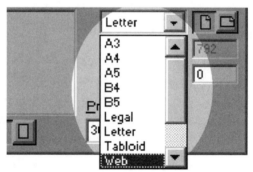

❸ *Use the* **x and y fields** *to set the dimensions of a custom page.*

❹ *Choose the* **Page tool** *in the Tools panel to visually manipulate pages on the artboard.*

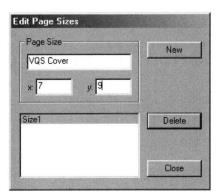

❺ *Use the Page tool to drag the handles around a page to change the size of the page.*

Edit Page Sizes

Page Size

New

VQS Cover

x: 7   y: 9

Size1

Delete

Close

❻ *The* **Edit Page Sizes dialog box** *lets you set custom page sizes that are displayed in the Page Size pop-up menu.*

Instead of changing the size of the page numerically, you can use the Page tool to visually drag the page so that it is the same size as your artwork.

To use the Page tool to create a custom-size page:

1. Choose the Page tool in the Tools panel **❹**.

2. Click the page you want to change. A set of handles appears around the edges of the page.

3. Drag one of the arrows to change the size of the page **❺**.

TIP Changing the page size does not change the size of any artwork on the page.

TIP Keep an eye on the Info toolbar to see the dimensions of the page as you drag.

If you create many custom-size pages, you can save those sizes as part of the page size list. This makes it easier to select those page sizes later on.

To add custom page sizes to the page size list:

1. Choose Edit from the bottom of the preset page size list. The Edit Page Sizes dialog box appears **❻**.

2. Click the New button to create a new page size entry.

3. Enter a descriptive name for the custom size.

4. Enter the horizontal size in the x field.

5. Enter the vertical size in the y field.

6. To enter additional custom sizes, click the New button.

7. Click the Close button to close the dialog box. The custom sizes appear in the Document panel menu.

TIP Click the Delete button to delete any sizes.

Adjusting Page Size and Orientation

You may want to reverse the horizontal and vertical sizes of your document. You can do this using the Document panel or the Page tool.

TIP Changing the orientation or rotating a page changes only the position of the artboard. It does not rotate any artwork on the page.

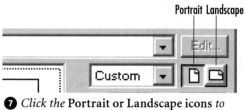

Portrait Landscape

7 *Click the* **Portrait or Landscape icons** *to change the orientation of a page.*

To set the orientation in the Document panel:

◆ To make the page wider than it is tall, click the Landscape icon in the Document panel **7**.

  or

  To make the page taller than it is wide, click the Portrait icon in the Document panel **7**.

TIP If the Portrait icon is selected, FreeHand does not accept measurements that would make a page wider than it is tall. Similarly, if the Landscape icon is selected, you can never specify a page that is taller than it is wide.

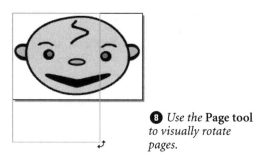

8 *Use the* **Page tool** *to visually rotate pages.*

To rotate a page using the Page tool:

1. Choose the Page tool in the Tools panel.

2. Click the page you want to change. A set of handles appears around the edges of the page.

3. Move the cursor outside a handle so that a curved arrow appears.

4. Drag the curved arrow to rotate the page **8**.

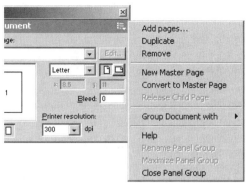

9 *Choosing* **Duplicate from the Document** **panel menu** *creates a new page the same size as the selected page.*

10 *Hold the Opt/Alt key as you drag with the Page tool to duplicate pages.*

11 *Add pages by clicking the* **new page icon** *at the bottom of the document window (Mac) or in the Status panel (Win).*

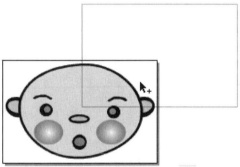

12 *Use the* **Add Pages dialog box** *to add multiple pages.*

Duplicating and Adding Pages

If you are creating a series of layouts for your client to choose from, you may want additional pages for different versions of the art. You can add new empty pages, or duplicate the current pages that may contain artwork.

To duplicate pages using the Document panel:

♦ Choose Duplicate from the Document panel menu. This creates a new page exactly the same size as the first page **9**.

TIP The new page also contains the same artwork as the original page.

To duplicate pages using the Page tool:

1. Choose the Page tool in the Tools panel.
2. Hold the Opt/Alt key **10**.
3. Drag the page to a new position.
4. Release the mouse button when the new page appears.

TIP Use the Shift key to select multiple pages. Then use the Opt/Alt key to duplicate the pages as you drag with the Page tool.

To add blank pages one at a time:

♦ Click the New Page icon in the Status panel (Win) or at the bottom of the document window (Mac) **11**.

To add many blank pages:

1. Choose Add Pages from the Document panel menu. This opens the Add Pages dialog box **12**.
2. Enter a number in the Number of new pages field.
3. Choose a size from the Page size pop-up menu.
4. Click the icon for orientation.
5. Set a Bleed size *(see page 43)*.
6. Set a master page *(see page 44)*.
7. Click OK to create the new pages.

Organizing Pages

You might want pages to touch so that you can spread artwork across the pages. Or you may want a page to come before another. You can move pages using the Page tool or the page thumbnails in the Document panel.

To move pages with the Page tool:

1. Choose the Page tool in the Toolbox.

2. Click to select a page. The handles indicate the page is selected.

3. If needed, hold the Shift key to select additional pages.

4. Press and drag inside the handles to move the pages ⑬.

5. Release the mouse button when the pages are in position.

TIP Hold the Shift key to constrain the motion to 45-degree angles.

To move pages with the page thumbnails:

◆ Drag the page thumbnail in the Document panel ⑭.

TIP If the thumbnail is too small, change the thumbnail magnification *(see below)*.

TIP Hold the Spacebar to switch to a Hand tool that can scroll around the thumbnail area in the Document panel.

To change the page icon magnification:

◆ Click the Magnification icons in the Document panel as follows ⑮:

• The **Small icon** shrinks the thumbnails to their smallest size.

• The **Medium icon** expands the thumbnails to their middle size.

• The **Large icon** expands the thumbnails to their largest size.

TIP Double-click a thumbnail in the Document panel to go to that page and fit the page in the window in one step.

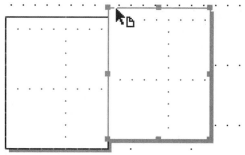

⑬ *The Page tool lets you select pages directly on the pasteboard and move them into position. The page icon shows that you are moving the page.*

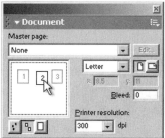

⑭ *As you move the page thumbnails in the Document panel you also change the arrangement of the pages on the pasteboard.*

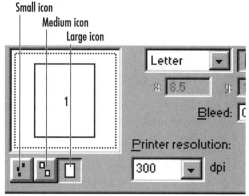

⑮ *The* **three magnification icons** *change the size of the page display in the preview area of the Document panel.*

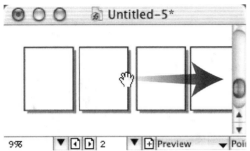

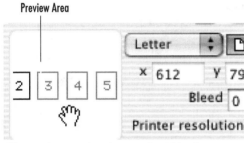

⓰ *Use the Hand tool to move from one page to another in the document window.*

Preview Area

⓱ *Use the Hand tool to scroll within the Preview Area of the Document panel.*

Moving Between Pages

With multiple pages in your document, you will need to move from one page to another. You can move between pages using the document window or by using the Document panel.

To move between pages in the window area:

1. Choose the Hand tool.

   or

   Hold the Spacebar to temporarily access the Hand tool.

2. Drag to move from one page to another ⓰.

To move between pages in the Document panel:

1. Position the cursor inside the Preview Area of the Document panel.

2. Hold the Spacebar to temporarily access the Hand tool.

3. Drag within the Preview Area ⓱. This allows you to click to move to a new page.

Where Are My New Pages?

In theory, each new page you add or duplicate should appear just to the right of the current page. Unfortunately this doesn't always happen. (The technical name for something like this is a *bug*.)

You may find that you add or duplicate pages, but you don't see the new pages on the pasteboard. If this happens, use the Hand tool to move all the way to the top-left corner of the pasteboard. You should see your missing pages there.

Why does this happen? The best reason I've been able to discover is that if you have changed the magnification icon to either the middle or large icon, there may not be enough room to add pages in the Document panel. In that case, FreeHand creates new pages all the way in the top-left corner of the pasteboard.

If your pages do appear in the wrong position, you can use the Page tool *(see the previous page)* or the Document panel to move the pages into the correct position.

Selecting and Deleting Pages

A FreeHand document must contain at least one page. That means you can never delete the only page in a document. However, if you have added pages to a document, you can delete one page at a time.

Before you delete a page, you need to select the page you want to delete.

To select a page in the Document panel:

◆ Click the page you want to select in the Preview Area of the Document panel. The selected page is indicated by a dark outline in the Preview Area ⓲.

To select a page in the FreeHand document window:

◆ Click the page you want to select in the document window.

  or

  Scroll through the document window so that the page you want to select is in the center of the window area.

  or

  Use the Page tool to select the page you want to delete.

TIP Hold the Shift key as you click with the Page tool to select multiple pages. Although multiple pages will be selected in the document window, only one page will be selected in the Document panel.

To delete a selected page:

◆ Choose Remove from the Document panel menu ⓳.

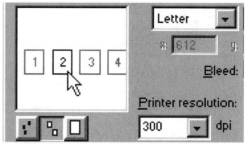

⓲ *A selected page appears with a dark outline in the Preview Area of the Document panel.*

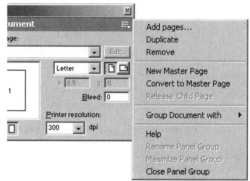

⓳ *Use the Remove command to delete a selected page.*

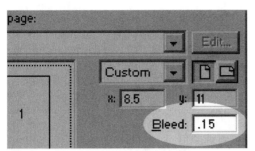

20 *Use the* **Bleed** *field to set the extra area around a page where artwork is printed.*

21 *The light gray line outside the work page indicates the bleed area.*

Setting a Page Bleed

Ordinarily, FreeHand doesn't print any part of an image that lies outside the page. If you want the artwork to print right to the edge of a page, you need to extend or bleed the artwork outside the edge of the page. (See the sidebar on this page "Why do I need to bleed?")

To set a bleed size:

1. Enter the desired bleed size in the Bleed field of the Document panel **20**.

2. Press Return or Enter. A light gray line appears around your work page. This is the bleed area **21**.

TIP Use the bleed area to hold elements that should print outside the live area of your artwork.

Why Do I Need to Bleed?

The reason is that the people who cut paper don't always trim pages exactly evenly. Take a look at the thumbtabs on the sides of this book. If you flip from page to page you will see that the gray area isn't always the same size. That's because when the paper for the book is cut to the final trim size, some of the pages will be cut slightly differently from others. (Yes, I know this will happen, even before the book is printed.)

If I had laid out the page so the gray area stopped right at the edge of the page, there might be some pages where the trim showed the white outside the page.

So instead of trusting that the trim position would always be perfect, I set a bleed to extend the gray area outside the size of the page. That way I don't have to worry if the trim is slightly off. I know that the gray area will still be visible outside the trim.

Unless your print shop is trying to trim pages in the middle of an earthquake, you shouldn't need more than a quarter-inch bleed. However, if you are in doubt, ask your print shop for the size bleed they would like you to specify.

Using Master Pages

If you have used a page layout program such as QuarkXPress or Adobe InDesign, you may be familiar with the concept of master pages. A master page is a page contains recurring elements which can be applied to ordinary document pages. Then any change you make to the master page is automatically applied to the document pages that are governed by the master page. The benefit of this is that you can make changes to many pages by making changes to a single master page.

FreeHand lets you create master pages that can then be applied to document pages.

To create and style a master page:

1. Choose New Master Page from the Document panel menu.

    or

    Choose New Master Page from the Library panel menu **22**. A new window that contains the master page appears.

    TIP You can tell you are on the master page because the title bar shows the name of the document followed by the name of the master page. Also, the preview area of the Document panel shows an un-numbered page **23**.

2. Add any items to the master page that you want to appear on the document pages.

3. Close the window containing the master page. This returns you to the document pages.

22 *Choose* **New Master Page** *from the Library menu to add a new master page.*

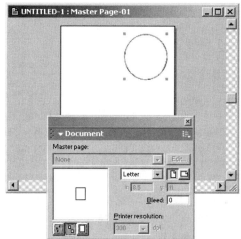

23 *The* **master page window** *is indicated in the title bar of the window and by the non-numbered page in the Document panel.*

Using Master Pages

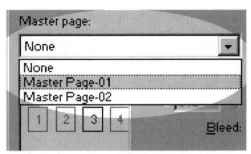

24 *You can apply a master page by choosing it from the Master page list in the Document panel.*

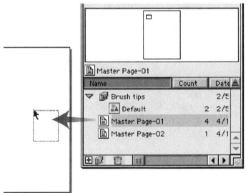

25 *Drag the icon of a master page from the Library panel onto a document page to apply that master page to the document page.*

As you work, you may realize that you would like a document page to act as a master page. Fortunately, it is easy to convert a document page into a master page.

To convert a document page into a master page:

1. Select the page you would like to have as a master page.
2. Choose Convert to Master Page from the Document panel menu. A new master page is created from the elements on the document page.

TIP When you convert a document page to a master page, the live items on the document page are deleted and the master page items are applied to the document page.

Once you have created a master page, you can apply it to document pages. You can use either the Document panel or the Library.

To apply master pages using the Document panel:

1. Select the page or pages using the Page tool, the Document panel, or click in the document window.
2. Choose the master page from the Master Page list in the Document panel **24**. The master page elements appear on the page.

To apply master pages using the Library:

♦ Drag the icon of the master page from the Library panel onto the page **25**. The master page elements appear on the page.

TIP You can apply a new master page to a document page at any time.

Using Master Pages

You can remove the master page elements by removing the master page applied to a document page.

To remove the master page from a document page:

1. Select the page or pages that you want to change.
2. Choose None from the Master Page list in the Document panel. The master page elements disappear from the page.

Master pages appear with a default name. However, you can rename a master page at any time.

To rename a master page:

1. Click to highlight the name of the master page in the Library ㉖.
2. Type the new name of the master page.
3. Press Return/Enter to apply the new name.

To edit a master page using the Library:

1. Double-click the icon of the master page in the Library. This opens the master page window.
2. Make whatever changes you want to the master page.
3. Close the master page window. The changes to the master page appear on those document pages that have the master page applied to them.

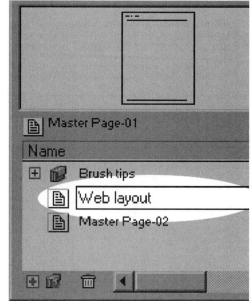

㉖ *Double-click the name of a master page in the Library to rename the master page.*

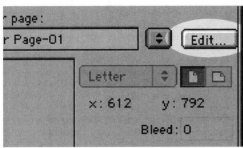

⚫ *The* **Edit button** *in the Document panel allows you to make changes to the master page.*

To edit a master page using the Document panel:

1. Select the master page in the Master Page list in the Document panel.

2. Click the Edit button **⚫**.

3. Make whatever changes you want on the master page.

4. Close the master page window. The changes to the master page appear on those document pages that have the master page applied to them.

Items that are on the master page are not editable when they appear on the document pages. If you want to modify those items on the document pages, you need to release those items from the master page.

To release master page items on document pages:

1. Select the document page that you want to release.

2. Choose Release Child Page from the Document panel menu. The items on the document page are no longer governed by the master page and can be freely edited.

Using Master Pages

PATH-CREATION TOOLS 5

One of the best ways to learn a vector drawing program is to create basic shapes. Rather than create these shapes from scratch, it is much easier to use FreeHand's many different tools that make all sorts of different objects.

For instance, if you want to draw a daisy, you can easily draw a few ovals around a circle using the ellipse tool. A house is easily created from several rectangles with a triangle on the top.

You can also use tools to create complicated mathematical shapes such as spirals and arcs. Finally, FreeHand lets you mimic the look of traditional pen and ink drawing tools.

Of course, you can also create paths with very defined shapes using two specialized tools called the Pen and the Bezigon. Those tools are covered in Chapter 6.

Understanding Paths

Almost all the objects you create within FreeHand are vector paths. Vector paths consist of anchor points that define the shape of the path and segments that join the points together.

For instance, in a vector-drawing program a circle is defined by placing four anchor points in position and joining them with curved segments ❶.

In a pixel-drawing program, each individual dot that creates the circle must be defined ❷.

To change the shape of a vector path, the anchor points or segments are modified. To change the shape of a pixel image, the original pixels must be erased and the new pixels placed into position.

Vector paths are usually used to create line artwork or illustration images ❸. Pixel images are the format used for scanned images and the photographs taken by digital cameras ❹.

One of the most important reasons to create objects using vector paths is that the size of the file is much smaller than the same image created using pixels. Also, unlike pixels, vector images can be scaled up with no loss of resolution.

Most people feel it is much easier to create photorealistic images using pixel-drawing programs. However, if you have the patience, you can create realistic images using vector objects. This includes special effects such as blends and gradients.

For more information on the differences between vector and pixel images and working with resolution, see *The Non-Designer's Scan and Print Book* by Sandee Cohen and Robin Williams.

❶ *A vector-drawing program defines shapes using anchor points (indicated by squares) connected by segments.*

❷ *A pixel-drawing program creates shapes using pixels (indicated by black and white squares).*

❸ *In this* **example of vector artwork,** *each shape is created by a separate vector path.*

❹ *In this* **scanned pixel image** *the artwork consists of millions of tiny, colored pixels.*

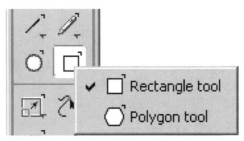

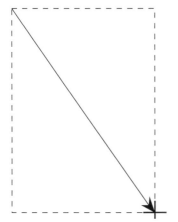

⑤ *The* **Rectangle tool** *selected from its toolset in the Tools panel.*

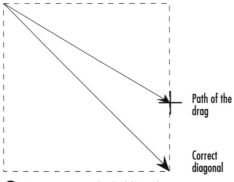

⑥ *To* **draw a rectangle,** *drag the cursor along the diagonal line between two corners.*

Path of the drag

Correct diagonal

⑦ **Draw a square** *by holding the Shift key while you drag with the Rectangle tool.*

Using the Rectangle Tool

One of the most basic objects you can create is a rectangle. This includes plain rectangles, squares, and rounded-corner rectangles.

To draw a rectangle:

1. Press the toolset to choose the Rectangle tool in the Tools panel **⑤**.

2. Position the plus sign cursor (+) where you want one corner of the rectangle and press to start the rectangle.

3. Drag diagonally to the opposite corner **⑥**.

4. Release the mouse button when you are satisfied with the size of the rectangle.

TIP Hold the Opt/Alt key to draw a rectangle outward from the center point.

TIP Once you draw the rectangle, you can still change its dimensions *(see page 52)*.

You may think of a square as different from a rectangle, but FreeHand doesn't make the distinction. The Rectangle tool creates squares which are also called perfect rectangles.

To draw a square:

1. Follow the steps to start creating a rectangle.

2. As you drag, hold the Shift key. This forces, or *constrains,* your rectangle into a square even if you do not follow the proper diagonal **⑦**.

TIP Whenever you hold a modifier, such as the Shift key, always release the mouse button first, then the modifier second.

TIP Hold both the Opt/Alt and the Shift keys to draw a square outward from the center point.

You can change the position and size of a rectangle using the Object panel.

To change the dimensions of a rectangle:

1. Select the Rectangle entry in the Object panel. This displays the dimensions fields for the rectangle ❽.

2. Set the dimensions as follows ❾:
   - The **x** field controls the horizontal position of the upper-left corner of the rectangle on the artboard.
   - The **y** field controls the vertical position of the upper-left corner of the rectangle on the artboard.
   - The **w** field controls the width of the rectangle.
   - The **h** field controls the height of the rectangle.

3. Press Return/Enter to apply the change.

You can modify rectangles so they have curved or rounded corners. The amount of the curve depends on the corner radius ❿. There are many different ways to create rounded corners for rectangles.

To set the corner radius for new rectangles:

1. Double-click the Rectangle tool in the Tools panel. This opens the Rectangle Tool dialog box ⓫.

2. In the Corner radius field, type the amount or drag the slider to set the number for the corner radius.

3. Click OK and draw your rectangle.

4. Press Return/Enter to apply the change.

TIP See page 72 for how to work with the Auto constrain option.

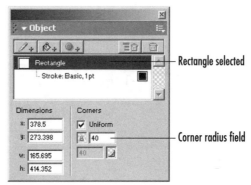

Rectangle selected

Corner radius field

❽ *Select the Rectangle entry in the Object panel to see the Dimensions and Corners controls.*

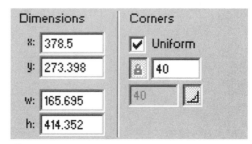

❾ *The Dimensions and Corners controls for a Rectangle selected in the Object panel.*

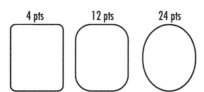

4 pts   12 pts   24 pts

❿ *Different* **Corner radius** *settings change the shape of rounded-corner rectangles.*

⓫ *The* Rectangle Tool *dialog box.*

Using the Rectangle Tool

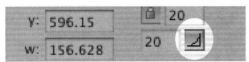

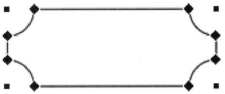

⓬ *The* **corner shape icon** *lets you change the curve from convex to concave.*

⓭ **Concave corners** *applied to a rectangle.*

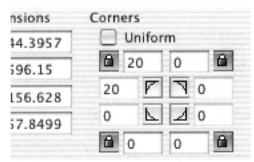

⓮ *Deselect Uniform to open the* **controls for each corner** *of the rectangle.*

⓯ *The* **non-uniform setting** *lets you apply different curves to each corner of a rectangle.*

You can also change the corner radius of a previously drawn rectangle using the Object panel.

To modify the corner radius for a rectangle:

1. Select the Rectangle entry in the Object panel.

2. Enter an amount in the Corner radius field. The higher the amount, the greater the curve of the corner radius.

3. Click the corner shape icon **⓬** to change the corner radius from convex to concave **⓭**.

TIP Do not ungroup the rectangle or you will no longer be able to enter a corner radius for the rectangle.

4. Press Return/Enter to apply the change.

Not all the corners have to have the same appearance. You can apply individual curves to each corner of the rectangle.

To apply individual curves to a rectangle:

1. Deselect the Uniform option to create individual settings for each corner of the rectangle **⓮**.

2. Enter a corner radius amount in each field. The rectangle displays the individual corner radii **⓯**.

3. Click the Concave icon to change the radius from convex to concave.

4. Press Return/Enter to apply the change.

You can also apply asymmetrical corner curves. This means one side of the curve is different from the other.

To apply asymmetrical curves to a rectangle:

1. Click the lock icon for corner control. This activates a second field for the curve ⑯.

2. Enter a radius amount for each side of the corner radius curve ⑰.

FreeHand also lets you visually drag to change the amount of the corner radius.

To manually modify the corner radius:

1. Select the rectangle.

2. Choose the Subselect tool in the Tools panel ⑱.

3. Move the cursor over a corner point and drag the corner radius control points ⑲. As you drag you see a preview of the radius applied to the object.

4. Release the mouse button when you are satisfied with the result.

TIP If the Uniform setting is unchecked in the Object panel, you can move the controls for each corner radius individually.

TIP If the lock icon is unlocked in the Object panel, you can adjust each side of the curve individually.

TIP You can use manual adjustment together with the numerical controls.

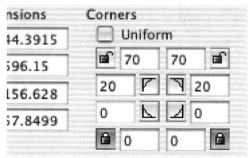

⑯ *The lock icon in the unlocked position allows you to apply unequal radius settings to each side of a curve.*

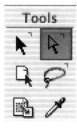

⑰ *An example of* **unequal curves** *applied to each side of the top corner radii.*

⑱ *The* **Subselect tool** *lets you manipulate the Corner Radius control points.*

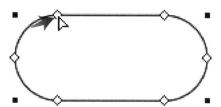

⑲ *Drag a* **Corner Radius control point** *to visually change the amount of corner radius applied to a rectangle.*

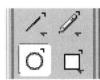

20 *The* **Ellipse tool** *selected in the Tools panel.*

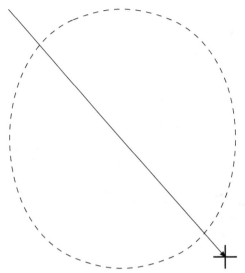

21 *To* **draw an ellipse**, *drag the cursor along the diagonal line between two sides.*

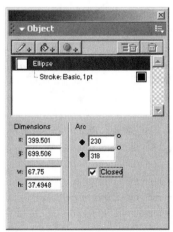

22 *Use the settings in the Object panel to change the attributes of an ellipse.*

Using the Ellipse Tool

Another type of object you can create is the ellipse. The Ellipse tool also creates circles.

To draw an ellipse or circle:

1. Click the Ellipse tool in the Tools panel **20**.
2. Position the cursor where you want one "corner" of the ellipse.
3. Press and drag to the opposite "corner" **21**.

TIP Hold the Shift key as you drag to constrain the ellipse to a circle.

TIP Hold the Opt/Alt key to draw the ellipse from the center outward.

TIP Combine both the Opt/Alt and Shift keys to draw a circle outward from the center point.

To change the dimensions of an ellipse:

1. Select the ellipse entry in the Object panel.
2. Change the Dimension settings in the Object panel as follows **22**:
   - The **x** field controls the horizontal position of the upper-left corner of the ellipse on the artboard.
   - The **y** field controls the vertical position of the upper-left corner of the ellipse on the artboard.
   - The **w** field controls the width of the ellipse.
   - The **h** field controls the height of the ellipse.
3. Press Return/Enter to apply the change.

The arc controls let you cut out a portion of the ellipse.

To create an arc from an ellipse:

1. Select the ellipse entry in the Object panel.

2. Set the Arc settings as follows ㉓:
   • Enter an amount in the diamond field to control the angle of the first arc segment ㉔.
   • Enter an amount in the circle field to control the angle of the second arc segment ㉔.

3. Click the Closed control to show or hide the segments from the edge of the arc to the radius of the ellipse ㉕.

You can also manually drag the arc segments into position.

To manually modify the arc from an ellipse:

1. Select the ellipse.

2. Choose the Direct Selection tool in the Tools panel.

3. Drag the diamond control point to change the angle of the first arc segment ㉖.

4. Drag the circle control point to change the angle of the second arc segment ㉖.

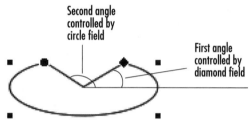

㉓ *Use the* **Arc settings in the Object panel** *to change the arc created by an ellipse.*

㉔ *The Arc settings in the Object panel change the arc created by an ellipse.*

㉕ *The difference between closed arcs (top) and open arcs (bottom).*

㉖ *Drag the arc control points to manually change the size of the arc.*

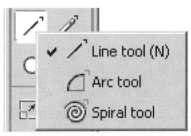

㉗ *The* **Line tool** *selected from its toolset in the Tools panel.*

㉘ *A* **straight line** *drawn with the Line tool.*

dx:39.7500	dy:39.7500	dist:56.2148	angle:45

㉙ *Watch the values in the Status panel to see the angles as you draw a line.*

Using the Line Tool

FreeHand is definitely the program for anyone who has said they cannot even draw a straight line. The Line tool makes it easy!

To draw a straight line:

1. Press the toolset to choose the Line tool in the Tools panel **㉗**.

2. Position the cursor where you want the line to start.

3. Press and drag along the direction the line should follow.

4. Release the mouse button where you want the line to end **㉘**.

TIP If you press the Shift key as you use the Line tool, your lines will be constrained to 45° or 90° increments of the Constrain axis *(see page 141)*.

You can't use the Object panel to change the settings of the path created by the Line tool. However, you can check the attributes of the line as you draw using the Info Toolbar.

To see the attributes of a line as you draw:

1. Start the drag to create the line.

2. Without releasing the mouse button, note the attributes in the Info Toolbar **㉙**:

   - The **x** shows the horizontal position of the first point of the line on the artboard.
   - The **y** shows the vertical position of the first point of the line on the artboard.
   - The **dx** shows the horizontal distance to the second point of the line.
   - The **dy** shows the vertical distance to the second point of the line.
   - The **distance** shows the actual length of the line.
   - The **angle** shows the angle of the line.

Using the Polygon Tool

There are two types of objects you can create with the Polygon tool: polygons and stars. Before you draw a polygon you have to set its attributes.

To set the attributes for a polygon:

1. Double-click the Polygon tool in the Tools panel 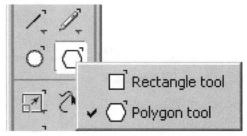. This opens the Polygon Tool dialog box.

2. If it is not already selected, choose Polygon from the Shape choices. The Polygon settings appear ③.

3. Use the Number of Sides field or slider to enter the the number of sides for your polygon. The Preview Area shows a representation of the polygon.

4. Click OK. The settings for the polygon are kept until the next time you change the dialog box.

To draw a polygon:

1. Position the cursor where you want the center of your shape.

2. Drag outward ②. As you drag, you will see the shape that defines your polygon.

3. Move the mouse to rotate the polygon to the position you want.

4. Release the mouse button when you are satisfied with the size and position of the polygon.

TIP If you set the Polygon tool to four sides, you can draw a rectangle that you can rotate as you drag. This is something you can't do with the regular Rectangle tool.

TIP Once you have drawn a polygon, you cannot use the settings to change its size or shape.

③ *The* **Polygon tool** *selected from its toolset in the Tools panel.*

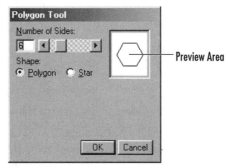

③ *The* Polygon Tool *dialog box.*

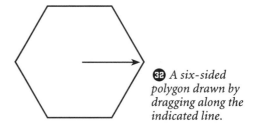

② *A six-sided polygon drawn by dragging along the indicated line.*

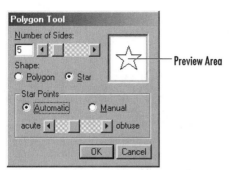

Preview Area

❸ Star choices *in the Polygon Tool dialog box.*

❹ *Stars set for Automatic alignment (top), an Acute angle (middle), and an Obtuse angle (bottom).*

A Minor Quibble

Strictly speaking, the Number of Sides label is incorrect. A star has twice the number of sides as it does points. The label should read Number of Outside Points when defining a star.

Stars are the second type of object that you can draw with the Polygon tool.

To set the attributes to create a star:

1. Double-click the Polygon tool in the Tools panel. This opens the Polygon Tool dialog box.

2. If it is not already selected, choose Star from the Shape choices. The Star settings appear ❸.

3. Use the Number of Sides field or slider to control the number of points of the star. The Preview Area shows a representation of the star.

4. Set the Star Points as follows:
   - **Automatic** creates a star that has its segments automatically aligned.
   - **Manual** lets you set your own angle for the alignment of the star sides.

5. If you have chosen the Manual setting for Star points, drag the slider between actute and obtuse settings ❹. The preview window shows the effect of the changes.

To draw a star:

1. Position the cursor where you want the center of your star.

2. Drag outward. As you drag, you will see the shape that defines your star.

3. Move the mouse to rotate the star to the position you want.

4. Release the mouse button when you are satisfied with the size and position of the star.

TIP Once you have drawn a star, you cannot use the settings to change its size or shape.

Using the Polygon Tool

Using the Pencil Tool

The Pencil tool allows you to draw lines that are both curvy and straight.

To set the Pencil tool options:

1. Double-click the Pencil tool in the Tools panel **35**. This opens the Pencil tool dialog box **36**.

2. Set Precision as follows:
   - Set a high value to have your path follow any minor variables as you drag.
   - Choose a low value to smooth out any minor variables as you drag.

3. If you drag too quickly, your stroke may not fill in correctly. Check the box for Draw dotted line. This creates a dotted line that follows your path. FreeHand then fills in that line with the actual path.

To draw with the Pencil tool:

1. Choose the Pencil tool in the Tools panel.

2. Drag the cursor along the path you want to create.

3. Release the mouse button when you have completed your line **37**.

4. Press the Opt/Alt key as you drag to create a straight line. Release the Opt/Alt key (but not the mouse button) to continue the path **38**.

5. Press the Cmd/Ctrl key and drag backward over the path to erase part of the path as you draw.

To close a path drawn with the Pencil tool:

1. Bring the line back to its origin and watch for a little square to appear next to the cursor.

2. Release the mouse button and the path will be closed.

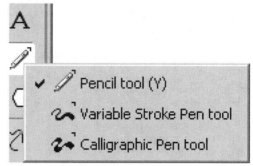

35 The **Pencil tool** *selected from its toolset in the Tools panel.*

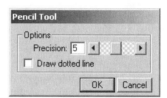

36 *The* **Pencil Tool** *dialog box.*

37 *The* **Pencil tool** *creates a line that follows the path you dragged.*

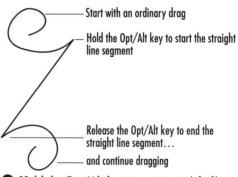

Start with an ordinary drag

Hold the Opt/Alt key to start the straight line segment

Release the Opt/Alt key to end the straight line segment…

and continue dragging

38 *Hold the Opt/Alt key to create straight lines with the Pencil tool.*

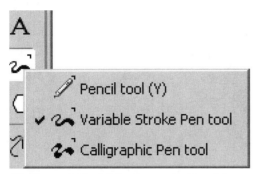

® The **Variable Stroke Pen tool** *selected from its toolset in the Tools panel.*

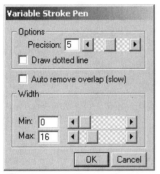

④ The **Variable Stroke Pen tool** *dialog box.*

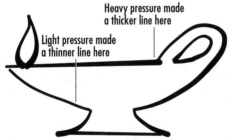

④ *Changing the pressure while drawing with a pressure-sensitive table changes the thickness of the line created in the* **Variable stroke mode**.

Using the Variable Stroke Pen Tool

The Variable Stroke Pen tool allows you to draw lines that are both curvy and straight.

To set the Variable Stroke Pen options:

1. Double-click the Variable Stroke Pen tool in the Tools panel **③**. This opens the Variable Stroke Pen tool dialog box **④**.
2. Set Precision as follows:
    *   Set a high value to have your path follow any minor variables as you drag.
    *   Choose a low value to smooth out any minor variables as you drag.
3. Check the box for Draw dotted line so that if you draw too quickly a dotted line follows your path.
4. In the Min field, enter the size for the thinnest part of your brush stroke (any size from 1 to 72 points).
5. In the Max field, enter the size for the thickest part of your brush stroke (any size from 1 to 72 points).
6. Choose Auto remove overlap (slow) to eliminate overlapping parts of the path. This makes it easier to reshape the path and avoid printing problems.

To draw with the Variable Stroke Pen tool:

1. Choose the Variable Stroke Pen tool in the Tools panel.
2. Drag to create the path.
3. If you have a pressure-sensitive tablet, any changes in the pressure you exert will change the thickness of your stroke **④**.

TIP Use the fill controls—not the stroke controls—to set the color of the object created with the Variable Stroke Pen. *(See Chapter 14, Fills, for how to set the fill color.)*

Using the Calligraphic Pen Tool

The Calligraphic Pen tool allows you to create the look of lines drawn with a calligraphy pen.

To set the Calligraphic pen mode:

1. Double-click the Calligraphic Pen tool in the Tools panel **42**. This opens the Calligraphic Pen tool dialog box **43**.

2. Set Precision as follows:
   - Set a high value to have your path follow any minor variables as you drag.
   - Choose a low value to smooth out any minor variables as you drag.

3. Check the box for Draw dotted line so that if you draw too quickly a dotted line follows your path.

4. Set the Width to Fixed to have a single width.

   or

   Set the Width to Variable to be able to set a minimum and maximum width.

5. If you have chosen Fixed width, use the slider or type the width in the field.

   or

   If you have chosen Variable width, use the slider for the Min field to enter the size for the thinnest part of your brush stroke (any size from 1 to 72 points).

   In the Max field, enter the size for the thickest part of your brush stroke (any size from 1 to 72 points).

6. Use the Angle wheel or type in the field to set the angle that the stroke uses for its calligraphic lines **44**.

7. Choose Auto remove overlap (slow) to eliminate overlapping parts of the path. This makes it easier to reshape the path and avoid printing problems.

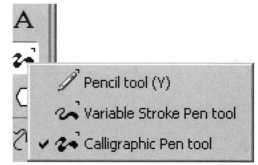

42 *The* **Calligraphic Pen tool** *selected from its toolset in the Tools panel.*

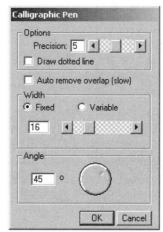

43 *The* **Calligraphic Pen tool** *dialog box.*

44 *Changing* **the angle for the Calligraphic pen** *changes the shape of the curves.*

Pen Tools or Strokes?

The Calligraphic Pen tool is not the same as the Calligraphic stroke option. Similarly, the Variable Stroke Pen tool is not the same as the Brushes stroke option. Both pen tools create a similar look of lines that become thinner and thicker.

Calligraphic or Brush strokes can be applied to any object drawn with any tool. Also you can easily reshape those paths.

The Pen tools, however, respond to the changes in a pressure-sensitive tablet. The stroke options don't.

Working with a Pressure-Sensitive Tablet

Many years ago I heard the statement that "drawing with a mouse is like drawing with a bar of soap." The solution to that cumbersome idea is to get a pressure-sensitive tablet such as those made by Wacom. I can't think of a better investment for any computer artist or graphic designer than a pressure-sensitive tablet.

In FreeHand, the Variable Stroke Pen and the Calligraphic Pen tools will respond to pressure exerted on the tablet's surface. This helps these two tools create natural-looking brush strokes. However, there's more than just artistic reasons to use a tablet.

Using a stylus keeps your hand in a more comfortable position than working with a mouse. This means you are less likely to develop hand strain or other problems.

To draw with the Calligraphic pen tool:

1. Drag to create the path.

2. As you change the direction of the path the angle determines the shape of the path. Pressure-sensitive tablets also respond to the changes in the angle that you hold the pen as you draw.

TIP Use the fill controls—not the stroke controls—to set the color of the object created with the Calligraphic Pen. *(See Chapter 14, Fills, for how to set the fill color.)*

Even if you don't use a tablet, you can still vary your stroke for the Variable Stroke Pen or the Calligraphic Pen tools.

To vary the pressure using the keyboard controls:

♦ To increase the thickness, press the right arrow or the number 2 key as you drag with the mouse.

   or

   To decrease the thickness, press the left arrow or the number 1 key as you drag with the mouse.

Using the Calligraphic Pen Tool

Using the Spiral Tool

FreeHand's Spiral tool provides you with more than enough options for creating all sorts of spirals.

To set the Spiral tool options:

1. Double-click the Spiral tool in the Tools panel **45**. This opens the Spiral dialog box **46**.

2. Choose between the Non-expanding and Expanding type.

TIP An Expanding spiral opens up its lines as it moves out from the center. The lines in a non-expanding spirals are evenly spaced.

3. If you choose Expanding, use the slider or enter a number in the Expansion field. The higher the number, the greater the expansion rate **47**.

4. Choose one of the following from the Draw by list:

   • **Rotations** lets you specify the Number of rotations in your spiral.
   • **Increments** lets you specify the amount of space between the curls in non-expanding spirals or the starting radius for expanding spirals.

5. Choose one of the following from the Draw from list:

   • **Center** starts at the center of the spiral.
   • **Edge** starts from the edge of the spiral.
   • **Corner** starts from the corner of the bounding box that holds the spiral **48**.

6. Click one of the Direction icons to choose either a counterclockwise or a clockwise spiral.

To create a spiral:

◆ Drag with the Spiral tool to create the spiral on the page.

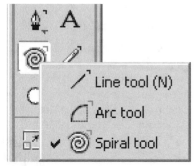

45 *The* **Spiral tool** *selected from its toolset in the Tools panel.*

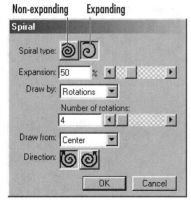

46 *The* **Spiral dialog box.**

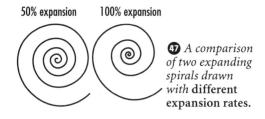

47 *A comparison of two expanding spirals drawn with* **different expansion rates.**

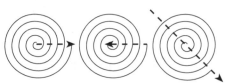

48 *Spirals drawn from the* **center** *(left), the* **edge** *(middle), and the* **corner** *(right). The dashed lines show the length and direction of the mouse drags.*

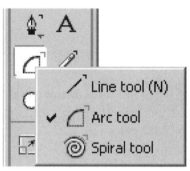

⑭ *The* **Arc tool** *selected from its toolset in the Tools panel.*

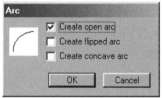

⑮ *The* **Arc dialog box** *allows you to choose from open, flipped, or concave arc settings.*

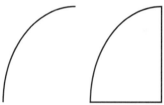

⑯ *Notice the difference between an* **open arc** *(left) and a* **closed arc** *(right).*

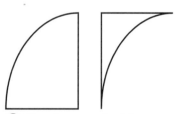

⑰ *Closed arcs can be either* **convex** *(left) or* **concave** *(right).*

Using the Arc Tool

This is definitely the tool for Indiana Jones—the Arc tool.

TIP You may want to use the Arc controls for ellipses if you want a little more numerical control when creating arcs.

To choose settings for the Arc tool:

1. Double-click the Arc tool in the Tools panel **⑭**. This opens the Arc dialog box **⑮**.

2. Choose Create open arc if you want a simple arc. Deselect this option if you want your arc to form a wedge shape **⑯**.

3. Choose Create flipped arc to reflect the arc from one direction to another.

4. Choose Create concave arc to create an arc that curves inside a corner.

To draw with the Arc tool:

1. With the Arc tool selected, drag to create the arc on the page.

2. Release the mouse button when you are satisfied with the arc.

TIP Hold the Cmd/Ctrl key after you start the drag to close or open the arc. This does not work if Create concave arc has been chosen.

TIP Hold the Opt/Alt key after you start the drag to flip the arc horizontally or vertically.

TIP Hold the Control key (Mac) to switch between either concave or convex settings **⑰**.

TIP Hold the Shift key to constrain the arc to quarter circles.

Using the Connector Tool

I spent too many years drawing organizational charts not to love this tool. The Connector tool lets you create lines that automatically stay connected to objects. This makes it easy to reposition objects while the attached connector lines move and reshape their positions.

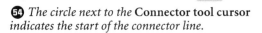

❸ *The* **Connector tool** *in the Tools panel.*

To draw a connector line between objects:

1. Choose the Connector tool in the Tools panel **❸**.

2. Position the cursor near the top, bottom, or sides of the object where you want the connector line to begin.

   TIP A small circle next to the cursor indicates you can start the connector line **❸**.

❸ *The circle next to the* **Connector tool cursor** *indicates the start of the connector line.*

3. Drag towards the top, bottom, or sides of the object that you want to connect to **❸**.

4. When you see the small circle appear, release the mouse button. The connector line automatically appears **❸**.

   TIP Connector lines automatically have arrowheads applied to the origin and end of the line. The arrowheads may be turned off or modified using the stroke controls *(see page 221).*

❸ *Drag with the Connector tool from one object to another.*

❸ *The circle next to the Connector tool cursor indicates the connector line will attach to the second object.*

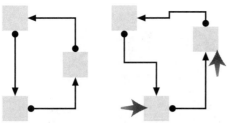

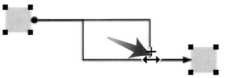

57 *The lines created by the Connector tool reshape as you move the objects to new positions.*

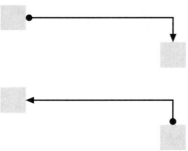

58 *Drag a connector line segment to reshape the connector line between two objects.*

59 *The **Reverse Direction command** changes the start and end points of the connection line.*

Once you have created connector lines, you can easily move the objects without having to redraw the connection.

To move objects connected by connector lines:

◆ Use either selection tool to move the object into a new position. *(See Chapter 8, Working with Objects, for more information on moving objects.)* The connector line automatically reshapes so that it connects the two objects **57**.

You can also reshape the connector lines without moving the objects they connect.

To reshape the connector lines:

1. Choose the Connector tool.

2. Position the cursor over a segment of the connector line. A plus sign and a double-headed arrow appears.

3. Drag the cursor to reshape the line **58**.

TIP Depending on the shape and position of the objects, you may create additional corners to the connector line.

You can also reverse the direction of a connector line so that the arrowheads appear on the opposite ends of the line **59**.

To reverse the direction of the line:

1. Select the connector line with either the Connector tool or the selection tools.

2. Choose **Modify** >**Alter Path** >**Reverse Direction**. The arrrowheads are reversed on the connector line **59**.

Using the Trace Tool

You may have scanned artwork that you want to convert into FreeHand paths. The Trace tool can recognize the different shapes in the artwork and convert them into vector paths. Before you use the Trace tool you need to import the scanned artwork into your FreeHand document.

To import artwork for tracing:

1. With your document open, choose **File > Import.**

2. Use the navigational tools to find the PICT, TIFF, or EPS file you want to trace. After the file is imported, your cursor changes to a corner symbol.

3. Click with the corner symbol to place the image on the page **60**.

TIP Though you can trace art on any layer, most people put imported images on layers below the horizontal line of the Layers panel. This lightens the image so it is easier to work with and ensures that it does not print *(see page 172).*

TIP For best results using the Trace tool, set the preference for Smart image preview resolution to Full Resolution *(see Appendix C).*

60 *An imported image appears on the page with four anchor points.*

Realistic Expectations for Using the Trace Tool

FreeHand's Trace tool is one of the best in the business—much better than its nearest competitor, and just about as good as the stand-alone tracing product, Adobe Streamline.

However, no automatic tracing tool or dedicated tracing program can do it all! Most likely, when you trace, you will have to manually clean up the image to get it to look good.

This is especially true if you are tracing company logos, text, or other artwork that has very graphic shapes.

You may find that it is easier to use FreeHand's other creation tools to manually trace that type of artwork. For instance, it is easier to use the Ellipse tool to trace a circle than try to get the Trace tool to create a perfect circle.

❻❶ *The* **Trace tool** *in the Tools panel.*

❻❷ *The* **Trace Tool dialog box** *lets you set the controls for how the Trace tool follows the shapes and colors of scanned images.*

Before you can use the Trace tool, you need to set its options, such as how many colors should be created, what kind of image you are working on, and so on.

To set the trace options:

1. Double-click the Trace tool in the Tools panel **❻❶**. This opens the Trace Tool dialog box **❻❷**.

2. Set the Color mode, Resolution, Trace layers, Path conversion, Trace conformity, Noise tolerance, and Wand color tolerance as detailed in the following exercises.

3. Click OK to apply the settings.

To set the Trace tool Color modes:

1. Use the pop-up list or type the number of colors or shades of gray that you want in the final image.

2. Choose between Colors or Grays for the final objects.

3. If you have chosen Colors, use the second list to select RGB or CMYK colors.

To set the Trace tool Resolution options:

◆ Set the Resolution options as follows:
   - **High** sets the Trace tool to look at the most details in the image.
   - **Normal** sets the Trace tool to look for less details.
   - **Low** sets the Trace tool to look for the fewest details.

TIP High-resolution traces take longer and require more memory.

To set the layers to be traced:

◆ Set the Trace layers options as follows:
   - **All** uses all the layers in the document.
   - **Foreground** uses just the foreground layers.
   - **Background** uses only those layers in the background of the Layers panel.

Using the Trace Tool

To set the how the paths are converted:

◆ Set the Path Conversions as follows:

- **Outline** traces the ouside border of the image to create closed, filled paths. This is the option most often used to trace scanned images.
- **Centerline** traces the center of graphic strokes. Use this option if you have an image that has many lines, but few filled areas.
- **Centerline/Outline** uses both options.
- **Outer Edge** traces only the outside contours of the image. Use this option if you want to mask the silhouette of an image against a background.

To set the sensitivity of the Trace tool:

◆ Set the three sensitivity sliders as follows:

- **Trace conformity** controls how close the traced objects follow the original. Set the value from 0 (lowest conformity) to 10 (highest conformity).
- **Noise tolerance** lets you eliminate any stray pixels, such as dirt or paper grain, in the scan. Set the value from 0 (more noise kept) to 10 (more noise eliminated).
- **Wand color tolerance** lets you set how broad a range of colors the Trace tool recognizes as one final color. Set the value from 0 (narrow range) to 255 (broadest range).

To trace an image:

1. Use the Trace tool to drag a marquee around the part of the image you want to trace **63**.

2. Release the mouse button to finish tracing the artwork. The traced objects appear on top of the original image **64**.

TIP When tracing photographic images, the Trace tool may create many objects. Choose **Modify** > **Group** to join the objects into an easily selected group.

63 Drag a marquee *with the Trace tool to trace an imported image.*

64 *A comparison of the original scanned image (top) and the traced image (bottom). Notice the small differences in the traced objects such as the flat lines in the shape of the clock or the outside circle.*

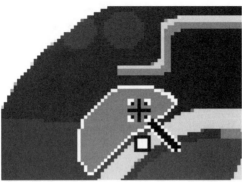

❺ *Click with the Trace tool to create a selection based on the color of the underlying image.*

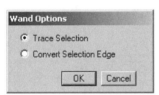

❻ *The* **Wand Options dialog box** *lets you choose how to convert the area selected with the Trace tool.*

❼ *An example of how individual elements can be traced by clicking with the Trace tool.*

Rather than draw a marquee around the image, you can also use the Trace tool to select individual areas of a scanned image. This makes it easy to isolate a particular area from the rest of the scan.

To trace specific areas of an image:

1. Click the Trace tool on the area you want to capture. A blue line appears around the area that has been selected **❺**.

2. If you want to add to the selection, hold the Shift key and click in another area of the image. Continue as many times as necessary to select all the areas you want.

3. Release the Shift key and click the Trace tool inside the selected area. The Wand Options dialog box appears **❻**.

4. Choose Trace Selection to trace the selected areas as if they had been part of a marquee selection.

   or

   Choose Convert Selection Edge to merge all the selected areas into one selection with a default color of black **❼**.

Using the Trace Tool

Auto Constrain

The Auto Constrain option is available for the Rectangle, Ellipse, and Line tools. Instead of holding the Shift key to constrain as you draw, the Auto Constrain option automatically constrains the object. This option makes it easy to draw squares and circles. It also makes it easy to draw horizontal, vertical, or 45-degree angled lines.

To use the Auto Constrain option:

1. Turn on the Auto Constrain option in the Rectangle, Ellipse, or Line tool dialog boxes.

2. Draw with the chosen tool. The tools are constrained as follows:
   - Rectangles are constrained to squares when you drag near the 45-degree angle.
   - Ellipses are constrained to circles when you drag near the 45-degree angle.
   - Lines are constrained to 0-degrees, 90-degrees, or 45-degrees when you drag near those angles.

TIP A small circle appears next to the cursor when the tool is constrained **68**.

Reposition While Drawing

As you draw, you may want to move the object to a new position. FreeHand lets you temporarily stop creating an object to move it to a new position.

To repositiion an object as you draw it:

1. Press the Spacebar as you draw the object. A four-headed arrow appears **69**.

2. Drag the object to the new position.

3. Release the Spacebar to continue drawing the object.

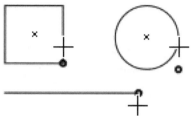

68 *The circle next to the cursor indicates that the object is being constrained by the* **Auto Constrain option.**

69 *Hold the Spacebar to reposition an object as you drag.*

70 *Compare an object drawn with the Pencil tool (top) and the Pen tool (bottom). Notice the uneven lines (circled) drawn by the Pencil tool object.*

Using the Pen and Bezigon Tools

There are two other creation tools in the Tools panel: the Pen and Bezigon tools. Both give much greater control over the shape of the path, especially when compared to the Pencil tool **70**.

However, these tools are not as simple to use as the other creation tools. Therefore I've given them their own chapter *(immediately following this one)* to cover how they work.

PEN AND BEZIGON 6

I remember the first time I tried to use the Pen tool in a vector-drawing program. I clicked the tool and dragged across the screen in a way that I thought would create a curve. Instead, I got a wild series of lines that shot out in different directions.

When I tried to change the shape of the lines, things got worse. I was so startled I closed up the program and didn't use the Pen tool again for a long, long, time.

When I finally got up enough nerve to try the Pen again, it took a lot of trial and error but eventually I got it! I saw that the principles of using the Pen are actually quite simple.

I just wish someone had written out some easy-to-understand, step-by-step instructions. So, think of this chapter as the instructions on the Pen and Bezigon tools that I wish I had back then.

This chapter contains everything you should need to master the Pen tool in FreeHand. However, if you would like to learn the Pen tool using movies and audio narration, may I suggest you visit **www.zenofthepen.org**. It has an online tutorial you can purchase that can help you learn the Pen tool in FreeHand as well as other programs such as Adobe Photoshop.

Working with the Pen Tool

Learning FreeHand's Pen tool makes it easier to learn the Pen tool in Macromedia Fireworks, Macromedia Flash, Adobe Photoshop, QuarkXPress, or Adobe InDesign.

To create straight sides with the Pen:

1. Choose the Pen tool from the Tools panel **❶**.

2. Position the cursor where you want the path to start and click. A corner point appears as a white square **❷**.

3. Position the cursor for the next point of the object and click. A line extends from the first point to the second point.

4. Continue clicking until you have created all the sides of your object **❸**.

5. Create a closed path by clicking the first point again.

TIP Once you finish a path, press Tab to deselect the path. This lets you start a new path instead of continuing the old one.

TIP Hold the Shift key to constrain your lines to 45° increments relative to the constrain axis.

❶ The **Pen tool** *selected from its toolset in the Tools panel.*

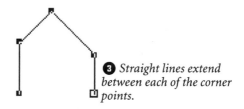

❷ *Clicking with either the Pen or the Bezigon creates a* **corner point** *shown as a hollow square.*

❸ *Straight lines extend between each of the corner points.*

The Difference Detween the Pen and Bezigon tools

Both the Pen and the Bezigon tools allow you to draw much more precisely than the Freehand tool. So what is the difference between the two tools? At first glance, there is very little difference. In fact, once a path has been created, there is no way to tell which tool created it.

The main difference is that the Pen tool allows you to manipulate handles as you place points. The Bezigon tool allows you to quickly click to place points, but all the point handles are set automatically. After you place points with the Bezigon tool, you must then go back to adjust the point handles. This makes the Bezigon tool easier to learn but makes the Pen tool faster when truly mastered.

These days I find find few people who use the Bezigon tool. However, mastering it or the Pen tool is vital to working with FreeHand.

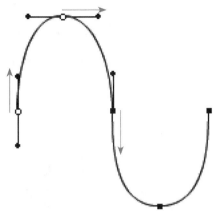

4 *To draw a smooth curved path with the Pen tool,* **drag to place curve points** *at each spot where the path changes direction.*

5 *To start the* **bumpy curved path,** *press the Opt/Alt key and drag with the Pen tool. This creates a corner point with a handle.*

6 *To create a* **corner point with two handles,** *drag down. When the handle extends backward enough, hold the Opt/Alt key and then drag in the direction of the second arrow.*

The Pen tool helps you draw smooth curves. A smooth curve makes the transition from one direction to another with no abrupt changes, like the curve created by a roller-coaster.

To draw a smooth curved path with the Pen:

1. Choose the Pen tool.

2. Click the first point and drag up. Do not release the mouse until you have created a handle that extends about a third of the way up the curve you want to create **4**.

3. Repeat the dragging process to place curve points at each spot where the path changes direction.

4. Press the Tab key to deselect the path when you have finished creating the path.

TIP You can modify a path by changing both the lengths of the point handles and their directions.

Life is not all smooth, and neither are paths. So, there may be times you need a bumpy path—a curved path that makes an abrupt change. Think of a bumpy curve as the path a bouncing ball takes.

To draw a bumpy curved path with the Pen:

1. Hold the Opt/Alt key as you drag with the Pen tool to create a corner point with a handle **5**.

2. Drag down at the second point. Two point handles extend out from the sides of the point. Do not release the mouse button.

3. When the point handle in the back has extended out enough, press the Opt/Alt key. Then rotate the front point handle so that it aligns properly **6**. You may then release the mouse button.

4. Drag to create the final point.

Working with the Pen Tool

Imagine you are riding in a car, and suddenly there is a bump in the road. As your car travels up and down the bump it follows the shape of a straight-to-bumpy path.

To draw a straight-to-bumpy path with the Pen:

1. Click to place the first corner point.
2. Click to create the next corner point.
3. To add a handle to this point, hold the Opt/Alt key and then drag **7**.
4. Drag to create a curve point at the end of the bump.
5. To add a straight line from the third point, hold the Opt/Alt key and move the Pen tool over the point. A small caret appears next to the Pen cursor.
6. Click on the point. This converts the point into a corner point and retracts the second handle **8**.

FreeHand has a special kind of point — the connector point — that is not found in most other vector-drawing programs. Connector points provide a smooth transition between straight lines and curves. Connector points ensure that the handle that defines the curve always stays aligned with the direction of the straight line **9**.

To create connector points using the Pen:

◆ (Mac) Hold the Control key and click to create a connector point.

(Win) Hold the Alt key and click with the right mouse button.

7 *To* **add a handle to a corner point,** *hold the Opt/Alt key and then drag on the point.*

8 *To retract a handle from a curve point, press the Opt/Alt key and click the point again.*

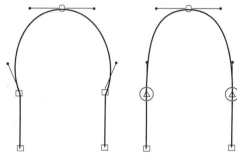

9 *Unlike the curve points (left) the* **connector points** *(circled) always stay aligned to the straight lines they are connected to.*

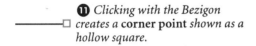

Pen tool

Bezigon tool (B, 8)

⑩ *The Bezigon tool selected from its toolset in the Tools panel.*

⑪ *Clicking with the Bezigon creates a **corner point** shown as a hollow square.*

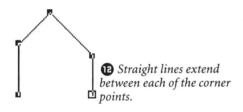

⑫ *Straight lines extend between each of the corner points.*

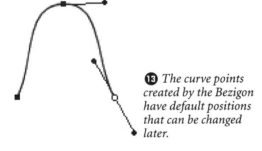

⑬ *The curve points created by the Bezigon have default positions that can be changed later.*

Creating Paths with the Bezigon Tool

If you find it difficult to remember all the moves with the Pen, you may find it easier to create objects with the Bezigon.

To create straight sides with the Bezigon tool:

1. Choose the Bezigon tool from the Tools panel **⑩**.

2. Position the cursor where you want the path to start and click. A corner point appears as a white square **⑪**.

3. Position the cursor for the next point of the object and click. A line extends from the first point to the second point.

4. Continue clicking until you have created all the sides of your object **⑫**.

5. Create a closed path by clicking the first point again.

TIP Once you finish a path, press Tab to deselect the path. This lets you start a new path instead of continuing the old one.

When you place curve points with the Bezigon, you only plot the position of each point. After you are done, you reshape the points to the exact shape of the curve.

To draw a smooth curved path with the Bezigon:

1. Choose the Bezigon tool and place your first curve point holding down the Opt/Alt key.

2. Hold the Opt/Alt key and click to create a second curve point. Although the segment between the points may not look correct, don't worry.

3. Keep holding the Opt/Alt key and click to create all the curve points.

4. Use the Pointer tool to adjust the point handles so the curve is the proper shape **⑬**.

When you use the Bezigon tool to create a bumpy path, you need an extra point at the top of the bump.

To draw a bumpy path with the Bezigon:

1. Click to create the first point, which is a corner point.

2. Hold the Opt/Alt key and click to add a curve point at the top of the bump. This adds a handle to the first corner point.

3. Click to create a corner point. A handle is added because this point is connected to a curve point.

4. Hold the Opt/Alt key and click to add a curve point at the top of the second bump. A handle is added to the previous corner point ⑭.

5. Click to create the final corner point. A handle is added because this point is connected to a curve point.

To draw a straight-to-bumpy path with the Bezigon:

1. Click to create a corner point.

2. Click again to create a corner point. The two points are connected by a line.

3. Hold the Opt/Alt key and click where the top of the bump should be. This creates a curve point. It also adds a handle to the corner point created in Step 2.

4. Click to create the next corner point ⑮. This adds a handle to the corner point that is connected to the curve point.

5. Click to create the final corner point that creates the straight line.

You create connector points with the Bezigon the same way as you do with the Pen.

To create connector points using the Bezigon:

◆ (Mac) Hold the Control key and click to create a connector point.

(Win) Hold the Alt key and click with the right mouse button.

⑭ *The Bezigon tool requires a curve point at the top of the bump to create a bumpy path.*

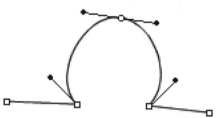

⑮ *The Bezigon tool automatically adds handles to the corner points that are connected to the top curve point.*

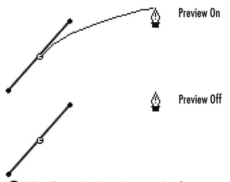

16 *The slash next to the cursor indicates that you can click or drag to add points to the path.*

17 *The* **Pen Tool dialog box** *lets you apply the Show Pen Preview command.*

Preview On

Preview Off

18 *The* **Show Pen Preview** *option lets you see where the next line segment will be placed.*

Adding Points to a Path

You may finish creating a path and later realize you want to add more segments to it. You then add points to the end of the path. (This only works with open paths. Closed paths have no endpoints.)

To add points to the end of a path:

1. Move the Pen or Bezigon over the endpoint that you want to continue. A slash appears next to the cursor **16**.

2. Click to create a corner point.

   or

   Drag to extend a handle out from the point.

3. Click to add more points to the path.

Pen Tool Options

The Pen tool has a preview option that helps you see what the next line segment will look like—before you place the next point. This is especially helpful when creating curved segments.

To apply the Pen tool preview:

1. Double-click the Pen tool in the Tools panel. This opens the Pen tool dialog box **17**.

2. Check the option for Show Pen Preview. This creates a preview of the next line segment before you place the next point on the path **18**.

Bezigon Tool Options

Like the Rectangle, Ellipse, and Line tools *(see Chapter 5)*, the Bezigon tool also has an auto constrain option.

To turn on the Bezigon tool Auto Constrain control:

1. Double-click the Bezigon tool in the Tools panel. This opens the Bezigon tool dialog box ⑲.

2. Check the option for Auto Constrain. This provides a visual feedback of where the 0-degree, 90-degree, and 45-degree lines are ⑳.

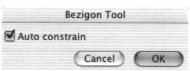

⑲ *The* **Bezigon Tool dialog box** *lets you apply the Auto Constrain option.*

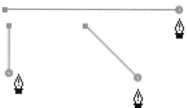

⑳ *The* **Auto Constrain** *option makes it easier to create lines on 0, 45, and 90-degree angles with the Bezigon tool.*

WORKING WITH POINTS 7

As you have seen in the previous chapters, all the objects created by the creation tools are called paths. And all paths consist of points that are joined by segments.

As soon as you start to change the shape of objects, it is necessary to understand what the different types of points are and how they can be modified. You also need to understand how to work with the handles that extend out from points.

Fortunately, Macromedia FreeHand gives you a wealth of powerful tools for working with points—either manually or automatically.

Understanding the Types of Points

If you are familiar with programs such as Macromedia Fireworks or Adobe Illustrator, you should understand the basic aspects of working with points.

The basics of points

There are three elements to working with points (also called *anchor points*). There is the point itself, the line segment that connects the point to other points on the path, and point handles that may extend out from the point 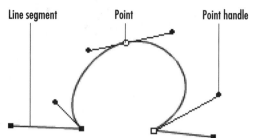.

TIP Points and point handles are displayed in the highlight color of the layer that they are on *(see page 174)*.

Handles are nonprinting lines that control the direction along which any path curves. Changing the direction of the handle changes the shape of the path ❷.

Point handles are also called Bézier (pronounced *Bay-zee-ay*) handles. They were named after the French mathematician Pierre Bézier. He invented the mathematical principles that control handles.

Three different types of points make up FreeHand objects: corner points, curve points, and connector points. In order to have a complete understanding of FreeHand, it is vital to understand how these points work.

Corner points

Corner points are anchor points that allow paths to have an abrupt change in direction. Depending on how they were created, there are three different types of corner points: points with no handles, points with two handles, and points with one handle ❸.

Line segment   Point   Point handle

❶ *The different elements that combine to create a path.*

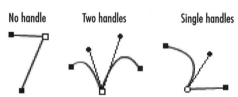

❷ *The results of moving the point handles in the directions indicated.*

No handle   Two handles   Single handles

❸ **Corner points** *are indicated by white squares and can have no handles (left), two handles (middle), or one handle (right).*

④ Curve points *are indicated by round dots and always have two point handles that govern the shape of the curve.*

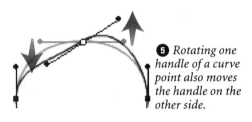

⑤ *Rotating one handle of a curve point also moves the handle on the other side.*

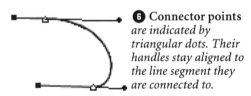

⑥ Connector points *are indicated by triangular dots. Their handles stay aligned to the line segment they are connected to.*

The One-Third Rule

The one-third rule says to limit the length of the point handles for any segment to no more than one-third of the length of that segment.

What happens if you break the one-third rule? Well, no one will come to arrest you, but you will find it difficult to edit your curves with long point handles that pivot all over the place.

Curve points

Curve points are anchor points that make a smooth, curved transition along the direction of the path. A curve point has two handles that extend out from both sides of the point. However, unlike corner points that may have two handles, the handles on curve points are linked so that as the handle on one side moves, the handle on the other side also moves. The length of the handle governs the shape of the curve **④**.

TIP If you rotate the point handle on one side of a curve point, the handle on the opposite side also moves. It is this "lever" action that makes the curve transition smooth **⑤**.

Connector points

The purpose of connector points is to constrain the transition between segments so that they cannot be moved out of alignment with their line segments **⑥**. Connector points are indicated by triangular dots and always have point handles.

Connector points can have one or two point handles. When a connector point occurs between a straight-line segment and a curved segment, there is only one point handle, which runs along the same direction as the straight line. When a connector point is between two curved segments, there are two point handles which are constrained by the position of the points on either side of the connector point.

TIP FreeHand provides two types of handles on the levers that come out of the points. The illustrations in this book show the small handles. If you find the small handles difficult to see, you can work with the large handles by switching the Preferences settings *(see Appendix C)*.

Understanding the Types of Points

Selecting Points

Anchor points define the shape of a path. So when you select and work with the points on a path, you also change the shape of the path. This is how great artwork begins.

FreeHand has two tools that select and move points: the Pointer tool and the Subselect tool. However, as you shall see, the Subselect tool can be found as an option when working with the Pointer tool.

To select points by clicking:

1. Click the Pointer tool in the Tools panel **7**.

2. Move the tip of the arrow of the Pointer tool on the path and click. This selects the path and makes its anchor points visible **8**. Although the anchor points are visible, they are not individually selected.

    TIP Do not use a path drawn with the Rectangle or Ellipse tools unless you have first ungrouped the objects *(see pages 97–98 for more information on grouping and ungrouping objects).*

3. Move the tip of the arrow over one of the points and click. The point is now selected and is shown as a hollow dot **9**. *(See the sidebar on this page regarding the display of selected points.)* If it has point handles, they will be visible.

4. Hold the Shift key and click with the Pointer tool to select additional points.

    TIP If you need to deselect a point, hold the Shift key and click on the selected point. This deselects the point without deselecting the path or other points.

7 *The Pointer tool in the Tools panel.*

8 *The anchor points of a path show up as dark squares when the entire path is selected.*

9 *A point on a path is displayed as a hollow dot when that single point is selected.*

For Adobe Illustrator Fans

Selected points on a path are usually displayed as hollow dots. Unselected points are usually solid. However, you can reverse this by choosing Show Solid Points in the FreeHand General Preferences *(see Appendix C).*

This setting displays selected points as solid dots and unselected points as hollow dots. This is how Adobe Illustrator displays points. Those who move from Illustrator to FreeHand may feel more comfortable working this way. (Sadly Adobe is not as welcoming for those moving from FreeHand to Illustrator.)

⑩ **Drag a marquee** *with the Pointer tool to select the points inside the marquee rectangle.*

⑪ *The* **Lasso tool** *in the Tools panel.*

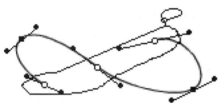

⑫ *Use the* **Lasso tool** *to select points within a non-rectangular area.*

Another way to select points is by using the Pointer to marquee an area around the points you want to select.

To select points with a marquee:

1. Place the Pointer tool outside the point or points you want to select.

2. Press and drag to create a rectangle that surrounds the points you want selected **⑩**. The area inside the rectangle is the *marquee.*

3. Release the mouse button. This selects all points inside the marquee.

TIP To select points in more than one area, create your first selection marquee. Then press the Shift key and create your next selection marquee.

TIP Hold the Cmd/Ctrl key to temporarily switch from another tool to the Pointer tool.

Sometimes creating a marquee may select points you don't want selected. In that case you may want to use the Lasso tool, which can select points in a non-rectangular area.

To select points within a non-rectangular area:

1. Choose the Lasso tool in the Tools panel **⑪**.

2. Place the Lasso tool outside the point or points you want to select.

3. Press and drag to create an area that surrounds the points you want selected **⑫**.

4. Release the mouse button. This selects all points inside the marquee.

To deselect points that are selected:

◆ Click elsewhere on the work page to deselect points.

Modifying Points and Handles

The shape of a path depends on the types of points on the path. You can change the shape of a path by changing the type of point or changing the point handles.

To modify points using the Object panel:

1. Use the Pointer tool to select one of the points on a path.

2. In the Object panel, click the entry for Path. This displays the point controls ⑬.

3. Use the Type icons to choose Curve point, Corner point, or Connector point ⑭.

4. Click the Handles icons to retract the handles going into and out of the point.

   TIP The left icon retracts the handle going into a point. The right icon retracts the handle coming out of a point.

5. With a curve point selected, choose the Automatic setting. This sets the point handles to the position and length that is best suited for the shape of the path ⑮.

   TIP The Bezigon tool creates points with the Automatic setting turned on.

6. Use the Point location x field to set the horizontal position of the point.

7. Use the Point location y field to set the vertical position of the point.

   TIP If you select multiple points on a path, you can change all the point attributes except their Point location.

To retract handles manually:

1. Select a point so that its handles are visible.

2. Place the Pointer tool or Subselect tool on the dot at the end of the handle.

3. Drag the handle into the anchor point ⑯.

⑬ *With a point selected, the Object panel displays the point controls.*

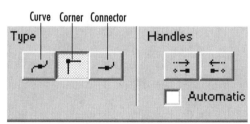

⑭ *You can change the type of point and retract the handles using the Object panel.*

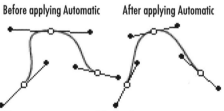

⑮ *A comparison of how the Automatic setting changes the position and length of point handles.*

⑯ *You can* **manually drag a point handle** *back into its anchor point.*

⓱ *Use the Subselect tool to* **manually extend a point handle** *out from a point.*

⓲ *Drag with the Subselect tool to* **manually extend point handles** *from both ends of the segment.*

⓳ *Place the Pen over a point (top) and click to* **retract the handles** *(bottom).*

⓴ *Drag with the Pen over a point to extend handles out from the point.*

To extend a single handle manually:

1. Use the Subselect tool to select the point from which you want to extend the handles.

2. Position the pointer over the selected point. A white curved arrowhead appears.

3. Drag to extend the handle out from the point ⓱.

TIP You can hold the Opt/Alt key while in the Pointer tool to access the Subselect tool.

You can also extend two handles at once from the points at either end of a segment. (This technique is sometimes called the "Bend-O-Matic.")

To extend two handles manually:

1. Use the Subselect tool to select the line segment between two points.

2. Drag the line segment. A handle extends out from each of the points on either side of the segment ⓲.

TIP If you use the Pointer tool, hold the Opt/Alt key to access the Subselect tool.

To retract handles with the Pen:

1. Move the Pen tool over the point. A small caret (^) symbol appears next to the cursor ⓳.

2. Click. The handles of the point are automatically retracted.

To extend handles with the Pen:

1. Move the Pen tool over the point. A minus sign (−) appears next to the cursor ⓴.

2. Drag but do not click. The point is converted to a curve point and handles extend out.

TIP If you click instead of drag, you will delete the point *(see the next page).*

Modifying Points and Handles

Modifying Points on a Path

As you create paths, you may need to delete or add points to make other modifications to the path.

To delete a selected point from a path:

1. Use any of the methods described earlier in this chapter to select the point or points you want to delete.

2. Press the Delete key. The point is deleted and the path reshapes **㉑**.

TIP If you delete an endpoint from a path, the path is reshaped, and the next endpoint is selected. You can then continue to delete each point along the path **㉒**.

You can also use the Pen or Bezigon tools to delete points from a path. This is helpful if you do not have your hands near the delete key on the keyboard.

To delete a point using the Pen or Bezigon tools:

1. Select the path.

2. Move the Pen or Bezigon tool over the point you want to delete. If the point has no handles, a minus sign (–) appears next to the cursor **㉓**.

3. If the minus sign appears, click to delete the point.

   or

   Click to retract the handles. You can then click again to delete the point.

TIP You can't use the Pen or Bezigon to delete an endpoint from a path.

㉑ *When you delete a point, you reshape the path.*

㉒ *When you delete an endpoint, the next point along the path is selected. This point can then be deleted and so on.*

㉓ *Click with the Pen or Bezigon tools to* **delete a point** *from a path.*

Open or Closed Paths

There are two types of paths: open and closed. Open paths have points at the end of the path called *endpoints*. A piece of string is an example of an open path.

Closed paths do not have endpoints. A rubber band is an example of a closed path.

24 *To* **add a point to a path,** *click with the Pen or the Bezigon tool on the path.*

25 *The* **Join command** *automatically created a new line segment connecting the points.*

26 *A point on the top path was selected and the* **Split command** *was applied. This created the bottom two paths. (Points were moved to show the separation.)*

You can also use the Pen or Bezigon tools to add points to a path.

To add a point to a path:

1. Select the path.

2. Move the Pen or Bezigon tool where you want the new point. A plus sign (+) appears next to the cursor **24**.

3. Click. A point appears where you clicked.

TIP If you click too far away from the path, you create a new point that is not part of the path.

To connect points:

1. Choose two open paths.

2. Choose **Modify > Join**. FreeHand creates a path between the two closest endpoints of the paths **25**. If the two points are on top of each other, FreeHand merges them into one point.

To split a point:

1. Choose a single point on a path.

2. Choose **Modify > Split**. FreeHand splits the point into two points on top of each other **26**.

TIP There is no indication that the points are separate; select the points and then move one manually to see the split.

Modifying Points on a Path

WORKING WITH OBJECTS 8

Sometimes I think of anchor points as the atomic particles of graphics. Think about it—the point is the nucleus and the handle contains the electrons that circle the nucleus.

Paths are the next level up from anchor points. In fact, you could think of paths as the molecules that string individual atoms together. Two curved points joined with a single corner point create one path. Three corner points joined together create another.

When you work with paths you do not change the attributes of the individual points, but you manipulate the path as a whole. This gives you more control over the look of your artwork.

Selecting and Moving Objects

Selecting and moving objects is vital to making changes to artwork.

To select and move an object:

1. Press with the Pointer tool on the objects. A four-headed arrow appears.

2. Pause a moment, and then drag to see a full preview as you move the object ❶.

   or

   Drag immediately to see just a keyline preview of the object ❷. A keyline preview allows you to work faster as FreeHand does not have to preview complex images.

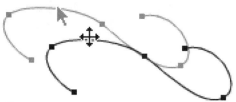

❶ *A path dragged with a* **preview.**

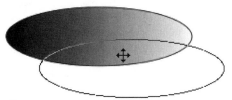

❷ *A path dragged with a* **bounding box.**

Ordinarily you move a path by dragging a line segment. But what if you want to line up two paths so that one point lies exactly on another point or guide? There is a special technique to move a path by dragging its point.

To move a path by dragging its point:

1. (Win) Deselect the path. (This step is not necessary on the Mac.)

2. Hold the Control key (Mac) or Ctrl key (Win).

3. Using the Pointer tool, position the arrow over the point you want to drag.

TIP If **View** > **Snap to Point** has been chosen, a dot appears next to the arrow. This indicates you are over a point ❸.

4. Drag the path to the new position.

TIP If Snap to Point has been chosen, a black dot appears next to the cursor. If you drag to a guide, a hollow dot appears.

❸ *A path dragged by its point.*

Selecting and Moving Objects

4 *When you move a selected point, you also change the shape of the path.*

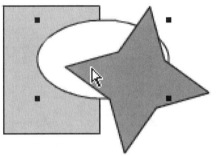

5 *Using the modifier keys, the ellipse was selected by clicking twice. The first click selected the star, the second click selected the ellipse.*

To move points on a path:

1. Select the points you want to move.

2. Move the Pointer tool over one of the selected points.

3. Drag the point to the new position. This changes the shape of the path **4**.

To delete an object:

1. Choose the object so that all its anchor points are visible or its group anchor points *(see page 97)* are visible.

2. Press the Delete key or choose **Edit > Clear** to delete the object.

You may find that you want to select objects positioned behind others. Rather than move your mouse to a new position, you can use a modifier key to select behind objects.

(Mac) To select behind objects:

1. Position the Pointer tool cursor over the area where you want to select an object.

2. Hold down Control+Opt keys.

3. Click as many times as necessary to select through to the object behind the others **5**.

(Win) To select behind objects:

1. Position the Pointer tool cursor over the area where you want to select an object.

2. Hold down Control+Alt keys.

3. Right-mouse click as many times as necessary to select through to the object behind the others **5**.

Selecting and Moving Objects

To select all the objects on a page:

◆ Choose **Edit** > **Select** > **All.** This selects all objects that touch the page. Objects on other pages or on the pasteboard are not selected ❻.

The above command only selects the objects on the page you are working on. However, you can also select all the objects on all the pages of the document.

To select all the objects in a document:

◆ Choose **Edit** > **Select** > **All in Document.** This selects all the objects on all the pages and any objects on the pasteboard ❼.

If you have many objects that you want to select, sometimes it is easier to select the one or two objects that you don't want selected and then invert the selection.

To swap the selected and unselected objects:

1. Select the objects that you ultimately do not want selected.

2. Choose **Edit** > **Select** > **Invert Selection.** This deselects the objects that were selected and selects all the other objects on the page.

To deselect an object:

◆ Click with the Pointer, Subselect, or Lasso tools anywhere else in the window.

   or

   Choose **Edit** > **Select** > **None.**

   or

   If you are not working in a text block press the Tab key.

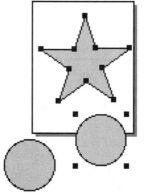

❻ *The* Select >All *command selects all the objects on or touching the currently active page.*

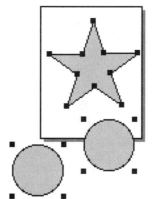

❼ *The* Select >All in Document *command selects all the objects on all the pages and the pasteboard.*

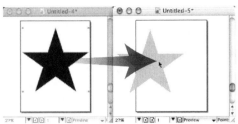

❽ *You can drag and drop objects from one document to another.*

The Computer Clipboard

The Copy and Cut commands place the selected objects into an area of the computer memory called the *clipboard*. The contents of the clipboard stay within the memory until a new Copy or Cut command is executed or the computer is turned off. You can even copy objects in FreeHand and paste them into other programs such as Macromedia Fireworks, Macromedia Flash, or Adobe Photoshop.

The clipboard can hold only one set of information at a time. So if you copy one object, and then later copy another, the first object is flushed from the clipboard and replaced by the second.

Using the Clone, Duplicate, Drag and Drop, and Opt/Alt-drag techniques allows you to make copies of objects without losing the current contents of the clipboard.

Copying and Duplicating Objects

One of the conveniences of working in a computer graphics application is that you can make infinite copies of objects.

To copy and paste an object on a page:

1. Select the object (or objects).
2. Choose **Edit** > **Copy**. This copies the object to the clipboard.
3. If desired, move to a new position on the page, a new page, or a new document.
4. Choose **Edit** > **Paste**. A duplicate of the object appears in the middle of the window.

When you copy an object, you leave behind the original. When you cut and paste, it moves from one position to another.

To cut and paste an object:

1. Select the object you want to cut.
2. Choose **Edit** > **Cut**. This deletes the object and copies it to the clipboard.
3. If desired, move to a new position on the page, a new page, or a new document.
4. Choose **Edit** > **Paste**. A duplicate of the object appears.

To drag and drop from one document to another:

1. Position the document windows so you can see both documents.
2. Using the Pointer tool, drag the object from one window across to the other.
3. When the bounding box is inside the second window, release the mouse button. The object appears in the second window **❽**.

TIP You can drag and drop from FreeHand to other applications such as Flash or Fireworks.

Copying and Duplicating Objects

FreeHand also gives you a command that duplicates objects. This command is useful if you don't want to change the previous contents of the clipboard.

To duplicate an object:

1. Select the object.

2. Choose **Edit** >**Duplicate.** The new object appears offset from the original **❾**.

TIP FreeHand's Clone command also duplicates an object, but the duplicate is positioned right on top of the original. The Clone command is useful when working with the transform commands *(see Chapter 10, "Move and Transform").*

When you copy to the clipboard, FreeHand uses the best format from the ones set in the Preferences *(see Appendix C).* The Copy Special command forces FreeHand to copy the selection as a specific file format.

To copy objects to a specific file format:

1. Select the object.

2. Choose **Edit** >**Special** >**Copy Special.** The Copy Special dialog box appears **❿**.

3. Choose the file format from the list.

4. Click OK. The specified format is copied to the clipboard.

TIP Some file formats in the Copy Special dialog box are available only on the Macintosh or Windows platforms.

You can also force objects copied in other applications to be pasted in a specific format into FreeHand.

To paste objects from other applications:

1. Copy the object in the application.

2. Switch to FreeHand and choose **Edit** > **Special** >**Paste Special.** The Paste Special dialog box appears **⓫**.

3. Choose the file format from the list and click OK.

❾ *The* **Duplicate command** *makes a copy of the original object and positions it away from the original.*

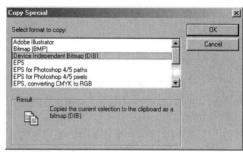

❿ *The* **Copy Special dialog box** *forces FreeHand to copy objects in specific formats.*

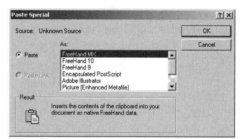

⓫ *The* **Paste Special dialog box** *lets you paste information from other applications.*

Copying and Duplicating Objects

⑫ *The anchor points of the selected objects are visible before the objects are grouped.*

⑬ *After the objects are grouped, the group displays* **four anchor points** *when selected.*

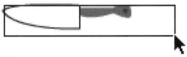

⑭ *Drag one of the group anchor points to resize a grouped object.*

⑮ *When a group is selected, the Object panel shows the coordinates and dimensions of the group.*

Automatic Groups

Objects drawn with the Rectangle and Ellipse tools are automatically grouped. However, unlike regular groups, you can't use the Subselect tool to select their points. You must ungroup those objects to select and modify their individual points.

Working with Groups

In order to protect the shape of an object, or to make it easier to select objects, you can group the points on the path or the multiple objects.

To group paths:

1. Select the path or objects you want to group **⑫**.
2. Choose **Modify > Group**. Instead of individual points, four points designate the corners of the grouped path or paths **⑬**.

To work with grouped objects:

1. To select a grouped object, click the Pointer tool on the object.
2. To resize a grouped object, drag on one of the four group anchor points that surround the object **⑭**.
3. To resize the object without distorting its shape, hold the Shift key as you drag one of the group anchor points.

Once you group objects, they are displayed in the Object panel as a group. This allows you to make changes to the group as a whole.

To modify a group in the Object panel:

1. Select the group.
2. Set the attributes in the Object panel as follows **⑮**:
   - Use the **x** field to change the horizontal position of the upper-left corner.
   - Use the **y** field to change the vertical position of the upper-left corner.
   - Use the **w** field to change the width of the group.
   - Use the **h** field to change the height of the group.
3. Press Enter/Return to apply the changes to the group.

To select individual points in a group:

1. Choose the Subselect tool in the Tools panel .

TIP Instead of the Subselect tool, you can use the Pointer tool while holding the Opt/Alt key.

2. Click one of the objects in the group. The individual points of the object appear.

3. Click the point you want to select. The point is displayed as a hollow dot 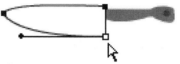.

4. To select additional points, hold the Shift key and click those points.

You can create levels of groups to make it easier to select objects. This is called nesting.

To nest grouped objects:

1. Select and group the first object.

2. After the object is grouped, deselect it.

3. Group any additional objects 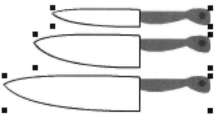.

4. Select all the individual groups and group them together as a single unit 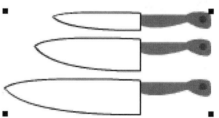.

Once you have taken the time to nest groups, you can easily select the individual groups within the nested group.

To work with nested groups:

1. Use the Subselect tool to select an object or point in a nested group.

2. Press the tilde (~) key. This selects up to the next level of the nest.

3. Continue to press the tilde key until you have selected all the levels you want.

To ungroup an object:

1. Select the grouped object.

2. Choose **Modify > Ungroup**. This ungroups the object.

3. If the object was part of a nested group, choose the Ungroup command again until you have completely ungrouped all the objects.

⑯ *The* **Subselect tool** *in the Tools panel.*

⑰ *Use the Subselect tool to* **select individual points** *of a grouped object.*

⑱ *The four anchor points around each of the knives indicate that each one has been grouped.*

⑲ *The four anchor points around all the knives indicate that they are all part of one group.*

Grouping Techniques

There is a limit of eight levels for nested objects. And even if you don't exceed that number, numerous nesting levels can cause problems when it comes to printing your file.

㉟ *To* **close a previously drawn path**, *drag one of the endpoints over the other.*

㉑ *A checkmark next to Closed in the Object panel indicates a closed path.*

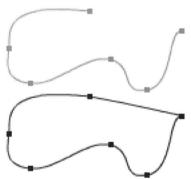

㉒ *Closing an open path (top) adds a segment between the two endpoints (bottom).*

Closing and Opening Paths

When I first started using FreeHand there were times it was absolutely vital to close an open path. For instance, you couldn't fill an object with a color unless it was a closed path. These days it isn't necessary to close a path to see its fill. However, you still may want to close the opening between the endpoints of a path.

To close a previously drawn path:

◆ Use the Pointer tool to drag one of the endpoints onto the other. As soon as the points touch, the path closes **㉟**.

TIP If Snap to Point is turned on, you see a small square next to the cursor when you are close enough to release the mouse button.

To open or close a path using the Object panel:

1. Select the path using the Pointer tool.
2. Select the path entry in the Object panel.
3. Click the checkbox next to the word Closed in the Object panel **㉑**. A line segment is extended between the endpoints of the path **㉒**.

Using the Contact-Sensitive Settings

When you use the Pointer or Lasso tools, ordinarily you have to completely encircle the object in order to select it. However, you can change the setting for those tools so that you can circle just a portion of the object and it will be selected. This is called the *contact-sensitive mode*.

To set the Pointer to be Contact sensitive:

1. Double-click the Pointer tool in the Tools panel. This opens the Pointer Tool dialog box ㉓.

2. Click the Contact sensitive control.

To work with the Contact-sensitive pointer:

◆ Drag a marquee around a portion of the object you wish to select. When you release the mouse button, the entire object will be selected ㉔.

To set the Lasso to be Contact sensitive:

1. Double-click the Lasso tool in the Tools panel. This opens the Lasso tool dialog box.

2. Click the Contact sensitive control.

To work with the Contact-sensitive lasso:

◆ Lasso an area around a portion of the object you wish to select. When you release the mouse button, the entire object will be selected ㉕.

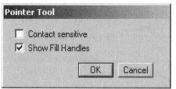

㉓ *The* **Pointer tool** *dialog box lets you turn on the options for the Contact-sensitive mode.*

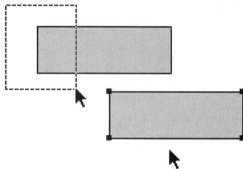

㉔ *When the* **Contact-sensitive mode** *is turned on for the Pointer tool, you can marquee just a portion of an object to select it.*

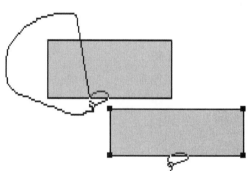

㉕ *When the* **Contact-sensitive mode** *is turned on for the Lasso tool, you can lasso just a portion of an object to select it.*

OPERATIONS AND XTRAS 9

Once you have created paths using any of the creation tools, you can modify those paths in a wide variety of ways. You can change the shape of a path using any of the commands called *path operations* or you can use the Xtra Operations and Xtra Tools to modify the shape or appearance of the path.

Path operations are actions that start with one or more paths and combine or manipulate them into new shapes. Xtra Operations are path operations that have been given their own toolbox to make them easier to apply.

You can also use the Xtra Tools to modify the shape and appearance of paths.

Joining Paths

Imagine you have created an illustration of a doughnut with a hole in the center. You need a special type of path to see through the hole. In FreeHand, these are called joined paths or composite paths.

TIP This type of effect is sometimes called a compound path in other programs.

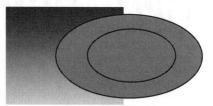

① *Two objects before they are joined.*

To create joined paths:

1. Select the objects that you want to join **①**.

2. Choose **Modify > Join.** This creates a hole in the object that you can see through **②**.

TIP If the second object is not completely contained inside the first, the hole will appear where both objects overlap **③**.

TIP After you apply the Join command, the objects have the same fill and stroke attributes.

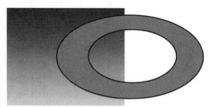

② *Two objects after they have been joined to make a* **joined** *or* **composite path.**

To split joined objects:

1. Select the entire joined object.

2. Choose **Modify > Split.** This releases the paths into separate objects.

To modify the paths of a joined object:

1. Use the Subselect tool to select one of the composite paths. The anchor points appear.

2. Move or modify the path as you would work with a grouped object *(see pages 97–98.*

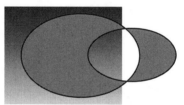

③ *The transparency between composite paths is visible where the two objects overlap.*

❹ *A* **clipping path** *is needed so that the rectangles are not visible outside the edges of the star.*

❺ *When the rectangles are* **pasted inside** *the star, the star acts as a clipping path.*

❻ *Drag the paste inside handle to reposition the objects pasted inside the clipping path.*

Masking

Have you ever seen those posters that show celebrity photos inside star shapes? Rather than cut the photo into the star shape, a mask is used to hide the parts of the image that are outside the star. Pasting an object inside another allows you to fill objects so that anything outside the objects will not be seen. The object that is filled is called a *clipping path* or *mask*.

To mask objects:

1. Position the objects to be masked over the object that is to act as the clipping path **❹**.

2. Select the objects and choose **Edit** > **Cut** to put those objects on the clipboard.

3. Select the object to be used as the clipping path and choose **Edit** > **Paste Inside** (Mac) or **Paste Contents**. (Win). The objects pasted from the clipboard are visible only inside the clipping path **❺**.

TIP Use the Subselect tool to select objects pasted inside the clipping path.

To move masked objects:

1. Click the "Contents" entry for the clipping path in the Object panel. A paste-inside handle appears.

2. Drag the handle to move the objects within the clipping path **❻**.

TIP To transform just the clipping path without affecting the objects pasted inside, make sure the Contents box in the Transform panel is not checked. *(See Chapter 10, "Move and Transform," for information on working with the Transform panel.)*

To release masked objects:

♦ Select the clipping path and choose **Edit** > **Cut Contents**. This removes the objects from inside the object.

Setting Path Direction

As you create paths, the path direction comes from the order that you create the anchor points. The first point you create is considered the start of the path and the last point the end. Even closed paths such as the rectangles and ellipses that FreeHand creates have a direction. Ordinarily it doesn't make too much difference what direction is applied to a path. However, there are sometimes when the path direction does matter.

To change the direction of a path:

1. Select the path you want to change.

2. Choose **Modify** > **Alter Path** > **Reverse Direction**.

   or

   Choose **Xtras** > **Cleanup** > **Reverse Direction**.

TIP The Reverse Direction command is obvious when applied to paths that are part of a blend ❼ or applied to the path that has text attached to it ❽. It is also useful to reverse the start and end arrowheads applied to connector lines.

❼ *When objects with the same direction are blended (on the left), the blend is smooth. When the direction of the top object (on the right) is reversed, the shape of the blend changes.*

❽ *The text on a path (top) is positioned on the top of the path and flows to the right. When the direction of the path is reversed (bottom), the text changes position and flows to the left.*

❾ *The **Knife tool** in the Tools panel.*

❿ *The **Knife tool dialog box.***

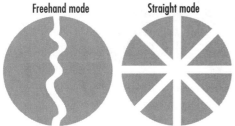

⓫ *Different effects that can be created with the Knife tool.*

Using the Knife Tool

FreeHand's Knife tool is truly a Swiss-army knife. With the Knife tool, you can open paths, slice objects into parts, punch holes in objects, and even erase parts of objects.

To set the Knife tool options:

1. Double-click the Knife tool **❾** in the Tools panel. This opens the Knife Tool dialog box **❿**.

2. Set the Tool Operation modes as follows:
   - **Freehand** allows you to create curved or wavy line cuts.
   - **Straight** constrains you to creating only straight-line cuts.

3. Set the width to control the space between the cuts. A width of 0 leaves no space between the objects created by the cuts. As you increase the width, the Knife acts as an eraser that erases portions of the object.

TIP You can also use the Eraser tool *(described on the next page)* to erase portions of objects.

4. Choose Close cut paths so that the objects created by the Knife are closed paths.

5. Choose Tight fit so that the Knife tool follows the movements of your mouse precisely.

To use the Knife tool:

1. Select the object you wish to cut.

2. Drag the Knife tool across the selected objects **⓫**.

TIP Hold the Opt/Alt key as you drag with the Knife to temporarily set the Knife for straight cuts.

TIP As you draw at the straight setting, hold down the Shift key to constrain your cuts to 45° angles.

Using the Knife Tool

Using the Eraser Tool

Strictly speaking you can't erase vector paths. An eraser tool in programs like Adobe Photoshop recolors or deletes the pixels in an image. FreeHand does have an Eraser tool that allows you to carve out parts of a path as if you were erasing it with a pixel eraser. This lets you reshape objects.

To set the Eraser tool options:

1. Double-click the Eraser tool in the Tools panel . This opens the Eraser tool dialog box .

2. Set the Width controls as follows:

   • **Min** sets the minimum amount of area that is erased when using a pressure-sensitive tablet. This is also the amount used with a mouse.

   • **Max** sets the maximum amount of area that is erased when using a pressure-sensitive tablet.

   TIP As mentioned on the previous page, the Knife tool can also erase areas of an object. However, the Knife tool does not respond to a pressure-sensitive tablet as the Eraser tool does.

To use the Eraser tool:

1. Select the object you wish to erase.

2. Drag the Eraser tool across the selected objects 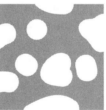. When you release the mouse button, the path reshapes .

   TIP Hold the Opt/Alt key as you drag to set the Eraser to erase straight line areas.

   TIP Hold the Opt/Alt+Shift keys to to constrain your erasing to straight lines at 0-, 45-, and 90-degree angles.

⑫ *The* **Eraser tool** *in the Tools panel.*

⑬ *The* **Eraser tool dialog box.**

⑭ *The black area indicates where the Eraser tool will reshape the path.*

⑮ *Use the Eraser tool to poke holes in a rectangle.*

⓰ *The* **Freeform tool** *selected from its toolset in the Tools panel.*

⓱ *The* **Push/Pull settings** *of the Freeform tool dialog box.*

Understanding the Freeform tool

There are subtle differences in the modes of the Freeform tool. The Push effect of the Push/Pull mode acts like a rolling pin that changes the shape of the object. The Pull effect of the Push/Pull mode acts like a magnet that draws out the shape of the object. The Reshape Area mode changes the shape of the object as if it were taffy that can be stretched into thin wisps.

Using the Freeform Tool

As a self-proclaimed "vectorbabe," I love Bézier handles. In case you don't share my enthusiasm, the Freeform tool allows you to reshape paths without modifying points or handles. There are two modes to the Free-form tool: Push/Pull and Reshape Area.

The Push/Pull tool allows you to pull to add new segments to a path or push to distort the shape of the segment.

To set the Push/Pull tool operation:

1. Double-click the Freeform tool in the Tools panel **⓰**. The Freeform Tool dialog box appears.

2. Set the Tool Operation to Push/Pull. This displays the Push/Pull options **⓱**.

3. Set the Size field to control the size of the area pushed by the tool.

4. Set the Precision field to control the precision amount—the greater the amount, the more sensitive the tool is to minor movements of the mouse.

5. Choose one of the following from the Pull Setting list:
   - **Bend By Length** pulls anywhere along a path
   - **Bend Between Points** restricts the pull to only between existing anchor points.

6. Set the Length field to control how much the Pull will alter the path.

7. If you have a pressure-sensitive tablet, check the Size and/or Length boxes to set how the pressure on the tablet affects the tool.

Using the Freeform Tool

To modify objects in the Push/Pull mode:

1. Select the object you want to modify.

2. Position the cursor as follows ⑱:

   - Move the cursor directly next to the object. A small **s** shape appears next to the cursor. This indicates you are in the pull mode.
   - Move the cursor inside or outside the object. A small **o** shape appears next to the cursor. This indicates you are in the push mode.

3. Drag to modify the object. In the push mode a circle appears that indicates the size of the area being modified ⑲. An arrow indicates you are working in the pull mode ⑳.

4. If you do not have a pressure-sensitive tablet you can modify the area as you drag as follows:

   - Press the 1, [, or left arrow keys as you drag to decrease the size of the Freeform tool effect.
   - Press the 2,], or right arrow keys as you drag to increase the size of the Freeform tool effect.

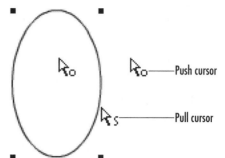

Push cursor

Pull cursor

⑱ *The Freeform tool has* **two different cursors** *in the Push/Pull mode.*

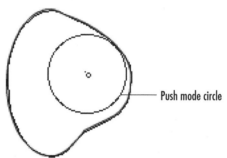

Push mode circle

⑲ *The* **Push mode circle** *indicates the size of the area that is distorted.*

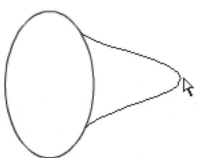

⑳ *The* **Pull arrow** *indicates that the Freeform tool adds a segment where the path is pulled.*

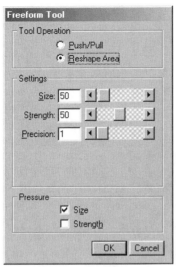

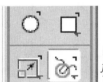

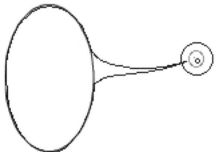

㉑ *The* **Reshape Area settings** *of the Freeform Tool dialog box.*

㉒ *The* **Reshape Area icon** *for the Freeform tool in the Tools panel.*

㉓ *The Reshape Area tool distorts a path into a new shape.*

In the Reshape mode, you distort the path by pulling out new segments from the existing path. The amount of distortion is set in the Reshape Area settings of the Freeform tool.

To set the Reshape Area tool operation:

1. Double-click the Freeform tool in the Tools panel. The Freeform Tool dialog box appears **㉑**.
2. Set the Tool Operation to Reshape Area. This displays the Reshape Area options.
3. Set the Size field to control the size of the Reshape Area tool.
4. Set the Strength field to control how long the tool will work during a drag—the greater the amount, the longer the tool distorts the path.
5. Set the Precision field to control the precision amount—the greater the amount, the more sensitive the tool is to minor movements of the mouse.

TIP The icon for the Freeform tool in the tools panel changes to the Reshape Area icon when the dialog box is set for Reshape Area **㉒**.

To modify objects in the Reshape Area mode:

1. Select the object you want to modify.
2. Drag to modify the object **㉓**.
3. If you do not have a pressure-sensitive tablet you can modify the area as you drag as follows:
   - Press the 1, [, or left arrow keys as you drag to decrease the size of the Freeform tool effect.
   - Press the 2,], or right arrow keys as you drag to increase the size of the Freeform tool effect.

Using the Freeform Tool

Path Commands

Instead of using a tool such as the Pointer or Knife to modify a path, you can also use commands. The Remove Overlap command changes a path so that areas that overlap each other are eliminated. This is very helpful when working with the Pencil tool.

To use the Remove Overlap command:

1. Select the object.

2. Click the Remove Overlap icon in the Xtra Operations toolbar **㉔**.

   or

   Choose **Modify** > **Alter Path** > **Remove Overlap**.

   or

   Choose **Xtras** > **Cleanup** > **Remove Overlap**. Notice that the overlapping areas are eliminated **㉕**.

Too many points on a path makes it difficult to reshape and work with paths. The Simplify command lets you remove excess points.

To use the Simplify command:

1. Select the object.

2. Click the Simplify icon in the Xtra Operations toolbar **㉖**.

   or

   Choose **Modify** > **Alter Path** > **Simplify**.

   or

   Choose **Xtras** > **Cleanup** > **Simplify**. The Simplify dialog box appears **㉗**.

3. Drag the slider to change the value in the Amount field. The greater the number, the more points will be eliminated **㉘**.

4. Click the Apply button to see the effects of the setting.

5. Click OK to execute the command.

㉔ *The* **Remove Overlap icon** *in the Xtra Operations toolbar.*

㉕ *The effects of applying the* **Remove Overlap command**.

㉖ *The* **Simplify icon** *in the Xtra Operations toolbar.*

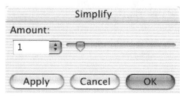

㉗ The **Simplify dialog box.**

㉘ *The effects of the* **Simplify** *command.*

㉙ *The* **Add Points** *icon in the Xtra Operations toolbar.*

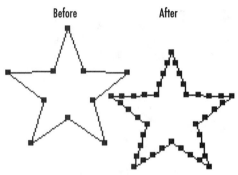

Before   After

㉚ *The results of the* **Add Points** *command.*

㉛ *The* **Intersect** *icon in the Xtra Operations toolbar.*

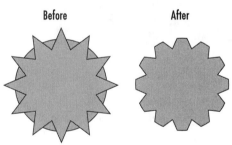

Before   After

㉜ *The effects of the* **Intersect** *command.*

Certain effects need additional points on the path to look good. For instance, more points create a different look when the Bend effect *(see page 237)* is applied. The Add Points command lets you add extra points to a path.

To use the Add Points command:

1. Select an object.
2. Click the Add Points icon in the Xtras Operations toolbar **㉙**.

   or

   Choose **Xtras > Distort > Add Points.**
3. Each time you choose the command, a new point is added between each existing pair of points **㉚**.

The Intersect command creates a new object from the area where two objects overlap.

To use the Intersect command:

1. Select two or more paths that overlap each other.
2. Click the Intersect icon in the Xtras Operations toolbar **㉛**.

   or

   Choose **Modify > Combine > Intersect.**

   or

   Choose **Xtras > Path Operations > Intersect.**
3. A new path is created that is the shape of the overlapping area **㉜**.

TIP The Intersect command deletes from the selection any objects that do not overlap.

Path Commands

The Union command allows you to take many objects and turn them into one path.

To use the Union command:

1. Select two or more objects that overlap each other.

2. Click the Union icon in the Xtras Operations toolbar .

   or

   Choose **Modify > Combine > Union.**

   or

   Choose **Xtras > Path Operations > Union.**

3. The multiple paths join into one .

TIP If the selected objects for the Union, Intersect, or Punch commands have different attributes, the resulting object has the attributes of the backmost object.

33 *The Union icon in the Xtra Operations toolbar.*

Before

After

34 *The effects of the Union command.*

The Punch command allows you to use one object to punch a hole in another.

To use the Punch command:

1. Select two or more overlapping objects.

2. Click the Punch icon in the Xtras Operations toolbar **35**.

   or

   Choose **Modify > Combine > Punch.**

   or

   Choose **Xtras > Path Operations > Punch.**

3. The top object punches through the bottom object **36**.

TIP To have multiple objects act as the punch, first apply the Union command.

TIP To save the original objects while creating new ones, hold the Shift key as you apply the Intersect or Punch commands or change the Preferences setting for Path operations consume original paths *(see Appendix C).*

35 *The Punch icon in the Xtra Operations toolbar.*

Before

After

36 *The effects of the Punch command.*

37 *The* **Divide** *icon in the Xtra Operations toolbar.*

Before   After

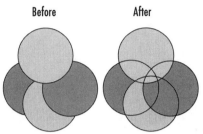

38 *The effects of the* **Divide** *command.*

39 *The* **Crop** *icon in the Xtra Operations toolbar.*

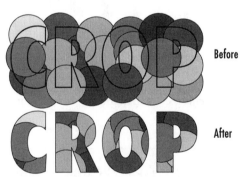

Before

After

40 *The effects of the* **Crop** *command.*

Crop or Mask?

The effects of the Crop command may remind you of what happens when you place objects inside a mask. The Crop command permanently deletes artwork that falls outside the cropping object. The objects hidden by a mask are not permanently deleted.

The Divide command creates new paths from the overlapping areas of objects.

To use the Divide command:

1. Select two or more objects that overlap each other.

2. Click the Divide icon in the Xtra Operations toolbar **37**.

   or

   Choose **Modify** > **Combine** > **Divide**.

   or

   Choose **Xtras** > **Path Operations** > **Divide**.

3. The paths divide into new paths wherever they overlapped **38**.

The Crop command allows you to use the top object as a cookie cutter that trims away parts of the path that are outside the top object.

To use the Crop command:

1. Select various objects with one object on top.

2. Click the Crop icon in the Xtra Operations toolbar **39**.

   or

   Choose **Modify** > **Combine** > **Crop**.

   or

   Choose **Xtras** > **Path Operations** > **Crop**.

3. All the objects at the bottom are trimmed so that only those portions that were under the topmost object remain **40**.

Path Commands

FreeHand offers you a way to convert lines or open paths to closed paths by using the Expand Stroke command. This allows you to convert stroked paths into closed paths that can have fills such as the Lens or Gradient fills. *(See Chapter 15, "Strokes," for more information on creating stroked paths.)*

To use the Expand Stroke command:

1. Select the stroked path you wish to convert.

2. Click the Expand Stroke icon in the Xtra Operations toolbar ④.

   or

   Choose **Modify** > **Alter Path** > **Expand Stroke**.

   or

   Choose **Xtras** > **Path Operations** > **Expand Stroke.** The Expand Stroke dialog box appears ④.

3. Enter the width you want for the final object.

4. Choose one of the Cap settings for the ends of the path. *(See page 218 for details of the Cap settings.)*

5. Choose one of the Join settings for the corners of the path. *(See page 218 for details of the Join settings.)*

6. Enter an amount for the Miter limit for the corners of the path. *(See page 219 for details of the Miter limit settings.)*

TIP Note that while these settings are the same as the settings for a stroke, the final object will actually be a filled path.

7. Click OK to create a new filled path ④.

④ *The* **Expand Stroke** *icon in the Xtra Operations toolbar.*

④ *The* **Expand Stroke** *dialog box.*

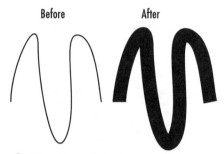
④ *The effects of the* **Expand Stroke** *command.*

Using the Repeat Xtra Command

Although many path operations are under the Modify menu, you have an extra feature if you choose the commands via the Xtras menu or the Operations toolbar. That command will be listed at the top of the Xtras menu as the Repeat [Xtra] command. This means that if you want to apply the command again, you can choose it from the top of the menu.

④ *The* **Inset Path icon** *in the Xtra Operations toolbar.*

④ *The* **Inset Path dialog box.**

④ *The menu for the Inset Path command.*

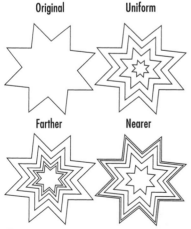

④ *The results of applying the* **Inset Path command** *at the different settings.*

The Inset Path command allows you to make multiple copies of an object. These copies can be smaller or larger than the original.

To use the Inset Path command:

1. Select a closed path.
2. Click the Inset Path icon in the Xtra Operations toolbar **④**.

    or

    Choose **Modify** > **Alter Path** > **Inset Path**.

    or

    Choose **Xtras** > **Path Operations** > **Inset Path**. The Inset Path dialog box appears **④**.
3. In the Steps field, enter the number of copies you want to create.
4. If the number of steps is greater than 1, choose one of the following from the inset menu **④**:
    - **Uniform** spaces each copy the same distance from the previous object.
    - **Farther** spaces each copy slightly closer than the previous object.
    - **Nearer** spaces each copy slightly further away from the previous object.
5. Use the slider to set the size of the new objects as follows:
    - **Positive numbers** place the new objects inside the original.
    - **Negative numbers** place the new object outside the original.
6. Click OK. This creates copies of the object inset from the original **④**.

TIP Multiples created by the Inset Path command are created as grouped objects.

Path Commands

115

The Emboss command allows you to create the look of raised or depressed areas on a background.

TIP The objects created with this Emboss command are discrete vector paths. If you want a more natural-looking embossed effect, you can use the Emboss effects in the Object panel *(see page 245)*.

To use the Emboss command:

1. Select one or more filled objects.

2. Click the Emboss icon in the Xtra Operations toolbar **48**.

   or

   Choose **Xtras** > **Create** > **Emboss**. This opens the Emboss dialog box **49**.

3. Click one of the top icons to choose from the five types of embossing effects: emboss, deboss, chisel, ridge, or quilt.

4. Set the Vary controls as follows:

   • **Contrast** lets you use the slider to control how much to change the existing colors in the object to create the light and dark portions of the emboss.

   • **Color** lets you set the color for the highlight and shadows of the emboss.

5. Set the Depth field for how obvious the embossing should be.

6. Set the Angle field to control where the light and dark areas of the emboss effect should be.

7. Click the Soft Edge box to make the transition less abrupt.

TIP Soft Edge is not available for all the embossed choices.

8. Click Apply to see how the settings affect the object.

9. Click OK when you are satisfied to view the results **50**.

48 *The* **Emboss icon** *in the Xtra Operations toolbar.*

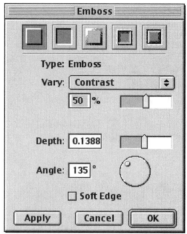

49 *The* **Emboss dialog box.**

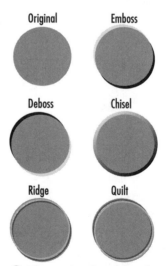

50 *The results of applying the* **Emboss** *command at the different settings.*

Path Commands

51 *The Fractalize icon in the Xtra Operations toolbar.*

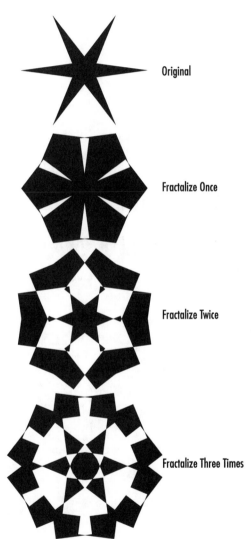

Original

Fractalize Once

Fractalize Twice

Fractalize Three Times

52 *The effects of the Fractalize command.*

I admit that not all commands are as useful as others. It takes a lot of creativity to find any practical uses for the Fractalize command. But it does create interesting kaleidescope or snowflake effects.

To use the Fractalize command:

1. Select the object.

2. Click the Fractalize icon in the Xtra Operations toolbar **51**.

   or

   Choose **Xtras > Distort > Fractalize**.

3. Repeat the command until you are satisfied with the effect **52**.

4. Make sure the Even/Odd fill box is checked in the Object panel.

TIP Without the Even/Odd fill box chosen, the image will appear as a solid fill, not a fractal effect.

TIP Apply the Fractalize command to different objects to create different effects.

What are fractals?

Fractals are geometric patterns that are repeated at ever smaller scales to produce irregular shapes and surfaces. These shapes are unique as they cannot be represented by classical geometry. Fractals are used in computer modeling of irregular patterns. They are also found in naturally occuring objects such as fern leaves, sea shells, and lightning bolts.

Path Commands

Xtra Tools

In addition to the Xtra Operations, there are also Xtra Tools that allow you to apply special effects to objects.

The Roughen tool, for example, takes clean, smooth paths and makes them irregular and ragged. This can be very useful in making artwork look hand-drawn, or less "perfect."

To set the Roughen tool options:

1. Double-click the Roughen tool in the Xtra Tools toolbar **53**. This opens the Roughen dialog box **54**.

2. Use the Amount slider to increase or decrease the number of segments per inch (how roughness is measured) that are added using the tool.

3. Set the Edge options as follows:

   • **Rough** adds corner points to create the rough edge.
   • **Smooth** adds curved points to create the rough edge. This creates a less harsh edge to the object.

To apply the Roughen effect:

1. Select the object or objects you want to modify.

2. Drag with the Roughen tool along the object. The further you drag, the greater the distortion **55**.

53 *The* **Roughen tool** *in the Xtra Tools toolbar.*

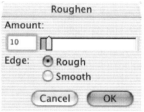

54 *The* **Roughen dialog box.**

NERVOUS   Smooth option

PANICKED   Rough option

55 *The results of applying the Roughen tool.*

5️⃣6️⃣ *The **Mirror tool** in the Xtra Tools toolbar.*

Preview area

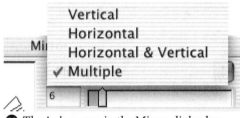

5️⃣7️⃣ *The Mirror dialog box.*

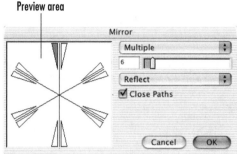

5️⃣8️⃣ *The **Axis menu** in the Mirror dialog box.*

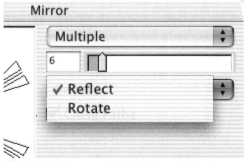

5️⃣9️⃣ *The **Mode menu** in the Mirror dialog box.*

The Mirror tool lets you create multiple rotated and reflected objects.

TIP Once you create objects with the Mirror tool, you must manually delete them and reapply the tool if you want to make changes. You can create a similar effect that can be easily changed later using the Duet effect *(see page 238)*.

To set the Mirror tool controls:

1. Double-click the Mirror tool in the Xtra Tools toolbar **5️⃣6️⃣**. This opens the Mirror dialog box **5️⃣7️⃣**.

2. Use the Axis pop-up menu to choose the axis as follows **5️⃣8️⃣**:
   - **Vertical** reflects the object from left to right.
   - **Horizontal** reflects the object from top to bottom.
   - **Horizontal & Vertical** reflects the object both ways at once.
   - **Multiple** reflects the object around multiple axes.

3. If you have chosen the Multiple setting, use the slider to control the number of axes the object reflects around. *(See the illustration on the next page for more details on the Multiple setting.)*

4. If you have chosen the Multiple setting, choose the Reflect or Rotate mode **5️⃣9️⃣**.

5. Click the Close Paths option to close any open paths that are created if the endpoints fall within the Snap To distance defined in the Preferences.

Xtra Tools

To use the Mirror tool:

1. Select the object you want to reflect. Choose the Mirror tool in the Xtra Tools toolbar.

2. Move the cursor onto the page area and press on the point around which the reflection should occur. A line extends out showing the axis that the object is reflected around ❻⓿. A preview of the reflection appears.

3. Drag the cursor until you are satisfied with the effect.

4. Release the mouse button to apply the Mirror tool effect ❻❶.

TIP Tap the left- or right-arrow keys to decrease or increase the number of axes in the multiple setting.

TIP Tap the up- or down-arrow keys to change the Multiple setting from reflect to rotate.

TIP Hold the Opt/Alt key to rotate the angle of the axis.

❻⓿ *As you press with the Mirror tool, you see the axis line and a preview of the effect.*

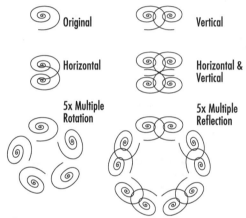

Original · Vertical · Horizontal · Horizontal & Vertical · 5x Multiple Rotation · 5x Multiple Reflection

❻❶ *Various effects created with the Mirror tool.*

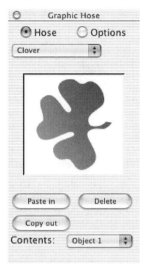

62 *The* **Graphic Hose tool** *in the Xtra Tools toolbar.*

63 *The* **Graphic Hose panel** *where you can store objects in the Hose sets.*

64 *The* **Graphic Hose menu** *lets you choose from the stored sets or create a new set.*

The Graphic Hose allows you to store objects and then drag on the page to paint with those objects. There are two parts to using the Graphic Hose: storing the objects in the Graphics Hose panel and setting the options for painting with the hose.

Objects for the Graphic Hose are stored as sets within the Graphic Hose panel.

To store objects in the Graphic Hose panel:

1. Double-click the Graphic Hose tool in the Xtra Tools toolbar **62**. This opens the Graphic Hose panel **63**.

2. Click Hose to display the Hose sets.

3. Choose New from the Sets pop-up menu to add a new set **64**. A dialog box appears where you can name the new set.

4. Copy the artwork to the computer clipboard.

5. Click Paste in. The artwork appears in the preview window as an object in the Contents pop-up menu.

6. Copy and paste additional artwork into the set. The artwork is added as a new object to the Contents menu.

TIP There is a limit of 10 objects for each set.

TIP Graphic Hose sets are not limited to just the FreeHand document they were created in. They are available for any FreeHand document and after you close and then relaunch FreeHand.

TIP You can use symbols as the elements for the Graphic Hose. *(See Chapter 21, "Styles and Symbols" for more information on using symbols.)* This allows you to modify the symbol element and all the objects created by the Graphic Hose update automatically.

Xtra Tools

Once you have created Hose sets, you need to set the Options to control how the Graphic Hose applies objects on the page.

To use the Graphic Hose tool:

1. Double-click the Graphic Hose tool in the Xtra Tools toolbar. This opens the Graphic Hose panel **65**.

2. Click the Options radio button to display the Options controls.

3. Use the Order menu to control the order that objects are placed on the page **66**:
   - **Loop** applies the objects in numerical order.
   - **Back and Forth** applies the objects in forward then reverse order.
   - **Random** applies the objects in no specific order.

4. Use the Spacing menu to control the distance between the objects **67**:
   - **Grid** applies the objects onto a grid with a size you set in the Grid field.
   - **Variable** applies the objects in a spacing that you set as Tight or Loose.
   - **Random** applies the objects with no specific distance between them.

5. Use the Scale pop-up menu to control the size of the objects **68**:
   - **Uniform** sets a certain size for all the objects.
   - **Random** applies the objects in no specific sizes.

6. Use the Rotate menu and angle wheel to control the rotation of the objects.
   - **Uniform** sets one angle for all objects.
   - **Incremental** applies rotations that change in specific increments from one object to the next.
   - **Random** rotates the objects without any order.

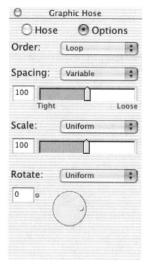

65 *The* **Graphic Hose Options** *controls let you change how the objects go on the page.*

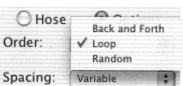

66 *The* **Order menu** *controls the order that the Graphic hose sprays objects on the page.*

67 *The* **Spacing menu** *controls the distance between the objects sprayed by the Graphic Hose.*

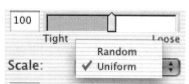

68 *The* **Scale menu** *controls the size of the objects sprayed by the Graphic Hose.*

69 *This circle of hearts and flowers was* **sprayed with the Graphic Hose**.

70 *The* **Bend tool** *in the Xtra Tools toolbar.*

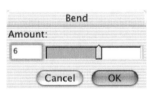

71 *The* **Bend dialog box** *allows you to control the number of points per inch that are added during a bend distortion.*

To create artwork with the Graphic Hose:

1. Choose the Graphic Hose tool from the Tools panel.

2. Drag the Graphic Hose across the page. The objects in the set are placed on the page **69**.

The Bend tool applies a distortion to objects to warp the path segments in or out.

To set the Bend tool options:

1. Double-click the Bend tool in the Xtra Tools toolbar **70**. This opens the Bend dialog box **71**.

2. Adjust the slider or enter an amount in the field to increase or decrease the number of points per inch that are added.

3. Click OK.

To use the Bend tool:

◆ With the object selected, drag down to create a rounded bend **72**.

   or

   Drag up to create a spiked bend **72**.

TIP The point where you start the drag is the center of the distortion.

TIP The longer you drag, the greater the amount of the bend.

Original

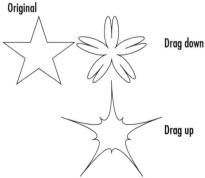

Drag down

Drag up

72 *The* results of applying the Bend tool.

MOVE AND TRANSFORM 10

Once you have created an object, most likely you will want to transform it at some other time. It is by moving and transforming objects that you can convert simple shapes into dramatic and sophisticated artwork.

Perhaps you want to enlarge an object, or rotate it on an angle, or skew its shape, or flip it so it is facing another direction. All those actions—scaling, rotating, skewing, and reflecting—are transformations. In fact, even moving an object from one position to another is considered a transformation.

FreeHand provides many different ways to transform objects. Some techniques let you view the results as you work. Other techniques let you enter numerical values for more precise results.

Viewing Transformations

As you transform an object you can see the details about the transformation in the Info Toolbar ❶. The Info Toolbar readings change depending on the position of your cursor, the tool chosen, or the action taken. The Info Toolbar has four fields: Object ❷, Position ❸, Info ❹, and Lock ❺. The following are the various categories seen on the Info Toolbar.

Label	Field	Indicates
object name	Object	Type of object
x	Position	Position of cursor along horizontal axis
y	Position	Position of cursor along vertical axis
dx	Info	Horizontal distance object is moved
dy	Info	Vertical distance object is moved
dist	Info	Total distance along which any angle object is moved
angle	Info	Angle along which any object is moved, created, or transformed
x	Info	Horizontal location of the centerpoint around which any object is being created or transformed
y	Info	Vertical location of the center point around which any object is being created or transformed
xscale	Info	Horizontal scale or skew of an object expressed as a ratio to an object's original size (e.g., 1.00 = 100%)
yscale	Info	Vertical scale or skew of an object expressed as a ratio to an object's original size (e.g., 1.00 = 100%)
width	Info	Width of a rectangle or ellipse
height	Info	Height of a rectangle or ellipse
radius	Info	Size of a radius of a polygon
sides	Info	Number of sides of a polygon
open padlock	Lock	(Mac) Indicates object is not locked
closed padlock	Lock	(Mac) Indicates object is locked
gray padlock	Lock	(Win) Indicates object is not locked
red padlock	Lock	(Win) Indicates object is locked

❶ *The* **Info Toolbar***.*

❷ *The* **Object field** *shows the type of object or the number of objects selected.*

❸ *The* **Position field** *shows the x and y coordinates of the cursor position.*

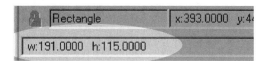

❹ *The* **Info field** *shows the various attributes of objects as they are created or manipulated.*

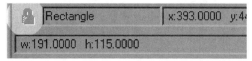

❺ *The* **Lock field** *shows if a selected object is locked or not.*

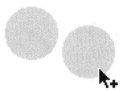

6 *Hold the Opt/Alt key to* **move and copy** *an object. The plus sign (+) next to the arrow indicates you are creating a copy.*

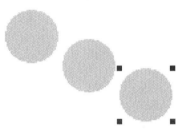

7 *Choose* **Edit > Duplicate** *as many times as necessary to create additional copies of the object.*

Moving Objects

As mentioned before, when you move an object you are actually transforming it. There are some special transformation techniques you can use when moving objects.

To move an object:

1. Select the object you want to move.
2. Use the Pointer tool to drag the object to a new position.

TIP When you move an object, the horizontal and vertical distances are recorded in the Move settings of the Transform panel *(see the next page)*. These settings can then be used to move other objects.

To move and copy an object:

1. Select the object you want to copy.
2. Start to drag the object to a new position.
3. Press the Opt/Alt key as you drag. The plus sign (+) next to the arrow indicates that you are creating a copy of the object.
4. When the object is in the correct position, release the mouse button first and then the Opt/Alt key. A copy of the original object is created at the point where you released the mouse **6**.

Once you have moved and made a copy of an object, you can continue to make copies of the object, each positioned the same distance, and the same direction, away from the previous copy.

To Duplicate the previous Move and Copy:

♦ With the object created in the previous exercise still selected, choose **Edit > Duplicate**. FreeHand duplicates the new object **7**.

TIP You can repeat this command over and over to create as many copies as you want.

Moving Objects

In addition to moving them manually, you can use the Transform panel to move objects numerically. You can also use the panel to make copies, each spaced the same distance, and in the same direction, from the previous copy.

To move using the Transform panel:

1. Select the object you want to move.

2. In the Transform panel, click the Move icon **8**. This switches to the Move controls **9**.

3. Set the Move distance as follows:
   - The x field controls the horizontal movement. Positive numbers move the object to the right. Negative numbers move the object to the left.
   - The y field controls the vertical movement. Positive numbers move the object up. Negative numbers move the object down.

4. Select Contents to move any items pasted inside along with the object *(see page 103)* **10**.

5. Select Fills to move any fills such as tiled fills *(see page 208)*.

6. Press Return or Enter to apply the move.

To copy and move using the Transform panel:

1. Select the object you want to copy and move.

2. Use the steps in the previous exercise to set the distance and attributes of the move.

3. Enter the number of copies in the Copies field.

4. Click the Move button or press Return or Enter to copy and move the object.

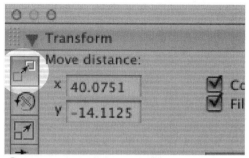

8 *The* **Move** *icon in the Transform panel.*

9 *The Transform panel set to the* **Move controls.**

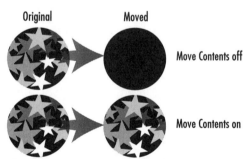

10 *When* **Move Contents** *is off (top) the stars pasted in do not move with the circle. When* **Move Contents** *is on (bottom) the stars pasted in move along with the circle.*

⓫ *The* **Snap To Point command** *causes an object to jump onto the point of another.*

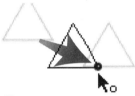

⓬ *The* **Snap To Object command** *causes an object to jump onto the point or line segment of another.*

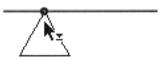

⓭ *The* **Snap To Guides command** *causes an object to jump onto a guide or page edge.*

Using the Snap To Commands

As you move an object, you can use the Snap To commands to have the object automatically jump to specific spots. This makes it easier to line up objects.

TIP The Snap To commands are controlled by the Snap To Distance in the Preferences *(see Appendix C)*. This is how close the object is before it snaps to its destination.

To use the Snap To Point command:

1. Choose **View > Snap To Point**.
2. Drag one object towards another. When the object gets near a point a small circle appears and the object jumps or snaps onto the position of the point **⓫**.

TIP A small square appears next to the arrow to indicate you are snapping to a point.

To use the Snap To Object command:

1. Choose **View > Snap To Object**.
2. Drag one object towards another. When the object gets near a point or path segment a small circle appears and the object jumps or snaps onto the position of the object **⓬**.

TIP A small circle appears next to the arrow to indicate you are snapping to an object.

To use the Snap To Guides command:

1. Choose **View > Snap To Guides**.
2. Drag one object towards a guide or edge of the page. When the object gets near the guide or edge of the page, a small circle appears and the object jumps or snaps onto the position **⓭**.

TIP A small triangle and line appears next to the arrow to indicate you are snapping to a guide or page edge.

Rotating Objects

Another type of transformation is rotation. Rotation allows you to change the orientation of an object.

To rotate an object by eye:

1. Select the object you want to rotate.

2. Choose the Rotate tool in the Tools panel **⑭**.

3. Move your cursor to the page. Your cursor turns into a star.

4. Position the star on the spot around which you would like the object to rotate **⑮**. This is the transformation point.

5. Press on the point you have chosen. *Do not release the mouse button.* A line extends out from the transformation point. This is the rotation axis **⑯**.

TIP You can transform an object around a point anywhere in the document.

6. Still pressing, drag the cursor away from the transformation point. Then move the rotation axis. The object rotates as you move the rotation axis **⑰**.

TIP Hold the Shift key to constrain the rotation to 45° increments.

7. Release the mouse button when you are satisfied with the position of the object.

TIP The farther you drag your cursor away from the transformation point during rotation or reflection, the easier it is to control the transformation.

To copy as you rotate an object:

1. Hold the Opt/Alt key as you drag to rotate the object. A plus sign (+) appears next to the star cursor.

2. Release the mouse button first and then the Opt/Alt key to create a copy of the object rotated to the position you chose.

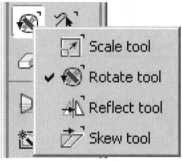

⑭ *The* **Rotate tool** *selected from its toolset in the Tools panel.*

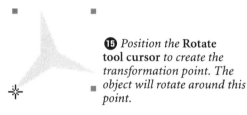

⑮ *Position the* **Rotate tool cursor** *to create the transformation point. The object will rotate around this point.*

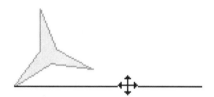

⑯ *Press with the Rotate tool to see the rotation axis—the line that will rotate the object.*

⑰ *The rotation axis and the preview show the position to which the object will be rotated.*

Rotating Objects

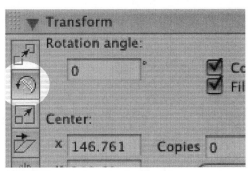

⓲ *The* **Rotate icon** *in the Transform panel.*

⓳ *The Transform panel set to the* **Rotate controls.**

To rotate using the Transform panel:

1. Choose the object you want to rotate.

2. Click the Rotate icon in the Transform panel ⓲. The Rotate controls appear ⓳.

3. Enter the number of degrees you want to rotate the object in the Rotation angle field.

4. To change the Center of the rotation, enter the coordinates you want in the **x** and **y** fields.

   or

   With the Rotate tool active, hold the Opt/Alt key and click to select a transformation point.

5. Select Contents to rotate any items pasted inside along with the object *(see page 103)* ⓴.

6. Select Fills to rotate any fills such as tiled fills *(see page 208).*

7. Click the Rotate button in the Transform panel.

   or

   Press Return or Enter to apply the rotation.

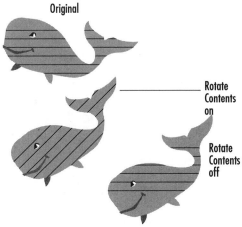

Original

Rotate Contents on

Rotate Contents off

⓴ *When* **Rotate Contents is on,** *the lines pasted in rotate along with the whale. When* **Rotate Contents is off,** *the horizontal lines pasted in do not rotate with the whale.*

Rotating Objects

Scaling Objects

If an object is too big or too small, it is a simple matter to scale it to a new size.

To scale an object by eye:

1. Choose the object you want to scale.
2. Choose the Scale tool in the Tools panel 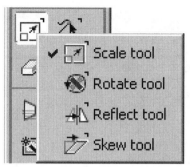.
3. Move your cursor to the page. Your cursor turns into a star ❷❷.
4. Position the star on the spot from which you would like the object to scale. This is the transformation point.
5. Press down on the point you have chosen. *Do not release the mouse button.*
6. Drag the cursor away from the transformation point. An outline of the object changes to show how the object is being scaled ❷❸.

TIP Hold the Shift key if you want to constrain the scale to a proportional change.

7. Release the mouse button when you are satisfied with the size of the scaled object. Your object scales into position.

To copy as you scale an object:

1. Hold the Opt/Alt key as you drag to scale the object. A plus sign (+) appears next to the star cursor.
2. Release the mouse button first and then the Opt/Alt key to create a copy of the original object scaled to the position you chose. The original object stays untouched.

❷❶ *The* **Scale tool** *selected from its toolset in the Tools panel.*

❷❷ *Position the* **Scale tool cursor** *on the point you want the object to scale from.*

❷❸ *Drag with the Scale tool to scale the object up or down.*

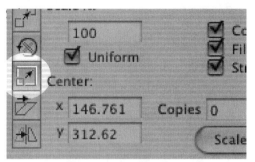

24 *The* **Scale icon** *in the Transform panel.*

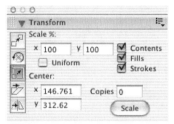

25 *The Transform dialog box set to the* **Scale controls.**

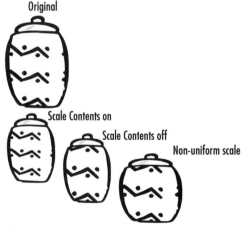

26 *With* **Scale Contents** *on the design pasted in scales along with the urn. With* **Scale Contents** *off the design does not scale with the urn.*

To scale using the Transform panel:

1. Select the object you want to scale.
2. Click the Scale icon in the Transform panel **24**. The Scale controls appear **25**.
3. Enter the percent you want to change the object.
4. For a proportional scale, keep the Uniform box checked.

   or

   To scale the object nonproportionally, deselect Uniform. This opens additional fields to enter the percentages to scale the object.
5. For a uniform scale, enter an amount in the Scale % field.

   or

   For a non-uniform scale, enter values in the **x** (horizontal) and **y** (vertical) fields.
6. To change the point of transformation from the center, enter the coordinates in the **x** and **y** fields.

   or

   With the Scale tool active, hold the Opt/Alt key and click to select a transformation point.
7. Check Contents to scale any items pasted inside along with the object *(see page 103)* **26**.
8. Check Fills to scale any fills such as tiled fills *(see page 208)*.
9. Check Strokes to scale the size of strokes along with the path.
10. Click the Scale button in the Transform panel.

    or

    Press Return or Enter to apply the scale.

Skewing Objects

Skewing (sometimes called *shearing*) is a way of distorting an object along an axis. This type of distortion is very common when making shadows.

To skew an object by eye:

1. Select the object you want to skew.

2. Choose the Skewing tool in the Tools panel **㉗**.

3. Move your cursor to the page. Your cursor turns into a star.

4. Position the star on the point around which you want the object to skew **㉘**. This is the transformation point.

5. Press down on the point you have chosen. *Do not release the mouse button.*

6. Drag the cursor away from the transformation point. The outline of the object changes its shape as you move the cursor **㉙**.

TIP Hold the Shift key to constrain the skew. Drag horizontally to constrain the skew to the horizontal axis. Drag in a vertical direction to constrain the skew to the vertical axis.

7. Release the mouse button when you are satisfied with the position of the skewed object. Your object skews into position.

To copy as you skew an object:

1. Hold the Opt/Alt key as you drag to skew the object. A plus sign (+) appears next to the star cursor.

2. Release the mouse button first and then the Opt/Alt key to create a copy of the original object skewed to the position you chose. The original object is left unchanged.

Skewing Objects

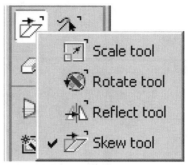

㉗ *The Skew tool selected from its toolset in the Tools panel.*

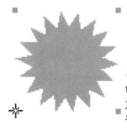

㉘ *Position the Skew tool cursor on the point you want the object to skew from.*

㉙ *Press and drag with the Skew tool to create a sheared or skewed image of the object.*

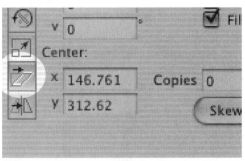

30 *The* **Skew** *icon in the Transform panel.*

31 *The Transform panel set to the* **Skew** *controls.*

To skew using the Transform panel:

1. Choose the object you want to skew. Click the Skew icon in the Transform panel **30**. The Skew controls appear **31**.

2. Enter the horizontal angle amount of the skew in the **h** field. Enter the vertical amount of the skew in the the **v** field.

3. To change the point of transformation from the center, enter the coordinates you want in the **x** and **y** fields.

   or

   With the Skew tool active, hold the Opt/Alt key and click to select a transformation point.

4. Check Contents to skew any items pasted inside along with the object *(see page 103)* **32**.

5. Check Fills to skew any fills such as tiled fills *(see page 208)*.

6. Click the Skew button in the Transform panel.

   or

   Press Return or Enter to apply the skew.

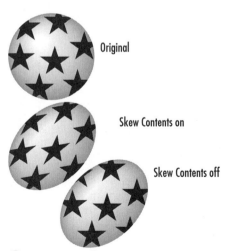

Original

Skew Contents on

Skew Contents off

32 *With* **Skew Contents on**, *the design pasted in skews along with the oval. With* **Skew Contents off**, *the design does not skew with the oval.*

Skewing Objects

Reflecting Objects

As the Wicked Queen in *Snow White* knew, reflecting allows you to create a mirror image of an object.

To reflect an object by eye:

1. Select the object you want to reflect.
2. Choose the Reflect tool in the Tools panel 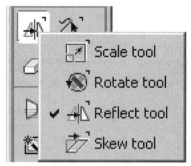.
3. Move your cursor to the page. Your cursor turns into a star.
4. Position the star on the point around which you want the object to reflect ❸❹. This is the transformation point.
5. Press on the point you have chosen. *Do not release the mouse button.* A line extends out from the star. This line is the reflection axis. (Think of the reflection axis as the mirror in which your object is being reflected.)
6. Drag the cursor away from the transformation point. The outline of the object changes its position and shape as you move the cursor ❸❺.
   TIP Hold the Shift key to constrain your reflection to 45° increments.
7. Release the mouse button when you are satisfied with the position of the reflected object. Your object is reflected into position.

To copy as you reflect an object:

1. Hold the Opt/Alt key as you drag to reflect the object. A plus sign (+) appears next to the star cursor.
2. Release the mouse button first and then the Opt/Alt key to create a copy of the original object reflected to the position you chose.

❸❸ The **Reflect tool** *selected from its toolset in the Tools panel.*

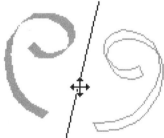

❸❹ *Position the* **Reflect tool cursor** *on the point you want the object to reflect around.*

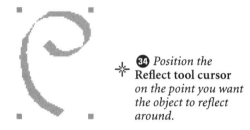

❸❺ *The reflection axis and the preview show the position to which the object will be reflected.*

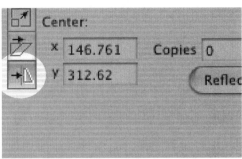

36 *The* **Reflect** *icon in the Transform panel.*

37 *The Transform panel set to the* **Reflect controls.**

Original

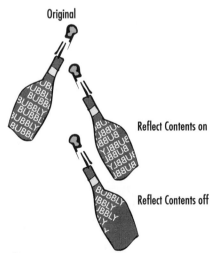

Reflect Contents on

Reflect Contents off

38 *With* **Reflect Contents on** *the text pasted in reflects along with the bottle. With* **Reflect Contents off** *the text does not reflect with the bottle.*

To reflect using the Transform panel:

1. Select the object you want to reflect.

2. Click the Reflect icon in the Transform panel **36**. The Reflect controls appear **37**.

3. In the Reflect axis field, enter the angle amount that you want the object to reflect around.

4. To change the point of transformation from the center, enter the coordinates you want in the **x** and **y** fields.

   or

   With the Reflect tool active, hold the Opt/Alt key and click to select a transformation point.

5. Check the Contents to reflect any items pasted inside along with the object *(see page 103)* **38**.

6. Check Fills to reflect any fills such as tiled fills *(see page 208)*.

7. Click the Reflect button in the Transform panel.

   or

   Press Return or Enter to apply the reflection.

Reflecting Objects

Using Power Duplicating

FreeHand offers two more techniques for copying and transforming objects. The first technique allows you to transform a copy of an object. You can then create additional transformed copies.

To create multiple transformed copies:

1. Hold the Opt/Alt key as you begin the transformation. A plus sign (+) appears next to the star cursor.

2. Release the mouse button first and then the Opt/Alt key to create a transformed copy of the original object ㊴.

   TIP If you do not see the plus sign (+), check that the Object Preference for Opt/Alt-dragging to create copies is selected (*see Appendix C*).

3. Choose **Edit > Duplicate** to create additional transformed copies ㊵.

The second technique allows you to store up to five transformations. You can then apply all the transformations as you make copies.

To combine transformations into Power Duplicating:

1. Select the object you want to transform.

2. Choose **Edit > Clone.** This creates a copy of the object on top of the original.

3. Move the clone or use any of the transformation tools to modify it.

4. Apply any of the other transformations. Each of the transformations is now stored.

5. Choose **Edit > Duplicate.** The object is copied and modified according to the stored transformations.

6. Choose **Edit > Duplicate** as many times as needed. Each command creates a new object. The new object is then transformed according to the stored transformation settings ㊶. This results in incremental changes to all the copies.

㊴ *The* **plus sign** *indicates that a copy of the object is being made as part of the transformation.*

㊵ *The* **Duplicate command** *creates additional copies of a rotated object.*

㊶ **Power Duplicating** *allows you to store transformations and reapply them to each new copy. In this case, the star is both rotated and scaled.*

42 *The* **Transformation handles** *around a grouped object.*

43 *The* **Move cursor** *indicates that you can move the objects and the Transformation handles.*

44 *Move the* **Transformation point cursor** *to change the point around which the transformation occurs.*

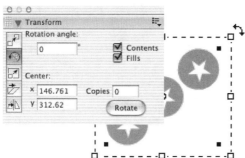

45 *As you use the Transformation handles, the information about the transformation is stored in the Transform panel.*

Using the Transformation Handles

At times it may be cumbersome to stop working on artwork to choose the scale or rotation tools. The Transformation handles let you modify objects directly on the page without changing tools.

To use the Transformation handles:

1. With the Pointer tool active, double-click the selected object. A rectangular box with eight Transformation handles appears **42**.

TIP Hold the Cmd/Ctrl key to temporarily switch to the Pointer tool.

2. Move the cursor near the handles to transform the selection as described in the following exercises.

3. Move the cursor inside the box. The four-headed arrow indicates you can move the objects to a new position **43**.

4. Drag the Transformation point icon away from the center of the object. This changes the point around which the transformation occurs **44**.

5. Double-click outside the box to clear the Transformation handles.

TIP Hold the Opt/Alt key as you drag with the Transformation handles to copy the object as it is transformed.

TIP As you use the Transformation handles, the information about the transformation is stored in the Transform panel **45**. You can then apply that numerical value to other objects.

TIP If you find the Transformation handles interfere with your work, turn them off using the Preferences *(see Appendix C)*.

To rotate using the Transformation handles:

1. Move the cursor near one of the handles. The curved arrow Rotation cursor appears ⓰.

2. Drag to rotate the object around the transformation point.

To scale using the Transformation handles:

1. Move the cursor directly onto one of the handles. The double-headed arrow Scale icon appears ⓱.

2. Drag to scale the object from the transformation point.

To skew using the Transformation handles:

1. Place the cursor between the handles. The split arrow Skew cursor appears ⓲.

2. Drag to skew the object from the transformation point.

⓰ *The* **Rotation cursor** *(circled) lets you use the Transformation handles to rotate an object.*

⓱ *The* **Scale cursor** *(circled) lets you use the Transformation handles to scale an object.*

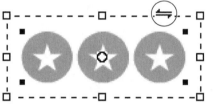

⓲ *The* **Skew cursor** *(circled) lets you skew the object around the Transformation point.*

Using the Transformation Handles

⑭ *Use the* **Constrain dialog box** *to change the horizontal axis along which objects are drawn.*

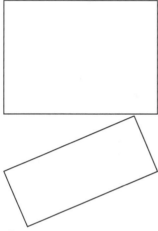

⑤ *The top rectangle was drawn with a Constrain axis of 0°. The bottom rectangle had a Constrain axis of 23°.*

Constraining Transformations

As you draw, move, or transform objects, the objects are positioned along an invisible line called the Constrain axis. The default setting of this axis is 0°. This means that your objects line up in an ordinary horizontal fashion. However, by changing the Constrain axis, you can make all your objects automatically align along any angle you choose.

To change the Constrain axis:

1. Choose **File** > **Document Settings** > **Constrain.** The Constrain dialog box appears **⑭**.

2. Enter the angle you want for the Constrain axis in the Angle field.

   or

   Rotate the wheel to enter an angle in the field.

3. Click OK. All objects will be drawn along the angle you have just set **⑤**.

TIP Changing the Constrain axis only affects those objects created from that point on. It does not affect previously created objects.

Constraining Transformations

Aligning Objects

You may want to move objects so that their
tops, bottoms, sides, or centers are in alignment. You may also want to move objects
so they are distributed equally. FreeHand
gives you several ways to align and distribute
objects.

To align using the Align menu:

1. Select the objects you want to align.
2. Choose one of the following from the
   Modify > Align menu:
   - **Top** aligns the objects along the top
     edge of their bounding boxes.
   - **Bottom** aligns the objects along the
     bottom edge of their bounding box.
   - **Center Horizontal** aligns the objects
     along the horizontal center of their
     bounding boxes.
   - **Center Vertical** aligns the objects along
     the vertical center of their bounding
     boxes.
   - **Left** aligns the objects along the left
     edge of their bounding boxes.
   - **Right** aligns the objects along the right
     edge of their bounding boxes.

To align using the Align panel menus:

1. Select the objects you want to align.
2. Choose **Window > Align** to open the
   Align panel 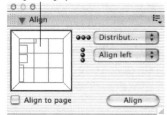.
3. In the Align panel, use the Horizontal
   menu to set the horizontal alignment of
   the objects 52.
4. Use the Vertical align menu to set the
   vertical alignment of the objects 53.
5. Click the Align button. The objects move
   into position.

Alignment graphic controller

51 *The* **Align panel** *lets you align or distribute
objects.*

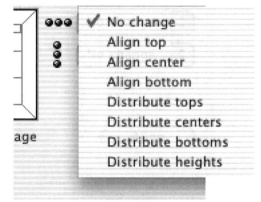

52 *The* **Horizontal align menu** *of the Align
panel.*

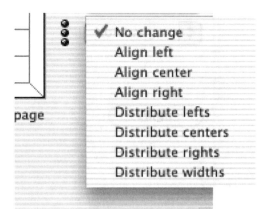

53 *The* **Vertical align menu** *of the Align panel.*

A	Top, no change vertical
B	Right, no change horizontal
C	Bottom, no change vertical
D	Left, no change horizontal
E	Top, left
F	Top, center horizontal
G	Top, right
H	Center vertical, left
I	Center vertical, center horizontal
J	Center vertical, right
K	Bottom, left
L	Bottom, center horizontal
M	Bottom, right

54 *Click each portion of the* **Alignment graphic controller** *to set different alignment options.*

To distribute using the Align panel menus:

1. Select the objects you want to distribute.
2. In the Align panel, use the Horizontal menu to set the horizontal distribution of the objects.
3. Use the Vertical menu to set the vertical distribution of the objects.
4. Click the Align button. The objects move into position.

To align or distribute to the page:

1. Click the Align to page option in the Align panel if you want the objects to align to the page.
2. Use any of the alignment features in the Align panel.

The Align panel also has a graphic controller that lets you click in certain areas to align objects. This is slightly faster than pulling down menus.

To use the Alignment graphic controller:

1. Select the objects you want to distribute.
2. Click one of the graphic controller areas in the Align panel **54**. The objects align into positon.

DIMENSIONAL EFFECTS 11

Strictly speaking, Macromedia Free-Hand is not a three-dimensional drawing program. Those programs let you create three-dimensional environments complete with shadows, reflections, and other lighting effects. If you're looking for that type of illustration work, Freehand is not the best choice.

That's not to say that Freehand limits you totally to two-dimensional effects. FreeHand has an impressive arsenal of three-dimensional tools. These include simple tools to rotate objects in space and add shadows. FreeHand also lets you distort or warp objects as if they were wrapped around dimensional objects.

FreeHand also lets you modify objects along a perspective. Finally, you can even take an ordinary object and apply sophisticated extrusions to give it a three-dimensional appearance.

Using the 3D Rotation Tool

The 3D Rotation tool applies a combination of transformations to make an object look like it is rotated in space.

To set the Easy 3D Rotation controls:

1. Double-click the 3D Rotation tool in the Xtra tools toolbar ❶. The 3D Rotation controls appear.

2. Click the Easy button to display the Easy (or less options) controls ❷.

3. Use the Rotate from menu to select the point from which the rotation should occur as follows:

   - **Mouse click** sets the rotation pivot point to the position where you click.
   - **Center of selection** makes the point the physical center of the object.
   - **Center of gravity** sets the rotation pivot point to the center of the object when adjusted for uneven shapes.
   - **Origin** sets the rotation pivot point to the bottom-left corner of the bounding box that surrounds the selection.

4. Set a Distance amount for how much distortion occurs. For the greatest distortion, enter small numbers.

TIP In the Easy mode, the projection point *(see the next exercise)* is set at the mouse click.

❶ *The* **3D Rotation tool** *selected from its toolset in the Tools panel.*

❷ *The* **3D Rotation controls** *in the Easy mode.*

Limitations of 3D Rotations

The 3D Rotation tool actually combines several transformations into a 3D effect. However, there is one important part of the 3D Rotation that is missing: Depth.

Unfortunately, the 3D Rotation tool doesn't show you any depth as it moves an object to its side. You can use the Extrude tool *(see page 158)* to add depth to a rotated object.

Also, the 3D Rotation tool isn't as powerful as the perspective grids. So unlike the grid, once you apply the 3D Rotation tool, you can't move the object to a new perspective position.

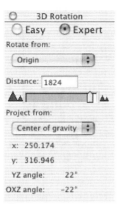

❸ *The* **3D Rotation controls** *in the Expert mode.*

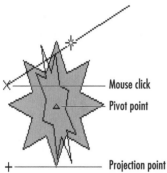

Mouse click

Pivot point

Projection point

❹ *As you drag with the 3D Rotation tool, a line extends from the mouse click. Drag along the line to control the distortion.*

Before After

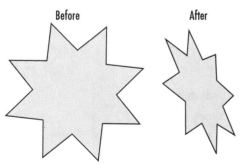

❺ *The results of applying the 3D Rotation tool.*

To set the Expert 3D Rotation controls:

1. Click the Expert button to display the Expert (more options) controls **❸**.

2. Use the Project from menu to select the *projection point* (the perspective vanishing point) as follows:

   - **Mouse click** sets the point to the position where you click.
   - **Center of selection** makes the point the physical center of the object.
   - **Center of gravity** sets the point to the center of the object when adjusted for uneven shapes.
   - **Origin** sets the point to the bottom-left corner of the bounding box that surrounds the selection.
   - **X/Y coordinates** sets the projection points from coordinates you enter in the fields.

To use the 3D Rotation tool:

1. Select the object or objects you want to modify.

2. Choose the 3D Rotation tool.

3. Press and drag the cursor away from the point where you pressed. A line extends out. The further along the line you drag, the greater the 3D rotation **❹**.

TIP As you press, a preview shows how the object is being modified.

4. When you are satisfied with the rotation, release the mouse button, and the object changes shape **❺**.

TIP In the Expert mode, watch the 3D Rotation tool panel to track the changes to the object as you drag along the line.

Using the 3D Rotation Tool

Using the Smudge Tool

The Smudge tool provides you with a quick and easy way to add a soft edge to an object.

To use the Smudge tool:

1. Select the object or objects you want to modify.

2. Choose the Smudge tool from the Xtra Tools toolbar **6**. Your cursor changes into the Smudge fingers.

3. Drag the fingers along the direction the smudge should take. A line extends from the object. That is the length of the smudge **7**.

4. Release the mouse button to create the smudge **8**.

TIP Spot colors used in a smudge are converted to process.

TIP Hold the Opt/Alt key to create a smudge from the center outward.

TIP The number of steps in a smudge is governed by the printer resolution in the Document inspector. If a smudge looks jagged, undo the smudge, increase the resolution, and then reapply the smudge.

If you are smudging objects over colors, the smudge should fade to those background colors. To do so, you change the smudge colors.

To change the smudge colors:

1. Double-click the Smudge tool in the Xtra Tools toolbar. This displays the Smudge dialog box **9**.

2. Drag colors from the Color Mixer or Color List into the Fill and the Stroke boxes.

3. Click OK and then apply the smudge as usual.

6 The **Smudge tool** *selected from its toolset in the Tools panel.*

7 *Dragging with the* **Smudge fingers** *cursor controls the length and direction of the effect.*

8 *The results of applying the* **Smudge tool.**

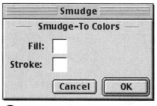

9 *The* **Smudge dialog box** *lets you set the colors that the fill and stroke fade into.*

🔟 The **Shadow tool** *selected from its toolset in the Tools panel.*

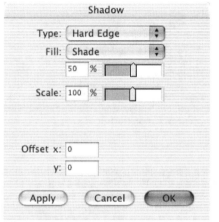

⓫ The **Shadow dialog box.**

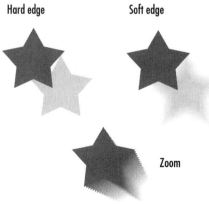

⓬ *The three different* **types of shadows.**

Working with the Shadow Tool

A more sophisticated version of the Smudge tool is the Shadow tool.

To apply a shadow:

1. Select the object or objects you want to modify.

2. Double-click the Shadow tool in the Xtra Tools toolbar 🔟. This opens the Shadow dialog box ⓫.

3. Choose one of the following from the Type menu:
   - **Hard Edge** uses a single object to create a crisp shadow.
   - **Soft Edge** uses a blend to create a shadow with a uniform soft edge.
   - **Zoom** creates a blend that is positioned to create a 3D effect.

4. Choose one of the following from the Fill menu:
   - **Color** lets you choose a specific color for the shadow.
   - **Shade** creates a shadow color that is a darker color of the original object.
   - **Tint** creates a shadow that is a lighter color of the original object.

5. Use the slider for the Color, Shade, and Tint fills to adjust the lightness or darkness of the shadow.

6. Use the Scale slider to set the size of the shadow element.

   TIP Less than 100% makes a shadow that is smaller than the original. Greater than 100% makes a shadow that is larger than the original.

7. Set the x and y offset amounts to position the shadow away from the original.

8. Click OK. The shadow is applied to the object ⓬.

   TIP If you ungroup the shadow and object, you can use the mouse to drag the shadow into new positions.

Working with the Fisheye Lens

In photography, a fisheye lens distorts the appearance of photos so that objects seem to be bulging out at the viewer. FreeHand lets you apply the same effect to graphics using the Fisheye Lens tool.

To set the Fisheye Lens tool:

1. Double-click the Fisheye Lens tool in the Xtra Tools toolbar ⓭. The Fisheye Lens dialog box appears ⓮.

2. Drag the Perspective slider or enter numbers in the Perspective field as follows:

   • **Convex** or positive numbers cause the object to bulge.
   • **Concave** or negative numbers cause the object to be pinched in.

   TIP The preview grid shows you a representation of what the setting will do to the object.

3. Click OK.

To use the Fisheye Lens tool:

1. Select the object you want to modify.

   TIP You must convert text to paths in order to apply the Fisheye Lens tool.

2. Select the Fishey Lens tool in the Tools panel.

3. Drag your cursor to create an oval over the area you want to distort.

   TIP Hold the Opt/Alt key to create a distortion from the center outward.

   TIP Hold the Shift key to constrain the distortion to a circular shape.

4. Release the mouse button to apply the distortion ⓯.

⓭ *The* **Fisheye Lens tool** *selected from its toolset in the Tools panel.*

Preview grid

⓮ *The* **Fisheye Lens dialog box.**

GAINING WEIGHT?

GAINING WEIGHT?

⓯ *The results of applying the* **Fisheye Lens** tool.

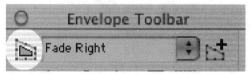

16 *The* **Envelope toolbar** *contains preset shapes you can choose among to distort an object.*

17 *The* **Create icon** *lets you apply the currently selected preset as an envelope shape.*

18 *Applying the circle envelope preset to an elongated object creates an elliptical text object.*

19 *The Circle preset was applied twice to text to create this elliptical shape.*

Working with Envelopes

Do you remember the logo for the Monkees rock group? That logo was the word "Monkees" stretched and distorted into the shape of a guitar. That guitar shape is called an *envelope*. FreeHand lets you apply electronic envelopes to distort text and other objects. Enveloping starts with 21 ready-made preset shapes that are stored in the Envelope toolbar. These shapes can be applied to either objects or text.

To apply an envelope to a graphic:

1. Select the object or text block you want to distort.

2. In the Envelope toolbar, select the envelope preset you want from the pop-up menu **16**.

3. Click the Create envelope icon to distort the selected object **17**.

   or

   Choose **Modify > Envelope > Create.** This uses the preset currently active in the Envelope toolbar **18**.

TIP Although you can apply envelopes to text objects, you may find you get better results if you first convert the text to paths *(see page 301)*.

TIP You may also find that some envelope shapes look better when they are applied a second time to an object **19**.

To modify the envelope applied to a graphic:

1. Use any of the selection tools to select the graphic. The envelope shape appears as a path.

2. Use any of the techniques that modify paths to change the shape of the envelope . This includes moving the points on the path, adding and deleting points, and using the transform tools.

TIP To edit text inside an envelope, Opt/Alt double-click with the Pointer tool. This opens the Text Editor where you can make your changes.

⓴ *You can modify the points on the envelope path.*

There are some limits to what you can do when an envelope is applied to a graphic. For instance, you can't use the enveloped graphic in a blend or apply a second envelope to the graphic. So you may want to release the envelope after you apply it to a graphic.

To release an envelope from a graphic:

◆ Choose **Modify** > **Envelope** > **Release.**

  or

  Click the Release icon in the Envelope toolbar **㉑**.

TIP When you release an envelope a path will return to being a path; a text block will become a group and the individual letters will have been converted to paths.

You may also want to remove an envelope so that it no longer distorts a graphic.

To remove an envelope from a graphic:

◆ Choose **Modify** > **Envelope** > **Remove.**

  or

  Click the Remove icon in the Envelope toolbar **㉒**.

㉑ *The* **Release icon** *applies the envelope shape to the graphic and then removes the envelope path.*

㉒ *The* **Remove icon** *removes the envelope shape from the graphic.*

23 *Create a path you want to use as an envelope preset.*

24 *The* **Paste as Envelope icon** *applies the contents of the clipboard as an envelope.*

25 *The results of pasting a path as an envelope.*

26 *The* **Save as Preset icon** *lets you save a custom shape as an envelope preset.*

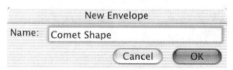

27 *The* **New Envelope dialog box** *lets you name a custom preset shape.*

You can also create your own custom envelope shapes from paths.

To use a path as an envelope:

1. Select the path you want to use as an envelope **23**.

2. Choose **Edit** > **Copy** to copy the path to the clipboard.

3. Select the object to which you want to apply the envelope.

4. Choose **Modify** > **Envelope** > **Paste as Envelope.**

 or

 Click the Paste as Envelope icon on the Envelope toolbar **24**. The envelope is applied to the object **25**.

Once you have a new envelope shape, you may want to save it to use on other objects. This includes shapes you have pasted as custom envelopes as well as preset paths you have modified.

To save a custom envelope:

1. Select the object that contains the envelope you wish to save.

2. Choose **Modify** > **Envelope** > **Save as Preset.**

 or

 Click the Save as Preset icon on the Envelope toolbar **26**. The New Envelope dialog box appears **27**.

3. Name the envelope shape and click OK. The envelope is listed in the preset list.

Working with Envelopes

To delete an envelope preset:

1. Select the envelope you wish to remove from the pop-up menu on the Envelope toolbar.

2. Choose **Modify > Envelope > Delete Preset.**

    or

    Click the Delete Preset icon on the Envelope toolbar ⓲.

FreeHand also lets you see the envelope map. This is the grid of lines that is used by the envelope as part of the distortion.

To see the envelope grid:

♦   Select the object that has the envelope applied and choose **Modify > Envelope > Show Map.**

    or

    Select the object that has the envelope applied and click the Show Map icon on the Envelope toolbar ⓲. The map appears inside the envelope ⓴.

After you have created an envelope to modify a path or a text block, you can convert it to a path for use in your document.

TIP Converting an envelope to a path is very helpful since you cannot apply fills or strokes to the paths used as envelopes.

To paste an envelope as a path:

1. Select the graphic that has the envelope you want to copy.

2. Choose **Modify > Envelope > Copy As Path.**

    or

    Click the Copy as Path icon on the Envelope toolbar ⓲.

3. Choose **Edit > Paste** to paste the shape into the document. You can add a fill or stroke to the path ⓲.

⓲ *The* **Delete Preset icon** *lets you delete any presets from the envelope preset list.*

⓲ *The* **Show Map icon** *lets you reveal or hide the grid used in the envelope distortion.*

⓴ *The* **Envelope Map** *displays the grid of lines used in the envelope.*

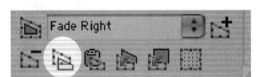

⓲ *The* **Copy as Path icon** *converts the envelope path into a path on the clipboard.*

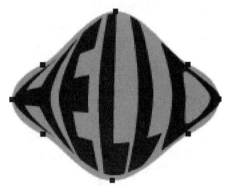

⓲ *Copy the envelope as a path and put it behind the original to put a fill behind the text.*

Working with Envelopes

③ *The* **Perspective tool** *selected from its toolset in the Tools panel.*

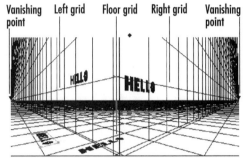

④ *The elements of a* **Perspective Grid.**

Using the Perspective Grid

The perspective grid gives you a very powerful set of tools for quickly and easily creating graphics that maintain a consistent perspective. Essentially, it allows you to create perspective envelopes that automatically adjust as they are moved around the page.

To view the Perspective grid:

◆ Choose **View** > **Perspective Grid** > **Show**. The grid appears on the page.

To attach objects to the Perspective grid:

1. Choose the Perspective tool from the Tools panel **③**.

2. Use the Perspective tool to drag an object to the desired place on the grid.

3. Without releasing the mouse button, tap one of the arrow keys on the keyboard as follows:

   • **Left arrow** attaches the object to the left grid.
   • **Right arrow** attaches the object to the right grid.
   • **Down arrow** attaches the object to the floor grid, oriented to the right vanishing point.
   • **Up arrow** attaches the object to the floor grid, oriented to the left vanishing point.

Using the Perspective Grid

Understanding the Perspective Grids

Perspective is the attempt to portray the appearance of a three-dimensional world in a two-dimensional graphic **④**.

If you look straight at a book, the cover is a rectangle, but if you put the book on an angle, the lines of the book change. Obviously the book itself doesn't change its shape—its appearance does. The angle that you slant the book is similar to the *left grid* or the *right grid* that the perspective grid aligns objects to. If you lay the book down, that is similar to aligning objects to a *floor grid*.

When you look down a road, objects seem to get smaller as they move away. The point where the objects are too small to be seen is called the *vanishing point*.

To move an object on the Perspective grid:

◆ Use the Perspective tool to move the object around the grid. As the object changes position it changes its shape to conform to the perspective grid ㉟.

TIP Hold the Opt/Alt key to copy an object while dragging it on the grid with the Perspective tool.

TIP Hold the Shift key to constrain its movement to the grid axes.

To define a Perspective grid:

1. Choose **View** > **Perspective Grid** > **Define Grids.** This opens the Define Grids dialog box ㊱.

2. Click New to add a new grid to the list.

3. Double click to change the name of the grid.

4. Use the Vanishing Point list to set the number of vanishing points in the grid ㊲.

5. Use the grid cell size to set how large the cells should be. A larger cell size creates fewer grid lines on the page.

6. Click the color wells to set the color for each portion of the grid.

7. Use the Delete button to delete grids.

8. Use the Duplicate button to make a copy of each grid.

9. Click OK to accept the settings and return to the document. The grids you define can be selected from the bottom of the **View** > **Perspective Grid** submenu.

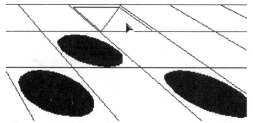

㉟ *As a circle is copied to different places on the perspective grid, it changes its shape.*

㊱ *The* **Define Grids dialog box** *sets the attributes of the Perspective grids in the document.*

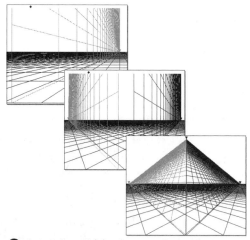

㊲ *A 1-point grid (top), a 2-point grid (middle), and a 3-point grid (bottom).*

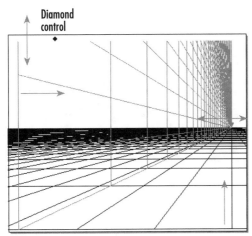

Diamond control

30 *Drag the* **Elements of a grid** *to change the characteristics of the grid on the page.*

To modify the page characteristics of a grid:

◆ Choose the Perspective tool. Modify the elements of the grid as follows **30**:

- To change the height of the grid, drag the diamond control up or down.
- To change the position of the vanishing point, drag the point to the right or left.
- To change the angle of a grid, drag the grid lines.
- To hide or show a left or right grid, double-click the grid's vanishing point.
- To hide or show the floor grid, double-click the horizon line.

TIP To protect a grid configuration, duplicate the grid in the Define Grid dialog box before you make changes.

To keep objects aligned as you modify a grid:

1. Select the objects.

2. Hold the Shift key as you modify the grid.

Objects aligned to a grid are inside envelopes. As with other envelopes, you can release an object leaving it distorted.

To release objects from the grid:

1. Select the object you want to release.

2. Choose **View > Perspective Grid > Release Perspective.**

You can also remove an object from the grid and return it to its original shape.

To remove objects from the grid:

1. Select the object you want to release and restore to its original shape.

2. Choose **View > Perspective Grid > Remove Perspective.**

TIP You can also choose **Modify > Envelope > Release** or **Modify > Envelope > Remove** as well as the Release and Remove buttons on the Envelope toolbar to release or remove objects from the grid.

Using the Perspective Grid

Using the Extrude Tool

The Extrude tool is the most sophisticated of FreeHand's dimensional effects. With the Extrude tool the shape of a flat object is extruded or projected into a three-dimensional appearance.

There are several steps you follow to create an extruded object.

39 *The* **Extrude tool** *selected from its toolset in the Tools panel.*

To create an extruded object:

1. Drag with the Extrude tool to apply an extrusion to an object. You can then manually adjust the perspective and depth controls *(see the following page)* **39**.

2. Use the Extrude tool to display and use the onscreen orientation ontrols *(see the following page)* **40**.

3. With the extruded object selected, click the Extrude icon in the Object panel to set the extrusion controls *(covered on page 160)*. This is where you control the basic appearance of the extruded object such as its depth and position.

4. Click the Surface icon to display the surface and lighting controls *(covered on pages 161 and 162)*. These are the controls that let you adjust the appearance of the object's surface and the lighting on the object.

5. Click the Profile icon to set the shape of the extrusion *(covered on page 163)*. This allows you to warp the object as it is extruded.

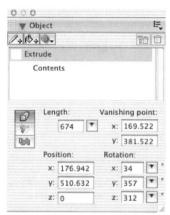

40 *The* **Extrude controls** *in the Object panel.*

Extrusions in the Real World

There are hundreds of examples of extruded objects in the real world. Toothpaste is extruded from a tube. The shape of the extruded toothpaste comes from the circle shape of the opening of the tube. The length of the extrusion comes from how hard and long you squeeze.

Most prepared snack foods are created by extrusion as are pastas and chopped meat.

Using the Extrude Tool

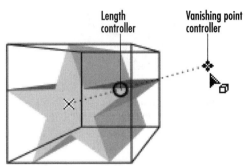

Length controller   **Vanishing point controller**

⑪ *You can adjust the appearance of an extruded object by dragging the* **onscreen perspective and depth controls**.

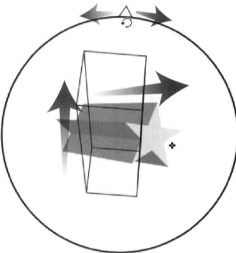

㊷ *You can change the spatial orientation of an extruded object by dragging the* **onscreen x, y, z orientation controls**.

Once you have created an extruded object, you can use the onscreen controls to manually adjust its depth, perspective, and position in space.

To extrude an object manually:

1. Select the object that you want to extrude.

2. Drag the Extrude tool in the direction that you want to extrude the object. This sets the vanishing point for the perspective applied to the object **⑪**.

3. Position the Extrude tool cursor over the length control. Drag to increase or decrease the length of the extrusion applied to the object.

TIP A bounding box appears to show the depth applied to the object.

TIP Use the Extrude tool to select a previously extruded object and drag to change either the vanishing point or the extrusion length.

To change the orientation manually:

1. Double-click with the Extrude tool on the object. The onscreen orientation controls appear **㊷**.

TIP Choose **Modify** > **Extrude** > **Release Extrude** to see the orientation controls.

2. Drag inside the orientation circle to change the x (horizontal) or y (vertical) orientation of the object.

3. Drag the outside control to change the z (depth) orientation of the object.

4. Double-click inside the orientation controls to to return to the bounding box controls.

TIP Choose **Modify** > **Extrude** > **Reset Extrude** to remove all orientation changes applied to the object.

You may find it easier to use the numerical controls in the Object panel to modify the perspective, depth, and orientation of an extruded object.

To set the numerical Extrude controls:

1. With the extruded object selected, click the Extrude icon in the Object panel 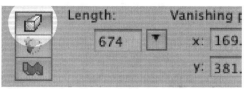. This displays the numerical Extrude controls .

2. Set the depth of the extrusion in the length field.

3. Use the Vanishing point fields to set the x (horizontal) and y (vertical) position of the vanishing point.

4. Use the x (horizontal), y (vertical), and z (depth) Position fields to set the position of the extruded object.

5. Use the x (horizontal), y (vertical), and z (depth) Rotation controls to set the orientation of the extruded object.

TIP The x and y Position controls are the same as moving the object up and down, or left and right on the page.

TIP The z Position control can only be set numerically in the Object panel. As you increase the z position, this has the effect of moving the object further away from the viewer which makes it smaller.

6. Press the Return or Enter key to apply the settings to the extruded object.

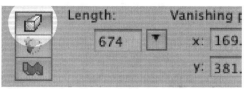

43 *The* **Extrude icon** *in the Object panel sets the extrude controls for an extruded object.*

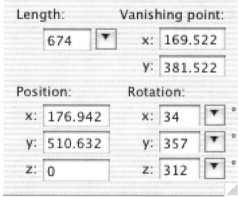

44 *The* **Extrude controls** *allow you to numerically change the appearance of an extruded object.*

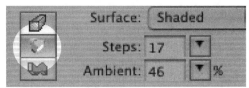

45 *The* **Surface icon** *in the Object panel sets the surface and lighting controls for an extruded object.*

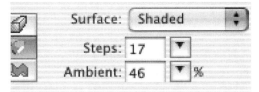

46 *The* **Surface controls** *for the appearance of the extruded object.*

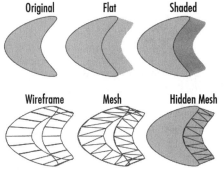

47 *The* **surface choices** *applied to an extruded object.*

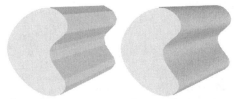

48 *The difference between 5 steps (left) and 25 steps (right) applied to a shaded object.*

The Surface options in the Object panel let you control the appearance of the shading and lighting applied to an object.

TIP An extruded object does not appear solid unless a fill color has been applied to the path *(see Chapter 14, "Fills").*

To set the surface options of the extruded object:

1. Click the Surface icon in the Object panel **45**. This displays the Surface controls **46**.

2. Use the Surface menu to choose one of the following **47**:

   - **Flat** applies the surface color with no lighting effects.
   - **Shaded** applies shaded contours to the object.
   - **Wireframe** displays a transparent frame structure for the object.
   - **Mesh** uses polygons to create a transparent structure for the object.
   - **Hidden Mesh** shows the exterior polygons and fill for the object.

3. Set the number of steps for the shading, wireframe, or mesh used to create the extrusion.

TIP In the Shaded option, the higher the number of steps, the smoother the shading **48**.

4. Use the Ambient control to increase or decrease the amount of light on the object.

TIP The Ambient control sets the general lighting of the object. See the next exercise for how to control the directional lighting.

Using the Extrude Tool

In addition to the ambient light applied to the surface of an object, you can also set options for two directional lighting sources.

TIP Only the Shaded surface option responds to changes in the lighting. The other surface options do not change their appearance from the lighting controls.

To set the lighting options of the extruded object:

1. Click the Surface icon in the Object panel. The Lighting controls appear at the bottom of the Object panel **49**.

2. Use the Direction menu to choose the direction for Light 1 and Light 2 **50**.

3. Use the Intensity controls to set the amount of light applied by Light 1 and Light 2.

TIP The higher the intensity of the light, the less color will be seen on the object. Extremely high lighting intensities can cause light-colored objects to appear white. Similarly, very little light on an object will make it appear black.

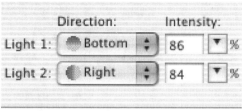

49 *The* **Lighting controls** *for the appearance of the extruded object.*

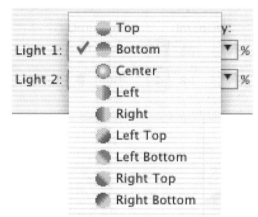

50 *The* **Direction menu** *for the appearance of the lighting on an object.*

How Lighting Affects Color

As you change the ambient lighting or the directional lighting, you change the color of an object. If you are creating Web graphics, you don't have to worry that much about these color changes. What you see on your screen is a good idea of what will be seen on the Web.

Print designers are not that lucky. They have to be very careful in how they apply the lighting controls as the colors of an object change. If you work with process colors, the lighting controls change the composition of those process colors.

If you work with spot colors, the lighting controls convert the spot colors from spot to process. This means you should not expect the spot colors to separate correctly. In addition, since many spot colors are defined using an RGB preview, the colors in the extruded object are converted to RGB. This could cause a problem if your final job needs to be produced using CMYK colors.

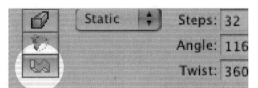

51 *The* **Profile icon** *in the Object panel displays the controls for modifying the shape of the extrusion.*

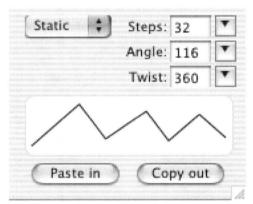

52 *The* **Profile controls** *for the appearance of the extruded object.*

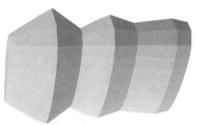

53 *A cylindrical extrusion changes its shape when a* **Bevel profile is applied**.

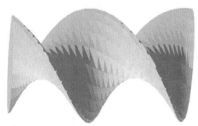

54 *The Twist control changes a cylindrical extrusion into a spiral ribbon.*

Perhaps the most sophisticated part of the extrusion controls is the ability to add a profile to the extruded object. A profile is a shape applied to the extruded side of an object. This allows you to add bumps and ridges to the object as it is extruded. For instance, when you crush a soda can from top to bottom, you change the profile of its extrusion.

To apply a profile to an extruded object:

1. Create an open path and copy it to the clipboard.

TIP Profiles must be open paths.

2. Select the extruded object and click the Profile icon **51**. This reveals the Profile controls **52**.

3. Change the Profile menu as follows:
   - **None** removes any profile.
   - **Bevel** applies the profile to the outside edge of the extrusion. This makes the extruded edge larger than the original shape **53**.
   - **Static** applies the profile within the original boundary of the extruded object.

4. Click the Paste in button. The profile appears in the preview area.

5. Use the Steps field to increase the amount of shading applied to the profile.

6. If you have applied a Static profile, you can use the Angle field to change how the profile is applied to the extrusion.

7. Increase the number in the Twist field to cause the extrusion to twist as it is created.

TIP Twists can be applied to an extrusion even if no profile has been applied **54**.

Using the Extrude Tool

In perspective drawings, all the objects in the drawing share a single vanishing point. If you create several different extruded objects, they each have their own vanishing point. Fortunately, it is very easy to make two extruded objects share the same vanishing point.

To apply the same vanishing point to objects:

1. Use the Pointer tool to select the extruded objects **55**.

2. Choose **Modify > Extrude > Share Vanishing Points.** The vanishing points appear and the extrude cursor becomes active.

3. Click with the extrude cursor. This forces the individual vanishing points to the same position **56**.

You may also want to modify the shape of an object after it has been extruded.

To modify an extruded object:

1. Choose the Subselection tool.

2. Select the extruded object. The points and segments become visible and can be modified **57**.

To convert an extruded object:

♦ Choose **Modify > Extrude > Release Extrude.** This converts the extruded areas into ordinary paths.

To remove the extrusion on an object:

♦ Choose **Modify > Extrude > Remove Extrude.** This removes all the the extruded areas from the object.

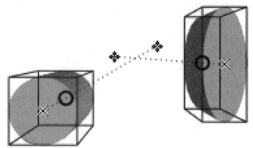

55 *Two different vanishing points create a mismatch between extruded objects.*

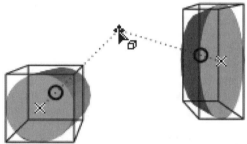

56 *A single vanishing point creates a better match for separate extruded objects.*

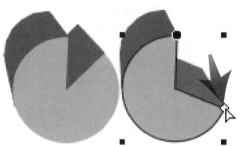

57 *Use the Subselection tool to modify the shape of an extruded object.*

LAYERS AND LAYERING 12

There were no computers when I started working in advertising. (Amazingly, we still managed to create artwork, logos, ads, and brochures even without any computers.) Instead, we pasted type and artwork on stiff mechanical boards that we sent to the printer to convert into printed materials.

If we needed to change the artwork, we would simply paste a new illustration or text on top of the old one. After a few weeks, we had many layers of paper on the board.

We also had acetate sheets that we would paste the artwork or text onto. This allowed us to flip the acetate over to see one version of the ad or cover it up with a second version.

Although it is electronic, Macromedia FreeHand works very similarly to the old boards. As soon as you put more than one path on your page, you already have layers of the artwork.

And you can also organize your artwork into electronic acetate sheets that can display different versions of the artwork.

Using the Arrange Commands

Objects are stacked on the page in the same order they were created. Though you may not see this when the objects are side by side, it is apparent when they overlap ❶ – ❷.

To move objects to the front of a layer:

1. Select an object in your artwork.
2. Choose **Modify** > **Arrange** > **Bring To Front** ❸ – ❹ to move the object to the front of the other objects in its layer.

To move objects to the back of a layer:

1. Select an object in your artwork.
2. Choose **Modify** > **Arrange** > **Send To Back** to move the object to the back of its layer.

TIP If you choose Bring To Front or Send To Back on a subselected object of a group, the object moves to the front or back of the group rather than the layer.

Sometimes you want to move an object in the middle of a layer. To do that, you use a different set of commands.

To move objects forward in a layer:

1. Select an object in your artwork.
2. Choose **Modify** > **Arrange** > **Move Forward** to move the object forward in its layer. This moves the object in front of the first object it was behind.
3. Repeat until the object is in the correct position in the layer ❺ – ❻.

To move objects backward in a layer:

1. Select an object in your artwork.
2. Choose **Modify** > **Arrange** > **Move Backward.** This moves the object backward in its layer.
3. Repeat until the object is in the correct position in the layer.

❶ *Although it may not be obvious, one object is in front of the other.*

❷ *When two objects overlap, it is obvious which object is in front of the other.*

❸ *If you want to move an object to the foreground...*

❹ *...select it and use the* **Bring To Front** *command.*

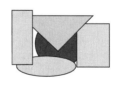

❺ *In this illustration, the circle needs to be in front of the triangle and square.*

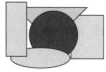

❻ *The same illustration after the* **Move Forward** *command was applied twice to the circle.*

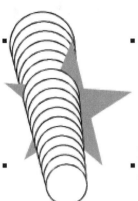

⑦ *To move an object using* **Paste Behind,** *select the object you want to move and then choose Cut.*

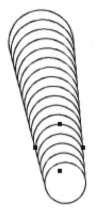

⑧ *Select the object that you want the object to be behind, in this case, the fifth circle.*

⑨ *Choose* **Paste Behind.** *The cut object appears behind the selected object.*

Using Paste in Front or Back

Since it may be tedious to choose Move Backward or Move Forward over and over, FreeHand offers two other ways to move objects within their layer.

To move objects using Paste Behind:

1. Select the object that you want to move.
2. Choose **Edit > Cut** **⑦**.
3. Select the object that you want in front of the original object **⑧**.
4. Choose **Edit > Special > Paste Behind.** The original object is pasted behind the object you chose **⑨**.

To move objects using Paste In Front:

1. Select the object that you want to move.
2. Choose **Edit > Cut.**
3. Select the object that you want behind the original object.
4. Choose **Edit > Special > Paste In Front.** The original object is pasted in front of the object you chose.

Using Paste in Front or Back

Locking and Unlocking Objects

As you work, there may be times when you want to lock a single object on a layer. This may be to avoid moving the object or to make sure it is not transformed.

To lock an object:

1. Select the object or objects you want to lock.

2. Choose **Modify** > **Lock.** The Lock icon in the Info toolbar indicates that the object is locked ⑩.

To unlock an object:

1. Select the object you want to unlock.

2. Choose **Modify** > **Unlock.**

If you have used programs such as Adobe Illustrator, you will find FreeHand treats a locked object differently. In Illustrator locked objects cannot be selected or modified. However, FreeHand does let you make some changes to locked objects. The chart on the right gives you a list of what you can — and cannot — do with locked objects.

⑩ *The* **Lock icon** *of the Info Toolbar indicates that an object is locked.*

Working with Locked Objects		
Select	Yes	
Modify fill	Yes	
Modify stroke	Yes	
Move		No
Resize		No
Transform		No
Delete		No
Copy	Yes	
Cut		No
Edit text	Yes	
Modify text formatting	Yes	

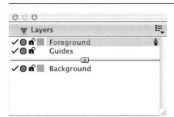

⓫ *The* **Layers panel** *shows the three default layers: Foreground, Guides, and Background.*

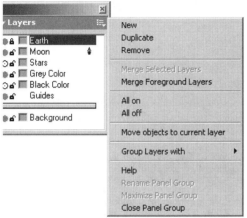

⓬ *The* **Layers panel menu** *lets you add, delete, duplicate, hide, or show the layers.*

Working with Layers

As your artwork becomes more complex, you may find that you need other ways of organizing objects. For instance, you may have many objects that overlap each other and you need to hide some objects while working on others. In that case, you will need to use FreeHand's Layers panel.

To view the Layers panel:

1. If you do not see the Layers panel on your screen, choose **Window >Layers.**

2. If you have not changed the default layers for your document, you should see three layers: Foreground, Guides, and Background ⓫.

Once you have created a new layer, you may want to rename it so that it reflects the items on that layer.

To rename a layer:

1. In the Layers panel, double-click the name of the layer you want to rename.

2. Type the new name of the layer.

3. Press Return or Enter, or click the Layers panel with the mouse.

To duplicate a layer:

1. Click the name of the layer you want to duplicate.

2. Choose Duplicate from the Layers panel menu ⓬. The layer and all of the objects on it will be duplicated.

TIP The Guides layer cannot be renamed or duplicated.

Working with Layers

To remove a layer:

1. Click the name of the layer you want to remove.

2. Choose Remove from the Layers panel menu. The layer and the objects on it are removed.

TIP You cannot delete the Guides layer or the very last drawing layer of a document.

TIP An alert box warns you if you try to remove a layer that has objects on it.

The layer at the top of the Layers panel is in front of the other layers. Layers do not have to remain in the order in which you created them. You use the Layers panel to reorder layers.

⓭ *In this illustration, the layer containing the Moon artwork is above the layer for the Earth.*

To reorder layers:

1. In the Layers panel, select the name of the layer you want to reorder **⓭**.

2. Drag the name of the layer to the spot on the list that represents where you would like the layer to be.

TIP (Win) A double-headed arrow cursor appears as you drag layers to new positions in the Layers panel.

3. Release the mouse button. The name of the layer disappears from where it was and reappears in its new position in the Layers panel. All objects on the layer are repositioned in the document **⓮**.

TIP If you want guides to appear in front of your artwork, drag the Guides layer above the layer that contains the artwork.

⓮ *The Earth layer is dragged above the Moon layer which changes the position of the artwork.*

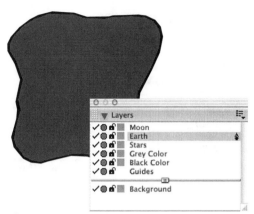

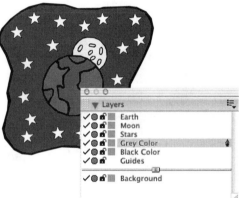

⓯ *In this illustration, the gray color is on the same layer as the Earth.*

⓰ *The same illustration after clicking the name of the Grey Color layer.*

When you are working, the objects you create go on the active layer, the one that has the pen icon on the Layers panel. You may want to move artwork from one layer to another.

To manually move objects between layers:

1. Select the artwork you want to move to a new layer. The layer to which it belongs is highlighted **⓯**.

2. Click the name of the layer that is the destination for the artwork. The artwork moves to that new layer **⓰**.

TIP To convert a path into a guide, move the path onto the Guides layer.

TIP You cannot move artwork onto a locked layer *(see page 174)*.

Some people do not like how easy it is to move objects from one layer to another. FreeHand lets you set a Preference that turns off the ability to move objects by clicking the name of a layer *(see Appendix C)*.

If you turn off the default setting, you must use the Layers panel menu to move objects between layers.

To use the menu to move objects between layers:

1. Select the artwork you want to move to a new layer.

2. Click the name of the layer that is the destination for the artwork.

3. Choose Move objects to current layers from the Layers panel menu. The artwork moves to the selected layer.

Working with Layers

A horizontal line divides the Layers panel. The layers above the line appear normal and print. The layers below the line appear dimmed and do not print. You may find you want to move layers from the printing to nonprinting areas of the list.

To create a nonprinting layer:

1. Drag the layer below the dividing line in the Layers panel.

2. Release the mouse button. The layer moves below the line, and any objects on the layer are dimmed and do not print **17**.

TIP Use nonprinting layers to hold images that have been placed for tracing *(see page 68)*.

To create a printing layer:

1. Drag the name of a nonprinting layer above the dividing line in the Layers panel.

2. Release the mouse button. The layer moves above the dividing line, and any objects on the layer will print.

TIP Objects on the Guides layer do not ever print, regardless of where the Guides layer is, either above or below the line.

To convert objects to guides:

1. Select the object you want to convert to a guide.

2. Click the Guides layer. The artwork is converted to a guide **18**.

TIP You must use the Guides dialog box *(see page 27)* to convert guides back into artwork.

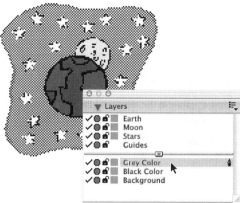

17 *To make a* **nonprinting layer,** *drag the name of the layer below the horizontal line.*

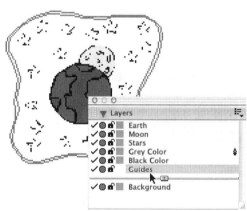

18 *Click the Guides layer to* **convert the selected objects to guides.**

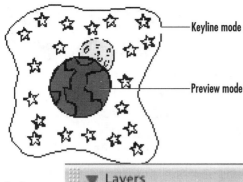

Preview
mode
Keyline
mode
Hidden

Displayed

⑲ *Use the Layers panels to control how artwork appears onscreen.*

⑳ *Select two or more layers in order to* **merge them into a single layer.**

You can also use the Layers panel to change the preview for the objects on each layer. This is especially helpful if you work with very complicated illustrations and need to select just certain elements.

To hide a layer:

◆ Click the check mark to the left of the layer name **⑲**. The check mark disappears, making the layer invisible.

To show a layer:

◆ Click the empty space for the check mark to make the layer visible **⑲**.

TIP Hold the Opt/Ctrl key as you click a check mark to show or hide all the layers.

TIP Use the *All on* or *All off* commands in the Options pop-up menu to quickly show or hide all layers.

To set a layer to the Keyline mode:

◆ Click the gray dot to the left of the layer name **⑲**. This creates a hollow dot that indicates the layer is in the Keyline mode *(see page 23).*

To set a layer to the Preview mode:

◆ Click the hollow dot to the left of the layer name **⑲**. This creates a gray dot that indicates the layer is in the Preview mode *(see page 22).*

TIP Hold the Opt/Ctrl key as you click a dot to switch the preview for all the layers.

You can also merge layers into a single layer. This is helpful when working with animations which create hundreds of layers.

To merge specific layers:

◆ Select the layers you want to merge and then choose Merge Selected Layers from the Layers panel menu **⑳**.

Working with Layers

You can also merge all the printing layers into a single layer.

To merge all the printing layers:

◆ Choose Merge Foreground Layers.

㉑ *Click an open padlock to lock a layer. Click a closed padlock to unlock a layer.*

There may be times when you want to see the objects on a layer, but you do not want to be able to select those objects. In this case, you need to lock the layer. This also lets you lock all the objects on the layer is which much quicker than locking the objects individually.

To lock a layer:

◆ Click the open padlock icon. This changes the icon to the closed position and locks all objects on the layer **㉑**.

To unlock a layer:

◆ Click the closed padlock icon. This changes the padlock to the open position and unlocks all objects on the layer **㉑**.

TIP Objects on locked layers cannot be selected, modified, or moved.

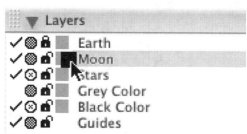

㉒ *To change the **path display color** of a layer, drag a color swatch onto the color box of that layer.*

When you select an object, the points and path outlines for that object are displayed in a color *(see Chapter 7, "Working with Points")*. You can change that display color by using the Layers panel.

To change the display color of a layer:

◆ Drag a color swatch from the Swatches or Mixer onto the color box for the layer **㉒**. The color box next to the name changes. All selected objects on that layer have their paths displayed in that color. *(For information on working with Swatches or the Mixer, see Chapter 13, "Working in Color".)*

WORKING IN COLOR 13

My first computer was a Macintosh SE that's currently serving as a bookend under my desk. It has a built-in screen that is even smaller than a page of this book. The screen only displays black and white images.

Still, I used it to create all sorts of full-color illustrations and designs. I just defined all my colors using numerical values and used my vivid imagination to visualize what the artwork would look like when it was finally printed.

I doubt you're using anything as primitive as my old computer. Today it's hard to even find a black-and-white monitor.

Interestingly, though, there are few differences in the principles of working in color from the old days to now. In fact, the basics of working in color aren't computer specific; they come from years and years of print shops printing color images.

Defining Colors

The Color Mixer panel is where you define or mix colors to use them in a document. There are five different modes for mixing colors: CMYK, RGB, HLS, Windows, and Apple.

TIP Even though the panel tab says Mixer, the full name of the panel used to define colors is the Color Mixer.

To use the Color Mixer:

1. Choose **Window** > **Color Mixer** to open the Color Mixer **①**.

2. Click the icon for the color mode you want to work in.

TIP Only four icons appear in the Color Mixer. The Windows mode is not available for the Macintosh. The Apple mode is not available for Windows.

The CMYK mode defines the color according to the *four process colors* used by most commercial printers—cyan, magenta, yellow, and black.

To define a CMYK color:

1. Click the CMYK icon in the Color Mixer **②**.

2. Click the cyan, magenta, yellow, or black fields and enter values for the color.

   or

   Drag the cyan, magenta, yellow, or black sliders to enter values for the color.

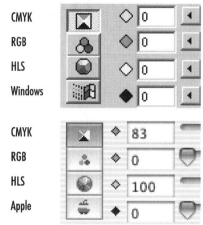

① *The five different icons in the Windows (top) and Macintosh (bottom)* **Color Mixer panels**.

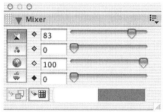

② *Use the four sliders to define colors in the* **CMYK mode**.

The 300% Ink Rule

When you define process colors, try to limit the total amount of ink to less than 300%. When colors contain more than 300%, it can cause problems during the printing and drying of the pages. If you are defining dark colors, try reducing the amount of cyan, magenta, and yellow inks, and increase the amount of black ink. However, check with your print shop if you are going to have a lot of dark colors on a page. They may ask you to limit the amount of ink even further.

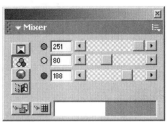

3 *Use the three sliders to define colors in the* **RGB mode.**

Color Wheel Slider

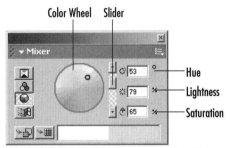

Hue

Lightness

Saturation

4 *Use the color wheel, slider, and fields to define colors in the* **HLS mode.**

The RGB mode defines the color according to *red, green, and blue components*. This is primarily a video color system and is the system used by your own monitor. Many people who design for multimedia and the Web use RGB to define colors.

To define an RGB color:

1. Click the RGB icon in the Color Mixer **3**.

2. Click the red, green, or blue fields and enter values for the color.

   or

   Drag the red, green, or blue sliders to enter values for the color.

The HLS system defines the color according to *hue, lightness,* and *saturation* components. The HLS system lets you pick different colors with similar values. For example, if you keep the lightness and saturation values the same, you can choose a red hue and green hue that belong together.

To define an HLS color:

1. Click the HLS icon.

2. Find the hue and saturation you want on the color wheel and click it **4**.

   or

   Enter the hue values (from 0 to 360 degrees) or the saturation amount (from 0 to 100 percent) in the fields.

3. Use the slider to adjust the lightness.

   or

   Enter the lightness value (from 0 to 100 percent) in the field.

Defining Colors

The Color Mixer (Win) also has a Windows button that opens the Windows colors where you can pick from the colors installed in the Windows operating system.

To define using the Windows Colors (Win):

1. Click the Windows icon. This opens the Windows Basic Colors dialog box ❺.

2. Select one of the colors displayed.

3. Click the OK button.

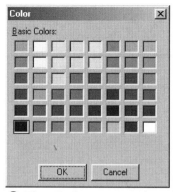

❺ *The* **Windows Basic Colors** *choices.*

The Color Mixer (Mac) also has an Apple button that opens the Macintosh color picker where you can pick colors according to a number of different models installed in the Mac OS.

To define using the Apple Color Picker (Mac):

1. Click the Apple icon. This opens the Apple Color Picker dialog box ❻.

2. Select one of the color systems on the top.

3. Define the color using the onscreen elements.

4. Click OK.

TIP The Apple Color Picker offers several different ways of choosing colors including the 216 Web-safe colors.

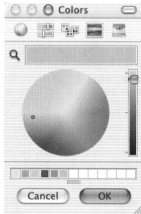

❻ *The* **Apple Color Picker** *lets you choose colors in a variety of systems.*

Which Color System Should You Use?

If you are defining a color for artwork that will be printed in a four-color printing process, the CMYK color system is the best choice. When you define the CMYK values, you choose the exact percentage of cyan, magenta, yellow, and black ink that will be used to create the color. CMYK colors are also called four-color or process colors. Rather than judge what CMYK colors look like onscreen, you should refer to a printed process color book such as the Trumatch Color Guide or the Agfa Process Color Guide.

If you are creating Web graphics or multimedia work, use the RGB colors. RGB system is based on the colors that are available on your monitor screen—the same way that Web pages and multimedia projects are displayed. Also, some colors are available in RGB that are not found in CMYK. HLS is a variation of the RGB color system. You can use HLS if you are trying to match the saturation or lightness of colors. Once you set one color, you can switch to HLS and then change only the hue value to get complimentary colors.

Defining Colors

❼ *Click the* **Add to Swatches button** *to add a color from the Color Mixer to the Swatches panel.*

❽ *The* **Add to Swatches dialog box** *allows you to rename the color and set it as process or spot.*

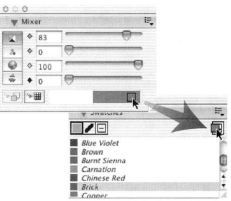

❾ *You can drag a swatch from the Color Mixer and drop it on the* **Swatches panel drop box.**

Using the Swatches Panel

Once you have defined a color in the Color Mixer, you need to store that color so you can define other colors. To do that, you use the Swatches panel.

To add a color to the Swatches panel:

1. Define the color in the Color Mixer.

2. Click the Add to Swatches panel button in the Color Mixer **❼**. The Add to Swatches dialog box appears **❽**.

3. Name the color.

4. Set the color as process or spot. *(See the sidebar, "Process or Spot?" on page 180.)*

5. Click OK. The color is added to the Swatches panel.

TIP The Add to Swatches panel button works even if the Swatches panel is not visible onscreen.

TIP Hold the Cmd/Ctrl key to bypass the Add to Swatches dialog box. The colors are defined according to the last setting in the Add to Swatches dialog box.

To drag colors to the Swatches panel:

1. Press and drag the color at the bottom of the Color Mixer.

2. Move to the drop box in the Swatches panel **❾**.

3. Release the mouse button. The color appears in the Swatches list.

To rename a color:

1. Double-click the name of the color in the Swatches panel. This highlights the name, indicating that it is selected **⑩**.

2. Type the new name for the color.

3. Press Return/Enter to complete the process of renaming the color.

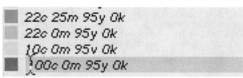

⑩ *Double-click or drag across a color name to rename the color.*

You can change any color from process to spot color, which is separated onto its own plate.

⑪ *The Swatches panel displays process colors in italics, spot colors in roman.*

To convert process to spot color:

1. Select the color you want to convert in the Swatches panel **⑪**.

2. Choose Make spot from the Swatches panel menu.

To convert spot to process color:

1. Select the color you want to convert from the Swatches panel.

2. Choose Make process from the Swatches panel menu.

Process or Spot?

Process colors are colors printed using small dots of the four process inks, cyan, magenta, yellow, and black. Spot colors are printed using special inks that are mixed to match a certain color.

For example, if you look at the process color green printed in a magazine, that color is actually a combination of cyan and yellow printed together in a series of dots. However, a spot color green is printed using actual green ink.

The benefit of spot colors is that you can exactly match a special color or use a specialty color such as fluorescents or metallics that could never be created using just process inks.

When you define a color as spot, you are designating that color to be separated on its own printing plate. When you define a color as process, you are designating that color to be broken down into its CMYK values.

Some people use spot colors instead of process colors for one- or two-color jobs. Others use spot colors in addition to process colors for five- or six-color printing.

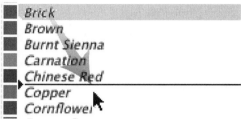

⑫ *You can drag colors from one position to another in the Swatches panel.*

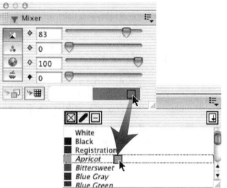

⑬ *Drag a color from the Color Mixer onto an existing color to redefine the color.*

When you add colors to the Swatches panel, they appear in the order that they were added. You may want to move the colors in the Swatches panel to different positions.

To change the order of the colors on the list:

1. Select the color you want to move.

2. Drag it to the new position and then release the mouse button ⑫.

TIP In Windows, a double-headed arrow indicates you are moving the color to a new position.

Once you have added a color to the Swatches panel, you can still change the color values. If you have used the color in your document, the changes will be applied to all the objects that use that color.

To redefine colors:

1. Use the Color Mixer to define the new color.

2. Drag the color swatch from the Color Mixer directly onto the name of the existing color ⑬. All objects that use the color will be redefined.

TIP If you have used the values to name the color, the color name is changed to reflect the new definition.

To duplicate colors:

1. Click the name of the color you want to duplicate.

2. Choose Duplicate from the Swatches panel menu. The duplicate color appears on the Swatches panel with the name "Copy of [Color Name]."

Using the Swatches Panel

You can remove colors from the Swatches panel.

To remove colors:

1. Click the name of the color you want to remove. The name highlights.

2. If you want to remove a group of adjacent colors, click the top name. Then hold the Shift key and click the bottom name. All the names between highlight.

3. Choose Remove from the Swatches panel menu. All the highlighted colors are deleted.

TIP If the color you remove is in use one of the following happens:

- Process colors are kept in use but are not listed in the Swatches panel.
- Spot colors are converted to process and then kept in use as un-named colors.

You can also direct FreeHand to replace one color with another.

To replace colors:

1. Click the name of the color you want to replace. The name highlights.

2. Choose Replace from the Swatches panel menu. The Replace Color dialog box appears ⓮.

3. Choose a replacement color from the current Swatches panel.

   or

   Choose a replacement from one of the Color Libraries *(see pages 185)*.

4. Click OK. The original color is replaced by the new one throughout the document.

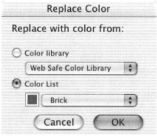

⓮ *The* **Replace Color** *dialog box lets you substitute one color in the Swatches panel for another.*

The Registration Color

You may notice that one of the default colors in the Swatches panel is called Registration. Registration is a color that has been specially defined so that it will print on all plates.

You should not use the Registration color for ordinary artwork. It will create objects that have much too much ink.

Use the Registration color for items such as crop marks or notes to the printer that you want to see on all the separations.

The Registration color is usually shown as black, but you can change its appearance by dragging a swatch onto the name.

⓯ *The* **Eyedropper** *icon in the Tools panel.*

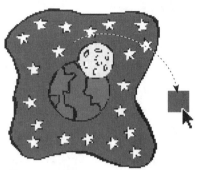

⓰ *Use the Eyedropper to drag colors from artwork and drop them into the Swatches panel.*

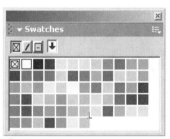

⓱ *The Swatches panel displays only the color swatches after choosing* **Hide** *names.*

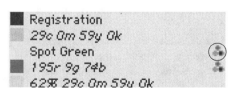

⓲ *Colors defined in the RGB or HLS mode display a small* **tricolored icon** *(circled) in the list.*

You can also add colors from objects or imported images to the Swatches panel.

To drag colors from objects to the Swatches panel:

1. Choose the Eyedropper tool from the Tools panel **⓯**.
2. Press and drag on an area of color. A swatch appears **⓰**.
3. Drag the swatch to the drop box of the Swatches panel.

TIP You can also use the Eyedropper tool to move colors directly from one object to another.

If it is difficult to scroll through a long list of color names. FreeHand lets you hide the names of the colors in the Swatches panel.

To hide the color names:

◆ Choose Hide names from the Swatches panel menu **⓱**.

To show the color names:

◆ Choose Show names from the Swatches panel menu to display the names.

FreeHand also lets you switch a color between the CMYK and RGB modes. This can be helpful if you are moving from print to the Web or vice versa.

To change the color mode:

1. Select the color you want to convert.
2. Choose Make RGB from the Swatches panel menu to change the color from CMYK to RGB.

   or

   Choose Make CMYK to change the color from RGB to CMYK.

TIP RGB colors may shift when converted to the CMYK mode.

TIP Colors defined using either the RGB or HLS mode have a small tricolored icon to the right of their name **⓲**.

Working with Tints

If you have defined a color, you can use that color as the basis for a tint. This is handy if you are working with spot colors and want to apply tints of those colors.

To define a tint of a color:

1. Define the color in the Color Mixer.

   or

   Add the color to the Swatches panel.

2. If you have not added the color to the Swatches panel, use the pop-up menu in the Tints panel to add the color to the Swatches panel .

   or

   Choose a color from the pop-up menu in the Tints panel.

3. Choose the tint percentage by one of the following methods:

   • Adjust the tint slider.
   • Type a percentage in the tint field.
   • Click one of the tint swatches.

To Add Tints to the Swatches panel:

1. With a tint percentage defined, click the Add to Swatches panel button in the Tints panel . The Add to Swatches panel dialog box appears .

   TIP Hold the Cmd/Ctrl key to bypass the Add to Swatches panel dialog box. The previous settings are used for the current swatch.

2. The name of the tint is shown as a percentage of the color's name. You can rename the color by typing in the field.

3. Click the Add button to add the tint to the Swatches panel.

⑲ *The* **Tints panel menu** *lets you choose a color or add the base color of a tint to the Swatches panel.*

⑳ *Use the* **Add to Swatches button** *to add the current tint setting to the Swatches panel.*

㉑ *The* **Add to Swatches dialog box** *for a tint.*

Understanding Tints

A *tint* is a screened or percentage value of a color. For example, a 50% tint means that only half of the fully saturated value of the color is applied. Tints are very useful for working with spot colors because they are the only way to create lighter versions of a spot color. Tints are not commonly used for process colors because it is just as easy to define the color using lower percentages of the CMYK colors.

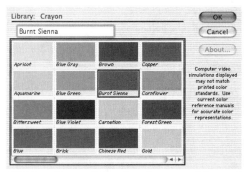

22 *The* **Library dialog box** *lets you add sets of predefined colors.*

Color-Matching System Libraries

FreeHand supplies you with various color libraries that are used by commercial printers, artists, and designers. Some of these color libraries are process color, some spot. They are customarily used with printed swatches that allow you to pick a name from the library and compare it to a specific printed color.

The color-matching systems that ship with FreeHand include Pantone (both process and spot), Toyo (spot), DIC (spot), Focoltone (process), and Web-safe colors. If you need more information on which color-matching system to use, consult with the print shop that will be printing your work.

My favorite libaries are Crayon and Greys. Neither the Crayon nor the Greys libraries are part of any standard color-matching system. They are included to give you an easy way to import a range of colors.

Working with Color Libraries

So far you have been defining your own colors. FreeHand also provides you with libraries of colors that are part of commerical color-matching systems.

To add colors from color-matching system libraries:

1. Choose the name of the color-matching system from the Swatches panel menu. The Library dialog box appears **22**.

2. Use one of the following techniques to choose a color from the Library:
   - Type in the name or code number of the color in the field.
   - Click a color in the preview area.

3. To select additional colors, hold the Shift key and click in the preview area.

   or

   Hold the Shift key and drag the mouse to select a range of colors.

4. Click OK. This adds the selected colors to the Swatches panel.

Once you have created your own list of colors in the Swatches panel, you can export those colors as your own custom color library, which appears in the Swatches panel menu.

To export a custom color library:

1. Choose Export from the Swatches panel menu. The Export Colors dialog box appears.

2. Select a single color.

    or

    Hold down the Shift key to select a continuous range of colors from the Export Colors list .

    or

    Hold down the Cmd/Ctrl key to select noncontiguous colors.

3. Click OK. This opens the Create color library dialog box 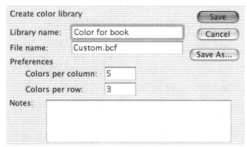.

4. Enter the Library name.

5. Enter the File name.

6. Under Preferences do the following:

    • Set the number of Colors per column.
    • Set the number of Colors per row.

7. Choose Save to place your custom color library in the Color folder located in the FreeHand application folder. The Library name appears in the Swatches panel menu along with the other color libraries.

    or

    Choose Save As which lets you save the file to a different folder or disk.

② *Use the Shift key in the* **Export Colors dialog box** *to select the colors to be exported.*

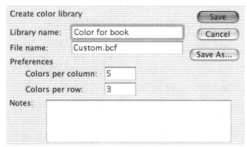

② *The* **Create color library dialog box** *allows you to group your own colors into a custom library.*

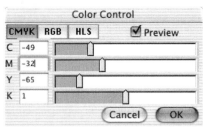

⑳ *The **Color Control dialog box** lets you choose HLS, RGB, and CMYK controls to change or adjust colors.*

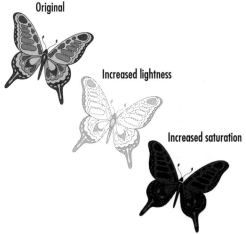

Original

Increased lightness

Increased saturation

㉖ *The Color Control dialog box in the HLS mode was applied to the original artwork to create the other two variations.*

Using the Xtra Color Commands

Once you have created and used colors, the Color commands under the Xtras menu provide many ways you can adjust the colors in your documents. The Color Control Xtra lets you shift the colors in selected objects.

To use the Color Control dialog box:

1. Select the objects you want to adjust.

2. Choose **Xtras > Colors > Color Control.** This opens the Color Control dialog box **⑳**.

3. Choose which color mode to use to adjust the colors:

   - **CMYK** lets you adjust the cyan, magenta, yellow, or black components of the color.
   - **RGB** lets you adjust the red, green, or blue components of the color.
   - **HLS** lets you adjust the hue, lightness or saturation components of the color.

   TIP The color can be defined in one color mode but adjusted in another.

4. Use the sliders or the fields to add or subtract color from the selected objects.

   - Positive numbers add color.
   - Negative numbers subtract color.

5. Check the Preview box to see how your adjustments affect the selected objects without actually applying the changes.

6. When you are satisfied with the color changes, click OK. Your changes are applied to the objects **㉖**.

   TIP The Color Control dialog box only works on objects that have been colored with process colors, not spot colors.

To darken or lighten colors:

1. Select the object or objects you want to change.

2. Choose **Xtras** > **Colors** > **Darken Colors** or **Lighten Colors** .

   - **Darken Colors** decreases the Lightness value of the color in 5% increments.
   - **Lighten Colors** increases the Lightness value of the color in 5% increments.

3. To continue to darken or lighten the colors, repeat the command as many times as necessary.

To saturate or desaturate colors:

1. Select the object or objects you want to change.

2. Choose **Xtras** > **Colors** > **Saturate Colors** or **Desaturate Colors.**

   - **Saturate Colors** increases the saturation value of the color in 5% increments. This makes muted colors more vibrant.
   - **Desaturate Colors** decreases the saturation value of the color in 5% increments. This makes colors less vibrant.

3. To continue to saturate or desaturate the colors, repeat the command as many times as necessary.

To convert colors to grayscale:

1. Select the object or objects you want to change.

2. Choose **Xtras** > **Colors** > **Convert to Grayscale.** All colors are converted to grays with the equivalent tonal value.

TIP Convert artwork to grayscale to be printed as one-color black. For instance, all the artwork created in FreeHand for this book was converted to grayscale.

Original

Darken   Lighten

The results of using the Darken Colors and Lighten Colors commands.

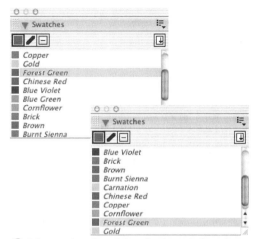

28 *The results of applying the* **Sort Color List by Name** *command.*

FreeHand offers several Xtras that help you manage colors in the Swatches panel and in your document.

To name all colors:

◆ Choose **Xtras > Colors > Name All Colors.** All colors used by objects in your document that are not named appear on the Swatches panel, with their names showing their CMYK percentages.

To sort the Swatches panel by name:

◆ Choose **Xtras > Colors > Sort Color List By Name.** This rearranges the Swatches panel. The default colors appear first, followed by the colors named by their CMYK and RGB compositions, and then named colors **28**.

To delete unused named colors:

◆ Choose **Xtras > Delete > Unused Named Colors.** Colors that are not applied to an object or a style are deleted. The default colors are not deleted even if they are not used.

TIP Delete unused colors before exporting artwork to layout programs such as Adobe InDesign or QuarkXPress.

To use the Randomize Named Colors Xtra:

◆ Choose **Xtras > Colors > Randomize Named Colors.** This command changes the values of the named colors in the Swatches panel. All objects with named colors applied to them are changed.

TIP While there aren't too many uses for this command for ordinary graphics, it does create interesting effects when applied to abstract art.

Using the Xtra Color Commands

Trapping Colors

Trapping is a technique printers use to compensate for misregistration of color plates in the printing process. FreeHand lets you create traps with the Trap Xtra. Although the Trap Xtra is very easy to apply, setting the proper values takes years of experience.

To use the Trap Xtra:

1. Select two or more objects in your illustration that you want to trap.

2. Choose **Xtras** > **Create** > **Trap**. The Trap dialog box appears ㉙.

3. Use the sliders or type in the Trap width suggested by your print shop.

4. If your print shop agrees, choose Use maximum value to make the trap color the strongest available.

   or

   Choose the Use tint reduction setting and enter the reduction amount suggested by your print shop.

5. Check the Reverse traps box to change the direction of the trap. (Reverse traps are sometimes called *chokes*.) Consult your print shop as to when you should do this.

6. Click OK. The traps are created ㉚.

TIP When you create traps, you create new objects set to overprint between the original objects. If you move or delete objects later, be careful that you do not leave the trap objects behind.

㉙ *The* Trap dialog box.

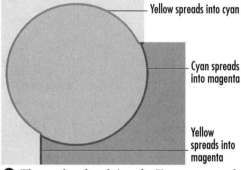

Yellow spreads into cyan

Cyan spreads into magenta

Yellow spreads into magenta

㉚ *The results of* applying the Trap command.

How to learn about trapping

Trapping is like buying a boat. If you have to ask the price of a boat, you can't afford it. If you have to ask what trapping is, you shouldn't do it.

If you want to set your own traps, talk to the print shop that will be printing your artwork. They are the best experts to teach you how much to trap, where to trap, and when not to trap.

Most print shops tell you not to trap. They often use their own software that traps automatically.

FILLS 14

The outline of a path is an empty shell waiting to be filled with a color or some other effect. Macromedia FreeHand offers a wealth of different ways to fill the empty path.

You can choose one of the solid colors in the Swatches panel. You can also combine those colors into gradients that change one color into another.

You can also apply special effects that fill one object so that it is transparent or it acts like a magnifying glass over other objects.

You can even create small illustrations that can be repeated, like a tiled floor, as the fill inside other objects.

Adding a fill to an object can change it from ordinary to exciting.

Choosing Fills

There are eight different types of fills you can apply to objects. The main place to apply and format fills is the Object panel.

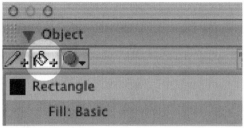

To apply a fill to an object:

1. Select the object.

2. Click the Fill icon in the Object panel ❶. A fill entry appears in the Attributes area.

❶ *Click the* Fill icon *in the Object panel to add a new fill.*

3. Choose one of the Fill options from the Fill menu in the Object panel ❷. The settings in the Object panel change depending on the type of fill chosen.

TIP You can add additional fills by repeating the above steps. However, unless you have applied one of the Effects to the object, you won't see much if one fill is added on top of another. *(See Chapter 16, "Effects and Attributes" for how to work with multiple fills.)*

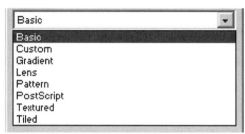

❷ *The* Fill menu *in the Object panel lets you choose the type of fill applied to objects.*

To delete a fill from an object:

1. Click the Fill entry in the Object panel.

2. Click the Remove Item icon. This removes the fill from the object ❸. *(See page 195 for additional ways to apply no fill to an object.)*

TIP The Remove Item icon also removes strokes and effects that have been selected in the Object panel *(see Chapter 15, "Strokes," and Chapter 16, "Effects and Attributes")*.

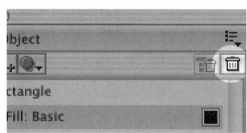

❸ *Click the* Remove Item icon *in the Object panel to remove a fill.*

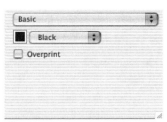

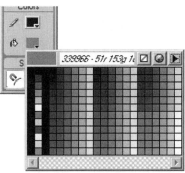

❹ *Choose Basic from the Fill menu to display the* **Basic fill** *options.*

❺ *The* **Fill color box** *in the Tools panel.*

❻ *The* **pop-up color palette** *in the Tools panel lets you choose fill colors.*

❼ *Use the* **pop-up palette menu** *to display the colors in the Swatches panel.*

Working with Basic Fills

TIP If you do not see the fills for open paths, check the object preferences. *(See Appendix C))*

The most common fill is the Basic fill. This is the equivalent of filling the object with a solid color. FreeHand provides you with many different ways to apply Basic fill.

To apply a Basic fill using the Object panel:

1. Select the object.
2. With the Object panel displayed, choose Basic from the Fill menu. This displays the Basic fill settings ❹.
3. Choose a color for the fill from the color list.

To apply a Basic fill using the Tools panel:

1. Select the object.
2. Click the triangle in the Fill color box at the bottom of the Tools panel ❺. This opens the pop-up color palette ❻.
3. Choose a color from the color palette.

The pop-up color palette is set by default to show the 216 Web-safe colors. You can change that setting to display the colors in the Swatches panel.

To change the display of the pop-up color palette:

1. Click the color box to open the pop-up color palette.
2. Click the palette triangle to open the options menu ❼.
3. Choose Swatches to display the colors from the Swatches panel.

Working with Basic Fills

To apply a fill color using the Swatches panel:

1. Select the object.

TIP Make sure that Basic is chosen in the Object panel. If another type of fill is listed, you may not see the color you choose.

2. Click the Fill drop box in the Swatches panel .

3. Click the name of the color you want as the fill in the Swatches panel.

   or

   Drag a color swatch from the Color Mixer onto the Fill drop box in the Swatches panel.

TIP The box next to the Fill drop box controls the stroke color. *(See Chapter 15, "Strokes.")*

TIP If no object is selected, any changes you make to the fill color are applied to the next object you create.

❽ *The* **Fill drop box** *in the Swatches panel indicates the fill color of the selected object.*

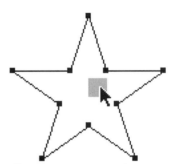

❾ **Drag a color swatch** *onto an object to apply a fill color.*

To change a fill color by dragging:

♦ Drag a color swatch from the Color Mixer or the Swatches panel directly onto the object **❾**.

TIP You do not have to select an object to drag a color swatch onto it.

TIP Hold the Shift key as you drag the color swatch onto the object to make sure that only the fill color changes.

Setting Overprinting

You may notice the Overprint settings for many of the fills. If you set an object to Overprint, that object will not knock out any colors below. Instead it will mix the colors in that object with the ones below.

You cannot see overprinting on your screen. Depending on the preference setting, objects that have an overprint applied will be displayed with a pattern of white Os on top.

You do not see overprinting in the output of most color printers. You need to make separations of your colors to see where the colors will overprint.

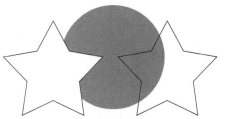

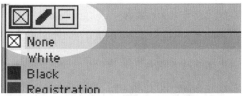

10 *Selecting a* **fill of None** *lets you see through an object, as seen in the star on the right.*

11 *Choose* **None** *in the Swatches panel to apply a transparent None fill.*

12 *Click the* **None icon** *in the Fill color box pop-up palette to apply a transparent fill.*

Applying a None Fill

In addition to the colors, there is another entry in the Swatches panel called *None*. While not a color *per se*, a None fill is very useful. When you apply the None fill to an object, the fill of the object becomes transparent **10**. There are three different ways to apply the None fill.

To change a fill to None:

1. Choose the object you want to become transparent.

2. Make sure the Fill drop box is selected in the Swatches panel.

3. Click None in the Swatches panel. An **X** appears in the Fill drop box, indicating that there is no fill **11**.

   or

   Click the None icon in the Fill color box pop-up palette **12**.

   or

   Click the Remove Entry icon in the Object panel *(see page 192)*.

TIP Objects with no fill color are invisible unless they have a stroke applied. *(See Chapter 15, "Strokes.")*

Working with Gradient Fills

Gradient fills start with one color and then change into others. There are six types of gradients: linear, radial, contour, logarithmic, rectangle, and cone ⓭. Each of the types of gradients creates a different shape within the path of the object.

To choose the type of gradient fill:

1. Choose Gradient from the Fill menu in the Object panel.

2. Choose one of the types of gradients from the Gradient menu ⓮:

   • **Linear** applies a color change in a straight transition using equal increments for the change.

   • **Radial** applies a color change in an elliptical shape.

   • **Contour** applies a color change that follows the shape of the path.

   • **Logarithmic** applies a color change in a straight transition using increments that get larger as the gradient progresses.

   • **Rectangle** applies a color change in a rectangular shape.

   • **Cone** applies a color change in 360-degree graduated sweep.

3. Once you have set the type of gradient, use the settings *(as described on pages 197–200)* to style the gradient.

4. You can also change the colors in the gradient ramp *(see page 201)*.

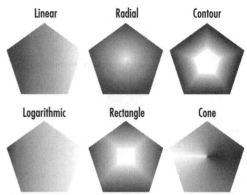

Linear   Radial   Contour

Logarithmic   Rectangle   Cone

⓭ *The* six different types of gradients.

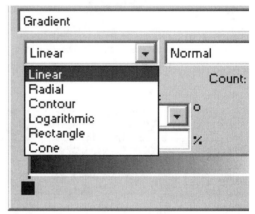

⓮ *The* **Gradient menu** *in the options for gradient fills.*

Working with Gradient Fills

⑮ *The difference between a* **Linear taper** *(left) and a* **Logarithmic taper** *(right), both set to 90° angles.*

⑯ *The controls for either a* **Linear or Logarithmic gradient.**

⑰ *Hold the Control/ Ctrl key as you drag a color swatch to apply a Linear Gradient to an object.*

The controls for Linear or Logarithmic gradients are identical. The main difference is that a Logarithmic gradient changes colors in unequal increments **⑮**.

To create a Linear or Logarithmic gradient:

1. Choose Linear or Logarithmic to open those gradient controls **⑯**.
2. Use the **x** field to enter a position for the horizontal start of the gradient.
3. Use the **y** field to enter a position for the vertical start of the gradient.

TIP The **x** and **y** positions are percentages of the width of the object. 0% starts at the edge of the object. 50% starts in the middle.

4. Enter an amount for the handle angle. This is the angle that the gradient moves along.
5. Enter a percentage for the length of the gradient.

TIP You can also set the start position, angle, and length of a handle visually using the gradient handles *(see page 202)*.

6. Use the Gradient ramp color controls *(see page 201)* to choose the colors in the gradient.

You can also create a Linear gradient by dragging a color swatch onto an object.

To apply a Linear gradient by dragging a color:

1. Press the Control/Ctrl key as you drag a color swatch onto an object that has one color already applied as a Basic fill. A diamond color swatch indicates you are creating a Linear Gradient **⑰**.
2. Release the mouse button on the object. A Linear gradient fills the object with the color of the swatch applied as the second color.

TIP Where you drop the swatch determines the angle of the gradient.

Working with Gradient Fills

The controls for Radial or Rectangle gradients are identical. The main difference between them is the shape of the gradient within the object. A Radial Gradient starts at the center and creates an ellipse. A rectangle gradient creates a rectangle.

 *The controls for either a* **Radial or Rectangle Gradient.**

To create a Radial or Rectangle gradient:

1. Choose Radial or Rectangle to open those gradient controls .

2. Use the **x** field to enter a position for the horizontal center of the gradient.

3. Use the **y** field to enter a position for the vertical center of the gradient.

4. Enter an angle for each of the handles.

5. Enter a percentage for the length of the two sides of the gradient.

TIP Radial and Rectangle Gradients have two handle controls.

6. Use the Gradient ramp color controls (*see page 201*) to choose the colors in the gradient.

TIP Position the centerpoint of a Radial Gradient off-center to create the effect of a 3D sphere 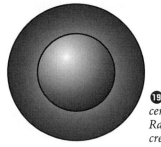.

Move the centerpoint of a Radial Gradient to create a 3D effect.

To apply a Radial Gradient by dragging a color:

1. Press the Opt/Alt key as you drag a color swatch onto an object that already has one color applied as a Basic fill. A circle color swatch indicates you are dragging a Radial Gradient onto the object.

2. Release the mouse button on the object. A Radial Gradient fills the object with the color of the swatch applied as the second color .

TIP The color of the swatch is applied as the inside color of the Radial Gradient.

TIP Where you drop the swatch determines the center of the Radial Gradient.

Hold the Opt/Alt key as you drag a color swatch to apply a Radial Gradient to an object.

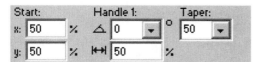

Start:	Handle 1:	Taper:
x: 50 %	△ 0 ▾ °	50 ▾
y: 50 %	⊢→⊣ 50 %	

㉑ *The controls for* **Contour gradient.**

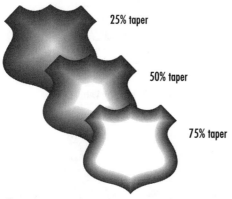

25% taper

50% taper

75% taper

㉒ *Adjusting the* **Taper control** *changes in how much of the object the Contour Gradient is seen.*

㉓ *Hold the Cmd-Opt keys (Mac) or Control-Alt keys (Win) as you drag a color swatch to apply a Contour Gradient to an object.*

A Contour Gradient creates a blend that follows the shape of the object. The settings for a Contour Gradient let you control the size of the interior blend.

To create a Contour Gradient:

1. Choose Contour to open the Contour Gradient controls **㉑**.

2. Use the **x** field to enter a position for the horizontal center of the gradient.

3. Use the **y** field to enter a position for the vertical center of the gradient.

4. Enter an amount for the handle angle. This is the angle that the gradient moves along.

5. Enter a percentage for the length of the gradient.

6. Enter an amount for the size of the taper. The higher the number, the more the gradient will fill the object **㉒**.

To apply a Contour Gradient by dragging a color:

1. Press the Cmd-Opt keys (Mac) or Control-Alt keys (Win) as you drag a color swatch onto an object that has one color already applied as a Basic fill. An irregular-shaped color swatch indicates you are dragging a Contour Gradient onto the object.

2. Release the mouse button on the object. A Contour Gradient fills the object with the color of the swatch applied as the second color **㉓**.

TIP The color of the swatch is applied as the inside color of the Contour Gradient.

TIP Where you drop the swatch determines the center of the Contour Gradient.

Working with Gradient Fills

A Cone gradient moves across an object in a circle that creates the appearance of a three-dimensional cone..

To create a Cone Gradient:

1. Choose Cone to open the Cone Gradient controls .

2. Use the **x** field to enter a position for the horizontal center of the gradient.

3. Use the **y** field to enter a position for the vertical center of the gradient.

4. Enter an amount for the handle angle. This is the angle that the gradient moves along.

5. Enter a percentage for the length of the gradient.

🥁 *The controls for a Cone Gradient.*

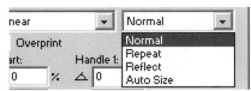

🥁 *The Gradient Behavior menu.*

In addition to the types of gradients, you can also set the behavior for how the gradient fills the object.

To set the gradient behavior:

1. Choose one of the following from the Behavior menu 🥁:

   - **Normal** sets the gradient to fill the object according the the start point and handle positions.

   - **Repeat** sets the gradient to repeat more than once in the same direction within the object.

   - **Reflect** sets the gradient to happen forwards and then backwards within the object.

   - **Auto Size** sets the gradient to fill the entire length of the object.

2. If you have chosen Repeat or Reflect, use the Count field to set how many times the gradient appears within the object 🥁.

🥁 *The difference between a gradient that repeats (left) or reflects (right).*

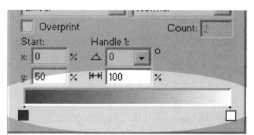

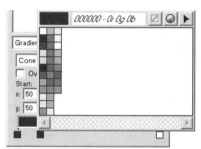

㉗ *The colors of a gradient appear as part of the Gradient Ramp at the bottom of the Object panel.*

㉘ *Click one of the color swatches in the gradient to open the Color panel.*

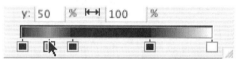

㉙ Drag a color control *to a new position or off the ramp.*

All gradients start with two default colors in the gradient ramp **㉗**. You can change those colors, add more colors, or change the position of the colors in the gradient.

To change the colors in the gradient ramp:

◆ Click one of the control colors in the gradient ramp. The Color panel appears **㉘**.

or

Drag a color swatch from the Swatches panel, Color Mixer, or Tools panel

To add colors to gradient fills:

◆ Drag a color swatch onto the gray area between the top and the bottom colors **㉙**. You can drag swatches from the Swatches panel, the Color Mixer, or the color boxes in the Tools panel.

or

Drag a color from either end color swatch.

or

Hold the Control/Alt key as you drag to copy the colors of existing color swatches.

To delete colors from gradient fills:

◆ Drag the color box off the gray area.

TIP You can't delete the left or right swatches of a gradient fill.

Working with Gradient Fills

You can also modify the appearance of a gradient by dragging the handles.

TIP If you do not see the gradient handles, double-click the Pointer or Subselect tools to open the Pointer tool dialog box. Turn on the option for Show Fill Handle.

To manually adjust the appearance of a gradient:

1. Use the Pointer tool to select the object with the gradient.

2. Click the entry for the gradient in the Object panel.

3. Drag the center point of the handles (designated with a circle) to define the start position ③⓪.

4. Drag the handle point (designated with a square) to define the length and angle of the gradient ③①.

5. Rotate the line segment of the handle to change the angle of the gradient without changing the length of the handle ③②.

TIP When you adjust the center point and handles, they obey the Snap To Guide, Snap to Point, Snap To Grid, and Snap To Object. This makes it easy to position the gradient exactly where you want it.

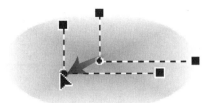

③⓪ **Drag the center point** *of the gradient handles to change the center of the gradient.*

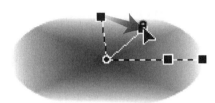

③① **Drag the handle point** *to change the length and angle of the gradient.*

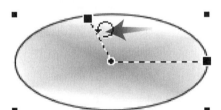

③② **Rotate the line segment of a gradient handle** *to change the angle of the gradient.*

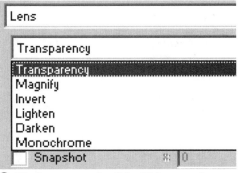

❸❸ *The* **Lens controls** *of the Object panel.*

Stacking Lens Objects

If you position one lens object over another, you will combine the effects of the lens fills. However, there is a limit of eight lens fills stacked over each other. If you add more than eight objects, the bottom-most objects will not be active as lens fills.

Working with Spot Colors

All of the lens fills convert spot colors to process. When you apply the lens fill, an alert box appears with the message that spot colors viewed through a Lens fill are converted to process colors. This means that if you work with spot colors you most likely will not want to apply any of the lens fills. To turn off the warning, check the Don't Show Again box.

Working with Lens Fills

One of the most dramatic features in FreeHand is the set of lens fills. These allow you to create transparency effects and to use one object to magnify others. There are six types of lens fills.

To choose the type of lens fill:

1. Choose Lens from the Fill menu in the Object panel.

2. Choose one of the types of lens fills from the Lens menu **❸❸**:
   - **Transparency** changes the appearance of the object so you can see objects behind it.
   - **Magnify** allows one object to increase the size of objects behind it.
   - **Invert** changes the colors of an object to their inverse.
   - **Lighten** lightens areas under the object that are darker than the original color.
   - **Darken** darkens areas under the object that are lighter than the original color.
   - **Monochrome** colorizes objects into a single color based on the color of the top object.

3. Once you have set the type of lens fills, use the settings (*as described on pages 204–207*) to style the appearance.

One of the Lens fills creates transparency. This is not the same as the transparency effect that is added to an object. One is a fill choice, the other is an effect.

To create a Transparent Lens fill:

1. With Lens selected, choose Transparency to open the transparency controls **34**.

2. Choose a color from the color pop-up menu

3. Use the Opacity slider or the field to set the amount of transparency for the lens. The lower the opacity, the more you will be able to see through the object **35**.

4. Click Objects Only to have the effects of the lens seen only on objects, not the page **36**.

5. See the exercise on the next page for working with the Centerpoint control.

6. Click Snapshot to freeze the lens fill within the object. The object may then be moved to another spot without changing the image within the lens **37**.

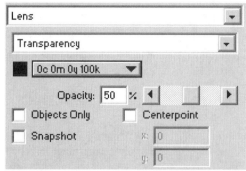

34 *The* **Transparency controls** *of the Lens fill in the Object panel.*

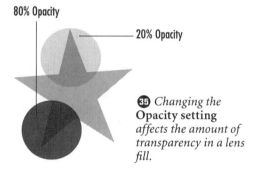

80% Opacity

20% Opacity

35 *Changing the* **Opacity setting** *affects the amount of transparency in a lens fill.*

36 *The* **Objects Only** setting *makes the lens work only on objects, not the page area.*

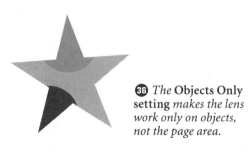

37 *The* **Snapshot** setting *freezes the image in the lens so you can move it.*

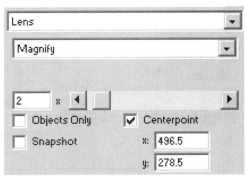

㊳ *The* **Magnify controls** *of the Lens fill in the Object panel.*

㊴ *A* **Magnify lens** *shows a closer view of an object.*

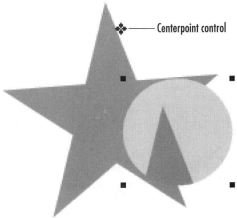

Centerpoint control

㊵ *Drag the* **centerpoint control** *to focus a lens over a certain area of the artwork.*

The Magnify Lens lets one object act as a magnifying glass on whatever objects it covers.

To create a Magnify Lens fill:

1. With Lens selected, choose Magnify to open the magnification controls **㊳**.

2. Use the Magnification slider or the field to set the amount of magnification for the lens.

TIP Magnification can be set from 1 (actual size) to 20 times bigger.

3. The object appears inside the lens as if it were scaled larger **㊴**.

There may be times when you want the lens object to be applied to an area that it is not located over. This is especially helpful for callouts of technical drawings or insets of maps. To accomplish this, use the centerpoint control.

To use the centerpoint control:

1. Position the Magnify Lens where you want it in your image—do not worry yet about what shows in the lens.

2. Check the Centerpoint box in the Object panel. A centerpoint control appears.

TIP If the centerpoint is not visible, check to see if the object is part of a group. If so, ungroup it.

3. Drag the centerpoint control to the center of the area you want to be visible within the lens **㊵**.

Working with Lens Fills

The Invert Lens inverts the colors of objects. This means that black objects turn white, red objects turn green, yellow objects turn blue, and so on .

To use the Invert Lens fill:

1. With Lens selected, choose Invert to open the invert controls ④.
2. Set the Centerpoint controls as described on page 205.

The Lighten Lens lightens the colors in the objects it passes over ④. This is similar to adding white to the colors.

To use the Lighten Lens fill:

1. With Lens selected, choose Lighten to open the lighten controls ④.
2. Use the Lighten slider or the field to increase or decrease the effect.
3. Set the Centerpoint controls as described on page 205.

④ *The* **Invert Lens** *reverses the colors of the objects the lens passes over.*

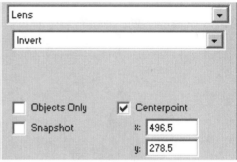

④ *The* **Invert controls** *of the Lens fill in the Object panel.*

④ *The* **Lighten Lens** *lightens the colors of the objects the lens passes over.*

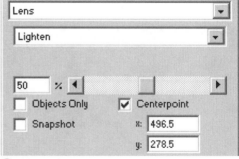

④ *The* **Lighten controls** *of the Lens fill in the Object panel.*

45 *The* **Darken Lens** *darkens the colors of the objects the lens passes over.*

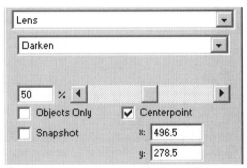

46 *The* **Darken controls** *of the Lens fill in the Object panel.*

47 *The* **Monochrome Lens** *changes the hue of the colors of the objects the lens passes over.*

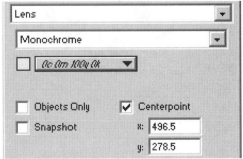

48 *The* **Monochrome controls** *of the Lens fill in the Object panel.*

The Darken Lens darkens the colors in the objects it passes over. This is similar to adding black to the colors **45**.

To use the Darken Lens fill:

1. With Lens selected, choose Darken to open the darken controls **46**.
2. Use the Darken slider or the field to increase or decrease the effect.
3. Set the Centerpoint controls as described on page 205.

The Monochrome Lens converts all the colors in the objects it passes over to a shade of the color applied to the monochrome object **47**.

To use the Monochrome Lens fill:

1. With Lens selected, choose Monochrome to open the monochrome controls **48**.

TIP The Monochrome Lens is a great way to tint part of a placed image.

2. Use the Color list to choose the monochrome color.
3. Set the Centerpoint controls as described on page 205.

Working with Lens Fills

Creating and Applying Tiled Fills

You have to create the next kind of fill—
called a Tiled fill—by yourself. Other programs may call this a pattern.

To create and apply a Tiled fill:

1. Copy the artwork that you want to repeat
   in other objects **49**.

2. Select the object you want to fill with the
   Tiled fill.

3. Choose Tiled from the Object panel.

4. Click Paste in. The artwork you copied
   appears in the Tiled preview box **50**. The
   selected object displays the Tiled fill **51**.

TIP To make the background of the Tiled
fill transparent, leave the artwork on an
empty area or on a rectangle with no fill.

TIP To give the Tiled fill a white or colored
background, place the artwork on a
rectangle filled with white or the color.
Select the artwork and the rectangle to
paste into the Tiled fill box.

TIP The more complex the tiled artwork, the
longer it takes for your screen to redraw
and for the artwork to print.

TIP Tiled fills cannot contain objects that
have Lens fills or Tiled fills applied to
them.

TIP Tiled fills cannot contain bitmapped
graphics.

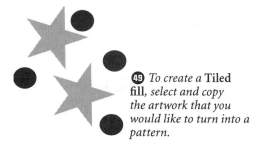

49 *To create a* **Tiled**
fill, *select and copy*
the artwork that you
would like to turn into a
pattern.

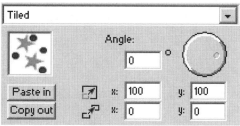

50 *Click* **Paste in** *to transfer the copied artwork*
into the Tiled fill settings box.

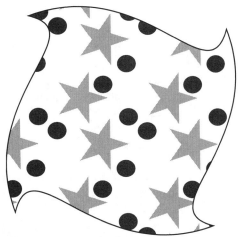

51 *The object selected displays the Tiled fill.*

Creating and Applying Tiled Fills

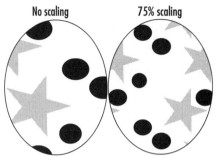

52 *The effects of* **scaling** *a Tiled fill object.*

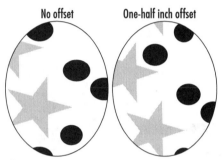

53 *The effects of* **offsetting** *a Tiled fill object.*

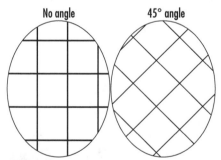

54 *The effects of* **changing the angle** *of a Tiled fill object.*

To adjust a Tiled fill:

1. Click the Tiled fill entry in the Object panel.

2. To change the size of the Tiled fill **52**, use the Scale % x and y fields. To scale the fill uniformly, use the same amounts for both the x and y fields.

3. To move a Tiled fill within the object **53**, enter positive or negative values in the Offset x and y fields.

TIP Positive x values in the Offset field move the fill to the right. Negative x values in the Offset field move the fill to the left. Positive y values in the Offset field move the fill up. Negative y values in the Offset field move the fill down.

4. To angle a Tiled fill within the object **54**, move the angle wheel or enter the exact angle in the Angle field.

Creating and Applying Tiled Fills

Using Custom and Textured Fills

Custom and Textured fills are premade graphics that simulate the look of various textures. After you choose a Custom or Textured fill, you can still make changes to the texture. *(See Appendix B for a printout of the Custom and Textured fills.)*

To apply a Custom or Textured fill:

1. Choose Custom from the fill choices in the Object panel.

   or

   Choose Textured from the fill choices in the Object panel.

2. Choose one of the Custom fills from the Custom menu 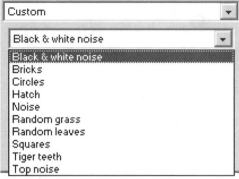.

   or

   Choose one of the Textured fills from the Textured menu ⑤⑥.

3. If applicable, change the color and make any other changes you want to the settings of the fill.

4. Instead of seeing a preview of the fill in the object, you see a series of Cs that fill the object ⑤⑦. You can only see the fill by printing the artwork ⑤⑦.

TIP If you use Adobe InDesign, you can also see the artwork on the InDesign page. This is because InDesign has a sophisticated PostScript rendering engine that allows you to see the effects of writing PostScript code. Neither QuarkXPress nor PageMaker provides this feature.

TIP Custom and Textured fills cannot be scaled with an object and do not print to non-PostScript printers.

⑤⑤ *The Custom fill choices.*

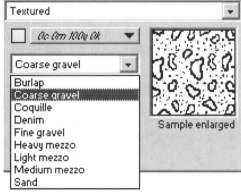

⑤⑥ *The Textured fill choices.*

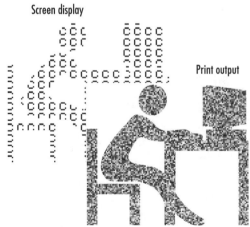

⑤⑦ *The difference between the display and the print output of a Custom or Textured fill.*

Using Custom and Textured Fills

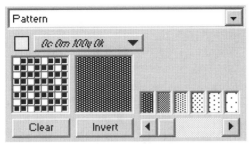

53 *The* **Pattern** fill settings *in the Object panel.*

59 *An object filled with a Pattern fill displays and prints that pattern.*

Writing PostScript Fills

When you choose a PostScript fill from the Object panel pop-up menu, you see a large box with the word "fill" in it. The purpose of this box is to allow you to type in specific PostScript code to create a pattern. Learning and working with PostScript code is much too advanced to cover here. If you are interested in working with PostScript in FreeHand, find an out-of-print copy of *Real World FreeHand* by Olav Martin Kvern (Peachpit Press).

Working with Pattern Fills

Pattern fills are bitmapped patterns that can be edited pixel by pixel. *(See Appendix B for a printout of the default pattern fills.)*

To apply a Pattern fill:

1. Choose Pattern from the fill choices in the Object panel. This opens the pattern controls **53**.

2. Use the slider bar to choose one of the Pattern fills from the series of small boxes.

3. Use the large preview box on the left to edit the pattern by clicking on each of the pixels. The large preview box on the right shows what your pattern will look like when applied to the object.

4. Use the Clear button to delete all the dark pixels from the large preview boxes to begin edit a pattern again.

5. Use the Invert button to change the black pixels into white and vice versa.

TIP Objects behind Pattern fills are not visible through the white spaces of the fills.

6. Use the color drop box to apply any color to the dark pixels of a pattern.

TIP Colors are applied to the solid-color portion of the fill. White areas remain white.

TIP Pattern fills appear the same way onscreen as they print **59**.

TIP Pattern fills cannot be transformed with an object.

TIP Pattern fills are designed for use on low-resolution printers, not high-resolution imagesetters or film recorders. They may also cause problems when part of Acrobat documents.

STROKES 15

Just as fills occupy the inside of objects, strokes surround the outside of objects. I always think of strokes as the shell that encases an egg, which is the fill inside. (However, unlike egg shells, the strokes in FreeHand don't crack if you accidentally bump them into another object.)

It's tempting to think of strokes as simply thin fill colors, but you'd be very much mistaken. There are so many other things you can do with strokes that you can't do with fills.

You can create dash patterns, add arrowheads, and change the thickness of the stroke color.

FreeHand also has a type of stroke, called Brushes, that resemble traditional paint brush strokes and calligraphic pen marks. But that's not all. Brushes also let you repeat objects along the a path.

As you'll see, strokes make up a very thick subject.

Choosing Strokes

There are six different types of strokes you can apply to objects. The main place to apply and format strokes is the Object panel.

To apply a stroke to an object:

1. Select the object.

2. Click the Stroke icon in the Object panel ➊. A stroke entry appears in the Attributes area.

3. Choose one of the Stroke options from the Stroke menu in the Object panel ➋. The settings in the Object panel change depending on the type of stroke chosen.

TIP You can add additional strokes by repeating the above steps. This allows you to create strokes with multiple colors *(see page 234)*.

To delete a stroke from an object:

1. Click the stroke entry in the Object panel.

2. Click the Remove Item icon ➌. This removes the stroke from the object.

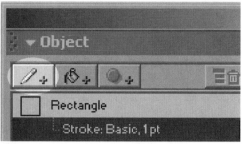

➊ *Click the* **Add Stroke icon** *in the Object panel to add a stroke to an object.*

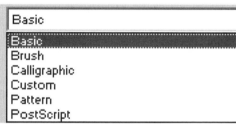

➋ *The* **Stroke menu** *in the Object panel lets you choose the type of stroke applied to objects.*

➌ *Click the* **Remove Item icon** *in the Object panel to remove a stroke from an object.*

④ *The* Stroke color box *in the Tools panel.*

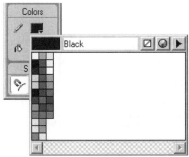

⑤ *The* pop-up color panel *in the Tools panel lets you choose stroke colors.*

⑥ *The* Stroke color drop box *in the Swatches panel indicates the stroke color of the selected object.*

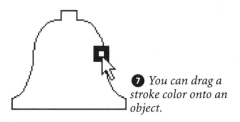

⑦ *You can drag a stroke color onto an object.*

Working with Basic Strokes

There are several ways to apply a Basic stroke. The simplest is just to choose the stroke color.

To apply a stroke color using the Tools panel:

1. Select the object.
2. Click the triangle in the Stroke color box at the bottom of the Tools panel ④. This opens the pop-up color panel ⑤.
3. Choose a color from the color panel.

To apply a stroke color using the Swatches panel:

1. Select the object.
2. Click the Stroke drop box in the Swatches panel ⑥.
3. Click the name of the color you wish to change the stroke to in the Swatches panel.

   or

   Drag a color swatch from the Swatches panel or the Color Mixer onto the Stroke color drop box ⑥.

To apply a stroke by dragging:

◆ Drag a color swatch onto the edge of an object.

   or

   Hold the Cmd key (Mac) or Ctrl+Shift keys (Win) as you drag. The cursor changes to a box, indicating that only the stroke will be affected ⑦.

TIP You can also use the same technique to change the color of an existing stroke.

You can also remove a stroke from an object by setting it to None.

To change a stroke to None:

1. Select the object to which you want to apply the None stroke to.

2. With the Stroke drop box selected, click None in the Swatches panel ⑧. An x appears in the Stroke drop box, indicating that there is no stroke.

   or

   Click the None icon in the Stroke color box pop-up panel ⑨.

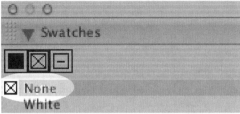

⑧ *Choose* **None** *in the Swatches panel to remove the stroke from an object.*

You can also set the color for a Basic stroke using the Object panel. This also lets you control the other settings of the Basic stroke.

To apply a Basic stroke using the Object panel:

1. Select the object.

2. With the Object panel displayed, choose Basic from the Stroke pop-up menu. This displays the Basic stroke settings ⑩.

3. Choose a color for the stroke from the color list.

⑨ *Click the* **None icon** *in the Stroke color pop-up panel to remove a stroke.*

⑩ *Choose Basic from the Object panel list to display the* **Basic stroke options.**

⓫ Use the **Width field** to change the stroke weight or thickness.

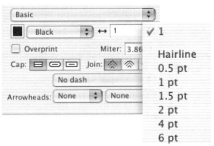

⓬ The **Width menu** provides a list of stroke widths to choose from.

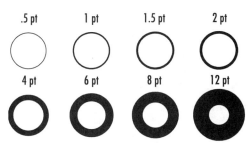

⓭ A sample of the **stroke weights** in the Width pop-up list.

Once you have applied a stroke, you can change the width, or how thick that stroke appears.

To change a stroke width using the Object panel:

1. Select the object you want to change.

2. With the Object panel set for Basic stroke, type the value for the thickness of the stroke in the Width field ⓫.

   or

   Choose a value in points from the pop-up menu next to the field. The thickness of the stroke changes ⓬.

3. Press Return/Enter to implement a value in the field ⓭.

TIP Half the width of a stroke is applied to the inside of the path. The other half is applied to the outside of the path.

To change a stroke width using keyboard shortcuts:

1. Select the object that has a stroke.

2. Use the following keyboard commands to increase or decrease the stroke weight by 1 point:

	Mac	Windows
Increase weight	Cmd-Opt-Shift->	Ctrl-Alt-Shift->
Decrease weight	Cmd-Opt-Shift-<	Ctrl-Alt-Shift-<

Working with Basic Strokes

Beware the Hairline Stroke

Unless you absolutely know what you are doing, don't apply the Hairline setting from the Width list.

A hairline stroke is defined as the thinnest possible stroke you can print. If you're printing to the office printer, the hairline will be pretty thin. If you then send the document out to be printed on a professional imagesetter, the hairline turns practically invisible.

As a general rule, don't specify a stroke width lower than .125 pt—and certainly never specify a hairline!

If you have an open path, you can change the appearance of the *cap* or the end of the path. If you have a stroke with corner points, you can change the appearance of the *join* or the point where the line segments meet.

To apply a cap to a stroke:

1. Select an open path that has a Basic stroke applied to it.

TIP If you cannot see the differences in the cap styles, trying zooming in or increasing the stroke width.

2. Choose the cap style as follows ⓮:
   - **Butt** ends the stroke with a straight line that stops exactly on the endpoint of the path ⓯.
   - **Round** ends the stroke with a half-circle that extends past the endpoint of the path ⓯.
   - **Square** ends the stroke with a square that extends past the endpoint of the path ⓯. The only difference between the Butt and Square caps is that the Square cap extends past the endpoints.

To change the join of a stroke:

1. Select an open path that has a Basic stroke applied to it.

TIP If you cannot see the differences in the join styles, trying zooming in or increasing the stroke width.

2. Choose the join style as follows ⓰:
   - **Miter** creates a pointed corner where the line segments intersect. The sharper the angle, the longer the pointed corner extends ⓱.
   - **Round** forms a curve between the two line segments ⓱.
   - **Bevel** creates a line that cuts off the segments at the anchor point that connects the segments ⓱.

TIP My favorite look is to combine a Round cap with the Round join. This creates a look similar to a marker pen.

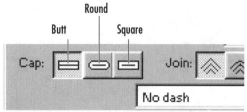

⓮ *Click the icons for the* **three Cap styles.**

⓯ *The three Cap styles applied to open paths. The endpoints are indicated by square white dots.*

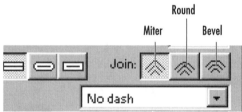

⓰ *Click the icons for the* **three Join styles.**

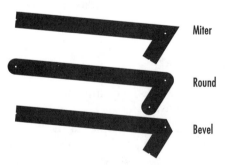

⓱ *The three Join styles applied to the corner point of a path. The anchor points are indicated by square white dots.*

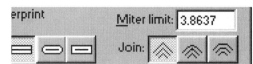

⓲ *The* **Miter limit field** *lets you set the maximum size for the spike of a Miter join.*

⓳ *A Miter limit of 7 points allows the top object to display a spike. A Miter limit of 6 points converts the bottom object's join to a Bevel.*

When you use a Miter join, you can also set the maximum size of the spike that extends out from the join. If the size of the spike exceeds the Miter limit, the join is converted to a Bevel join.

To change the Miter limit:

1. Select a path with a miter join.

TIP In order to see the effects of changing the miter limit, choose a rather thick width such as 24 points and create two line segments with a very acute angle between them. If the miter limit is high enough, the extension should look like a spike.

2. In the Object panel, use the Miter limit field to lower the size of the Miter limit **⓲**.

TIP A low number such as 1 or 2 points converts the Miter join to a Bevel join **⓳**.

Moving Basic Strokes to Flash

One of the benefits of working with FreeHand is you can easily copy and paste artwork into Macromedia Flash. If you intend to use FreeHand with Flash, there are some limitations to how the Basic strokes are converted into Flash objects.

Flash only has round caps and round joins. This means that if you need a particular cap or joint (other than round) you should use the Expand Stroke command *(see page 114)* to convert the stroke to a filled path.

Also, Flash doesn't have all the options for custom dashes *(see the next page)*. This means that some of FreeHand's dashed lines may appear in Flash, but others are converted into solid strokes.

Finally, any arrowheads *(see page 221)* will be converted into discrete objects. Their orientation to the path may also shift.

Working with Basic Strokes

Creating Dashed Strokes

Instead of a solid basic stroke, you can create dashed lines like the ones used for coupons.

To apply a premade dash pattern:

1. Set the stroke to Basic.

2. In the Object panel, use the Dash pop-up menu to choose from the default list of premade dash patterns **㉕**.

TIP The spaces between the dashes of a stroke are transparent, not white. If you lay your dashed stroke over another object, you will see through the spaces to that other object.

㉕ *The* Dash patterns menu.

In addition to the dash patterns that ship with FreeHand, you can create your own custom dash patterns.

To edit a dash pattern:

1. With the Object panel displayed, hold down the Opt/Alt key as you click to select one of the dash patterns from the Basic stroke settings. The Dash Editor dialog box appears **㉑**.

2. Set the length of the visible portion of the dash by entering a number in the On field.

3. Set the length of the space between the dashes by entering a number in the Off field.

4. You can enter up to four different sets of On and Off values.

5. When you have finished entering the pattern, click OK. The dash pattern is added to the bottom of the dash list.

TIP You can also create different effects with dashed patterns by setting the caps to Round or Square.

㉑ *The* Dash Editor dialog box *lets you create your own dash patterns. Choose up to four sets of On and Off patterns.*

Working with Multiple Strokes

Don't forget you can apply multiple strokes to a path. This allows you to create very sophisticated looks—especially with dash patterns. See page 234 for how to work with multiple strokes.

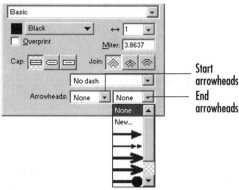

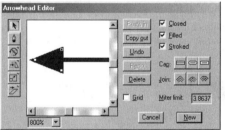

22 *The* **Arrowheads pop-up menu** *lets you add arrowheads to open paths made with Basic strokes.*

23 *The* **Arrowhead Editor dialog box** *lets you modify the program's arrowheads or create your own custom arrowheads.*

Adding Arrows to Strokes

Basic strokes can also have arrowheads that are automatically applied to the front and back of open paths.

To apply arrowheads:

1. Select an open path with a Basic stroke.

TIP Arrowheads take their size from the point size of the stroke.

2. Choose one of the Arrowheads pop-up menus in the Object panel **22**. The left menu controls the start of the path, the right menu controls the end of the path.

3. Using the appropriate menu, choose an arrowhead.

TIP Choose None to remove an arrowhead from a path.

To create new arrowheads:

1. Open either Arrowheads pop-up menu and choose New. The Arrowhead Editor dialog box appears **23**.

2. Use any of the Arrowhead Editor tools to draw the arrowhead.

3. Click New. The new arrowhead appears at the end of both arrowhead menus.

To edit arrowheads:

1. Hold down the Opt/Alt key as you select one of the arrowheads from the pop-up menu.

2. In the Arrowhead Editor that appears, modify the arrowhead.

3. Click New to complete your edit. The original arrowhead is modified and all objects that use the arrowhead change.

TIP Use the Paste in and Copy out buttons to transfer arrowheads between the Arrowhead Editor and the work page. This allows you to use all the FreeHand tools to create arrowheads.

Applying Brush Strokes

One of the limitations to Basic strokes is they are so — well, um — *basic.* Brushes are a special type of stroke that allow you to simulate the look of pen and ink as well as other special effects.

TIP Although Brush strokes can be applied to any path, you will most likely want to use them as the setting for the Pencil tool.

To use Brush strokes to draw objects:

1. With no object selected, click the Add Stroke button in the Object panel.

TIP If you choose a setting for the Object panel with no object selected, you make that setting the default for all new objects that are created.

2. Choose Brush from the Strokes menu in the Object panel. This displays the Brush settings ㉔.

3. Choose a brush tip from the Brushes menu ㉕.

   - **Default Paint** creates a brush stroke that stretches along the shape of the path.
   - **Default Spray** repeats the brush stroke in a pattern along the path.

TIP Each new FreeHand document always contains a default paint brush and a default spray brush ㉖. Although these brushes are rather plain, you can convert your own artwork into brushes *(see the opposite page).*

4. Enter a number in the Width field to change the size of the brush.

5. Use the Pencil tool (or any other creation tool) to draw paths. Each new path is styled with the Brush stroke.

TIP You can also apply a Brush stroke to any existing path.

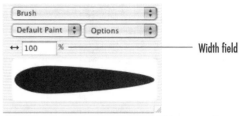

Width field

㉔ *The* **Brush settings** *in the Object panel.*

㉕ *Choose one of the default brush tips from the* **Brushes menu**.

㉖ *The* **default paint brush** *and* **default spray brush** *applied to Pencil stroke.*

Brush Colors?

As you apply Brush strokes, you will notice there is no setting for the color of the Brush stroke. That's because brushes are colored by the color of the object used to define the Brush stroke. A black ellipse creates a black Brush stroke. You have to change the color of the ellipse to change the color of the Brush stroke.

Applying Brush Strokes

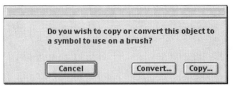

27 *An example of how a custom piece of art (upper left) becomes a wispy stroke when converted into a brush tip.*

28 *You have a choice as to how to use the object selected as a brush tip.*

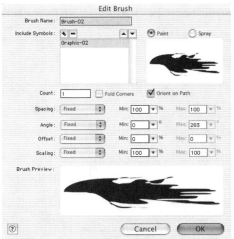

29 *The* **Edit Brush dialog box** *lets you control how custom artwork is used as a brush tip.*

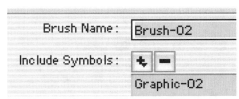

30 *New brush tips are automatically named. Also the symbols used as the brush tip are automatically created and named.*

Creating Brushes

Although the two default brushes are useful, they hardly demonstrate all the aspects of Brush strokes. You can use your own artwork as brushes.

To convert selected objects to a brush:

1. Select the object that you want to use as the brush tip.

TIP An irregular object can simulate the look of traditional sable brushes **27**.

2. Choose **Modify** > **Brush** > **Create Brush**. A dialog box appears asking how you would like to use the selected object **28**.

3. Choose **Copy** to create a symbol used as the brush tip. This leaves the selected object unchanged.

   or

   Choose **Convert** to create a symbol used as the brush tip. This replaces the selected object with an instance of that symbol.

4. In the Edit Brush dialog box that automatically opens **29**, use the Brush Name field to change the name automatically created for the brush **30**.

TIP A new symbol, also automatically named, is created and applied to the brush in the Include Symbols field. *(See Chapter 21, "Styles and Symbols" for more information on working with symbols.)*

5. Set the options as described in the following exercises.

6. Click OK. The brush tip is available to be applied to paths.

Creating Brushes

To set the brush mode:

1. Click Paint to create a brush tip that stretches along the length of the path .

   or

   Click Spray to create a brush tip that repeats along the path ③.

2. If you choose Paint, enter a number from 1 to 500 in the Count field ②. This sets how many times the brush tip appears along the path.

To control the orientation of the brush:

◆ Check Orient on Path to have the artwork follow the orientation of the path to which it is applied ③.

To set the spacing options:

1. Use the Spacing list ④ to choose one of the following options for the space between each instance of the brush tip ⑤:

   • **Fixed** sets a specific space.
   • **Random** lets you set minimum and maximum amounts that are applied randomly.
   • **Variable** lets you set the minimum and maximum amounts that are applied linearly.

2. If the Spacing is set for Fixed, enter an amount between 1% to 200% in the Min field.

   or

   If the spacing is set for Random or Variable, set an amount in both the Min and Max fields.

TIP The percentage of spacing is based on the width of the symbol used as the artwork.

③ *Click the* **Paint or Spray buttons** *to set the type of Brush stroke.*

② *Use the* **Count field** *to set how many times a Paint brush repeats along a path.*

③ *The* **Orient on Path option** *controls how the brush tips align themselves to the path.*

④ *Use the* **Spacing controls** *to set the space between each instance of a brush tip.*

⑤ *The effects of the* **Spacing controls** *on the look of a brush.*

36 Use the **Angle controls** to set the rotation of each brush tip as it is applied to the path.

Brush tip

Fixed

Random

Variable

37 The effects of the **Angle controls** on the look of a brush.

38 Use the **Offset controls** to set the rotation of each brush tip as it is applied to the path.

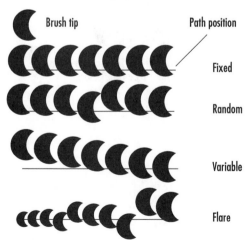

Brush tip | Path position

Fixed

Random

Variable

Flare

39 The effects of the **Offset controls** on the look of a brush.

To set the angle options:

1. Use the Angle list **36** to choose one of the following options for the rotation of each instance as it is applied to the path **37**:
   - **Fixed** sets a single rotation for all instances.
   - **Random** lets you set minimum and maximum rotations that are applied randomly to each instance.
   - **Variable** lets you set the minimum and maximum amounts that are applied linearly to the instances.
2. If the Angle is set for Fixed, set an amount from 0° to 359° in the Min field.

   or

   If the spacing is set for Random or Variable, set an amount in both the Min and Max fields.

To set the offset options:

1. Use the Offset list **38** to choose one of the following options for the distance of the brush tip from the path **39**:
   - **Fixed** sets a single offset for all instances.
   - **Random** lets you set minimum and maximum amounts that are applied randomly to each instance.
   - **Variable** lets you set the minimum and maximum amounts that are applied linearly to the instances.
   - **Flare** is available for Spray brushes. Flare lets you change the offset amount according to the Scaling amounts.
2. If the Offset is set for Fixed, set an amount from -200% to 200%° in the Min field.

   or

   If the spacing is set for Random or Variable, set an amount in both the Min and Max fields.

Creating Brushes

To set the scaling options:

1. Use the Scaling list  to choose one of the following options for the size of the instances ⓐ:

   - **Fixed** sets a single size for all instances.
   - **Random** lets you set minimum and maximum sizes that are applied randomly to each instance.
   - **Variable** lets you set the minimum and maximum sizes that are applied linearly to the instances.
   - **Flare** is available for Paint brushes. Flare lets you change the scale amount according to the minimum and maximum scaling values ⓑ.

2. If the Offset is set for Fixed, set an amount from -200% to 200%° in the Min field.

   or

   If the spacing is set for Random or Variable, set an amount in both the Min and Max fields.

ⓐ *Use the* **Scaling controls** *to set the size of the object used as the Brush stroke.*

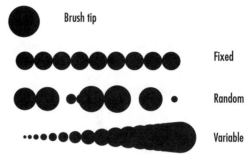

ⓐ *The effects of the* **Scaling controls** *on the look of a brush.*

ⓑ *The effects of the* **Scaling controls** *on a Paint brush set for three repetitions.*

43 *An example of how two symbols can be combined into a single brush stroke.*

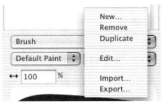

44 *The* **Options menu** *for the Brush settings.*

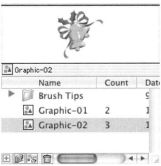

45 *The symbols for brushes are contained in the Library panel.*

Add symbol   Move up
    Delete symbol   Move down

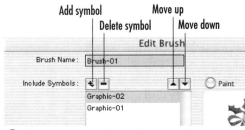

46 *Use the* **Include Symbols** *controls to apply multiple brush tips.*

You're not limited to using only one piece of artwork as a brush tip. FreeHand also lets you use several brush tips within one brush stroke.

To use multiple tips in a brush:

1. Select the graphic you want to use as a brush tip.

2. Choose **Modify > Symbol > Copy to Symbol.** This creates a symbol of the artwork that is available in the Library **43**.

3. Repeat steps 1 and 2 to create as many symbols as necessary.

4. With the Object panel list set to Brush, choose New from the Object panel Options menu **44**. This opens the Edit Brush dialog box.

5. Click the Add Symbol button to choose a symbol from the Library. The name of the symbol is displayed in the symbol list **45**.

6. Add as many other symbols from the Library as you would like.

7. Use the Move up or Move down buttons to change the stacking order of the symbols in the brush.

8. Set the rest of the options in the Edit Brush dialog box as described in the previous exercises.

TIP You can have both Paint and Spray brush tips in the same brush.

9. Click OK. The brush is now available to be used on paths **46**.

Creating Brushes

Working with Brushes

As you create and apply brushes, you will want to control and manage those brushes.

To edit a brush:

1. Use the brush list in the Object panel to choose the brush you want to edit.

2. Choose Edit in the Options menu for the Brush settings.

3. Make whatever changes you want to the brush and click OK. If the brush is in use, a dialog box appears 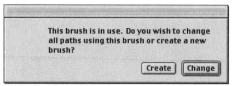.

4. Click Change to apply those changes to the existing brush graphic.

   or

   Click Create to create a duplicate of the original brush with the changes. This leaves previously created artwork untouched.

   TIP If you want to edit the artwork used to create a brush, you need to edit the symbol for that artwork *(see Chapter 21, "Styles and Symbols.")*.

Before you edit a brush, you may want to keep its original settings. The easy way to do this is to make a duplicate of the brush.

To duplicate a brush:

◆ Use the brush list in the Object panel to choose the brush you want to duplicate.

This brush is in use. Do you wish to change all paths using this brush or create a new brush?

Create   Change

47 *You can control what happens when you edit a brush that is is use.*

Confessions of a Brushes Addict

I admit it—I'm addicted to using brushes. My favorite activity is to create some sort of blobby shape and then watch what happens when I turn it into a brush.

I also love taking plain silhouette shapes and watching what happens when I apply different paint brush strokes. I especially like to simulate the look of pen and ink and other traditional media.

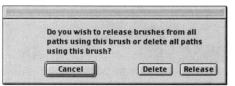

48 *You can control what happens to paths when you delete a brush.*

49 *When you use the* **Release Brush** *and* **Release Instance commands***, you can then modify the individual elements.*

Brushes are stored in the document that originally created them. As you add more and more brushes to the document, the list of brushes may become unwieldy. You may then want to delete one or more brushes from the document.

To delete a brush:

1. Select the brush from the Brush list in the Object panel.

2. Choose Remove from the Object panel menu. If the brush has been applied to a path, a dialog box appears **48**.

3. Choose Delete to remove the brush from the brush list as well as delete any paths that had the brush applied to them.

   or

   Choose Release to convert the brush to discrete objects and remove the brush from the brush list.

You may want to manipulate the artwork in the brush itself—for instance to recolor an object. You do so by releasing the brush.

To release a brush from a path:

1. Select the object.

2. Choose **Modify** >**Brush** >**Release Brush.** This converts the brush artwork into discrete instances of the symbol used to define the brush tip.

TIP The instances can be moved, but not individually modified.

3. If you want to modify an instance, select the instance and choose **Modify** > **Symbol**> **Release Instance.** This converts the instances into paths **49**.

Working with Brushes

To import brushes:

1. With Brush chosen in the Object panel list, choose Import from the Object panel menu.

2. Navigate to find the file you want to import brushes from. The Import Brushes dialog box appears 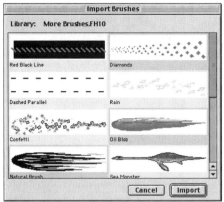.

3. Select the brushes you want to import.

TIP Use the Shift key to select a range of brushes. Use the Cmd/Ctrl key to select multiple brushes.

4. Click Import. The brushes are added to the document.

To export brushes:

1. With Brush chosen in the Object panel list, choose Export from the Object panel menu. The Export Brushes dialog box appears ⑤.

2. Select the brushes you want to export.

TIP Use the Shift key to select a range of brushes. Use the Cmd/Ctrl key to select multiple brushes.

3. Click Export. The Save dialog box appears.

4. Name and save the file.

⑤ *The* **Import Brushes dialog box** *lets you choose brushes to import from other documents.*

What's Imported with the Brushes?

When you import a brush into a file, you also import any named colors that are used in the artwork for the brush. You also import any symbols that are used as the brush tip.

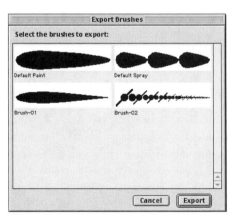

⑤ *Use the* **Export Brushes dialog box** *to choose the brushes to be exported into their own file.*

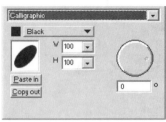

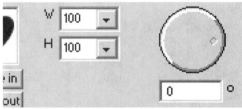

52 *The* **Calligraphic stroke controls** *of the Object panel.*

53 *Use the width, height, and angle controls to change the appearance of a calligraphic stroke.*

54 **Unequal width and height settings** *change the top stroke to the two bottom strokes.*

Calligraphic Strokes

Calligraphic strokes simulate the look of calligraphy pens. They can be applied to an existing objects or drawn on the fly with any tool. They are most useful when used with the Pencil tool.

To use Calligraphic strokes to draw objects:

1. With no object selected, click the Add Stroke button in the Object panel.

TIP If you choose a setting for the Object panel with no object selected, you make that setting the default for all new objects that are created.

2. Choose Calligraphic from the Strokes menu in the Object panel. This displays the Calligraphic settings **52**.

3. Use the **W** and **H** fields to set the width and height of the stroke **53**.

TIP Unequal amounts in the two fields create a more angular look to the stroke **54**.

4. Use the Angle wheel or enter an amount in the Angle field. This controls how the calligraphic stroke is applied to the path.

5. Use the Color menu to apply a color to the stroke.

TIP You can also drag colors from the Color Mixer onto the color box or click the color box to display the color pop-up panel.

The Stroke is Mightier Than the Pen!

The Calligraphic stroke is more flexible than the Calligraphic Pen tool. Calligraphic strokes can be applied to any type of object. They also can be reshaped easily. The Calligraphic Pen tool can only draw its own paths. It cannot be applied to other objects. However, the Calligraphic Pen tool does respond to the changes in pressure when working with a pressure-sensitive tablet.

Calligraphic strokes are created from a calligraphic shape. The default tip is an angled ellipse. However, you can create your own calligraphic shapes .

To use your own calligraphic shapes:

1. Use any of the creation tools to create the object you want to use for the calligraphic shape. Create the object as follows:

   • The object must be a closed path.
   • It must be a single object.
   • It should be styled with a basic fill set to black. All other fill or stroke choices will be discarded and converted to a basic, black fill.

2. Choose **Edit** > **Copy** to copy the object to the clipboard.

3. Click the Paste in button in the Calligraphic stroke controls 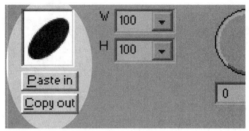. The new object appears in the preview area.

TIP If the Paste in button is not available, it means the object on the clipboard is not suitable to use as a calligraphic shape.

You can also copy the object used as a calligraphic shape to the working area.

To copy a calligraphic shape:

1. Click the Copy out button in the Calligraphic controls ⑤⑥.

2. Choose **Edit** > **Paste**. The object appears on the page.

⑤⑤ *The difference between an ellipse and a triangle applied as calligraphic shapes.*

⑤⑥ *Use the* **Paste in and Copy out controls** *to change the calligraphic shape used in a calligraphic stroke.*

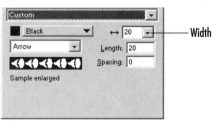

57 *The Custom stroke settings in the Object panel.*

58 *Three sample custom strokes.*

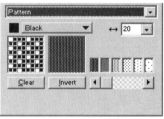

59 *The Pattern stroke settings in the Object panel.*

Writing PostScript Strokes

When you choose a PostScript stroke from the Object panel pop-up menu, you see a large box with the word "stroke" in it. Like the PostScript fills, the purpose of this box is to allow you to type in specific PostScript code to create a pattern. Since learning PostScript is beyond the scope of this book, I suggest you find an out-of-print copy of *Real World FreeHand* by Olav Martin Kvern (Peachpit Press).

Specialty Strokes

Just as there are Custom fills, FreeHand provides Custom stroke patterns. *(See Appendix B for a printout of the Custom stroke patterns.)*

To apply a Custom stroke pattern:

1. Choose Custom from the Stroke menu of the Object panel **57**.
2. Choose a stroke from the Effect menu.
3. Choose the color from the Color menu.
4. Use the Width menu or field to set the thickness of the stroke.
5. Enter an amount in the Length field to control the size of the repeating element in the stroke.
6. Enter an amount in the Spacing field to control the space between each repeating element.

TIP FreeHand displays custom strokes as a solid line. They are visible when printed to a PostScript device or placed in Adobe InDesign **58**.

Pattern strokes are bitmaps that can be edited pixel by pixel.

To apply a Pattern stroke:

1. Select the object and choose Pattern from the Object panel.
2. Use the slider to choose one of the Pattern strokes **59**.
3. Use the preview box to edit the pattern.
4. Use the Clear button to clear all the pixels from the preview boxes.
5. Use the Invert button to change the black pixels into white pixels and vice versa.
6. Use the color drop box to apply a color to the dark pixels.

TIP Use pattern strokes for low-resolution or non-PostScript printers.

Creating Multiple Strokes

One of the more exciting ways to work with strokes is to apply multiple strokes to an object. As each stroke is added to the Object panel, they stack up on the path 🙿. You can mix solid and dashed basic strokes, basic strokes with gradient strokes, or combine brush strokes with calligraphic strokes. There are endless ways to work with multiple strokes.

TIP This exercise deals with multiple strokes. For working with multiple fills and effects, see page 251.

To create multiple strokes:

1. In the Object panel, format a stroke for an object.

2. Click the Add Stroke icon in the Object panel. Format this second stroke as desired.

3. Add as many more strokes to the object as you desire.

4. Drag the strokes up or down in the list so that the thicker strokes do not obscure the thinner ones.

TIP Strokes need to be stacked with the thickest stroke as the bottom of the list and the thinnest stroke at the top 🙿.

🙿 *Three strokes combined in one object.*

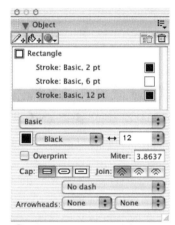

🙿 *An example of how three basic strokes can be combined in the Object panel.*

EFFECTS AND ATTRIBUTES 16

Have you ever watched a child eat his or her first birthday cake? I remember when my niece, who had never tasted any sweets, had her first birthday party.

Her mother put a fingertip covered with icing into the baby's mouth. At first the child's face registered confusion as she tried to understand this new, and very intense taste. Slowly, her eyes widened and she broke into a huge smile. This was a great thing she had discovered. In just a few minutes, the child was grabbing and eating the cake herself.

You may experience something similar learning how to use Effects and Attributes. These are the sweet treats that change the look of paths, add drop shadows or soft feathered edges, or transform strokes and fills.

On first exposure they may seem confusing and hard to appreciate. Give it time. In a short while you will see that these are FreeHand's special treats that you will truly enjoy using.

Choosing Effects

Effects are applied through the Object panel. There are six vector effects that modify paths. There are five raster effects that convert objects into raster images. *(See page 50 for an explanation of the differences between vector and raster objects.)*

To apply an effect to an object:

1. Select the object.

2. Click the Add Effect icon in the Object panel ❶. The Effects menu appears.

3. Choose one of the Effects ❷. The settings in the Object panel change depending on the type of effect chosen.

TIP The effects listed above the line are vector effects. The effects listed below the line are raster effects.

Once you have selected an effect in the Object Panel, you can use the Current Effect menu to replace one effect with another.

To change an effect:

1. Select the effect entry in the Object panel.

2. Click the Current Effect menu to choose a replacement effect ❸.

To modify the effect applied to an object:

1. Click the effect entry in the Object panel. The effect controls appear.

2. Change the settings for the effect.

To delete an effect from an object:

1. Click the effect entry in the Object panel.

2. Click the Remove Item icon. This removes the entry from the object.

❶ *Click the* Add Effect icon *in the Object panel to open the Effects menu.*

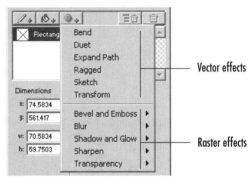

❷ *The* Effects menu *is divided into Vector effects (top) and Raster effects (bottom).*

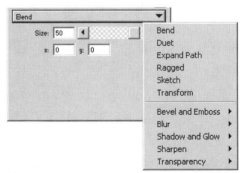

❸ *The* Current Effect menu *lets you replace one effect with another.*

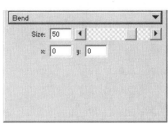

4 *The* **Bend Effect controls** *in the Object panel.*

5 *Use the* **Size slider** *to change the amount of distortion applied in a bend effect.*

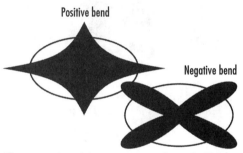

Positive bend

Negative bend

6 *Examples of the* **two types of Bend effects.**

Applying Vector Effects

FreeHand comes with several Vector effects that bend, twist, duplicate, and otherwise transform vector objects. You can access them from the Effects menu.

The Bend Effect allows you to apply a warp to objects.

To apply the Bend effect:

1. Select Bend from the Effects menu. This displays the Bend controls **4**.

2. Use the Size slider to set the amount of bending applied to the object as follows **5**:

   - Positive numbers warp the line segments into concave arcs **6**. This creates sharp points where the arcs meet.
   - Negative numbers warp the line segments into convex arcs **6**. This pulls the ends of the arcs into the center of the object.

3. Use the x and y fields to set the center point of the effect. *(See page 242 for how to manually move the center point:)*

Applying Vector Effects

The Deja Vu of Vector Effects

As you look through the Vector effects, you may feel like you've seen these commands before. You're right; almost all of the Vector effects have equivalent commands elsewhere in FreeHand. The Bend effect is just like the Bend tool. The Duet effect is similar to parts of the Mirror tool. The Roughen effect is like the Roughen tool.

So why should you choose effects when there are tools that do similar things? The primary reason is that when you use a tool to change an object, you permanently modify the shape of the object. If you Bend an ellipse into a curved diamond and then change your mind the next day, you no longer have the original ellipse shape. Not so with effects; the original shape of an object is retained even after you apply an effect.

Also, effects are considered "live." Unlike tools, you can change the settings of an effect at any time. This means if you want to see more or less of the effect, you can go back and change the controls at any time.

The Duet effect automatically creates rotated or reflected copies of the selected artwork. This is similar to the Mirror tool.

To apply the Duet effect:

1. Select Duet from the Effects menu. This displays the Duet effect controls **7**.

2. Choose one of the following:
   - **Reflect** creates a single reflection of the object.
   - **Rotate** creates multiple copies rotated around a center point.

3. Use the **x** and **y** fields to set the position of the center point of the effect. This is the point where the rotation or reflection occurs. *(See page 242 for how to manually move the center point.)*

4. If you have chosen Rotate, use the Copies field to set the number of copies **8**.

5. Choose Joined to connect the original shape to the copies.

6. Choose Closed to close open paths if the copies are near each other.

7. Choose Even/Odd fill to make overlapping areas between the copies transparent.

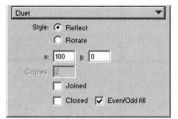

7 *The **Duet effect controls** in the Object panel.*

8 *An example of how the original ellipse (shown with the white stroke) can be rotated into multiple copies using the Duet effect.*

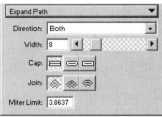

⑨ *The* **Expand Path effect controls** *in the Object panel.*

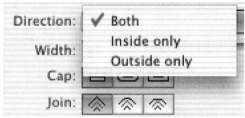

⑩ *The* **Direction menu** *of the Expand Path effect.*

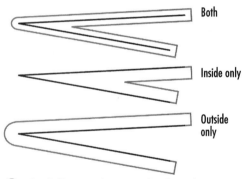

Both

Inside only

Outside only

⑪ *The differences between the three direction settings for the Expand Stroke effect.*

The Expand Path effect works similarly to the ordinary Expand Stroke command *(see page 114)*. However, as an effect it offers a direction option that is not available in the ordinary Expand Stroke command.

To apply the Expand effect:

1. Select Expand Path from the Effects menu. This displays the Expand Path effect controls **⑨**.

2. Choose one of the following from the Direction menu**⑩**:

   - **Both** expands the path equally on both sides of the path **⑪**.
   - **Inside only** expands the path only on the inside portion of the path **⑪**.
   - **Outside only** expands the path only on the outside portion of the path **⑪**.

3. Use the Width slider to set the size of the expanded path. This is similar to the width size of a stroke.

4. Choose one of the Cap icons.

5. Choose one of the Join icons.

6. Set the Miter Limit for how corner points are displayed.

TIP The caps, joins, and miter limit settings are the same as the controls for a Basic stroke *(see pages 218–219)*.

Applying Vector Effects

The Ragged effect works similarly to the Roughen tool. As an effect it lets you make copies as you modify the path.

To apply the Ragged effect:

1. Select Ragged from the Effects menu. This displays the Ragged effect controls 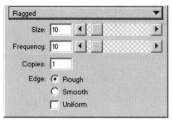.

2. Use the Size slider to control how much the path is positioned away from the original object.

3. Use the Frequency slider to control how many points are added to the new path.

4. Use the Copies field to set how many new paths are created. These new paths are randomly altered from the other copies.

5. Choose one of the following Edge options:
   • **Rough** adds sharp, corner points ⓭.
   • **Smooth** adds curved points ⓭.

6. Choose the Uniform option to make all the points the same distance from the path and each other ⓭.

⓬ *The* **Ragged effect controls** *in the Object panel.*

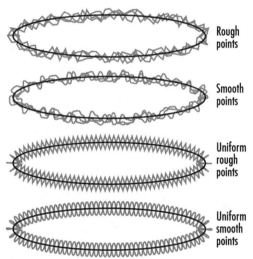

Rough points

Smooth points

Uniform rough points

Uniform smooth points

⓭ *Examples of the differences between the* **Rough and Smooth edges** *and the effect of the* **Uniform setting.**

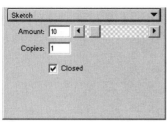

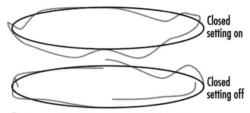

⓮ *The* **Sketch effect controls** *in the Object panel.*

⓯ *Examples of how the Closed setting creates a single sketched path, or two open sketched paths.*

⓰ *Examples of setting multiple copies to the sketch effect.*

The Sketch effect modifies the path as if an artist were quickly tracing the path.

To apply the Sketch effect:

1. Select Sketch from the Effects menu. This displays the Sketch effect controls **⓮**.

2. Use the Amount slider to control how faithful the sketch line is to the original path.

3. Deselect Closed to break the original path into smaller, open paths **⓯**.

TIP When the Closed option is deselected, open paths are created between each set of points on the original path.

4. Use the Copies field to set how many new paths are created. These new paths are randomly altered from the other copies **⓰**.

Applying Vector Effects

The Transform effect allows you to apply live transformations to objects. This allows you to combine several transformations together as well as create copies of the transformed objects.

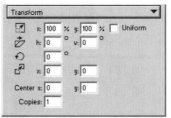

⓱ The **Transform effect controls** *in the Object panel.*

To apply the Transform effect:

1. Select Transform from the Effects menu. This displays the Transform effect controls **⓱**.

2. Choose each of the transform fields as follows **⓲**:
   - The **Scale** fields increase or decrease the size of the object.
   - The **Skew** fields warp the object along an axis.
   - The **Rotate** field changes the orientation of the object.
   - The **Move** field moves the object to a new position.

3. Use the x and y fields to position the center point of the transition.

4. Enter the number of copies for the object. To create no copies, enter 0 in the Copies field.

TIP The transformation applied to the copies is cumulative. Each copy is transformed from the previous copy.

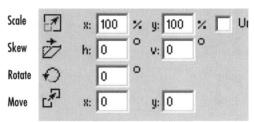

⓲ *The* Scale, Skew, Rotate, *and* Move *fields.*

⓳ *The* **center point control** *inside a Bend effect.*

Instead of trying to judge the x and y coordinates to locate the center point, you can manually move the point on the screen.

To change the center point of an effect:

1. Use the Pointer tool to select the object that contains the effect.

2. Select the Effect entry in the Object panel. The center point appears **⓳**.

3. Position the cursor over the center point and drag it to a new position **⓴**.

TIP Double-click the center point to reset it to the middle of the object.

⓴ *Drag the center point effect to change the appearance of an effect.*

② *The* **Raster Effects Settings dialog box** *controls the resolution for all objects in the document.*

② *The* **Object Resolution dialog box** *allows you to set a different resolution for a specific object in the document.*

Raster Effects and Spot Colors

If you apply a raster effect to an object that contains a spot color, the spot color will be converted to RGB for the screen display. Then, that RGB color will be converted to CMYK process during printing. Unless you want spot colors to be converted, do not use any raster effects with spot color artwork.

Working with a Temporary Resolution

High resolutions for raster effects cause the screen to redraw slowly. One solution is to set the document resolution to a low number as you create the artwork. Then, change the resolution to a higher amount before printing. This will change the appearance of the effect, but will help you work faster. Just remember to change the resolution before final putput.

Applying Raster Effects

Raster effects allow you to apply effects such as shadows, glows, bevels, and transparencies. These effects require the final print output to convert the vector object into a raster image. This means you need to set the resolution for the final raster image before you work on it. You can set the resolution for the document as a whole or set the resolution for a specific Raster effects object.

To set the Raster effects document resolutions:

1. Choose **File** > **Document Settings** > **Raster Effects Settings**. This opens the Raster Effects Settings dialog box **②**.

2. Enter an amount in the Resolution field.

TIP The default is 72 dpi which is used primarily for Web work or rough comps. Higher amounts, such as 300 dpi, are used for high-end professional printing.

3. Select Optimal CMYK Rendering to render the objects without using FreeHand's color management settings.

TIP Use Optimal CMYK Rendering only if all the objects in the document are CMYK.

You can also set a specific resolution for objects. For instance, effects such as shadows and glows can use a lower resolution while effects such as sharpen, applied to images, require higher resolutions.

To set the Raster Effects object resolutions:

1. Select the object that you want to control.

2. Choose Raster Effects Settings from the Object Panel menu. This opens the Object Resolution dialog box **②**.

3. Deselect Use document Raster Effects Resolution.

4. Enter an amount in the Resolution field.

Bevels can be applied to the inside or the outside of an object.

To apply a Bevel effect:

1. Click the Effects icon in the Object panel. This opens the Effects menu.

2. Choose Bevel and Emboss and then pick one of the submenu effects as follows:

   - **Outer Bevel** adds a bevel to the outside of the object . The Outer Bevel controls appear 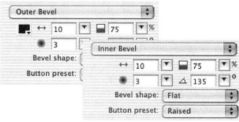.
   - **Inner Bevel** adds a bevel inside the object . The Inner Bevel controls appear .

3. Use the Width field to set the size of the bevel edge 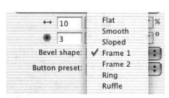.

4. Use the Contrast field to set the difference in appearance between the highlight and shadow on the bevel .

5. Use the Blur field to add a blur to eliminate any harsh lines in the bevel shading .

6. Use the Angle field to set the direction for the light that appears on the bevel .

7. If you have chosen Outer Bevel, use the color box to choose a color for the outer bevel.

8. Choose an appearance from the Bevel shape menu **26**.

9. Use the button preset menu to change the appearance of the object **27**.

TIP The button presets are simply an easy way to apply a slight color change to the appearance of the object. They do not actually create an interactive button.

23 *Examples of an* **inner bevel** *(left) and* **outer bevel** *(right).*

24 *The* **Outer Bevel** *and* **Inner Bevel** *controls in the Object panel.*

Width   Blur   Contrast   Angle

25 *Use the* **Width, Blur, Contrast,** *and* **Angle** *fields to style the size and appearance of the bevel.*

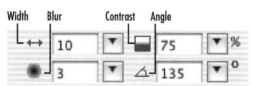

26 *The* **Bevel shape menu** *for bevel effects.*

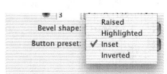

27 *The* **Button preset menu** *for bevel effects.*

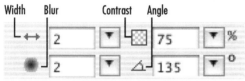

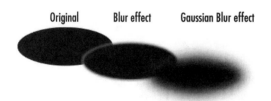

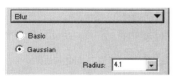

②⑧ *Examples of an* **inset emboss** *(left) and* **raised emboss** *(right).*

②⑨ *The* **Emboss controls** *in the Object panel.*

Width   Blur   Contrast   Angle

③⓪ *Use the* **Width, Blur, Contrast, and Angle** **fields** *to style the size and appearance of the emboss.*

Original   Blur effect   Gaussian Blur effect

③① *Examples of applying the* **Blur** *and* **Gaussian Blur** *effects.*

③② *The* **Blur controls** *in the Object panel.*

Embossing creates the effect that the object is raised or depressed into the page **②⑧**.

To apply an Emboss effect:

1. Click the Effects icon in the Object panel. This opens the Effects menu **②⑨**.

2. Choose Bevel and Emboss and then pick one of the submenu effects as follows:

   - **Inset Emboss** adds an emboss as if the object is pressed down into the page.
   - **Raised Emboss** adds an emboss as if the object is pushed up from the page.

   TIP Although they apply different effects, the Inset Emboss and Raised Emboss have the same controls **②⑨**.

3. Use the Width field to set the size of the emboss edge **③⓪**.

4. Use the Contrast field to set the difference in appearance between the highlight and shadow on the emboss **③⓪**.

5. Use the Blur field to add a blur to eliminate any harsh lines in the emboss shading **③⓪**.

6. Use the Angle field to set the direction for the light that appears on the emboss **③⓪**.

The Blur effects allow you to change crisp, clean lines, into fuzzy, hazy images.

To apply a Blur effect:

1. Click the Effects icon in the Object panel. This opens the Effects menu.

2. Choose Blur and then pick one of the submenu effects as follows:

   - **Blur** applies a blur to create an unfocused appearance **③①**.
   - **Gaussian Blur** applies a blur to create a hazy appearance **③①**.

3. Use the Radius field to set the amount of blur—the higher the number, the greater the blur **③②**.

Applying Raster Effects

The Shadow effects allow you to create the appearance of light casting a shadow from the object. There are two types of shadow effects.

To apply a Shadow effect:

1. Click the Effects icon in the Object panel. This opens the Effects menu.

2. Choose Shadow and Glow and then pick one of the submenu effects as follows:

   • **Drop Shadow** creates the effect of an object casting a shadow onto the page .

   • **Inner Shadow** creates the effect of the object cutting cutting a hole in the page and then casting a shadow into the hole .

   TIP Although they apply different effects, the Drop Shadow and Inner Shadow have the same controls .

3. Use the Distance field to set the position of the shadow from the edge of the object .

4. Use the Opacity field to set the transparency of the shadow .

5. Use the Blur field to apply a blur to the edge of the shadow .

6. Use the Angle field to set the direction for the light that appears on the shadow .

7. Use the color box to set the color of the shadow.

8. Choose Knockout to hide the object, leaving only the shadow 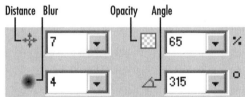.

③ *Examples of a* **drop shadow** *(left) and an* **inner shadow** *(right).*

③ *The* **Shadow controls** *in the Object panel.*

Distance Blur   Opacity Angle

③ *Use the* **Distance, Blur, Opacity, and Angle** fields *to style the size and appearance of the shadow.*

③ *Examples of a* **regular shadow** *(left) and* **knockout shadow** *(right).*

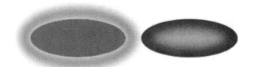

37 *Examples of a* **glow** *(left) and an* **inner glow** *(right).*

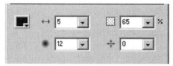

38 *The* **Glow controls** *in the Object panel.*

Width   Blur   Opacity Offset

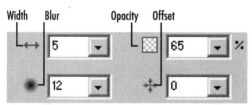

39 *Use the* **Width, Blur, Opacity, and Offset fields** *to style the size and appearance of the glow.*

The Glow effects allow you to create soft glows of colors around objects. There are two types of glow effects.

To apply a Glow effect:

1. Click the Effects icon in the Object panel. This opens the Effects menu.

2. Choose Glow and then pick one of the submenu effects as follows:
   - **Glow** creates a glow that surrounds the outside of an object **37**.
   - **Inner Glow** creates a glow that is contained within the object **37**.

   TIP Although they apply different effects, the Glow and Inner Glow have the same controls **38**.

3. Use the Width field to set the size of the glow **39**.

4. Use the Opacity field to set the transparency of the glow **39**.

5. Use the Blur field to apply a blur to the edge of the shadow **39**.

6. Use the Offset field to set the size of a space between the object and the glow **39**.

7. Use the color box to set the color of the glow.

Applying Raster Effects

The Sharpen effects allow you to take slightly out of focus images and sharpen them so they look crisper.

TIP Although the sharpen effects can be applied to vector objects, they are most useful when applied to imported images. *(See page 342 for information on importing images.)*

To apply a Sharpen effect:

1. Click the Effects icon in the Object panel. This opens the Effects menu.

2. Choose Sharpen and then pick one of the submenu effects as follows:

   - **Sharpen** applies a crispness equally to all the parts of the image ㊵.
   - **Unsharp Mask** applies an increased contrast to the edges of images to increase the difference between the edges ㊵.

3. Use the Amount field to set the degree of sharpening—the higher the number, the greater the sharpness ㊶.

4. If you have chosen Unsharp mask, use the Pixel radius field to set the size of the area that the sharpness is applied to. Higher numbers means the sharpness is applied to a wider area.

5. If you have chosen Unsharp mask, use the Threshold field to set the amount of difference between pixels that should be sharpened. As you increase this number, less sharpness is applied to the image.

㊵ *Examples of applying the* **Sharpen** *and* **Unsharp mask effects.**

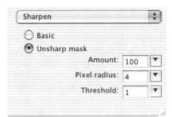

㊶ *The* **Sharpen controls** *in the Object panel.*

Unsharp Masking?

Despite the name, the unsharp mask effect is actually the most sophisticated way to sharpen images.

The ordinary Sharpen command sharpens all the pixels in an image equally. This can cause some parts of an image to appear noisy or grainy.

The Unsharp Mask command allows you to specify the threshold of what parts of the image are sharpened. This avoids noise problems in the image.

The term *unsharp mask* comes from a traditional photographic technique where an out of focus (or unsharp) duplicate of the original image was used as a mask to sharpen the original. For more information about today's digital imaging, see *Photoshop Color Correction* by Michael Kieran, published by Peachpit Press.

42 *A* **Basic Transparency** *applied to the top object on the right allows you to see the bottom object on the left.*

43 *The* **Basic Transparency controls** *in the Object panel.*

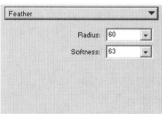

44 *The* **Feather controls** *in the Object panel.*

| Radius: 10 | Radius: 20 | Radius: 20 |
| Softness: 10 | Softness: 20 | Softness: 100 |

45 *Changing the radius and softness in a feather changes the appearance of the opacity around an object.*

The Basic Transparency effect changes the opacity of one object so you can see through it to the objects below **42**.

To apply a Basic Transparency effect:

1. Click the Effects icon in the Object panel. This opens the Effects menu.

2. Choose Transparency and then choose Basic Transparency from the submenu. This opens the Basic Transparency controls.

3. Use the Opacity field to set the amount of transparency **43**.

The Feather effect applies an opacity fade to just the edge of an object.

To apply a Feather effect:

1. Click the Effects icon in the Object panel. This opens the Effects menu.

2. Choose Transparency and then choose Feather from the submenu. This opens the Feather controls **44**.

3. Use the Radius field to set how far inside the object the opacity is applied **45**.

4. Use the Softness field to control the thickness of the opacity fade. High numbers create a larger fade **45**.

TIP If you apply too large a feather amount, the fill disappears.

Applying Raster Effects

The Gradient Mask effect allows you to fade an object or image according to the shape and appearance of a gradient fill .

TIP Strictly speaking, gradient masks aren't actual gradient fills. Rather they are their own type of gradient. However, they use the exact same controls as the gradient fills. *(See page 196 for imformation on gradient fills.)*

To apply a gradient mask effect:

1. Click the Effects icon in the Object panel. This opens the Effects menu.

2. Choose Transparency and then choose Gradient Mask from the submenu. This opens the Gradient Mask controls ⓬.

3. Use the Shape menu to choose the shape for the fade.

4. Use the Start fields to position the start of the fade *(see page 197)*.

5. Use the handle controls to position the angle and length of the fade *(see page 197)*.

TIP You can also modify the handle manually *(see page 202)* ⓭.

6. Use the Repeat menu to choose how the gradient repeats or fills the object *(see page 200)*.

7. If you choose a repeat behavior, set the number of repetitions in the Count field *(see page 200)*.

8. Use the Gradient Mask ramp to set the appearance of the transparency *(see page 201)*. Black creates no transparency. White creates 100% transparency ⓬.

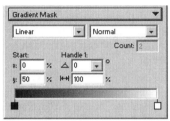

⓬ *A* **Gradient Mask** *allows you to create a transparent effect according to the shape of a gradient fill.*

⓬ *The* **Gradient Mask controls** *in the Object panel.*

⓭ *The* **Gradient Mask handle** *allows you to manually adjust the appearance of the fade.*

Applying Raster Effects

49 Multiple fills *are visible in a single object when the Sketch effect is applied to each fill.*

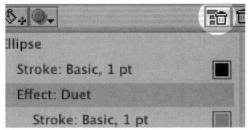

50 *Multiple* **branches of effects** *converted a single ellipse into these multiple objects.*

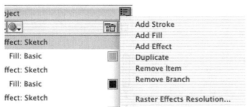

51 *Click the* **Remove Branch icon** *in the Object panel to all the attributes under an effect.*

52 *The* **Object panel menu** *allows you to add, delete, and duplicate attributes and attribute branches.*

Working with Attributes

Every time you add a stroke, fill, or effect to an object, you add another attribute to the Object panel. How these attributes are added affects the appearance of an object. You can also modify the attributes of an object to create different looks. For instance, the order that effects appear in the Object panel changes the appearance of an object.

To set the order of attributes:

◆ Drag an effect up or down the Object panel list as follows:

- Fills and strokes are visible in the order they are listed in the Object panel **49**. Attributes at the top of the list are visible above the attributes below.
- Effects are applied only to the fills or strokes below them.

To apply effects to individual fills or strokes:

◆ Drag a fill or stroke so that it is nested under an effect. This creates a *branch* effect **50**.

TIP The effects in a branch extend down only until the next branch.

TIP Branches may contain fills and strokes or other effects. The order that the attributes appear under a branch determines the appearance of the object.

To delete a branch and its attributes:

1. Select the effect that defines the top of a branch.

2. Click the Remove Branch icon in the Object panel **51**.

   or

   Choose Remove Branch from the Object panel menu **52**.

Working with Attributes

You may also want to replicate an attribute or branch in the Object panel to then apply it to another fill or stroke in the list.

TIP This technique makes it easy to apply complicated effect settings to multiple fills or strokes

To replicate an attribute or a branch:

1. Select the attribute or top element in the branch.

2. Choose Duplicate from the Object panel menu.

I find it thrilling to be able to apply multiple attributes to objects. I love working with live effects that can be edited at any time. However, at some point, you may want to separate all the attributes applied to an object to work with them as separate objects.

To convert attributes into separate elements:

1. Select the object.

2. Choose **Modify** > **Separate Attributes**. The single object is converted into a group that contains the individual components created from the multiple attributes or branches.

BLENDS 17

When I first started working with Macromedia FreeHand, blends were the only way we could create certain effects.

Way back then we used blends to create subtle shading and lighting contours. We used them to create soft edges for shadows. We relied on them to make one shape morph into another. And we used blends to make a series of objects follow a path.

Today, however, FreeHand has many other features that create all those effects without using blends. Gradient fills make it much easier to add subtle shading to objects. The raster effects create shadows and glows. The Spray brushes *(covered in Chapter 15)* give you much more control to make objects follow a path.

That's not to say there are no more uses for blends. They are great for creating very specialized effects or transitions. It's just you don't have to rely on them as much as I did back in the old days.

Understanding Blends

Although there are hundreds of thousands of different looks you can create with blends, they are all variations of three basic effects: color change, shape change, or distributing objects.

Color changes

Color changes are similar to the look of gradients. However, blends give you more control over the appearance of the color change ❶.

Shape changes

Shape changes create the effect of one object turning into another. Some shape changes use hundreds of intermediate styles which make a subtle change between the objects ❷. Other shape changes use few steps which lets you see how each object changes ❸.

Distributing objects

You can distribute objects by blending one object to an identical copy of itself. The intermediate steps are also identical objects, but they can easily be distributed in a straight line or along a path ❹.

❶ *The top three color changes were created by gradients, but a blend is needed for the more complicated color change on the bottom.*

❷ *The difference between a blend with just a few steps (left) and one with over two hundred steps (right).*

❸ *An example of how a blend can make one object change its shape into another.*

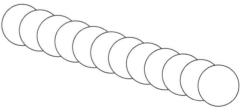

❹ *An example of how a blend between two identical circles creates a distribution of circles.*

⑤ *Two objects selected to create a blend.*

⑥ *After applying the* **Blend command,** *the objects are blended with intermediate steps.*

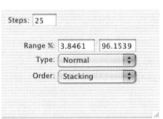

⑦ *Use the* **Steps** *field to set the number of steps between the original objects in a blend.*

Blending Paths

No matter what type of blend effect you create, they all start with the same basic blend command.

To create a simple blend:

1. Select two or more shapes you want to blend **⑤**.
2. Choose **Modify > Combine > Blend.** The objects blend together **⑥**.

TIP Blends are created in straight lines between objects. To make a blend follow a curve, you attach the blend to a path *(see page 260).*

Once you have a blend, you may want to change the number of steps. You might want to make the blend as smooth as possible or modify it to show the intermediate steps.

To change the number of steps in a blend:

1. Select the blend. The blend controls appear in the Object panel.
2. Enter the number of steps between the original objects in the Steps field **⑦**.
3. Press Return/Enter. The blend re-forms with the new number of steps.

Blending Paths

Using the Blend Tool

While the Blend command is handy, the Blend tool is more flexible and easier to use.

To blend between objects using the Blend tool:

1. Select the Blend tool in the Tools panel **8**.

2. Drag the Blend tool from the first object that you want to blend. A line extends out from the object **9**.

3. Drag the line to the next object that you want to blend. The intermediate steps of the blend are visible **10**.

4. Release the mouse button. The blend between those two objects is completed.

TIP Use the Blend controls in the Object panel if you want to change the number of steps in the blend.

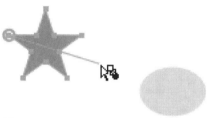

8 *The* **Blend tool** *in the Tools panel.*

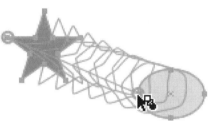

9 Drag the Blend tool *from one object to another.*

To add objects to the end of the blend:

1. Drag from the blend to the object you want to add to the blend **11**.

2. When you see the preview of the intermediate steps, release the mouse button. The new object is added to the end of the blend.

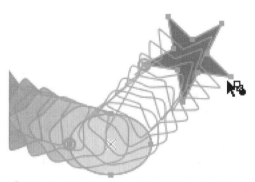

10 *When you see the previews of the intermediate steps, release the mouse to create the blend.*

To add objects to the start of the blend:

1. Drag from the new object to the blend.

2. When you see the preview of the intermediate steps, release the mouse button. The new object is added to the start of the blend.

11 *Use the Blend tool to add* **additional objects to the blend.**

⑫ A **custom blend** *between two objects created by selecting two points (circled).*

⑬ A **custom blend** *created by selecting two different points (circled).*

By default, FreeHand automatically calculates the blend using the points that will create the most uniform blend. However, there may be times when you want to force a blend to happen from specific points. You can use the Blend tool to pick those specific points **⑫** and **⑬**.

To change the points used in a blend:

◆ After the blend has been created, drag from the point that is used in the blend to another on the same object **⑭**. The blend is reshaped.

TIP Blend points are indicated by a circle around the point.

TIP You can also pick the specific points in a blend by selecting the points with the direct selection tool before you choose the Blend command.

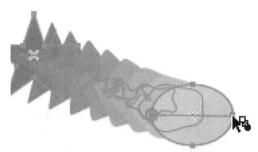

⑭ *Drag with the* **Blend tool** *to change the points used for defining a blend.*

The Rules of Blends

There are limitations to which objects can be used in a blend. You cannot blend between paths that have different types of strokes or fill. For example one object cannot contain a basic fill and the other a gradient.

Blends between two spot colors must remain grouped in order to mix as spot colors. If you ungroup, the intermediate steps will be converted to process colors.

You cannot blend between objects that have lens fills.

You cannot mix types of gradient fills. For instance, you cannot blend between a linear and a radial gradient. Gradients must contain the same number of colors.

Using the Blend Tool

Blending Composite Paths

Composite paths are those objects that have had the Join command applied. If you use composite (joined) paths in a blend, you have some extra controls as to how the blend is drawn. *(For more information on composite paths, see page 102.)*

To use composite paths in a blend:

1. Select the composite paths you want to blend.

TIP Some or all of the objects in the blend can be composite.

2. Choose **Modify** > **Combine** > **Blend**.

3. Set the Type list options in the Object panel as follows 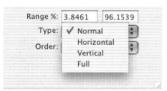:

   - **Normal** uses the normal appearance of the composite object for the blend. This is the best setting for most composite paths ⓰.
   - **Horizontal** gives the best appearance when the composite paths do not overlap and are arranged in a horizontal alignment.
   - **Vertical** gives the best appearance when the composite paths do not overlap and are arranged in a vertical alignment.

4. Set the Order list options in the Object panel as follows ⓱:

   - **Positional** blends the objects based on their position on the page ⓲.
   - **Stacking** blends the objects based on their stacking order.

ⓖ *The* **Type menu** *is used to control the appearance of composite shapes in a blend.*

⓰ *These three composite ovals have been blended to the bottom oval with the settings of* **Type: Normal and Order: Stacking.**

ⓗ *The* **Order menu** *is used to control how blends of composite shapes are created.*

ⓘ *The same composite ovals have been blended to the bottom oval with the settings of* **Type: Horizontal and Order: Positional.**

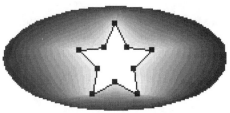

⑲ *To modify an object in a blend, use the Subselect tool to select one of the original objects in the blend.*

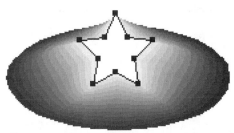

⑳ *Make whatever changes you want to the object. The blend automatically redraws.*

㉑ *When the top blend is ungrouped, the original objects are released. The intermediate steps are grouped together.*

Modifying Blends

Once you create a blend, you can still make changes to the objects in the blend. For instance, you may want to change the shape of one of the original objects in the blend.

To modify a blend shape:

1. Use the Subselect tool to select one of the original objects of the blend **⑲**.

2. Use the Pointer tool or Subselect tool to make any changes to specific points on the object or move the object into a new position.

3. The blend automatically redraws when you release the mouse button **⑳**.

To modify the objects in a blend:

1. Use the Subselect tool to select one of the original objects of the blend.

2. Use any of the onscreen panels, inspectors, or tools to change the colors, fills, or strokes in the blend.

TIP If you add an attribute to one object in a blend that is not in the other objects, the blend will not redraw.

Blends are actually special types of groups. You use the Ungroup command to release the objects in the blend.

To release a blend:

◆ With the blend selected, choose **Modify > Ungroup.** The original objects of the blend are released along with the intermediate steps.

TIP The intermediate steps are themselves grouped and can be deleted or modified **㉑**.

Modifying Blends

Attaching Blends to a Path

Once you have created a blend, you can then align the blend to a path. This feature allows you to create all sorts of effects, the most exciting of which is the ability to create your own custom strokes.

TIP This feature was much more important before FreeHand added the Spray brushes. If you want to repeat the same object along a path, the Spray brush will probably be easier to use. However, if you want to repeat elements that change color or shape, then you will most likely need to use a blend on a path.

To align a blend to a path:

1. Create a blend and a path . Select both the blend and the path.

2. Choose **Modify > Combine > Join Blend to Path.**

3. The blend automatically aligns to the shape of the path .

4. To see the path, click Show path in the Object panel 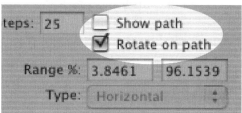.

5. To make the objects in the blend rotate along with the orientation of the path, click Rotate on path in the Inspector palette **㉕**.

To release a blend from a path:

1. Select a blend that has been aligned to a path.

2. Choose **Modify > Split.**

3. The blend separates from the path.

TIP Blends that have been aligned on a path can still be modified using the Subselect tool *(see previous page).*

㉒ *To* **align a blend to a path,** *create the blend and the path to which you want to align it.*

㉓ *The results of aligning a blend to a path.*

㉔ *The* **Blend on a path controls** *in the Object panel.*

㉕ *A blend with Rotate on path selected (top) and unselected (bottom).*

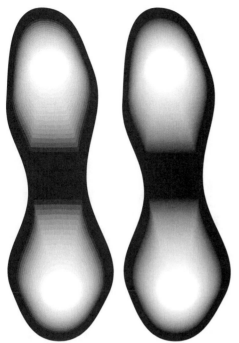

 A blend with **banding** *(left). The same blend with more steps to decrease the banding (right).*

Printing Blends

If you are printing to a low-resolution device such as a laser printer, you may not be satisfied with the printout of the blend. That is because those printers cannot reproduce all the tones necessary to create a smooth blend.

If you are printing on a high-resolution device such as an imagesetter, your blend should print smoothly. However, sometimes blends produce an effect called *banding* . The following may help you avoid banding when printing on PostScript devices. (*For more information on printing, see Chapter 28.*)

To avoid banding in blends when printing

- Print at high resolutions. For most work, this is a minimum of 2400 dpi.
- Lower the screen ruling if you see banding. This is especially helpful when printing to laser printers.
- Avoid blends over 7 inches long. This is especially true if you are outputting to a PostScript Level 1 device. If you are outputting to a PostScript Level 2 device, you may not need to limit the length of your blends.
- Examine the difference between the percentages of each of the CMYK colors. If you are getting banding, try increasing the difference between the percentages.

BASIC TEXT 18

Most people think of Macromedia FreeHand only as a program for creating graphics. However, hidden beneath the graphic tools lies the heart and soul of a full-fledged text-layout program.

In fact, FreeHand has text controls that are not found in page layout programs such as QuarkXPress or Adobe PageMaker. For instance, the tab controls in FreeHand allow you to easily format complex data into tables. Also, the copyfitting commands help you automatically balance columns.

And don't let the chapter title "Basic Text" fool you. These may be the basic text features, but they are exceptionally sophisticated and powerful.

Working with Text Blocks

All text in FreeHand starts inside a text block. There are two types of text blocks: Standard and Auto-expanding.

Standard text blocks have a fixed height and width.

❶ *The* **Text tool** *in the Tools panel.*

To create a standard text block:

1. Select the Text tool from the Tools panel ❶.

2. Drag across the page. How far you drag determines the size of the text block.

3. Release the mouse button to see the text block and the text ruler ❷.

4. Start typing. The text automatically wraps within the text block.

TIP If you do not see the text ruler, choose **View > Text Rulers.**

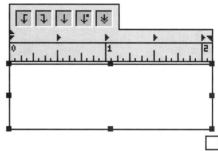

❷ *A* **text block** *with a text ruler.*

Auto-expanding text blocks shrink or expand depending on the amount of text.

To create an auto-expanding text block:

1. Click with the Text tool. A blinking insertion point and a text ruler appear.

2. Start typing. The text block is set to horizontal auto-expansion. *(See the sidebar on this page for a description of the auto-expansion settings.)*

TIP If your text does wrap within the box, check your Preferences settings for auto-expansion of text blocks *(see Appendix C).*

If you deselect the text block before typing in it, you leave an empty text block on the page. These empty blocks contain font information that may confuse your print shop.

To delete empty text blocks:

◆ Choose **Xtras > Delete > Empty Text Blocks.** All text blocks with no characters in them are automatically deleted.

Standard or Auto-Expanding Text Blocks

A standard text block is a fixed-size container. As you type, the text wraps from one line to another. The text block fills from the top and automatically wraps to the next line until it reaches the bottom.

Auto-expanding text blocks never fill up. If the horizontal control is set to auto-expand, the text block just keeps growing wider. You have to manually type a Return/Enter or Shift-Return/Enter to start a new line.

If the vertical auto-expand feature is selected, the text wraps within the text block, but the height of the text block continues to grow taller and taller. Text blocks set to auto-expand never overflow *(see page 266).*

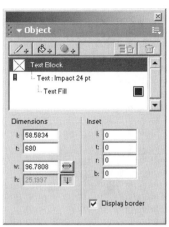

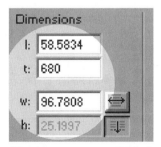

❸ *Select the Text Block entry in the Object panel to display the* **Text Block controls.**

Auto-expansion off

Auto-expansion on

❹ *The* **Auto-expansion icons** *control the behavior of the text block.*

Any person in Government service should or wishing to engage in Government service should:

❺ *To manually* **change the size of a text block,** *drag one of the corner points of the block.*

Dimensions

l: 58.5834

t: 680

w: 96.7808

h: 25.1997

❻ *The* **Dimensions fields** *let you move a text block to a specific position.*

To change the auto-expansion settings:

1. Select the entry for Text Block in the Object panel. This displays the Text Block controls in the Object panel **❸**.

2. Change the expansion icons as follows **❹**:
    - When the icon is in the up state (light), the field is not set for auto-expansion.
    - When the icon is in the down state (dark), the field is set for auto-expansion as new text is entered.

3. Change the handles on the right and bottom of the text block as follows:
    - Double-click a black handle to turn it white. This indicates that auto-expansion is turned on.
    - Double-click a white handle to turn it black. This indicates that auto-expansion is turned off.

To change the size of a standard text block:

◆ Use the Selection tool and drag one of the corner points of the text block **❺**.

or

With the text block selected, open the Object panel. Under Dimensions, change the measurements in the **w** (width) or **h** (height) fields **❻**.

To position a text block numerically:

1. Select the entry for Text Block in the Object panel.

2. In the Object panel set the Dimensions fields as follows:
    - **l** controls the position of the left edge of the text block.
    - **t** controls the position of the top edge of the text block.

3. Press Return or Enter.

Working with Text Blocks

The little square at the bottom of the text block is called the Link box. The different states for the Link box convey important information about the text.

To recognize the status of the Link box:

- If the Link box is white, then all the text in the block is visible ❼.

- A black circle inside the Link box means there is more text than can fit inside the text block ❽. This is called an *overflow*.

- Small arrows inside the Link box mean the text block has been linked to another object *(see page 281)* ❾.

Another way to resize a text block is to shrink the block to fit the size of the text.

To automatically shrink a text block:

1. Select a text block that has extra space that is not filled by text.

2. Using the Selection tool, double-click the Link box of the block ❿. The text block automatically shrinks to fit the text.

🄣🄘🄟 If there is no text in a text block, double-clicking the Link box deletes the text block.

(see page 281)

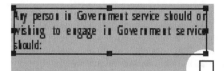

❼ *An* open link box *indicates that all the text is visible in the text block.*

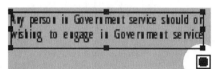

❽ A circle in the link box *indicates an overflow.*

❾ Two arrows in the link box *show that the text is continued in another text block.*

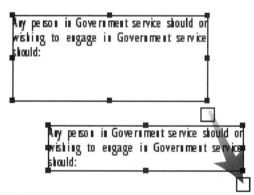

❿ Double-click the Link box *to shrink a text box with extra space to the actual size of the text.*

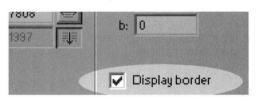

⑪ Check **Display border** *to see a stroke applied to a text block.*

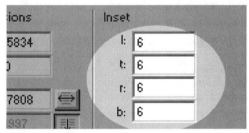

⑫ *The Stroke inspector applies a border to a text block. Here a dashed line was applied.*

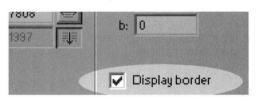

⑬ *The* **Inset fields** *set text away from the edges of a text block.*

```
Amendment III
No Soldier shall, in time of peace be quartered
in any house, without the consent of the
Owner, nor in time of war, but in a manner
to be prescribed by law.
```

⑭ *This text is set away from the border by 6 points to make the text more legible.*

Just as in a page-layout program, FreeHand lets you stroke or frame the outside border of a text block.

To apply a border to a text block:

1. Select the emtry for the Text block in the Object panel.
2. Click the Display border box **⑪**. This allows you to see the border, but it does not create the stroke.
3. Click the Add Stroke icon to add an entry for a stroke in the Object panel.
4. Select the stroke entry in the Object panel.
5. Format the stroke using any of the stroke styles. The border appears around the text block **⑫**.

Once you have given a text block a border, you will probably want to inset the text to add some white space between the text and the border.

To inset text:

1. Select the text block.
2. In the Object panel set the Inset fields as follows **⑬**:
   - l controls inset for the left edge.
   - t controls the inset for the top edge.
   - r controls the inset for the right edge.
   - b controls the inset for the bottom edge.
3. Press Return/Enter to set the amounts **⑭**.

TIP Negative values extend the text outside the borders of the block.

Working with Text Blocks

Selecting Text

You need to select text to change it. There are several different ways to select text.

To select all the text in a text block:

1. Click with the Text tool inside the text block.

2. Choose **Edit** > **Select** > **All**.

TIP Selecting the text block with the Pointer tool also selects all the text in the text block .

To select text within a text block:

◆ Click with the Text tool inside the text block. Use the following techniques to select text:

- **Double click** to select a word.
- **Triple click** to select a paragraph.
- **Drag** to select a range of text .

Although you can drag to select text, it may not be practical to drag to select a long range of text—especially if the text extends over many pages. In that case, you can use the following technique.

To select a range of text:

1. Click with the Text tool to place the insertion point where you want the selection to begin 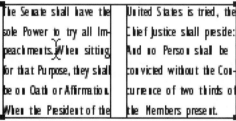.

2. Hold the Shift key and click where you want the selection to end .

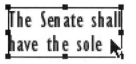

⑮ *A selected text block also selects all the text inside.*

⑯ *Drag to select text within a text block.*

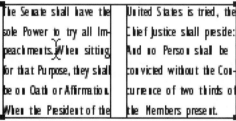

⑰ *Click to place the insertion point where you want to start the text selection.*

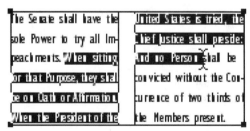

⑱ *Hold the Shift key and click in a second position to select all the text between.*

Selecting Text

⓲ *Select the Text entry in the Object panel to display the* **Text controls.**

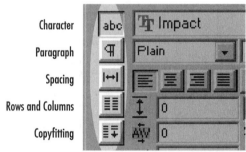

Character
Paragraph
Spacing
Rows and Columns
Copyfitting

⓳ *The five* **Text icons in the Object panel** *display the different text controls.*

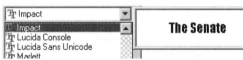

The Senate

⓴ *You see a* **preview of the typeface** *as you choose from the font list.*

㉒ *The* **Style controls** *in the Object panel.*

Changing Character Attributes

FreeHand gives you several places to change character attributes. The Object panel contains a full range of all the text attributes.

The Text toolbar contains some of the text attributes. *(For information on customizing the toolbars, see Chapter 29, "Customizing FreeHand.")*

To see the Character settings in the Text controls:

1. Click the Text entry in the Object panel. The Text controls appear **⓳**.

2. Click the Character icon. The Character settings appear **⓴**.

To change the typeface:

◆ Choose a typeface from the Font list in the Object panel or Text Toolbar.

 or

 Choose **Text > Font** and choose a typeface from the submenu.

TIP If you format without selecting any text, any text you type afterwards will be styled accordingly.

TIP A sample of the typeface is shown next to the Font list in the Object panel **㉑**.

To change the style:

◆ Use the Style list in the Object panel or Text Toolbar to apply Bold, Italic, or BoldItalic **㉒**.

 or

 Choose **Text > Font Style** and choose a listing from the submenu.

To change the point size:

◆ Use the Size list in the Object panel or Text Toolbar to select one of the preset point sizes ㉓.

or

Enter a specific amount in the Size field in the Object panel or Text Toolbar.

or

Choose **Text** > **Size** and select a size from the submenu.

Alignment is the horizontal position of the text within the text block. Strictly speaking, alignment is a paragraph attribute, since it affects the entire paragraph. However you control the alignment in the character area of the Object panel.

To change the text alignment:

◆ Click one of the alignment icons in the Object panel or Text Toolbar to position the text as follows ㉔:

• **Left** sets the text to align with the left margin ㉕.

• **Centered** sets the text to align at a point exactly halfway between the two margins ㉕.

• **Right** sets the text to align with the right margin ㉕.

• **Justified** sets the text to align at both the left and right margins ㉕.

or

Choose **Text** > **Align** and select a setting from the submenu.

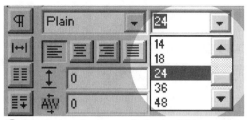

㉓ *The* **Point size controls** *in the Object panel.*

㉔ *The* **Alignment icons** *in the Object panel.*

Left aligned

The Senate shall have the sole Power to try all Impeachments. When sitting for that Purpose, they shall be on Oath or Affirmation. When the President of the United States is tried, the Chief Justice shall preside: And no Person shall be

Center aligned

The Senate shall have the sole Power to try all Impeachments. When sitting for that Purpose, they shall be on Oath or Affirmation. When the President of the United States is tried, the Chief Justice shall preside: And no Person shall be

Right aligned

The Senate shall have the sole Power to try all Impeachments. When sitting for that Purpose, they shall be on Oath or Affirmation. When the President of the United States is tried, the Chief Justice shall preside: And no Person shall be

Justified

The Senate shall have the sole Power to try all Impeachments. When sitting for that Purpose, they shall be on Oath or Affirmation. When the President of the United States is tried, the Chief Justice shall preside: And no Person shall be

㉕ *The* **four alignment options** *change how text is positioned in a text block.*

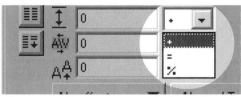

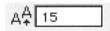

@ *The* **Leading pop-up menu** *in the Object panel.*

@ *A* **Kerning** *value of -10.5 has been applied to the letters T and r in the bottom word, decreasing the separation between the letters.*

@ *A* **Range kerning** *value of 15 has been applied to the letters U, S, and A in the bottom initials.*

@ *A* **baseline shift** *of 15 has been applied to the letter Y, moving it higher than the other letters.*

Leading (pronounced *ledding*) is the amount of space between lines of text.

To change the leading:

1. Use the leading pop-up list to change the leading as follows @:
   - **+ sign** adds space between the lines in addition to the space used by the characters.
   - **= sign** sets an amount of space that does not change if the text size changes.
   - **% sign** adds an amount of space that is a percentage of the point size of the text.
2. Enter the amount of leading in the leading field.

TIP Drag the top or bottom side handles of a text block to increase or decrease the leading of an entire text block.

To change the kerning:

1. Click between two letters.
2. Enter a value in the Kerning field. Positive values increase the space. Negative values decrease the space @.

To change the range kerning:

1. Drag across the text.
2. Enter a value in the Range kerning field. Positive values increase the space. Negative values decrease the space @.

TIP Drag the left or right side handles to increase or decrease the Range kerning of an entire text block.

TIP Hold down the Opt/Alt key as you drag the left or right side handles to change the Range kerning between words.

To change the baseline shift:

- ◆ Enter an amount in the Baseline shift field. Positive values raise the text above the normal baseline for the text. Negative values lower the text @.

Changing Character Attributes

Setting Paragraph Attributes

Once you have text inside a text block, you can format its paragraph attributes.

To change the paragraph attributes:

◆ Click the Paragraph icon in the Object panel. This displays the paragraph options 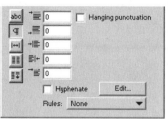.

If you want more space between paragraphs, you should use the Above or Below fields to add space before or after the paragraph. You should *not* use extra paragraph returns which can cause problems if you have to copyfit or need to have others work on your text.

To add space between paragraphs:

◆ Enter the amount of space you want under Paragraph spacing in the Above or Below fields ③.

Ordinarily, text expands to the sides of the text block. The margin indents let you control where the text is positioned in the text block.

To change the margin indents:

◆ Enter the amount of space as follows in the margin indent fields ③:
  • The Left margin indent changes the position of the left margin of a paragraph.
  • The Right margin indent changes the position of the right margin of a paragraph.
  • The First line indent changes the position of the first line of a paragraph.

TIP Use a negative First line indent to create a hanging indent for bullets and numbered lists ③.

③ *The **Paragraph controls** in the Object panel.*

Space above

Space below

③ *The **Above** and **Below** fields let you add space above or below paragraphs.*

Left margin indent

Right margin indent

First line indent

③ *The **Margin indent** fields let you indent the margins and first lines of a paragraph.*

> • Put loyalty to the highest moral principals and to country above loyalty to Government

③ *A negative indent applied to the first line moves the bullet outside the left margin.*

Text Inset or Margin Indent?

The Text Inset command *(see page 267)* indents all the text within a text block.

The Margin indent can be applied to individual paragraphs within a text block.

Left First line   Right
margin margin   margin

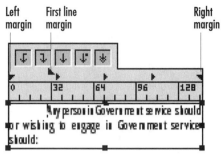

34 *Dragging the* **margin indent triangles** *of the text ruler allows you to change text margins.*

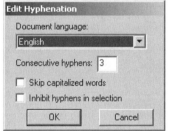

35 *An example of* **hanging punctuation.** *Notice how the quotation marks float outside the margins of the paragraph.*

36 *The* **Edit Hyphenation dialog box.**

FreeHand also lets you use the text ruler to set the margin indents **34**.

To change margin indents using the text ruler:

1. Select the text you want to modify.

2. If the text ruler is not visible, choose **View > Text Rulers.**

3. Select the paragraph you want to change.

4. Drag the margin indent triangles as follows:
   - The bottom of the left indent triangle controls the position of the left margin.
   - The top part of the left indent triangle controls the position of the first line.
   - The right indent triangle controls the position of the right margin.

To create hanging punctuation:

♦ Select Hanging punctuation in the paragraph attributes of the Object panel. This keeps paragraphs from looking ragged **35**.

To turn on hyphenation:

♦ Click the Hyphenate option in the Paragraph settings of the Object panel.

To control the hyphenation:

1. Click the Edit button in the Object panel. The Edit Hyphenation dialog box appears **36**.

2. Use the pop-up menu to choose any foreign language dictionaries.

3. To limit the number of consecutive lines that may end with hyphens, enter the number in the Consecutive hyphens field.

4. To prevent capitalized words from being hyphenated, click Skip capitalized words.

5. To prevent a specific word (such as a company name) from being hyphenated, select the text and click Inhibit hyphens in selection.

6. Click OK to apply the settings.

Setting Paragraph Attributes

Changing the Spacing Options

Space—the final frontier! Or for FreeHand users: Spacing—the third option in the Object panel.

To change the spacing attributes:

◆ Click the Spacing icon in the Object panel. This displays the spacing options .

Horizontal Spacing is an electronic distortion of the text. Small amounts of horizontal scale are sometimes used to fit a few extra characters into a paragraph.

TIP Extreme amounts (more than 10%) of horizontal scaling are unacceptable to professional designers. If you need condensed or expanded type, you should use a typeface that is designed that way.

To change the horizontal scaling of the typeface:

1. Select the text.

2. Enter the amount you want to horizontally scale the text in the Horizontal scale field . Values lower than 100% compress the text. Values higher than 100% expand the text.

TIP Hold the Opt/Alt key and drag a corner handle to change the horizontal scale of all the text in a text block.

③⑦ *The* **Spacing controls** *in the Object panel.*

JULY 4

JULY 4

③⑧ *A* **Horizontal scale** *value of 75% has been applied to the text on the bottom, distorting the characters.*

Changing the Spacing Options

Put loyalty to the highest moral principals and country above loyalty to Government persons, party, or department.

Put loyalty to the highest moral principals and country above loyalty to Government persons, party, or department.

Spacing %:	Min	Opt	Max
Word:	70	100	100
Letter:	-20	0	0

39 *Changing the values for* **Word spacing** *and* **Letter spacing** *compresses the space between letters and words in the second paragraph.*

Keep together off	Keep together on
The President shall be Commander in Chief of the Army and Navy of the United States, and of the Militia of the several States, when called into the actual Service of the United States; he may require the Opinion, in writing, of the principal Officer in each of the	The President shall be Commander in Chief of the Army and Navy of the United States, and of the Militia of the several States, when called into the actual Service of the United States; he may require the Opinion, in writing, of the principal Officer

40 *An example of applying* **Keep together selected words** *to keep a phrase on one line.*

A well regulated Militia, being necessary to the security of a free State, the right of the people to keep and bear Arms, shall not be infringed.	No Soldier shall, in time of peace be quartered in any house, without the consent of the Owner, nor in time of war, but in a manner to be prescribed by law.

41 *An example of applying* **Keep together lines** *to force a paragraph to start in a new column.*

Word spacing controls the space between words. Letter spacing controls the space between characters in a word.

To change word and letter spacing:

1. Select the paragraphs you want to change.
2. Set the Word spacing amounts as follows **39**:
   - **Min** sets the minimum amount of space FreeHand will allow.
   - **Opt** sets the preferred space.
   - **Max** sets the maximum amount of space FreeHand will allow.
3. Set the Letter spacing amounts as follows **39**:
   - **Min** sets the minimum amount of space FreeHand will allow.
   - **Opt** sets the preferred space.
   - **Max** sets the maximum amount of space FreeHand will allow.

Sometimes it is important to keep selected words together. For instance, you may have a title or proper noun that should not be broken across line.

To keep words together:

1. Select the text.
2. Click Selected words **40**.

You can also force FreeHand to keep the lines in a paragraph together rather than breaking across a column. For example, you may want the text for a paragraph not to break across a column.

To keep lines together:

1. Select the text.
2. Enter the number of lines that you want to keep together in the Keep lines together field **41**.

Converting Text Case

Once you have text on your page, you may want to convert the case from upper to lower, or vice versa. FreeHand has several sophisticated Convert Case commands.

To apply the Convert Case commands:

1. Select the text to be converted.
2. Choose **Text** > **Convert Case** and then choose one of the following from the submenu **42**:
   - **Upper Case** changes all the text to uppercase.
   - **Lower Case** changes all the text to lowercase letters.
   - **Small Caps** changes the text size to simulate the look of a small caps font.
   - **Title Case** changes the initial letter of every word to uppercase.
   - **Sentence Case** changes the initial letter of the selected text to uppercase.

To set the Small Caps appearance:

1. Choose **Text** > **Convert Case** > **Settings**. This opens the **Settings** dialog box **43**.
2. Set the Small Caps percentage of point size to whatever proportion you want the text reduced for Small Caps.

You can also set certain words that should not be converted using the Convert Case commands. For instance, you would not want the letter USA converted to lowercase.

To set the Convert Case exceptions:

1. Choose **Text** > **Convert Case** > **Settings**. This opens the **Settings** dialog box.
2. Click the Add button.
3. Type the word you want to make an exception to the Convert Case command.
4. Check which Convert Case commands should not be applied to that word.

CODE OF ETHICS —— Uppercase
code of ethics —— Lowercase
CODE OF ETHICS —— Small Caps
Code Of Ethics —— Title
Code of ethics —— Sentence

42 *An example of applying the* **Convert Case** *commands.*

43 *The* **Settings dialog box** *for the Convert Case commands.*

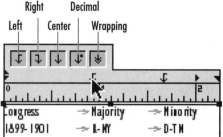

44 *To set a tab position, drag a* **tab arrow** *directly to the text ruler.*

Congress	Majority	Minority
1899-1901	→ R-NY	→ D-TN
1901-1903	→ R-NY	→ D-TN

45 *Text set with* **Left alignment tabs.** *Arrows mark where the tab characters were entered.*

	Congress →	Majority →	Minority
→	1899-1901→	R-NY →	D-TN
→	1901-1903→	R-NY →	D-TN

46 *Text set with* **Right alignment tabs.**

→	Congress	→	Majority	→	Minority
→	1899-1901	→	R-NY	→	D-TN
→	1901-1903	→	R-NY	→	D-TN

47 *Text set with* **Center alignment tabs.**

Years	Income	Expense
1899-1901	→ 2.5M	→ 4.2M
1901-1903	→ 3.05M	→ 1.75M

48 *Text set with* **Decimal alignment tabs.**

Sereno E. Payne, R-NY→ → James D. Richardson, D-TN

Sereno E. Payne, R-NY   John Sharp Williams, →→ D-MS

49 *Text set with* **Wrapping tabs.**

Working with Tabs

There are two separate ways to working with tabs. The first part is to insert a tab character into the text. This tells FreeHand that the text needs to be aligned at that point.

To insert tab characters in the text:

1. Place the insertion point where you want a tab space to occur.
2. Press the Tab key to insert a tab character into the text.

TIP FreeHand sets default left alignment tabs at half-inch intervals.

The second part to working with tabs is to set the alignment tab stop. FreeHand also offers the ability to align text using five different types of tab stops.

To set the tabs by dragging:

1. Select the text.
2. If the text ruler is not visible, choose **View > Text Rulers**.
3. Drag the appropriate tab arrow from the top of the text ruler down to the area just above the numbers **44**. Each of the tab stops aligns the text in a specific way:
   - Left alignment tabs position the left side of the text at the tab position **45**.
   - Right alignment tabs position the right side of the text at the tab position **46**.
   - Center alignment tabs position the center the text at the tab position **47**.
   - Decimal alignment tabs position a decimal point at the tab position **48**.
   - Wrapping tabs position the left edge of the text at the tab position. Any text that does not fit into the tab space is moved down into a new line to form a column **49**.
4. Release the mouse button when the tab arrow is where you want it. The text realigns.

To set the tabs numerically:

1. Double-click any of the tab icons at the top of the ruler. This opens the Edit Tab dialog box .

2. Choose the type of tab you want from the Alignment pop-up menu 🖸.

3. Enter a number in the Position field for where you want the tab located. This number is in relation to the left side of the text block.

4. Click OK to apply the settings.

A tab *leader* is a character that repeats to fill the space created by inserting a tab. The table of contents of this book contains tab leaders that fill the space with periods 🖾.

To set a tab leader:

1. Double-click any of the tab icons at the top of the ruler. This opens the Edit Tab dialog box.

2. Enter a character in the Leader field.

   or

   Select a character from the Leader pop-up menu 🖾.

3. Click OK to apply the settings.

TIP To change the appearance of a tab leader, double-click the characters in the text and change their size, font, color, and so on.

To delete existing tabs:

◆ Drag the tab arrow down off the ruler and then release.

To move a tab to a new position:

◆ Drag the tab arrow along the ruler to the position you want.

🖸 *The* **Edit Tab dialog box.**

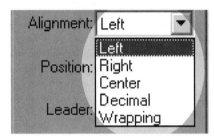
🖸 *The* **Tab Alignment pop-up menu.**

Chapter one..............................5
Chapter two...........................17
Chapter three 29
🖾 *An example of a* **tab leader.**

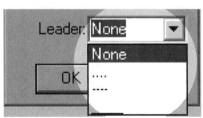
🖾 *The* **Leader pop-up menu.**

Columns

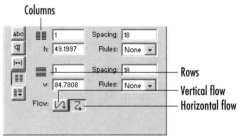

Rows
Vertical flow
Horizontal flow

54 *The* **Rows and Columns controls** *in the Object panel.*

January 27 Senate convenes at 12:00	February 14–23 President's Day Recess
April 3–20 Spring Recess	May 22–June 1 Memorial Day Recess

55 *An example of using rows and columns to create a text table.*

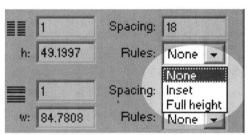

56 *Use the* **Rules menu** *to choose the style of rules around columns and rows.*

January 27 Senate convenes at 12:00	February 14–23 President's Day Recess
April 3–20 Spring Recess	May 22–June 1 Memorial Day Recess
January 27 Senate convenes at 12:00	February 14–23 President's Day Recess
April 3–20 Spring Recess	May 22–June 1 Memorial Day Recess

57 *The difference between* Inset rules *(top) and* Full rules *(bottom).*

Working with Rows and Columns

FreeHand gives you the ability to divide text blocks into columns and rows.

To create columns and rows:

1. Click the Rows and Columns icon of the Object panel **54**.
2. Set the column controls as follows:
   - Enter the number of columns in the column field.
   - Enter the column height in the h field.
   - Enter the space between columns in the spacing field.
3. Set the row controls as follows:
   - Enter the number of rows in the row field.
   - Enter the width in the w field.
   - Enter the space between rows in the spacing field.
4. Click the Flow icons as follows:
   - Horizontal flow fills the columns from left to right and then moves down.
   - Vertical flow fills the rows from top to bottom and then moves to the right.

TIP Although FreeHand doesn't have actual tables, rows and columns can be used instead of tables **55**.

FreeHand also lets you create rules that fit in the spaces between columns or rows.

To add rules to columns and rows:

1. Apply columns or rows to a text block.
2. Select a rule style from the Rules menu as follows **56**:
   - **Full width** creates rules that cross over the space between columns **57**.
   - **Full height** creates rules that cross over the space between rows **57**.
   - **Inset** creates rules that break between the columns or rows **57**.
3. With the text block still selected, use the Stroke controls in the Object panel *(see page 216)* to apply and style the stroke applied to the rules.

Copyfitting Text

If you have multiple columns of text next to each other, you may want the columns to have the same number of lines. You use FreeHand's *copyfitting* commands to adjust your text.

To copyfit text:

1. Click the Adjust Columns icon of the Object panel **58**.

2. Click the Balance option to adjust the columns so there are an equal number of lines in each. This may leave extra space at the bottom of the text block **59**.

3. Click the Modify leading option to adjust the leading. This increases the leading so that the lines fill the text block **60**.

4. To adjust the columns by changing the point size of the text, enter values in the Minimum and Maximum fields. Values below 100 will reduce the point size. Values above 100 will increase it **61**.

5. Enter an amount in the First line leading field to move the first line down from the top of a column.

TIP Copyfitting is a sophisticated feature that, unless you understand what you are doing, can cause more problems than it solves. Use it with caution.

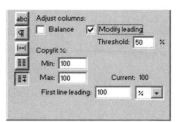

58 Click the **Adjust columns icon** *of the Object panel to see the copyfitting controls.*

| The Senate shall have the sole Power to try all Impeachments. When sitting for that Purpose, they shall be on Oath or Affirmation. When the President of the | United States is tried, the Chief Justice shall preside: And no Person shall be convicted without the Concurrence of two thirds of the Members present. |

59 *Copyfitting by* **balancing the columns.**

| The Senate shall have the sole Power to try all Impeachments. When sitting for that Purpose, they shall be on Oath or Affirmation. When the President of the | United States is tried, the Chief Justice shall preside: And no Person shall be convicted without the Concurrence of two thirds of the Members present. |

60 *Balancing the columns and* **modifying the leading** *to fill the text box.*

| The Senate shall have the sole Power to try all Impeachments. When sitting for that Purpose, they shall be on Oath or Affirmation. When the President of the United | States is tried, the Chief Justice shall preside: And no Person shall be convicted without the Concurrence of two thirds of the Members present. |

61 *Copyfitting by* **changing the type size** *fills the text block and keeps leading proportional.*

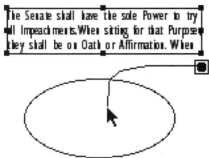

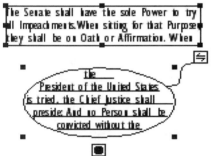

🗲 *To* link text, *drag from the Link box to another text block or object.*

🗲 *Text linked from a text block to an ellipse.*

Linking Text

While it is very easy to create columns within a text block, you may want to have text flow from one text block to another. Or, you may want your text to flow onto an open path or into a closed path. You can link the text in these ways by using the Link box in the text block.

To link text between objects:

1. Select a text block you want to link to another object.

2. Using the Selection tool, drag from the Link box of the text block. You will see a wavy line extend out 🗲.

3. Drag the wavy line onto the object to which you want to link your text 🗲.

4. Release the mouse button. If you had an overflow of text, the text flows into the new object and you see arrows in the Link box.

TIP If you did not have an overflow, you still see arrows in the Link box. This indicates that if you add text or decrease the size of the first text box, the text will appear inside the new object.

TIP You can link text within a page or across pages.

Importing and Exporting Text

If you are working with long documents, you ought to import the text from a word processing program rather than typing it in FreeHand. To prepare text for exporting, in the word processor save your work in one of two formats:

- **RTF Text** (rich text format) keeps the text formatting.
- **ASCII** (pronounced As-kee) keeps only the characters without any formatting.

To import text:

1. Choose **File** > **Import** and choose the text file you want to import. Your cursor changes into a corner symbol **64**.

2. Position the corner symbol where you want your text to start.

3. If you want your text block to be a certain size on the page, drag the corner symbol to create a rectangle the size you want the text block to be **65**.

    or

    If you just want the text anywhere on the page, click. A text block is created and filled with text.

To export text:

1. Select the text blocks you want to export. If you select no text blocks, FreeHand exports all the text in the document.

2. Choose **File** > **Export**. This opens the Export Document dialog box **66**.

3. Name the file and specify its destination.

4. Choose one of the following formats:
    - RTF text.
    - ASCII text.

TIP Unlinked text blocks export in their stacking order from back to front, first page to last page.

64 *The* **corner symbol** *indicates that you have text ready for importing.*

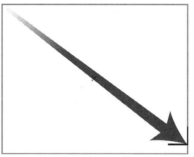

65 **Drag the corner symbol** *to size placed text.*

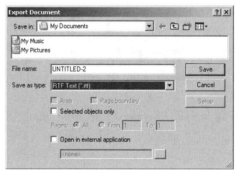

66 *The* **Export Document dialog box** *lets you choose a format to export text.*

TEXT TOOLS 19

Many years ago I wrote copy for print ads and direct mail letters. I'm a pretty fast typist so instead of writing out the text by hand, I typed my copy directly onto the page in the typewriter.

Years later, when I switched to writing on a computer, something interesting happened. Instead of quickly typing and finishing each job, I was more likely to spend more time fussing over each line of text.

I would try the copy with one set of words, and then change it to another set. I moved phrases from the top of the copy to the end. I was much more willing to spend time playing with the text—not because I suddenly became more fastidious about what I was writing, but because changing the words around was so easy.

Macromedia FreeHand offers you the same tools for editing text you'll find in any good, basic word processor.

Using the Text Editor

The Text Editor lets you view and change text all in one place without the formatting.

To open the Text Editor:

1. Select the text block or path with the selection tools, or click with the Text tool inside the text.

2. Choose **Text** > **Editor.** This opens the Text Editor dialog box ❶.

3. If desired, click 12 Point Black to view the type in that point size and color.

TIP Use this option when the text on the page has been styled in such a way that makes it difficult to read within the Text Editor. For instance, white text on a black background may be visible on the page but is not visible in the Text Editor.

4. Make whatever changes you want via the Text menu or the Object panel.

5. To see the text changes in the text block or path, click Apply. When you are satisfied with your changes, click OK.

TIP Hold the Opt/Alt key as you double click in a text block to open the Text Editor.

To open the Text Editor for a new text block:

◆ Hold the Opt/Alt key as you click with the Text tool. This opens the Text Editor and creates an auto-expanding text block.

or

Hold the Opt/Alt key as you drag with the Text tool. This opens the Text Editor and creates a standard text block.

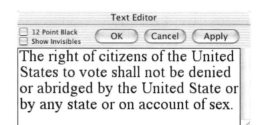

❶ *The* **Text Editor** *lets you work with text that might be difficult to read on the document page.*

Using the Text Editor

When vacancies happen in the Representation from any state, the executive authority thereof shall issue writs of election to fill such vacancies. The House of Representatives shall	choose their speaker and other officers; and shall have the sole power of impeachment.

When vacancies happen in the Representation from any state, the executive authority thereof shall issue writs of election to fill such vacancies.	The House of Representatives shall choose their speaker and other officers; and shall have the sole power of impeachment.

❷ *Text before (top) and after (bottom) inserting the* **End of Column character** *in front of the second paragraph.*

to which the Laws of Nature and of Nature's God

to which the Laws of Nature and of Nature's God

❸ *Text before (top) and after (bottom) inserting the* **End of Line** *character in front of the word "Laws."*

We congratulate Ms. DuPrât on her success.

We congratulate Ms. DuPrât on her success.

❹ *Text before (top) and after (bottom) inserting a* **Non-Breaking Space** *character before the name "DuPrât."*

Space Regular
Space   Em
Space En
Space Thin

❺ *Compare the spaces to see how the different types of* **spaces** *appear.*

Working with Special Characters

Special characters help improve the look of the text or control the flow of the text.

To use the special characters:

1. Place your insertion point where you would like the special character.
2. Choose **Text > Special Characters** and then choose from the submenu.

TIP You can also use keystrokes to insert the characters into your text as you type. *(See the sidebars on the next page.)*

End of Column

Inserts an invisible character that forces the text to the next column or next text block **❷**.

End of Line

Inserts an invisible character that forces the text to the next line **❸**.

Non-Breaking Space

Inserts a space that does not break across lines **❹**.

Em Space

Inserts a space the width of the type size **❺**.

En Space

Inserts a space one-half the width of the type size **❺**.

Thin Space

Inserts a space that is fixed as 10% of an em in width **❺**.

TIP A thin space is often used to add a small amount of space between characters. For instance, I use a thin space on either side of the greater than symbol when I give directions such as **Text > Special Characters**.

Working with Special Characters

Em Dash

Inserts an em dash, that is the length of one em (a typographic unit). It is used to indicate an abrupt change in thought .

En Dash

Inserts an en dash, that is the length of one-half em . It is used to indicate duration.

Discretionary Hyphen

Inserts a hyphen that is visible only if the word breaks across lines.

Invisible characters such as the End of column character do not print and are not visible on your page. However, you can use the Text Editor to view these invisible characters.

To see the invisible character:

1. Open the Text Editor and click the Show Invisibles box.
2. Invisible characters such as spaces, paragraph returns, end of column markers, and tabs show up in the text as gray symbols .

Pop-up menu

Nothing—I meant nothing.

April–July

 Compare how the different types of **dashes** *appear: (top to bottom) hyphen, em dash, en dash.*

 Show Invisibles *in the Text Editor let you see the nonprinting characters for tabs, returns, special spaces, and so on.*

Special Characters Keystrokes (Mac)	
End of column	Cmd-Shift-Enter
End of line	Shift-Enter
Non-breaking space	Alt-Spacebar
Em space	Cmd-Shift-M
En space	Cmd-Shift-N
Thin space	Cmd-Shift-T
Em dash	Alt-Shift-Hyphen
En dash	Alt-Hyphen
Discretionary hyphen	Cmd-Hyphen

Special Characters Keystrokes (Win)	
End of column	Ctrl-Shift-Enter
End of line	Shift-Enter
Non-breaking space	Alt-Spacebar
Em space	Ctrl-Shift-M
En space	Ctrl-Shift-N
Thin space	Ctrl-Shift-T
Em dash	Alt-1, 5, 1
En dash	Alt-1, 5, 0
Discretionary hyphen	Ctrl-Shift-Hyphen

8 *Use the* **Spelling dialog box** *to check the spelling in a document.*

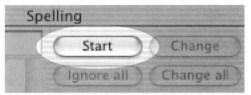

9 *Click the* **Start button** *to start a spell check.*

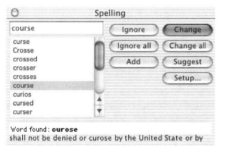

10 *The* **Spelling checker** *looks for unknown words, capitalization errors, and duplicate words.*

11 *The* **Change button** *changes the word to one of the suggested alternates.*

Checking Spelling

You may want to make sure the text in your document is spelled correctly. To do so, you can use the spelling checker.

To use the spelling checker:

1. Use the Selection tool to select the text block or path.

   or

   Place your insertion point at the point in the text where you would like the spelling check to start.

2. Choose **Text** > **Spelling**. The Spelling checker appears **8**.

3. To start checking the spelling of your text, click Start **9**. The spelling checker looks through the text and stops when it finds an error **10**.

TIP If no text blocks are selected, the spelling checker checks the entire document.

4. If the spelling checker finds a word it does not know, it displays the word in the top field. If possible, it shows alternates.

TIP The spelling checker is not a grammar checker or a proofreader. It does not find typos such as *He was reel good,* since the word "reel" is a known word.

To use the Change button:

1. If the original word is incorrect, choose one of the alternates from the list of suggestions.

2. If none of the alternates are correct, type the correct word and then click Change **11**. The incorrect word is deleted and the correct word is inserted.

Checking Spelling

To use the Change All button:

◆ If you suspect that other uses of the word are incorrect in the document, choose one of the alternates and then click Change All .

⑫ *The **Change all button** changes all instances of the word.*

To use the Ignore button:

◆ If the original word is correct, click Ignore ⑬. The spelling checker skips over that instance of the word, but stops again if the word is elsewhere in the text chain.

⑬ *The **Ignore button** skips the word.*

To use the Ignore All button:

◆ If all the instances of the original word are correct, click Ignore All ⑭. The spelling checker ignores all instances of that word until you quit that session of FreeHand.

⑭ *The **Ignore all button** skips all instances of the word.*

To use the Add button:

◆ If the spell check flags a word that is spelled correctly, click Add ⑮. This adds the word to the spelling dictionary and stops the spelling checker from identifying the word as mis-spelled in the future.

TIP To change how the spelling checker finds and adds words, change the spelling preferences (*see Appendix C*).

⑮ *The **Add button** adds the word to the dictionary that FreeHand uses during a spelling check.*

To use the Suggest button:

◆ To see the list of suggested words, click Suggest ⑯.

TIP To check the spelling of just a portion of a lengthy text block, use the Text tool to select just that portion and then run the spelling checker.

⑯ *Click the **Suggest button** to see the list of suggested alternates.*

Checking Spelling

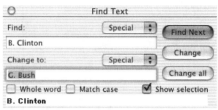

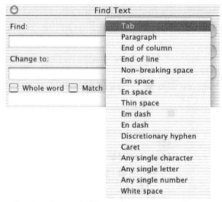

17 *The* **Find Text dialog box** *allows you to search and replace text strings or invisible characters.*

18 *The* **Special characters menu** *allows you to insert special characters into the Find and Change to fields.*

19 *The* **Find First button** *starts the search process.*

20 *The* **Change and Change All buttons** *allow you to make changes to the text.*

Replacing Text

If you are dealing with long passages of text, you may need to use FreeHand's Find Text dialog box.

To use the Find Text dialog box:

1. Place your insertion point in the text block, or select the text block or path with the selection tool.

2. Choose **Edit** > **Find & Replace** > **Text** to open the Find Text dialog box **17**.

3. In the Find field, type the text string you want to search for. In the Change to field, type the text string you want as a replacement.

4. To search for only the word listed, click the Whole word box. If you want to search for the text exactly as typed in uppercase and lowercase, click Match case.

5. Click to open the Special characters menus **18**. This lets you insert the codes for the special characters into the Find and Change fields.

TIP If you know the codes, you can type or paste them directly into the fields.

6. Click the Find First button to find the first instance of the text string **19**.

7. Click Change to change the text **20**.

    or

    Click the Find Next button to find the next instance of the text string.

    or

    Click Change All to change all occurrences of the text string **20**.

TIP To see the text currently being searched by the Find Text dialog box, click Show selection **17**.

Replacing Text

Working with Missing Fonts

When you open a FreeHand file that contains text, you need to have the fonts used in the text installed on your machine. If you don't have those fonts, you need to decide how the missing fonts are handled.

To work with missing fonts:

1. Open the FreeHand file. If the fonts are not installed on your machine, the Missing Fonts dialog box appears 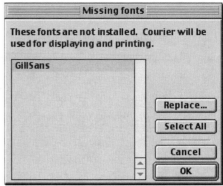.

2. Select one of the fonts listed in the dialog box.

   or

   Use the Select All button to select all the missing fonts.

3. Click the Replace button. This opens the Replace Font dialog box.

4. Use the Replace with menu to choose a font to replace the missing font .

5. Use the Text style menu to choose the type style for the font .

6. Click OK to make the replacement.

7. If necessary, repeat steps 2–6 for any additional missing fonts.

The Missing Fonts dialog box lets you know which fonts are not installed in the system.

Use the Replace Font dialog box to choose the typeface and text style for a missing font.

TEXT EFFECTS 20

With Macromedia FreeHand, you can create looks for text that would be difficult, if not impossible, to create using an ordinary page-layout program. This makes FreeHand an excellent choice for adding special effects to text.

For instance, FreeHand makes it easy to attach text to a path as well as apply special effects such as highlights and three-dimensional zooms.

You can also create more routine effects such as adding rules above and below paragraphs. You can also wrap text around graphics. You can also create inline graphics that allow images to become part of the text flow.

Finally, FreeHand lets you convert text into artwork that can be further modified.

Working with Text on a Path

One of the most popular effects in graphic design is to align text to a path. The path can be open or closed, with curve or corner points. The text can even be linked to other paths or text blocks.

To attach text to a path:

1. Select both the text block and the path to which you want the text aligned **❶**.

2. Choose **Text** >**Attach To Path.** The text aligns with the selected path **❷**.

TIP If you are aligning text to a closed path, such as an oval, insert a paragraph return in the text to align the text to both the top and bottom of the path **❸**.

TIP If the path is not long enough to display all the text, the overflow box fills.

TIP To remove text from a path, select the path and choose **Text** >**Detach From Path.**

TIP Use the Text tool to select text on the path.

To change the direction in which the text flows:

1. Hold the Opt/Alt key and click with the Pointer tool to select just the path.

2. Choose **Modify** > **Alter Path** >**Reverse Direction.** The text flows in the opposite direction **❹**.

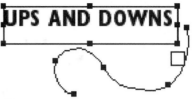

❶ *Text and a path selected.*

❷ *The results of applying the* **Attach To Path** *command.*

❸ **Insert a paragraph return** *to cause the text to attach to both sides of an ellipse.*

❹ *The* **Reverse Direction** *command causes the text (top) to change its direction (bottom).*

5 Drag the white triangle *next to the text to move the text along the path.*

6 *The* Text on a path options *in the Object panel.*

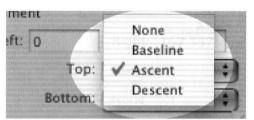

7 *Use the* Text Alignment menu *to control where the text sits in relation to the path.*

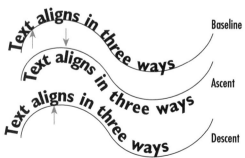

8 *The ways text can be aligned to a path.*

To move the text along the path:

1. With the Pointer tool, click the path. A small white triangle appears.

2. Drag the triangle to move the text in either direction along the path **5**.

You can control the vertical alignment of the text in relationship to the path. This is especially helpful if you have descending characters in the text.

To change the text alignment:

1. Click the Text on a path entry in the Object panel. This displays the Text on a path options **6**.

2. Use the Top and Bottom Text alignment pop-up menus to control where the text sits in relation to the path **7**:

   - **Baseline** puts the baseline of the characters on the path **8**.
   - **Ascent** puts the ascenders, such as the tops of the letter t on the path **8**.
   - **Descent** puts the descenders, such as the bottom of the letter g, sit on the path **8**.

   TIP The None option is not used to align the text, but rather indicates that no text is on the top or bottom of the path.

   TIP The Top menu controls text before any paragraph return. The Bottom menu controls text after any paragraph return.

You can also control the orientation of the text in relationship to the path. This allows you to simulate the look of 3D text rotating around an object.

To change the orientation and rotation:

Use the Orientation pop-up menu to change how the the text is oriented to the path **9**.

- **Rotate around path** keeps the text in a perpendicular orientation as it moves around the path **10**.
- **Vertical** makes each character stand up straight no matter how the path curves **10**.
- **Skew horizontal** exaggerates the text's horizontal tilt up to a 90° rotation and distorts the characters shapes as the text follows the path **10**.
- **Skew vertical** maintains a vertical rotation but distorts the characters' shapes as the text follows the path **10**.

To move text numerically:

- Set the amounts in the Left and Right Inset fields.

To display and print the path:

1. Check Show path in the Object panel.
2. Use the Fill and Stroke Inspectors to style the path.

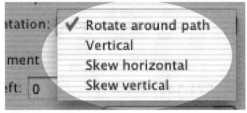

9 *Click the* **Remove Entry icon** *in the Object panel to remove a fill.*

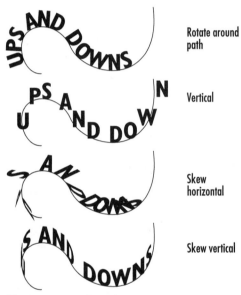

Rotate around path

Vertical

Skew horizontal

Skew vertical

10 *The ways text can be oriented to a path.*

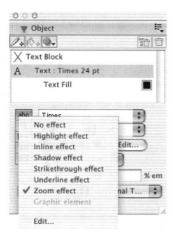

⑪ *Use the* **Text Effects menu** *of the Object panel to apply the special text effects.*

We, the people of the United States

⑫ *The* Highlight effect *on text.*

We, the ~~folks~~ people of the

⑬ *The* Strikethrough effect *on text.*

establish justice, ensure domestic

⑭ *The* Underline effect *on text.*

GO TEAM USA

⑮ *The* Inline *effect on text.*

We the People...

⑯ *The* Shadow effect *on text.*

⑰ *The* Zoom effect *on text.*

Special Text Effects

Perhaps some of the greatest unknown features in FreeHand are the special text effects. Quite frankly I've never seen any graphics or page-layout program offer anything like these effects.

To apply any of the special text effects:

1. Select the text.

2. Choose the Character options of the Object panel.

3. Choose one of the following from the **Text > Effect** submenu or the Text Effects menu in the Object panel **⑪**.

   - **Highlight** creates a color or tint block around the text **⑫**.
   - **Strikethrough** draws a line that runs across the text **⑬**.
   - **Underline** runs a line underneath the text **⑭**.
   - **Inline** creates a number of outlines around the text **⑮**.
   - **Shadow** adds a drop shadow image behind the text **⑯**.
   - **Zoom** adds a 3D perspective effect **⑰**.

4. Use the dialog box for each effect to edit the appearance of the effect. *(See the following exercises for how to edit the effects.)*

TIP You can turn the visual display of the text effects on or off by changing your Redraw preferences settings *(see Appendix C)*.

To change the settings for the text effects:

1. Select the text that has the effect.

2. Choose one of the effects from the **Text > Effect** submenu. The effect dialog box reopens.

   or

   Choose Edit from the Text Effect menu in the Object panel.

3. Make any changes to the effect settings.

Highlight, Underline, and Strikethrough effects are actually just variations on the same effect so the settings work the same way for all three.

To edit the Highlight, Underline, and Strikethrough effects:

1. Choose Highlight, Underline, or Strikethrough. The dialog box appears ⓲.

2. In the Position field, enter the distance from the baseline for the effect.

3. In the Stroke Width field, enter the value of the thickness for the effect.

4. To change the color of the effect, use the color pop-up menu.

5. To apply a dash pattern, choose a pattern from the Dash pop-up menu.

6. Overprinting is one way of compensating for slight misregistrations in the printing process. To allow the effect to overprint the original text, click Overprint.

The Inline effect creates outlines of strokes and colors that surround the text.

To edit the Inline effect:

1. Choose the Inline effect. The Inline Effect dialog box appears ⓳.

2. In the Count field, enter the number of sets of outlines you want to surround the text.

3. In the Stroke Width field, enter the width of the stroke ⓴.

4. To change the color of the stroke, choose from the color pop-up menu.

5. In the Background Width field, enter the width of the background color that will be between the stroke and the text ⓴.

6. To change the background color, choose from the color pop-up menu.

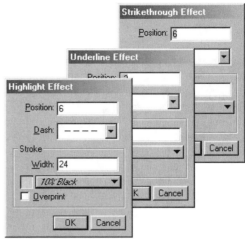

⓲ *The* **Highlight, Underline, and Strike-through effects dialog boxes** *all have the same settings.*

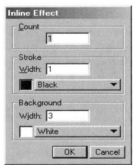

⓳ *The* **Inline Effect** *dialog box*

⓴ *The two elements of the Inline effect.*

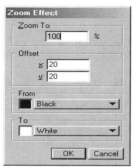

㉑ *The* **Zoom Effect** *dialog box.*

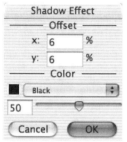

㉒ *The* **Shadow Effect** *dialog box.*

Zoom creates a 3D effect where the text has one look in the background and changes into another in the foreground.

To edit the Zoom effect:

1. Choose the Zoom effect. The Zoom Effect dialog box appears **㉑**.

2. In the Zoom To field, enter the percentage for the foreground object.

TIP A value of 100% keeps the foreground the same size as the background. A value greater than 100% makes the foreground object larger than the background for a greater perspective effect.

3. In the x and y Offset fields, enter the distance you want to move the foreground object from the original text.

4. To change the color of the background object, use the From pop-up menu.

5. To change the color of the foreground object, use the To pop-up menu.

The Shadow effect creates an automatic drop shadow behind the text.

To edit the Shadow effect:

1. Choose the Shadow effect. The Shadow Effect dialog box appears **㉒**.

2. Use the x and y Offset fields to control the distance that the shadow is positioned away from the text.

TIP The distance size is a percentage based on the point size of the text.

3. Use the Color menu to choose a color.

4. Use the Tint slider to lighten the color of the shadow.

Special Text Effects

Paragraph Rules

Rather than use the Line tool for each paragraph, FreeHand lets you create automatic paragraph rules 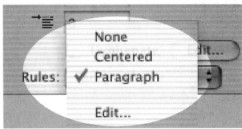. The benefit of paragraph rules is that you can add or delete text and the rules reflow with the text. Once again, this is the type of feature found in page layout programs—and hardly ever in illustration programs.

To create paragraph rules:

1. Select the paragraphs where you want the rules.

2. Choose the following from the Rule pop-up menu of the paragraph controls of the Object panel ㉔.

   - **Centered** positions the rule centered on the last line or column.
   - **Paragraph** moves the rule along with the alignment for the paragraph.

3. Make sure Display border is checked in the Object panel for the text block.

4. Click the Add Stroke icon in the Object panel.

5. Use the stroke controls to style the stroke for the rules. The rules appear under the paragraph that were selected.

To edit the paragraph rules:

1. Select the paragraph that you applied rules to.

2. Choose Edit from the Rule pop-up menu. This opens the Paragraph Rule Width dialog box ㉕.

3. Use the % field to set the length of the rule.

4. Choose the following from the pop-up menu:

   - **Last line** extends the rule the width of the last line of text.
   - **Column** extends the rule the width of the column.

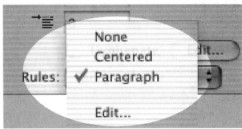

┌─────────────────────────────────┐
│   Senate Calendar: │
│   │
│   January 27 Senate convenes   │
│   at 12:00 Noon ET/9:00 am PT │
│   │
│ February 14 - 23 President's Day Recess │
│   │
│   April 3 - 20 Spring Recess │
└─────────────────────────────────┘

㉓ **Paragraph rules** *that are aligned to the text.*

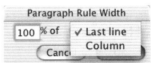

㉔ *The* **Paragraph Rules** *menu.*

㉕ *The* **Paragraph Rule Width** *controls.*

Runaround off

Flow Around Selection

Runaround on

Standoff

Left: 0

Right: 0

Top: 0

Bottom: 0

Cancel   OK

26 *The* **Flow Around Selection** *dialog box lets you enter the Standoff distances or how far the text is from the graphic.*

We hold these truths to be self-evident, that all men are created equal, that they are endowed by their Creator with certain unalien- able that among these are Life, Liberty and the pursuit of Happiness

Rights,

27 *A* **Text wrap** *around a graphic element.*

Working with Text and Graphics

FreeHand lets you position graphics so that the text automatically flows around the graphic. This is called text wrap or *run- around*.

To wrap text around a graphic element:

1. Select the graphic element you want the text to wrap around.

2. Move the graphic so that it is in the proper position in relation to the text.

3. Make sure the graphic is in front of the text block.

4. With the graphic still selected, choose **Text > Flow Around Selection.** This displays the Flow Around Selection dialog box **26**.

5. Click the Runaround on icon to display the Standoff distances fields. The Standoff is the space between the text and the edges of the graphic.

6. Enter the standoff amount for each side of the graphic.

7. Click OK when you are finished. The text automatically runs around the graphic **27**.

TIP To get more control over the flow, draw an outline around the object. Do not give this outline a fill or a stroke. Give this object the text wrap. You can then manipulate the outline to create a more precise text wrap.

To change a text wrap:

1. Select an object with a text wrap.

2. Choose **Text > Flow Around Selection**.

3. Change the amounts in the Standoff distances fields as necessary.

To undo a text wrap:

1. Select an object with a text wrap.

2. Choose **Text** > **Flow Around Selection**.

3. Click the top left icon of the FlowAround Selection dialog box.

You can also add inline graphics to text. This lets you create elements, such as ornate letters or logos, that are part of the text. So if the text reflows, the inline graphic flows along with the text.

To create an inline graphic:

1. Create the graphic you want to place inline. Examples of these graphics may be FreeHand objects, text on a path, text blocks, or placed TIFF or EPS images.

2. Use the Selection tool to select the graphic, and choose Copy or Cut from the Edit menu **28**.

3. Use the Text tool to place an insertion point in the text where you want the inline graphic.

4. Choose **Edit** > **Paste**. The inline graphic appears and flows along with the text **29**.

TIP To remove an inline graphic from text, use the Text tool to drag across the graphic as you would a text character. Choose **Edit** > **Cut** or **Edit** > **Clear**.

TIP To move the inline graphic up or down on the baseline, drag across the graphic as you would a text character. Change the Baseline shift.

TIP If you select an inline graphic, the Effects pop-up menu displays the words *Graphic Element*. Click Edit and use the Text Wrap dialog box to add more space around the inline graphic.

TIP If you select all the text in a text block, including the inline graphic, and then change the point size of the text, the inline graphic scales up or down along with the text.

We hold these truths to be self-evident, that all men are created equal

28 *To create an* **inline graphic,** *select the graphic and choose Copy or Cut.*

We hold these ⭐ truths to be self-evident, that all men are created equal

29 *The* **inline graphic** *as it appears within the text.*

30 *Text that has been* **converted to paths** *and manipulated as art.*

So far, all the effects you have created with text have kept the text as text. This means that you can still edit the text. There may be times, however, when you will prefer to convert the text to paths that can be worked with as graphic objects **30**.

To convert text into paths:

1. Use the Selection tool to select the text block or the text on a path you want to convert.

2. Choose **Text > Convert To Paths.**

TIP If you convert text aligned to a path, the path disappears, leaving only the text.

3. To manipulate the individual paths of the characters, choose **Modify > Ungroup** or hold the Opt/Alt key as you click each individual path.

TIP Text that has been converted to paths does not require fonts installed for it to print.

TIP You cannot change the font, spelling, or characters of text that has been converted to paths.

TIP Characters that have holes, such as the letters **A**, **O**, or **B**, are converted as a joined or composite path *(see page 102)*.

TIP Text must be converted to paths in order to use the Paste Inside command to have the text act as a mask *(see page 103)*.

TIP You must convert text to paths in order to apply most of the FreeHand and third-party Xtras that create special effects.

Working with Text and Graphics

STYLES AND SYMBOLS

If you have worked in a word processing program or a page-layout application, you may have used styles to automate text formatting. Macromedia FreeHand has both text styles and object styles. So in addition to changing text, you can use styles to change the fills, strokes, colors, and other attributes of objects.

Symbols are even more powerful than styles. If you have used Macromedia Flash, you are most likely very familiar with symbols. Unlike styles, which can only control an object's attributes, symbols let you control both an object's shape and attributes. As in Flash, FreeHand's symbols not only streamline the use of repetitive elements, they also help minimize file sizes.

Using styles or symbols, you can change the look of an entire document with just a few actions.

Using the Normal Styles

Every FreeHand document comes with three default "Normal" styles. These are the styles for drawing new objects, creating new text, or applying new connector lines.

To apply a Normal style:

◆ Draw an object, or type some text, or add a connector line. The Normal style is automatically applied.

TIP You can see the Normal styles highlighted in the Styles panel.

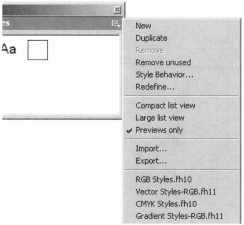

● *The* **Styles panel menu** *contains commands for working with styles.*

There are three display modes for the Styles panel.

To change the Styles panel display:

◆ Choose one of the following from the Styles panel ●:

• **Previews only** displays a thumbnail representation of the style in the Styles panel ❷.

• **Compact list view** displays a smaller thumbnail representation of the style with the name next to it ❷.

• **Large list view** displays a thumbnail representation of the style with the name next to it ❷.

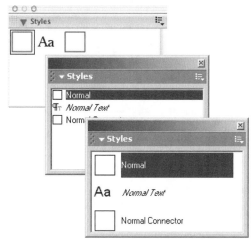

❷ *The* **three display options for the Styles panel** *from top to bottom: Previews only, Compact list view, Large list view.*

Using the Normal Styles

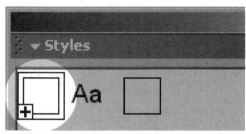

3 *The* plus sign in the Styles panel *indicates that modifications have been made from the original style.*

When to Use Styles

Most of my designer and illustrator friends would never be caught dead applying styles to objects. Their work is much too freeform to use the same styled object over and over.

However, my cartographer friends (map makers), use FreeHand's object styles extensively. They define a thick stroke to use as major highways and a thinner stroke for back roads. Then they apply the style to their artwork.

Also, people who use FreeHand to design Web pages use styles to maintain a consistent look for all their pages. That includes working with both object styles and text styles.

I use styles extensively when I create long-text documents—especially if I have copy with lots of subheads, lists, and captions.

Working with Styles

The three Normal default styles are hardly enough to work with. You need to define your own styles. The easiest way to define a style is to create the object or text and then use it as the reference to define the style.

To define a style by example:

1. Draw an object or type some text.
2. Use the Object panel to style the object or format the text.
3. With the object or text block selected, choose New from the Styles panel menu.
4. A new style appears in the Styles panel. This style contains all the attributes of the selected object.

TIP Text styles in FreeHand are paragraph styles—that is, they can not be applied to just some of the characters in a paragraph. If you need that type of local formatting, you need to do it manually.

You can also define a style by modifying the Normal styles with no object selected.

To create a style by modifying the Normal styles:

1. Deselect any objects.
2. Select one of the Normal styles. The style appears in the Object panel.
3. Use the Object panel to add or modify any of the attributes listed. A plus sign in the Styles panel indicates that the style has been modified **3**.
4. Choose New Style from the Styles panel. The new style appears with the default name Style-#.

You can also create a style by dragging the
Object panel preview into the Styles panel.

To create a style by using the Object panel:

1. Use the Object panel to create any set of
   attributes. It doesn't matter if an object is
   selected or not.

2. Drag the preview of the attributes from
   the Object panel onto an empty space in
   the Styles panel. The new style appears in
   the Library panel with the default name
   Style-# ❹.

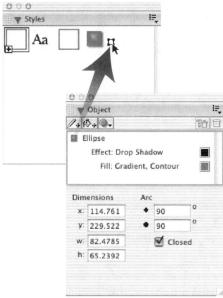

Once you have defined styles, you can then
apply them to objects.

To apply styles to selected objects:

1. Select the object that you want to apply
   the style to.

2. Click the style in the Styles panel.

❹ **Drag the Object panel preview** *into the
Styles panel to create a new style.*

To apply styles to unselected objects:

◆ Drag the style swatch from the Styles
  panel onto the object ❺.

❺ **Drag the style swatch** *onto an object to
apply the style.*

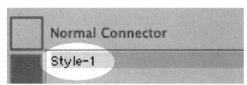

❻ *Double-click the name of a style to change the style name.*

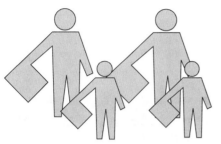

❼ *The style for these objects was defined with a 20% black fill and a black stroke.*

❽ *Redefining the style to a black fill and white stroke changed all the artwork without selecting any objects.*

❾ *This alert box lets you choose to redefine a style or create a new style.*

Once you add a style, it is easy to change the name of the style.

To rename a style:

1. Choose Large list view or Compact list view from the Styles panel menu to see the style names.

2. Double-click the name of the style in the Styles panel to highlight the name ❻.

3. Type the new name of the style.

4. Press Return or Enter to apply the new name.

Styles do more than just make it easy to apply formatting. If you redefine a style, you also change the appearance of all the objects that have that style applied to them ❼ and ❽. There are several different ways to redefine styles.

To redefine a style by dragging:

1. Drag the attribute preview from the Object panel onto the style swatch in the Styles panel. A dialog box appears.

2. Click Redefine to change the style based on the attribute preview ❾. Any objects that have the style applied are automatically updated.

   or

   Click New style to create a new style based on the attribute preview.

Working with Styles

To redefine a style using the Styles panel:

1. Use the Object panel to create a set of attributes.

2. Choose Redefine from the Styles panel. The Redfine style dialog box appears ❿.

3. Choose the style you want to change.

4. Click OK to change the style.

To redefine a style using the Object panel:

1. Deselect any objects or text.

2. Select the style you want to redefine.

3. Use the Object panel to modify the attributes of the style.

4. Click the Attributes: Redefine button in the Object panel ⓫.

To duplicate a style:

1. Choose the style you want to copy.

2. Choose Duplicate from the Styles panel menu. A new style with the preface *Copy of* appears.

To remove a style:

1. In the Styles panel, click the name of the style you want to delete. Use the Shift key to select any additional styles you want to delete.

2. Choose Remove from the Styles panel menu. The style is deleted.

TIP If you delete a style that has been applied to objects or paragraphs, those objects or paragraphs keep their attributes.

To remove an unused style:

◆ Choose Remove Unused from the Styles panel menu. All styles not applied to objects or text are removed.

❿ *The* **Redefine Style dialog box** *lets you choose which style should be redefined.*

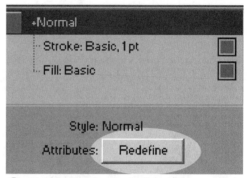

⓫ *Click the* **Attributes: Redefine button** *in the Object panel to change the style definition to the current attributes.*

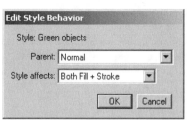

⓬ *The* **Edit Style Behavior dialog box** *to apply a parent style to a child style.*

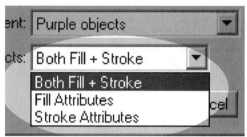

⓭ *Use the* **Style affects menu** *to choose which attributes a parent style should change.*

Original Parent style

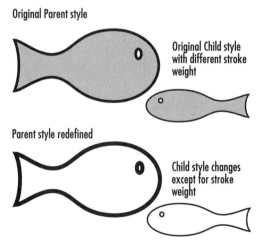

Original Child style with different stroke weight

Parent style redefined

Child style changes except for stroke weight

⓮ *An example of what happens in a* **Parent and Child** *relationship when the Parent style is changed.*

You can also set one style to act as the master of other styles. This is called a *style behavior.* Think of a style behavior as similar to the relationship between a parent and child. The child style changes according to changes applied to the parent—which is *not* true of most real parents and kids!

To apply a style behavior:

1. Define two object styles or two text styles in the Styles panel.

TIP To make it easier to understand Parent/Child styles, define only one difference (for instance, stroke weight or point size) to the second style.

2. Select the second style and choose Style Behavior from the Styles panel menu. The Edit Style Behavior dialog box appears **⓬**.

3. In the Edit Style Behavior dialog box, use the Parent menu to choose the style you want to govern the child style.

4. Use the Style affects menu to choose how the parent style affects the child **⓭**.

5. Click OK. The child style is now linked to the parent style.

TIP One Parent style can have many different Child styles based on it.

To work with parent and child styles:

◆ Use the Object panel or the Styles panel *(see the exercises on the previous page)* to redefine the attributes for the Parent style. Notice how the changes have been applied to the objects or paragraphs. Only those attributes that are shared by both the Parent and Child styles will change after editing the Parent style **⓮**.

Working with Styles

Importing and Exporting Styles

You don't have to define new styles every time you open a new FreeHand document. You can easily import styles you've already defined from other FreeHand documents.

To import styles:

1. Choose Import from the Styles panel menu.

2. Navigate to find the FreeHand document you want to import styles from.

3. Click Choose/Open. The Styles Library for that document appears ⓯.

4. Select the styles that you want to import.

5. Click Import. The styles are imported from one document into another.

TIP FreeHand ships with four files called *Button Styles, Gradient Styles, Raster Styles,* and *Vector Styles.* You can open these object styles by choosing from the Styles panel menu.

TIP If you copy an object or text with a style and paste it into a new document, the object or text styles appear automatically in the second document.

You can also export styles from a document. This is useful if you want to create a library of just a few of the styles used in a file.

To export styles:

1. Choose Export from the Styles panel menu. The styles for the document appear ⓰.

2. Select the styles you want to export.

3. Click Export. The Save File dialog box appears.

4. Name the document and file it in the location you want.

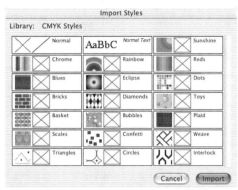

⓯ *The* **Import Styles dialog box** *lets you choose styles from one document to import into another.*

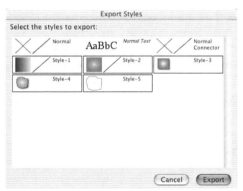

⓰ *The* **Export Styles dialog box** *lets you choose the style in a document to export.*

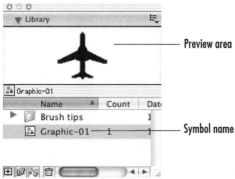

⑰ *A new symbol appears in the Library under the name Graphic-01.*

⑱ *Use the Library panel menu to create and control symbols.*

New Symbol
New Group
Swap Symbol
Remove

⑲ *The Library icons let you create and control symbols.*

Working with Symbols

Symbols are even more powerful than styles. Symbols can be made from paths with a variety of strokes and fills, groups, or text blocks.

To create a symbol using the menu commands:

1. Select the object you want to convert into a symbol.

2. Choose **Modify** > **Symbol** > **Convert to Symbol**. This creates a symbol of the selected object and makes the selected object into an instance of that symbol ⑰.

   or

   Choose **Modify** > **Symbol** > **Copy to Symbol**. This creates a symbol of the selected object, but the selected object remains unchanged and does not become an instance of the new symbol.

TIP New symbols appear in the Library and are given the name Graphic-##.

To create a symbol using the Library:

1. Select the object you want to convert.

2. Choose New Graphic from the Library menu ⑱.

   or

   Click the New Symbol icon at the bottom of the Library ⑲. This creates a symbol of the selected object but leaves the original object unchanged.

To duplicate a symbol:

1. Select the symbol you want to duplicate.

2. Choose Duplicate from the Library menu. A new symbol appears with the prefix Copy of before the name.

To change the name of a symbol:

1. Choose Rename from the Library menu. This highlights the name ②⓪.

2. Type the new name for the symbol.

TIP You can also double-click to highlight the name.

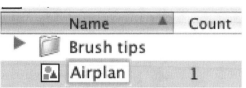

②⓪ *To rename a symbol, highlight the name of the symbol and then type the new name.*

An *instance* is a representation of a symbol that changes when you change the appearance of the symbol. Once you have a symbol in the Library you can apply instances of the symbol in your document.

TIP The actual symbol itself is never on the document page. Only the instance is applied on the page.

To create instances of a symbol:

1. Select a symbol from the Library.

2. Drag the symbol from the preview area or from the list onto the page ②①. This creates an instance of the symbol.

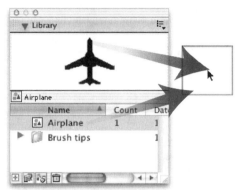

②① *Drag the symbol preview or symbol name from the Library onto the page to create an instance of that symbol.*

Working with Instances

When you have an instance of a symbol on a page, there are some tools and commands you can use on the instance and others that you can't.

Select	Yes	
Subselect		No
Modify fill or stroke		No
Move	Yes	
Resize	Yes	
Transform	Yes	
Use Freeform tool		No
Copy	Yes	
Cut	Yes	
Paste	Yes	
Edit or modify text		No

Recognizing Instances

Unfortunately there is little difference between the appearance of instances and ordinary artwork.

Here are a few ways to tell if you have selected the instance of a symbol:

An instance of a symbol displays no options for either fill or stroke in the inspectors or the Tools panel.

You can't select any of the points of an instance with the Subselect tool.

Document name

Symbol icon | Symbol name

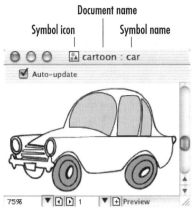

○ ○ ○ | cartoon : car

☑ Auto-update

75% ▼ ◁ ▷ 1 ▼ ⊞ Preview

㉒ *The* **Symbol window** *is where you edit the artwork for a symbol.*

Nesting Symbols

One special technique for working with symbols is to use the instance of one symbol to be part of the artwork for another symbol. This is called nesting symbols **㉓**. When you nest symbols, you can edit the nested symbol and it changes all the instances in the document—including those instances used in other symbols.

㉓ *Instances of the Wheel are used as* **nested symbols** *in the Car symbol. Editing the Wheel changes both instances used in the Car.*

Once you create a symbol, you edit the graphics that are used in the symbol in the Symbol window. If you have created any instances of the symbol, the instances are modified.

To open the Symbol window:

1. Select the instance of the symbol you want to edit.

2. Choose **Modify** > **Symbol** > **Edit Symbol**.

   or

   Double-click the Preview Area of the Symbol in the Library.

   or

   Double-click the icon of the Symbol in the Library.

   or

   With the symbol selected in the Library, choose Edit from the Library menu.

To make changes in the Symbol window:

1. In the Symbol window, use any of the tools or commands to modify the object.

2. Check the Auto-Update option at the top of the Symbol window to see the changes in the document window as you make the changes to the symbol.

3. Close the Symbol window. The changes are applied to all instances.

TIP You can tell you're working in the Symbol window by the following clues **㉒**:

- The name of the symbol follows the document name in the title bar
- A symbol icon appears in the title bar.

Although you can't edit an instance on the page, you can release it so that it is an ordinary graphic.

To release an instance:

1. Select the instance.

2. Choose **Modify > Symbol > Release Instance.** This converts the symbol into an ordinary graphic which can be edited like a regular graphic.

You can also use the Library to replace a symbol with new artwork.

To replace a symbol:

1. Create the new artwork for the symbol.

2. Drag the artwork onto the name of the original symbol. An alert dialog box is displayed **24**.

3. Click one of the following buttons:

   - **New Symbol** creates a new symbol from the artwork dragged into the Library.

   - **Replace** changes the original symbol to the new artwork. All instances of the symbol are also changed **25**.

   - **Convert** changes the original symbol to the new artwork. All instances of the original symbol are converted into ordinary graphics.

   TIP When one symbol replaces another, the new instances inherit any transformations previously applied **25**.

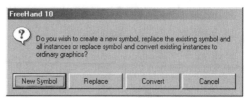

24 *An alert box lets you control how artwork should be added to the Library.*

Transformed instances

25 *The female icon was replaced by the male icon. Transformations applied to the first symbol's instances were applied to the new instances.*

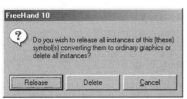

26 *An alert box lets you control what happens to the instances of a symbol that is removed.*

The Two Other Types of Symbols

As mentioned earlier, master pages are actually a type of symbol. Although master pages are created using the Document inspector, they are stored in the Library with the other symbols. When you apply a master page, you are actually applying instances of the symbol to the page. That's why you can't edit any of the master page items.

The artwork for brushes are also symbols. However, their instances are stretched or duplicated along the brush path. When you edit the brush shape, you are editing the symbol. Then those edits are applied to the instances applied to the path.

You can also select instances or objects on the page and apply a new symbol to those instances or objects.

To swap the symbol applied to instances or objects:

1. Select the instances or objects on the page.

2. Choose the new symbol you want to apply to those instances or objects.

3. Click the Swap Symbol button at the bottom of the Library panel. The instances and objects are replaced with instances of the new sysmbol.

TIP Transformations are maintained during the swap.

To delete a symbol:

1. Click the name of the symbol.

2. Click the Remove Symbol icon in the Library.

   or

   Choose Remove from the Library menu. If the symbol is in use, an alert dialog box appears **26**.

3. Choose one of the following from the alert dialog box:

   • **Convert/Release** changes all instances into ordinary art.

   • **Delete** removes the symbol and its instances.

Working with Symbols

As you work, you may find it helpful to organize your symbols into different categories. These categories can be for each graphic, category, or page—you decide whatever is right for you.

To create a symbol group:

◆ Click the New Group icon in the Library ㉗.

or

Choose New Group from the Library menu.

To add symbols to a group:

◆ Drag the symbol from the Library list into the group ㉘.

To open or close a group:

◆ (Mac) Click the twist triangle in the Library list ㉙.

or

(Win) Click the plus or minus signs in the Library list ㉚.

To delete a group:

1. Select the name of the group.
2. Click the Remove icon.

or

Choose Remove from the Library menu.

New Group

㉗ *The* **New Group** *icon lets you create groups to help organize symbols.*

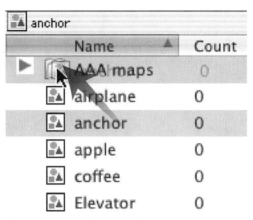

㉘ *Drag a symbol into a group to organize the symbols in the Library.*

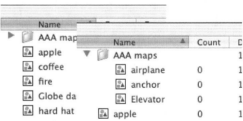

㉙ *(Mac) Use the twist triangle to open and close the groups in the Library.*

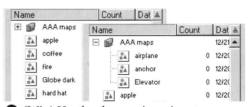

㉚ *(Win) Use the plus or minus signs to open and close the groups in the Library.*

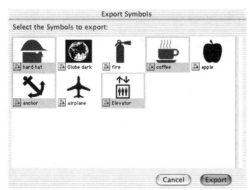

③ *Choose the symbols you want to export from the* **Export Symbols dialog box.**

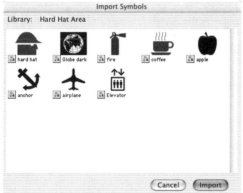

③ *Choose the symbols you want to import from the* **Import Symbols dialog box.**

Importing and Exporting Symbols

Symbols created in one document can be exported as libraries that can then be opened for use in other documents.

To export symbols:

1. Choose Export from the Library panel menu. The Export Symbols dialog box opens **③**.
2. Select the symbols you want to export.
TIP Use the Shift key to select a range of symbols. Use the Cmd/Ctrl key to select non-adjacent symbols.
3. Click Export. The Save *(Mac)* or Export Symbols *(Win)* panel opens.
4. Assign a name to the library you are creating and click Save.

You can import symbols from any FreeHand document.

To import symbols:

1. Choose Import from Library panel menu. The operating system dialog box opens.
2. Navigate to the document you want to import symbols from and click Choose/ Open. The Import Symbols dialog box opens **③**.
3. Select the symbols you want to import.
TIP Use the Shift key to select a range of symbols. Use the Cmd/Ctrl key to select non-adjacent symbols.
4. Click Import. The symbols appear in the Library of the current document.

Importing and Exporting Symbols

Changing the Library Display

You can also control how the Library panel displays symbols.

To change the order of the symbol display:

◆ Click the controls in the Library as follows **33**:

- **Name** arranges the items alphabetically.
- **Count** arranges the items by the number of times they are used in the document.
- **Date** arranges the items by their creation date.
- The **toggle triangle** reverses the order of the list **34**.

To hide or show the symbol previews:

◆ Choose Preview from the Library menu to hide the display of the symbols in the Library. Choose Preview again to show the symbol displays.

To display or hide the graphic symbols:

◆ Choose Show Graphics from the Library menu to hide the graphic symbols in the Library. Choose Show Graphics again to show the graphic symbols.

To display or hide the master page symbols:

◆ Choose Show Master Pages from the Library menu to hide the master page symbols in the Library. Choose Show Master Pages again to show the master page symbols.

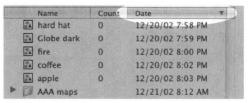

33 *Click the* **category** *button to order symbols by their name, count, or date.*

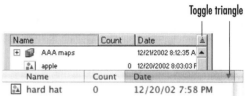

34 *Click the Toggle triangle to see the items in reverse sort order.*

AUTOMATING FREEHAND 22

As you have seen, styles and symbols let you make changes to many objects at once. Unfortunately both styles and symbols require some advance preparation for them to be helpful.

So what happens if you want to make changes to a file that doesn't have any styles or symbols? Fortunately, there is another way to quickly make changes to objects using the Find & Replace panel.

This chapter is all about automating repetitive tasks and getting your work done as efficiently as possible.

Note: If you are paid by the hour and saving time through increased productivity is not important to you, please feel free to skip this chapter entirely!

Finding and Replacing Graphics

This is one of the most sophisticated features of its kind. I know of no other graphics program that lets you search for such a wide range of objects and then change them into something else. For instance, you can find all objects with a certain shape and change them to another without losing the original fill and stroke settings.

To use the Find & Replace Graphics:

1. Choose **Edit > Find and Replace > Graphics.** This opens the Find & Replace panel.

2. Click the Find and Replace tab to open that section 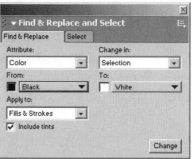.

3. Use the Attribute menu to select those features you want to find ❷. Each attribute displays different choices for the From and To sections. *See the exercises that follow for specifics on how to set each attribute.*

4. Set the Change in menu as follows ❸:

   • **Selection** searches only the selected objects.

   • **Page** searches through just the current page.

   • **Document** searches through all the pages and the pasteboard.

5. Set the From choices on the left side of the box to select the features or what you want to find the objects.

6. Set the To choices on the right side of the box to select the features you want to end up with in the objects.

7. Click Change. FreeHand automatically changes the objects from one set of attributes to another.

TIP The number of objects that change is listed at the bottom of the Find & Replace panel ❹.

❶ *The* **Find & Replace panel** *of the Find & Replace and Select dialog box.*

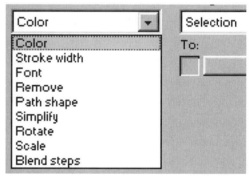

❷ *The* **Attribute choices** *that can be changed using the Find & Replace feature.*

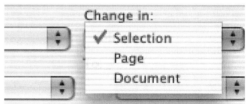

❸ *The* **Change in menu** *lets you control where the replacements are made in the document.*

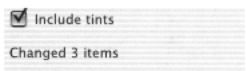

❹ *The* **number of changed items** *document is displayed at the bottom of the panel.*

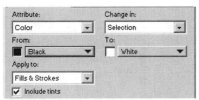

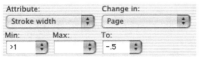

⑤ *The* **Color section** *of the Find & Replace panel.*

⑥ *The* **Apply to menu** *of the Find & Replace panel.*

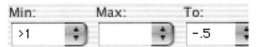

⑦ *The* **Stroke width section** *of the Find & Replace panel.*

Min: Max: To:

⑧ *In this example, FreeHand will find all stroke widths greater than 1 point and decrease their size by .5 points.*

The color attributes allow you to find one color and replace it with another.

To set the color attributes:

1. Use the color list under the From side to choose the color that you want to find **⑤**.

2. Set a color under the To side that you want to replace.

TIP These choices are the named colors listed in the Swatches panel.

3. Set the Apply to menu to change only fills, only strokes, or fills and strokes **⑥**.

4. Check Include tints to change (or find) tints of the swatches.

The stroke width attributes allows you to search and replace the size of strokes applied to objects.

To set the stroke width attributes:

1. With Stroke width selected, enter a value in the Min field to specify the smallest stroke width to find **⑦**. For example, you can search for all 1 pt. strokes.

2. Leave the Max field blank.

TIP Use the greater than (>) or less than (<) signs to find strokes larger or smaller than the specified weight **⑧**.

3. Enter the new stroke width in the To field. For example, you can change the stroke weight to .5 pt.

Platform Differences

Look carefully, and you'll see there is a slight difference between the Macintosh and Windows versions of the Find & Replace panels. On the Windows platform, the panel can be docked with the other onscreen panels. The Macintosh panel can not be docked. Also, the name of the panel is called *Find & Replace and Select* for Windows. It is *Find & Replace Graphics* for Macintosh. Rather than list both names, I'll refer to them both as the *Find & Replace* panel in this book.

Finding and Replacing Graphics

You can also set a range of stroke widths to replace.

To set a range of stroke width values:

1. Enter a value in the Min field to specify the smallest stroke width to find.

2. Enter a value in the Max field to specify the largest stroke width to find.

3. Enter the new stroke width in the To field. This lets you change all the strokes to an absolute amount such as .5 pt.

   or

   Use the + or - sign before a number in the To field to increase or decrease all the stroke widths by that amount. For instance, if you enter +2 pt, then all the strokes will be increased by 2 points.

   or

   Use the * sign before a number in the To field to multiply all the stroke widths by that amount 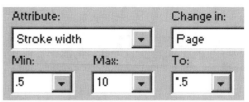. For instance, if you enter *.5, then all the strokes will be changed to 50% of their size.

In this example, FreeHand will find all stroke widths from .5 to 10 points and then decrease them to 50% of their size.

Find & Replace Strategies

For most work, you shouldn't have to rely on the Find & Replace panel. As you work, you can place objects on their own layers or in groups to make it easier to select them later.

You can also assign styles or create symbols to make it easier to change many objects at once.

However, if you are a production person working on files that were not created carefully, the Find & Replace panel is very helpful.

Changing Stroke Weights

Most of my students can't imagine any reasons why they might need to search and replace stroke weights. Before you move to the next page, consider the following.

Every time you scale objects up or down, you may change the stroke weight applied to those objects. This means that all your .5- and 1-point strokes may scale down to .1 and .2 points. Those weights are just too small to be printed correctly.

Rather than manually changing the stroke weight, it is much easier to use the Find & Replace panel. You can set the minimum weight to .1 point and the maximum to .2 point. Then you enter an amount of .5 point for all the objects. That weight can be printed correctly.

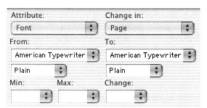

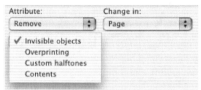

⑩ *The* **Font section** *of the Find & Replace panel.*

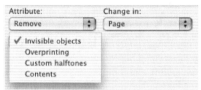

⑪ *The* **Remove choices** *of the Find & Replace panel.*

Selecting and Replacing Text Attributes

The Find & Replace controls let you search for various text attributes such as font, point size, text effects, and type styles in a text block.

But these commands can't find text attributes that are selectively applied to only some of the text in a text block. They only work if the attribute has been applied to all the text in the text block.

If you need to make to change individual words within a text block, you need to use the **Edit > Find and Replace > Text** command *(covered on page 289)*.

You can also search and replace for text attributes.

To set the font attributes:

1. Set a typeface in the From side that you want to find **⑩**.

2. Set a typeface in the To side that you want to replace.

3. Set the style in the From side.

4. Set the style in the To side.

5. Set the point sizes to search for in the Min and Max fields in the From side.

6. Set the point size in the Change field.

TIP Leave the point size fields empty to find all type sizes.

TIP You can use the <, >, +, –, or * characters to specify the point size values.

You may discover that you have applied attributes to objects that you want to remove. The remove attributes list lets you search for those attributes and remove them from the objects.

TIP The remove attributes are especially useful for production managers who may need to fix a file before printing.

To set the remove attributes:

◆ With Remove selected, choose one of the following from the list **⑪**:

- **Invisible objects** deletes all objects with no fill or stroke settings.

- **Overprinting** removes any overprint setting applied to fill or strokes.

- **Custom halftones** removes any special halftone settings applied to objects *(see page 405)*.

- **Contents** removes any objects pasted inside other objects.

This may sound impossible, but you can even ask FreeHand to look for all objects that have a certain shape and replace them with another object.

To set the path shape attributes:

1. Copy an object that has the same shape as the ones you want to find 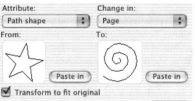.

2. Click the Paste in button in the From side. The shape appears in the Preview box.

3. Copy an object that you want to replace.

4. Click the Paste in button in the To side.

5. Check Transform to fit original to keep any transformations that were applied to the original objects.

TIP This feature is very useful if you have many objects on the page that you want to turn into a symbol. Search for the object shape and then paste in an instance of the symbol. The object will be replaced with instances of the symbol.

⑫ *The* **Path shape choices** *in the Find & Replace panel show the shapes being searched and replaced.*

The simplify attributes allow you to search for objects that have a certain number of points and then simplify them so they have fewer points. This is especially helpful if you use clip art that have many points in its objects. Simplifying makes it easier to modify the artwork and easier to print it.

To set the simplify attributes:

1. With Simplify selected, enter the number of points in the Apply to paths with field ⑬.

TIP Use the < or > signs in front of the number to find objects with less than or greater than a number of points.

2. Set the slider to set the amount of simplification to be applied to the object. *(See page 110 for information on using the Simplify command.)*

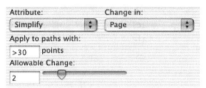

⑬ *The* **Simplify options** *of the Find & Replace panel.*

Path Shape Expectations

There are limitations to the miracle of searching for specific path shapes. For instance, although the path shapes may be exactly the same, the command won't find objects that have different number of points.

However, the Find & Replace command will find rectangles that are different sizes and proportions. The command looks at the number of points in the object and the angles of the line segments.

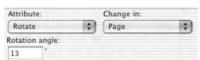

⓮ *The* **Rotate options** *of the Find & Replace panel.*

Tool or Command?

When you use the Rotation tool on multiple items, the items rotate as a group around a single transformation point. When you use the Find & Replace Rotate on multiple items, each item rotates individually around its center point. This creates a different effect than the Rotation tool or transform command **⓯**. The same is true for the Find & Replace Scale command.

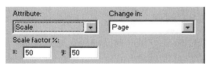

⓯ *The Rotation tool (left) rotates the items as a group. The Find & Replace Rotate command (right) rotates each item individually.*

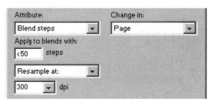

⓰ *The* **Scale options** *of the Find & Replace panel.*

⓱ *The* **Blend steps options** *of the Find & Replace panel.*

The rotate attributes allow you to change the orientation of many objects.

To set the rotate attributes:

◆ With Rotate selected, enter a rotation amount in the Rotation angle field **⓮**.

The scale attributes allow you to change the scaling applied to objects.

To set the scale attributes:

1. Enter a horizontal scale amount in the x field **⓰**.
2. Enter a vertical scale amount in the y field.

TIP Like the Rotate attributes, the Scale attributes command scales objects from their own center points. This means that each of the objects in a group will increase their individual size rather than increasing the overall size of the group.

The default number of blend steps is 25. If you're like me, it is possible to create many blends and then realize they all have the wrong number of steps. The blend steps attributes allow you to quickly change the steps in all the blends in the document.

To set the blend steps attributes:

1. Enter the number of steps to find in the Apply to blends with field **⓱**.

TIP Use the < or > signs in front of the number to find blends with less than or greater than a number of steps.

2. Choose from the following options:
   - **Change** lets you enter a number of steps to change the blend to.
   - **Resample** at lets you set a resolution amount. The blend is then changed so that it looks smooth at that resolution.

Finding and Replacing Graphics

Selecting Graphics

The other tab of the Find & Replace dialog box opens the Select panel. Although not quite as powerful as the other side of the panel, the Select commands let you find many more types of objects. Once you have found the objects, you can manually change them, or move them to separate layers, or apply styles to them.

To select objects by attribute:

1. Choose **Edit > Find & Replace > Graphics** to open the Find & Replace panel.

2. Click the Select tab to open that panel of the dialog box .

3. Use the Attribute menu to specify those features you want to select . Each attribute displays different choices to control what objects are selected. *See the exercises that follow for specifics on how to set each attribute.*

4. Set the Search in menu as follows 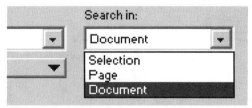:
   - **Selection** searches only the selected objects.
   - **Page** searches through just the current page.
   - **Document** searches through all the pages and the pasteboard.

5. Choose Add to selection to add the selected object to the objects currently selected.

6. Click Find. The objects that fit the search criteria are selected.

TIP The number of objects found in a search are listed at the bottom of the Select tab of the Find & Replace dialog box.

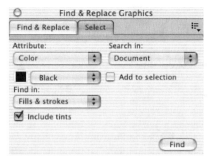

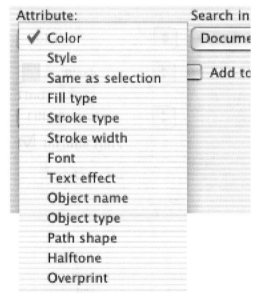

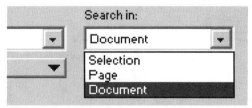

⑱ *The* **Select panel** *of the Find & Replace dialog box.*

⑲ *The* **Attributes choices** *that can be selected using the Select panel.*

⑳ *The* **Search in menu** *controls where the selections will be made.*

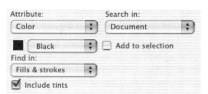

㉑ *The* **Color options** *of the Select panel.*

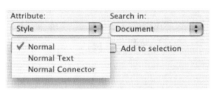

㉒ *The* **Style options** *of the Select panel.*

㉓ *The* **Select same as selection options** *of the Select panel.*

You may need to select all the objects that have the same color applied to them. For instance, you may want to make sure that extremely dark swatch colors have not been applied to very small text or strokes.

To set the color attributes:

1. Use the color menu to select a color that you want to find **㉑**.

TIP These choices are the named colors in the Swatches panel.

2. Set the Find in menu to find only fills, only strokes, or fills and strokes.

3. Check Include tints to find tints of the color.

You may want to select all the objects that have been formatted with a particular style.

To set the style attributes:

♦ Use the style list to choose the style that you want to find **㉒**.

TIP Text styles must be applied to the entire text block, not just part of the text.

Sometimes the easiest way to organize items is to group them if they have the same fill or stroke attributes. This can be easily done by selecting one object and finding all the others just like it.

To set the same as selection attributes:

1. Select the object that you want to use as the model for the selection.

2. Use the Match list to choose which attributes should be the same in the final selection **㉓**.

Selecting Graphics

You may find that you need to change all
the objects styled with a particular fill. For
instance, if you are printing to an ink jet
printer, the custom fills will not appear. In
that case, you can select all those particular
fills and change them.

To set the fill type attributes:

1. Use the Fill menu to select the type of fill
   as follows 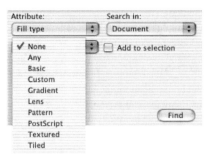:

   - **None** chooses objects that have no fill
     type.
   - **Any** chooses an object that contains
     any type of fill.

   or

   - Choose one of the fill types to find a
     specific fill.

2. If you have chosen the Gradient fill, use
   the Gradient menu to select the type of
   gradient as follows 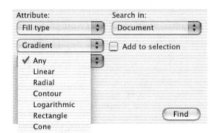:

   - **Any** chooses an object that contains
     any gradient fill.

   or

   - Choose one of the gradient types to
     find a specific gradient.

Just as you can select a particular type of
fill, you can also select objects that have a
particular type of stroke.

To set the Select stroke type attributes:

- Use the Stroke menu to select the type of
  fill as follows :

  - **None** chooses objects that have no
    stroke type.
  - **Any** chooses an object that contains
    any type of stroke.

  or

  - Choose one of the stroke types to find a
    specific stroke.

*The **Fill type options** of the Select tab of the Find & Replace dialog box.*

*The **Gradient menu** of the Select panel.*

*The **Stroke type options** of the Select panel.*

Selecting Graphics

27 *The* **Stroke width options** *of the Select tab of the Find & Replace dialog box.*

28 *The* **Font options** *of the Select tab of the Find & Replace dialog box.*

Selection Strategies

Although the Selection tab only selects objects, that doesn't mean you can't then make changes to the selection.

Once you have run the selection command, you can easily apply a style to all the selected objects. You can use the Swap Symbol command *(see page 315)* to change the ordinary objects into instances of a symbol.

You can also move objects to a separate layer or group them to make it easy to select them later on.

You can also select objects by their stroke width.

To set the stroke width attributes:

1. With Stroke width chosen, enter a value in the Min field to specify the smallest stroke width to find **27**.

2. Enter a value in the Max field to specify the largest stroke width to find.

TIP Leave the Max field blank to select a specific stroke width.

TIP Use the greater than (>) or less than (<) signs to find strokes larger or smaller than the specified weight. *(See the exercise on page 322 on changing stroke width using these characters.)*

To set the font attributes:

1. With Font chosen, set a typeface that you want to find **28**.

2. Set the style that you want to find.

3. Set the point sizes to search for in the Min and Max fields in the From side.

TIP Leave the point size fields empty to find all type sizes.

TIP Use the < or > characters to search for point sizes less than or greater than a specific size.

TIP Text styles will only be selected if they're applied to the entire text block, not just part of the text.

If you need to, you can select any text blocks that contain special text effects.

TIP To be found, the text effect must be applied to the entire text block, not just part of the text.

To set the text effect attributes:

◆ Use the Effect menu to select the type of effect as follows :

- **Any effect** chooses a text block that contains any text effect.

  or

- Choose one of the text effects to choose a specific effect.

29 *The* **Text effect options** *of the Select panel.*

Objects can also have names applied to them. You can then search for all objects with a specific name.

To set the object name attributes:

◆ Enter the name of the object that you want to find in the object name field .

TIP The object name is applied using the Set Note command *(covered on page 332)*.

Object name field

30 *The* **Object name options** *of the Select panel.*

Sometimes it is necessary to search for a particular type of object.

To set the object type attributes:

1. Use the list to choose the type of object you want to find 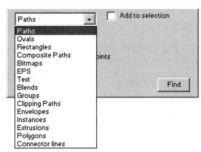.

2. If you choose Paths, you can choose to find open paths only or paths with a certain number of points .

TIP Use the greater than (>) or less than (<) signs to find objects with a larger or smaller number of points.

31 *The* **Object type options** *of the Select panel.*

32 *The* **Path options** *of the Object type controls Select panel.*

③ *The* **Path shape options** *of the Select panel.*

③ *The* **Halftone options** *of the Select panel.*

③ *The* **Overprint options** *of the Select panel.*

You can also select objects that have the same shape.

To set the path shape attributes:

1. Copy the path that has the shape you want to find.

2. With Path shape chosen, click the Paste in button **③**. The path appears in the preview box.

3. If you want to select objects that may or may not have the same fill or stroke, select the options as follows:

   - **Shape** searches for objects with the same shape.
   - **Fill** searches for objects with the same fill.
   - **Stroke** searches for objects with the same stroke.

A custom halftone means that the object has a special type of screen applied to it. Your production house may ask you to change that custom halftone.

To set the halftone attributes:

♦ Choose Halftone from the attributes menu to select all objects that have a custom halftone applied **③**. *(See page 405 for more information on working with custom halftone screens.)*

You may want to adjust the colors in objects that have overprinting applied to them.

To set the Select overprint attributes:

♦ Choose Overprint from the attributes menu to select all objects that have an overprint applied **③**. *(See pages 210 and 404 for more information on working with overprinting.)*

Selecting Graphics

Copying and Pasting Attributes

While not as powerful as styles or the Find & Replace dialog box, there is another way to quickly make changes to graphic attributes.

To use Copy Attributes

1. Select an object with a set of attributes that you want to apply to another object.

2. Choose **Edit > Special > Copy Attributes**.

To use Paste Attributes:

1. Select the object or objects that you want to change.

2. Choose **Edit > Special > Paste Attributes**. The second object does not change its shape but does change its attributes, such as fill and stroke, to match the first 🗣.

Naming Objects

You can name an object using the Navigation panel.

TIP The primary use of the Navigation panel is to add actions to objects that are used in SWF files. *(For more information, see Chapter 27, "Animations and Actions.")*

To name an object:

◆ In the Navigation panel, enter a name for the object in the Name field 🗣.

🗣 **Copy Attributes** *was applied with the hat in the left image selected. The hat, pants and shoes of the right image were selected and* **Paste Attributes** *was applied.*

🗣 *Use the* **Name** field in the Navigation panel *to name an object.*

CHARTS AND GRAPHS 23

Here's where Macromedia Free-Hand gets down to business—creating mathematically correct charts and graphs. Even if you don't understand the mathematics of graphs—and I know few designers who do—you can still create exceptional graphs using FreeHand's charts and graph commands.

Whether column graphs or piecharts, FreeHand gives you the tools to transform data into visually appealing information.

Unfortunately, the integrity of the data can be easily compromised when translated into a graphic display. For an excellent study on maintaining graphical integrity in charts, see *The Visual Display of Quantitative Information* by Edward R. Tufte, published by Graphics Press.

Creating Charts or Graphs

To create a chart or graph, you need to open a *worksheet* and enter the data.

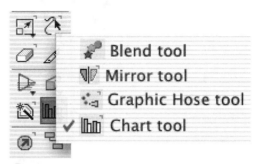

● *The* **Chart tool** *selected from its toolset in the Tools panel.*

To open the worksheet:

1. Choose the Chart tool in the Tools panel ●.

2. Drag the + sign cursor to create a rectangle on your work page. (The size of the rectangle determines the size of the chart.) The Chart worksheet appears ●.

Each piece of data is entered into the cells in the worksheet. If you have a very simple chart, you can enter the data directly into the worksheet.

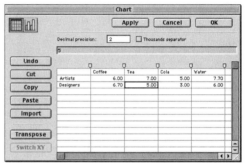

● *The* **chart worksheet** *is where you enter data for a chart or graph.*

To enter data:

1. Click the cell where you want to enter data ●.

2. Type the data in the data entry area at the top of the worksheet area ●.

3. Apply the data and navigate to new cells as follows:

   • Press Return or Enter to apply the data to the cell and move to the cell below. Type the data for that cell.

   • Press Tab to apply the data to the cell and jump to the cell to the right.

   • Use the up, down, left, or right arrow keys to move to different cells.

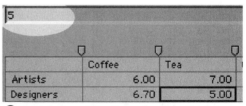

● *Type information for each cell in the* **data entry area** *at the top of the worksheet.*

You can also import data created from a spreadsheet program. This data must be saved as *tab-delimited text.*

To import data:

1. Click the Import button.

2. Navigate and select the text file. The data is imported into the cells of the worksheet.

Creating Charts or Graphs

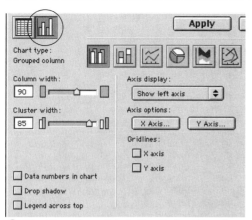

❹ The **Chart icon** (circled) switches from the worksheet to the controls for styling charts and graphs.

Once you have entered the data, you choose the type of graph or chart you will create.

To style a graph or chart:

1. Click the Chart icon at the top of the Chart window. The worksheet disappears and the styling selections appear **❹**.

2. Click one of the six chart type icons **❺**: grouped column, stacked column, line, pie, area, and scatter.

TIP To see the effects of changing the style and features of your graph, click Apply at the top of the Chart window.

TIP Use the Subselect tool to select an individual element in a chart.

To modify an existing chart:

◆ With the chart selected, double-click the Chart tool in the Xtra Tools toolbar.

 or

 Choose **Xtras > Chart > Edit.** The Chart worksheet opens.

TIP Don't ungroup a chart or graph, or you will lose the link to the worksheet information.

Type of Chart	Icon ❺	When to use it
Grouped Column Graph		Use a grouped column graph to compare data. Each bar represents one data cell.
Stacked Column Graph		Use a stacked column graph to compare the progress of data. Each stacked bar represents one row of data.`
Line Graph		Use a line graph to compare the trend of data over time. Each line represents a column of data.
Pie Chart		Use a Pie chart to display data as percentages of the total. Each wedge represents one data cell. Each row creates a separate chart.
Area Graph		Use an area graph to compare the trend of data over a period of time. Each area represents a column of data. Each column's value is added to the previous column's total.
Scatter Graph		Use a scatter graph to plot data as paired sets of coordinates. Each coordinate represents a row of data containing two cells.

Creating Charts or Graphs

Formatting Column Graphs

Once you have entered data in the worksheet and picked the style of the graph, you can still modify various elements of the graph. These controls change depending on the type of graph selected.

To change the column width:

1. Click the icon for grouped column or stacked column graphs.

2. To change the width that each column takes up within its cluster, drag the slider or enter the amount in the Column width field **6**.

3. Click Apply to see the effects on the graph **7**.

To change the cluster width:

1. Click the icon for a grouped column or stacked column graph.

2. To change the width of the cluster of the columns, drag the slider or enter the amount in the Cluster width field.

3. Click Apply to see the effects on the chart **8**.

All the graphs except area graphs let you display the data values in the graph itself.

To show the data values:

◆ Click the Data numbers in chart checkbox to see those values.

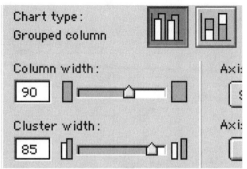

6 *The controls for* **Column width** *are available for grouped column and stacked column graphs.*

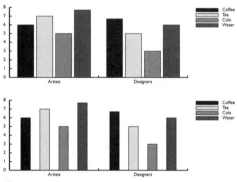

7 *A* **column width** *of 85 (top) and 50 (bottom).*

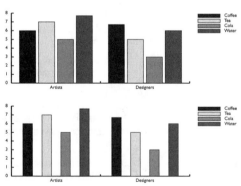

8 *A* **cluster width** *of 90 (top) and 50 (bottom)*

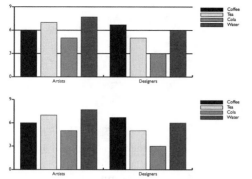

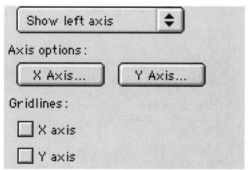

❾ *X axis* **gridlines** *turned off (top) and turned on (bottom).*

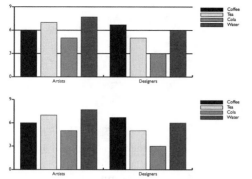

❿ *The* **Gridlines** *boxes show and hide the* **x** *axis and* **y** *axis gridlines.*

Charts are always created using shades of black. However, you can change the colors applied to the charts.

To color a chart:

◆ Drag colors onto individual elements.

   or

   Subselect objects and change them through the color list.

TIP You can also use the Find and Replace Graphics dialog box to change each color globally.

All the graphs except line and scatter graphs let you add a drop shadow behind the graph.

To add a drop shadow:

◆ Click the Drop shadow checkbox to see the effect.

Each of the graphs can contain a *legend* which explains what the different colors or symbols for the chart represent. You can choose where the legend is positioned.

To reposition the legend:

◆ Click the Legend across top checkbox. This repositions the legend from the top-right corner to across the top of the chart.

All the graphs except the pie chart allow you to control whether or not gridlines are displayed along the x or y axis **❾**.

To create gridlines:

1. Check the **x** axis box to display horizontal gridlines.

2. Check the **y** axis box to display vertical gridlines **❿**.

Formatting Column Graphs

337

The most powerful part of modifying a column graph is in working with the x (horizontal) axis and the y (vertical) axis.

To modify the axis values:

1. With a chart selected and the Chart dialog box open, click either the x axis or y axis buttons under Axis options. The Options dialog box appears **⓫**.

2. Under Axis values, click Calculate from data if you want the numbers along the axis to be calculated from the data entered in the worksheet.

   or

   Under Axis values, click Manual to enter your own values for the axis.

3. Choose the following from the Major Tick marks pop-up menu **⓬**:

   - **Across axis** positions the tick marks so they straddle the axis.
   - **Inside axis** positions the marks inside the axis line.
   - **Outside axis** positions the marks outside the axis line.

4. Choose the following from the Minor Tick marks pop-up menu:

   - **Across axis** positions the tick marks so they straddle the axis.
   - **Inside axis** positions the marks inside the axis line.
   - **Outside axis** positions the marks outside the axis line.

   TIP Many designers like to position the major tick marks across the axis, and the minor tick marks inside the axis **⓭**.

5. Enter the number of minor tick marks in the Count field.

6. Use the Prefix and Suffix Axis value labels to add a prefix (such as $) in front of the data or a suffix (such as /hour) after the data in the axis.

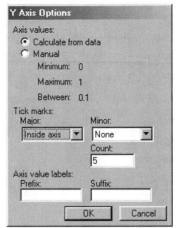

⓫ *The* Y Axis Options *dialog box.*

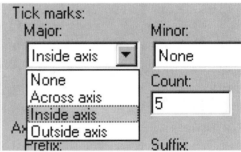

⓬ *The* Tick marks Options.

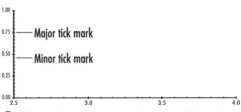

⓭ *The display of major and minor tick marks.*

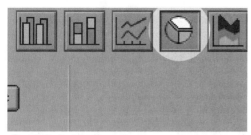

⑭ *Click the* **Pie chart icon** *to see the options.*

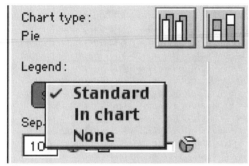

⑮ *The* **Legend options** *for a pie chart.*

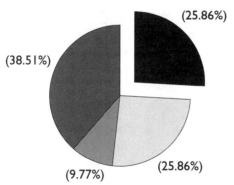

⑯ *A* **Separation amount** *of 28 has moved the black wedge away from the rest of the pie chart.*

Working with Pie Charts

When you create a pie chart, you have special controls for working with the wedges.

To create a pie chart:

◆ Click the pie chart icon in the Chart dialog box. The pie chart options appear **⑭**.

To modify a pie chart legend:

◆ Choose the following from the Legend pop-up menu **⑮**:
   • **Standard** positions the legend on the side of the chart.
   • **In chart** positions the legend next to each wedge.
   • **None** hides the legend.

The first cell of data creates a wedge that can be moved away from the other segments.

To change the wedge separation:

◆ Drag the slider or enter an amount in the Separation field. This moves the first wedge away from the rest of the chart **⑯**.

TIP To enter numbers as labels, not graph data, insert quotation marks around the numbers. For example, the year 1997 would be entered as "1997."

Working with Pictographs

FreeHand also lets you put graphics into the columns of your charts. These graphics, called *pictographs*, give visual representations of the type of data being shown.

To insert a pictograph in a chart:

1. Find the graphic that you would like to have in the chart.

   TIP You can use a FreeHand graphic or an imported file as the pictograph image.

2. Select the graphic and copy it.

3. Select one column of the series to which you want to apply the pictograph.

4. Choose **Xtras** > **Chart** > **Pictograph.** The Pictograph dialog box appears.

5. Click Paste in. The copied graphic appears in the preview window **⓱**.

6. To repeat the graphic within the column, click the Repeating box. To stretch a single graphic within the column, leave the box unchecked.

7. Click OK. The Pictograph replaces the column of the chart **⓲**.

   TIP Use the Copy out button to copy the pictograph artwork to the clipboard. You can then paste the pictograph artwork onto the FreeHand page to modify the pictograph.

⓱ *The* **Pictograph box,** *where you can paste in a graphic to represent data.*

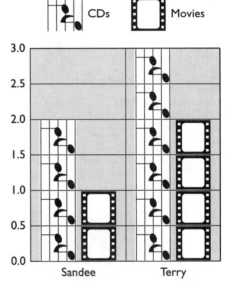

⓲ *An example of a chart that uses repeating pictographs for the columns.*

RASTER IMAGES 24

When my artist friends and I first started using drawing programs such as Macromedia FreeHand, we had the slightly arrogant attitude that we would never mix raster images with vector objects. Somehow we felt vector artwork was "too pure" to be mixed with photographs and scanned images.

But it soon became very clear to all of us that it was a great idea to add photographs and scanned artwork to FreeHand documents. This allowed us to use FreeHand as a complete page-layout program.

You can easily import raster images onto the FreeHand pages and work with them the same way you would in programs such as QuarkXPress or Adobe InDesign. In fact, just as Freehand gives you more options for styling text, it also offers you more options for working with raster images than are found in a typical page layout program.

Importing Raster Images

FreeHand has several different ways to import raster images into a document. *(See page 350 for how to import Fireworks raster images.)*

To import artwork using the File menu:

1. Choose File > Import.

2. Use the dialog box to find the image you want to import. The cursor changes into a corner symbol ❶.

TIP If you are going to print your artwork, import a TIFF or EPS file.

3. Click the corner symbol to import the file in its original size.

   or

   Drag the corner symbol to set the image to a specific size ❷.

TIP Unless you have changed the Import Preferences settings, the placed image is a proxy that's only linked to the FreeHand file. You must send the original image along with the FreeHand file for it to print properly.

To import artwork by copying and pasting:

1. Open the file from which you want to import artwork.

2. Select the artwork you want to import and copy it to the clipboard.

3. Bring the FreeHand document to the front and choose **Edit > Paste**.

TIP The artwork is imported as a group which becomes an embedded TIFF when ungrouped. *(See pages 347—348 for understanding embedded images.)*

TIP (Mac) You can drag and drop artwork from other applications onto the FreeHand document.

❶ *The* **corner symbol** *indicates that you have a file ready for importing.*

❷ **Drag the corner symbol** *to resize an image as you place it.*

3 *Drag a corner handle to change the size of an imported image.*

4 *The* **Object panel** *lets you resize images.*

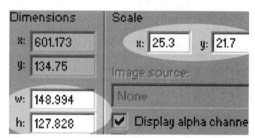

5 *Use the* **Scale x or y fields** *to change the width (w) or height (h) fields of a placed image.*

Modifying Raster Images

Once you have imported an image, there are many ways to modify that image.

To resize raster images by dragging:

1. Place the Pointer tool on one of the corner handles of the raster image.

2. Drag to change the size of the image **3**.

TIP Hold the Shift key to retain the horizontal and vertical proportions of the image.

To resize raster images numerically:

1. With the image selected, open the Object panel **4**.

2. Enter a percentage in the **Scale x** and **y** fields to change the size of the image **5**.

   or

   Enter an actual amount in the **w** and **h** fields.

3. Press Return or Enter to apply the changes.

TIP Enter the same percentage in both the **Scale x** and **y** fields to resize the object proportionally.

If you only know one dimension that you want to change, you can change the object's size proportionally.

To change the object's size using one dimension:

1. Enter the amount that you want to change the object in either the **w** or **h** field. A percentage appears in one of the scale fields.

2. Copy the percentage that appears in the scale field and paste it into the other field so they are equal. The object is scaled proportionally.

You can also use any of the transform commands to modify a raster image.

To transform a raster image:

1. Double-click the image.

2. Use the transformation handles to rotate, skew or scale the image ❻.

    or

    Use any of the transformation tools (rotating, scaling, reflecting, skewing) to modify the image.

❻ *You can modify raster images with the transformation handles or the transformation tools.*

FreeHand also lets you change the color of grayscale or black-and-white TIFF, PICT, and BMP images.

To colorize a raster image:

1. Select a black-and-white or grayscale image.

2. Drag a color swatch from the Color List or Color Mixer onto the color box for the image in the Object panel ❼.

    or

    Drag a color swatch onto the image ❽.

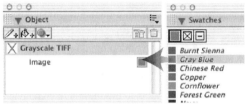

❼ **Drag a color swatch** *onto the Image color box to colorize a grayscale TIFF or PICT image.*

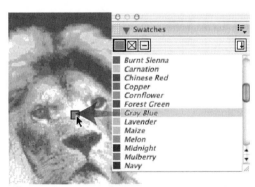

❽ **Drag a color swatch** *onto black-and-white or grayscale TIFF or PICT to colorize the image.*

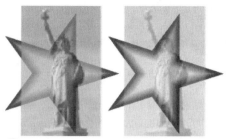

9 *An example of how the transparency effect changes the opacity of a raster image.*

Before, an opaque image   After, a transparent image

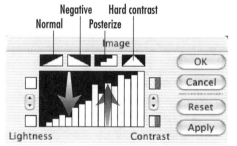

10 *The results of applying the* **Transparent option** *to a grayscale image.*

Negative   Hard contrast
Normal   Posterize

11 *Drag the bars up or down to* **change the appearance of the raster image.**

You can apply any of the raster effects to raster images. This includes applying the transparency effect to the image *(see page 249)*. However, that transparency is applied uniformly to the black and white areas of the image **9**. A different effect is created by making just the white areas of an image transparent.

To make a raster image transparent:

1. Select a grayscale image.

2. Click Transparent in the Object panel. This sets the white areas of the image to be transparent. This lets objects behind your image show through the transparent areas **10**.

TIP The image must be grayscale or the Transparent checkbox will not be active.

FreeHand also lets you change the shade, or lightness and contrast, of grayscale or black-and-white TIFF, PICT, and BMP images.

To change the shade of an imported image:

1. Select a black-and-white or grayscale image.

2. Click the Edit button in the Object panel. The Image dialog box appears **11**.

3. Click the controls for Lightness or Contrast.

   or

   Adjust the slider bars.

   or

   Click one of the preset controls.

TIP You can change the shade or color of a portion of an image by putting one of the transparency lens fills over a raster image *(see page 203)*.

Modifying Raster Images

Rasterizing Graphics

Importing graphics isn't the only way to get raster images into FreeHand. You might want to convert FreeHand's vector graphics into their pixel-based equivalents.

TIP You automatically convert vector objects to pixel-based images when you apply any of the raster effects.

To rasterize an image:

1. Select the vector objects you want to convert.

2. Choose **Modify > Convert to Image.** The Convert to Image dialog box appears **⑫**.

3. Set the resolution to the amount you need.

TIP Most print work uses a resolution of 300 dpi. Web graphics need only 72 dpi.

4. Set the anti-aliasing amount. This smooths lines or edges in the image with a slight blur.

TIP High resolutions and high anti-aliasing require more memory for the FreeHand application.

5. Click OK. The objects turn into rasterized art embedded in the file **⑬**.

TIP If you have converted vector objects using the raster effects, you control the resolution using raster effects resolution settings *(see page 243)*.

⑫ *The* **Convert to Image** *dialog box controls how artwork is converted into a raster image.*

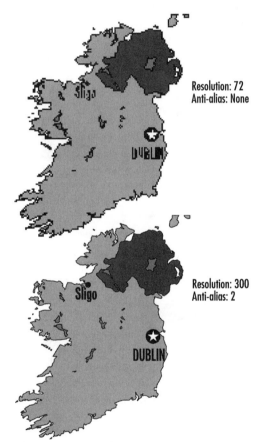

Resolution: 72
Anti-alias: None

Resolution: 300
Anti-alias: 2

⑬ *The result of using the Rasterize command at two different resolutions and anti-aliasing amounts.*

⑭ *The* **Links** *buttons at the bottom of the Object panel.*

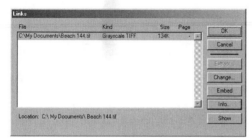

⑮ *The* **Links dialog box** *shows a list of all the imported images in the FreeHand file.*

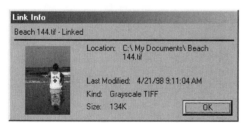

⑯ *The* **Link Info dialog box** *displays the specific information for each linked image.*

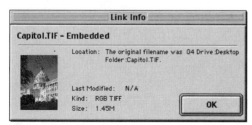

⑰ *The Link Info dialog box also shows the former name for embedded images.*

Linking and Embedding Images

As mentioned earlier, the images you import into FreeHand are not actually included in the file. Rather, these proxy images are linked to the original raster file. FreeHand makes it easy to work with linked images.

To view the link information:

1. With the raster image selected, click the Links button in the Object panel **⑭**.

   or

   Choose **Edit** > **Links**. This opens the Links dialog box **⑮**.

2. Click the Info button. This opens the Link Info dialog box which contains the specific information for the imported image **⑯**.

Ordinarily, you want to keep raster images linked to their outside files. This helps reduce the size of the FreeHand file. However, if the imported image is small enough, you can embed it in the FreeHand document. When you embed an image, the FreeHand file contains all the information necessary to print and edit the file.

TIP When you apply any of the raster effects to an image, it is automatically embedded in the FreeHand document.

To embed a linked image:

1. Select the name of the linked image in the Links dialog box.

2. Click the Embed button. FreeHand changes the status of the file from linked to embedded.

TIP The Link Info dialog box displays the information for an embedded image including the original filename **⑰**.

Linking and Embedding Images

FreeHand looks for linked images where they were when imported. If you move a linked file, a missing link is created.

To open a file with a missing link:

1. Open the file. The Locate file dialog box alerts you that the link is missing 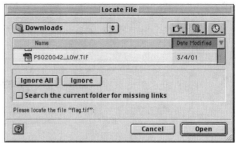.

2. Click the Ignore All or Ignore buttons to open the file without updating the link.

   or

   Navigate to find the missing link file.

3. Click Search the current folder for missing links to update any additional missing links.

You can also update missing links using the Links Info dialog box.

To update a missing link:

1. Open the Links Info dialog box. The missing link is displayed in italics 🔟.

2. Select the missing link entry.

3. Click the Change button 🔟 *(previous page)*. This opens the Open dialog box.

4. Navigate to find the missing link and click Open. This re-establishes the link.

Embedded images add to the file size. So you might want to turn the embedded images into proxy images linked to an external file.

To extract an embedded image:

1. Select the image that is embedded in the FreeHand file.

2. Click the Links button in the Object panel to open the Links dialog box.

3. The Extract button opens the Save (Mac) or Extract Import (Win) dialog box. This lets you choose a name and destination for the extracted image.

🔟 *Use the* **Locate** *dialog box to re-establish the link to a linked image.*

🔟 *The italic typeface and question marks indicate that an imported file is missing its link.*

Linking and Embedding Images

20 *This dialog box asks you to confirm that you want to edit the image in another application.*

21 *The* **Editing in Progress** *dialog box lets you choose when you have finished editing a file in an external application.*

Editing Raster Images

You can use commands within FreeHand to open the application, such as Macromedia Fireworks or Adobe Photoshop, that created the linked image. This lets you easily modify the image and update it in the FreeHand file.

To edit an image with an external application:

1. Select the image you want to edit.

2. Choose **Edit** > **Edit in External Editor**. A dialog box asks to confirm that you want to open an external application **20**.

3. Click OK. This opens the image using the application specified in the Object preferences *(see Appendix C)*.

TIP If you have not specified an external editing application, a dialog box appears which asks you to choose an application. This application becomes the default until you change it in the Preferences dialog box.

4. When you have completed your edits, save your changes in the external application.

5. Return to your FreeHand document and click Done in the Editing in Progress dialog box to implement your changes or click Cancel to leave the graphic as it was **21**.

TIP You can also activate the external editing function by holding the Opt/Alt key and double-clicking on a graphic.

Working with Fireworks

There's a special relationship between Macromedia FreeHand and Macromedia Fireworks. This includes how FreeHand imports Fireworks files. It also lets you use Fireworks as FreeHand's raster editing program.

TIP Do not use Fireworks to edit images if you need to maintain an image as a grayscale or CMYK document. Fireworks will always convert those files into RGB documents.

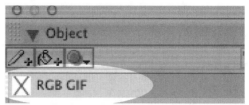

② *A flattened Fireworks file appears as a single image in the Object panel.*

There are two types of Fireworks files that can be imported into FreeHand documents. Native Fireworks PNG files are special types of pixel-based images that contain separate objects and layers. Exported Fireworks files are GIF, JPEG, TIFF, or PNG files that are flattened into a single raster image. Exported images should be used when you don't need to manipulate the individual objects in the file. *(See the Fireworks MX Visual Quickstart Guide published by Peachpit Press for more information on working with Fireworks.)*

To import flattened Fireworks files:

1. Choose **File > Import** and select the file that was exported from Fireworks. The corner symbol appears.

2. Drag or click the corner symbol to place the image in the FreeHand document. The file appears as a single raster image ②.

Working with Fireworks and FreeHand

A native Fireworks PNG file can look a lot like a FreeHand page. In both cases, individual objects can be stacked on top of each other; objects can appear in layers; and each of the objects can be styled with fills, strokes, and effects. If you import a native Fireworks PNG file into FreeHand, each object is converted into a separate FreeHand item. This allows you to change the stroke, fill, or effects applied to the object. You can also edit text.

When you optimize and export a Fireworks file, all the objects are flattened into one raster image. This image can be used in a FreeHand document, but you can't edit the individual objects. The benefit of importing a flattened image is that you don't have to worry about inadvertently moving or changing the objects.

Fortunately, FreeHand allows you to have the best of both types of Fireworks files. You can import flattened images, but still edit the original Fireworks file *(see page 352)*.

23 *The* **Fireworks PNG Import Settings** **dialog box** *let you set how the objects from a native Fireworks file are imported into the FreeHand document.*

24 *The* **File Conversion menu** *lets you control how Fireworks frames are imported into FreeHand documents.*

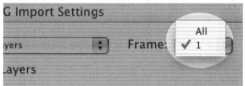

25 *The* **Frame menu** *lets you choose which frames are imported into the FreeHand file.*

Native Fireworks PNG files should be used if you want to modify the imported Fireworks objects in the FreeHand document.

To import native Fireworks files:

1. Choose **File** > **Import** and select the native Fireworks PNG file. The Fireworks PNG Import Settings dialog box appears **23**.

    TIP You can also use **File** > **Open** to open Fireworks PNG files.

2. Choose one of the following from the File Conversion menu **24**:
    *   **Open frames as pages** opens each Fireworks frame as a separate page.
    *   **Open frames as layers** converts the frames into FreeHand layers.

3. Use the Frame menu to choose a specific frame or all the frames **25**.

    TIP All is available if you select the Open frames as layers option.

4. Check Remember Layers to keep the Fireworks objects on their original layers.

5. Choose one of the Objects options:
    *   **Rasterize if necessary to maintain appearance** may convert Fireworks objects into rasterized objects.
    *   **Keep all paths editable** will force the Fireworks objects into FreeHand objects. This may change the objects' appearance.

6. Choose one of the Text options:
    *   **Rasterize if necessary to maintain appearance** may convert Fireworks text into rasterized text.
    *   **Keep all text editable** converts Fireworks text into FreeHand text.

7. Check **Import as a single flattened bitmap** to convert the Fireworks objects into a single pixel-based image.

Working with Fireworks

You can use Fireworks as the image editor to make changes to imported files. However, if the imported image came from a native Fireworks PNG file, you can open the Fireworks PNG file. This allows you to place flattened files in FreeHand, and yet retain the ability to edit the layered Fireworks objects.

To edit placed images with Fireworks:

1. With the image selected, click the Edit with Fireworks button in the Object panel . The Find Source for Editing dialog box appears .

2. Click the Yes button to launch Fireworks and open the original layered Fireworks file. If necessary, you may be prompted to locate the original Fireworks PNG file.

   or

   Click the No button to launch Fireworks and open the flattened verson of the file.

3. Make whatever changes you want to the file.

   TIP The special Done button at the top of the document window indicates you are working in a special "launch-and-edit" session of Fireworks 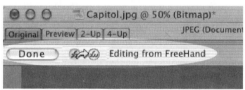.

4. Click the Done button to close the Fireworks document and return to the FreeHand file. The changes you made are automatically applied to the imported file.

   TIP Use the menu in the Find Source for editing dialog box to choose one of the following:

   - **Always Use Source PNG** will always open the PNG source file.
   - **Never Use Source PNG** will always open the flattened file.
   - **Ask When Launching** will open the dialog box .

26 *The* **Edit with Fireworks button** *is used to launch Fireworks to edit placed images.*

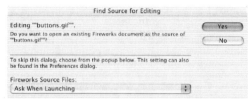

27 *The* **Find Source for Editing dialog box** *lets you choose to edit the placed file or the original Fireworks source file.*

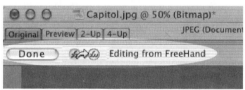

28 *The* **Done button and logo information** *indicate that Fireworks is editing a FreeHand image.*

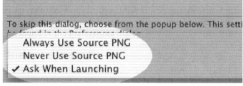

29 *Use the menu in the Find Source for Editing dialog box to control how Fireworks files are opened.*

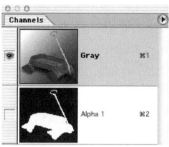

30 *The* **Channels** *palette (shown here in Adobe Photoshop) displays the image information including the additional alpha channel for the image silhouette.*

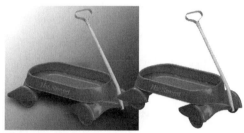

31 *An image with the* **alpha channel turned off** *(left) is displayed inside a rectangle. An image with the* **alpha channel turned on** *(right) is displayed inside the channel silhouette.*

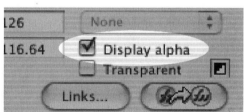

32 *Click the* **Display alpha checkbox** *to show or hide the effects of an image's alpha channel.*

Working with Alpha Channels

An alpha channel is the technical term for an extra image of information that is added to the regular channels of color of a file. For instance, instead of just four channels of color information or one channel of a grayscale image, you can add extra channels of information to an image. These extra channels can be created in a program such as Adobe Photoshop and can be any shape or appearance you want **30**. The most common use for alpha channels is to draw a silhouette around an image. If you are unfamiliar with how to create an alpha channel, you should consult the manual for the program that created the graphic.

Once you have created an alpha channel for an image, you can use FreeHand to show or hide the alpha channel. If the alpha channel is visible, then you see the image only through the white or light areas of the image **31**. Any parts of the image that are behind the black parts of the alpha channel will be transparent. If the alpha channel is not visible, then you see the complete image.

TIP FreeHand lets you display the alpha channels applied to TIFF, Photoshop, PNG, and GIF images.

To control the alpha channel display:

1. Select the placed image.
2. Click the Display alpha checkbox to show or hide the effects of the alpha channel **32**.

TIP The Display alpha checkbox is only available if there is an alpha channel applied to the image.

EXPORTING 25

I t's not enough to save files in the Macromedia FreeHand format. Today's designers need to convert files into many different formats.

For instance, you may want to add your FreeHand graphics to Microsoft Word or Microsoft PowerPoint files. If you save your graphics in the FreeHand EPS format, you will find that the file doesn't print well to a non-PostScript printer such as an ink-jet printer. So you will need to convert the file into a format that prints well on an ink-jet printer.

You might need to send your file to someone who uses (gasp!) Adobe Illustrator. Fortunately, you can easily change the FreeHand file to the Illustrator format.

Converting FreeHand files from one format to another is called *exporting*.

Basic Exporting

FreeHand offers you many different ways to convert or export your files into formats that can be read by other applications. Because some formats change the look of your file, pick your format according to your needs.

To export a document:

1. Choose File > Export.

2. In the Export dialog box, enter a name for the file and select a location where it will be saved 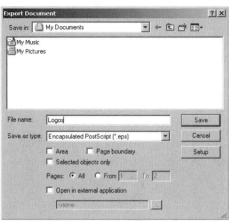.

3. Choose the format from the Save as Type menu (Win) or the Format menu (Mac).

4. Select the Selected Objects Only option to export only selected objects.

TIP The Selected Objects Only option is not available when exporting to a FreeHand file format.

5. Click Setup to select options for the export file format. *(See the options listed in the next sections for information on the individual export options.)*

6. Click Export.

To open the exported file in another application:

1. Choose File > Export.

2. In the Export dialog box, check Open in External Application.

3. Use the dialog box to navigate to the application that will open the image.

4. Click OK.

① The **Export dialog box** *is where you can name and set the format for an exported file.*

Export File Formats

The following are the available export file formats:

Adobe Illustrator: Illustrator 1.1, 88, 3/4, 5.5, 7.

Macromedia FreeHand: FreeHand 8, 9, 10.

EPS Vector files: Generic EPS, Macintosh EPS (Win), MS-DOS EPS (Mac), EPS with TIFF Preview (Win), QuarkXPress EPS, DCS2 EPS.

Other Vector formats: Windows Metafile (Win), Windows Enhanced Metafile (Win), Macromedia Flash, PDF.

Raster files: TIFF, PNG, GIF, JPEG, BMP, Targa, PICT (Mac).

Adobe Photoshop: Photoshop 3 EPS, Photoshop 4/5 RGB EPS, Photoshop 5.

Text files: ASCII text, RTF text.

Basic Exporting

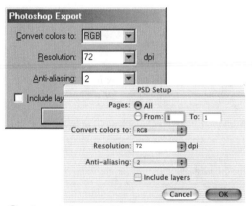

② *The* **Pages option** *is available for some export formats in the Windows Export dialog box.*

③ *The Windows (left) and Macintosh (right) export options. On the Mac the* **Pages option** *is integrated into the Setup dialog box.*

Once you have exported a file, you may make some changes to the original FreeHand document. You can then re-export the file without having to go through setting the Export dialog box.

To re-export a document:

◆ Choose **File** > **Export Again**. FreeHand uses the previous export settings to export a new version of the document.

Because FreeHand is a multi-page program, you have the chance to choose which pages are exported. On the Macintosh platform this is built into the options for each of the file formats. On the Windows platform, this is part of the Export dialog box.

TIP If the file format does not support multiple pages, FreeHand creates individual files for each page.

To set the pages for export (Win):

◆ In the Export dialog box, set the number of pages to be exported as follows ②:
  - **All** exports all the pages into the selected file format.
  - **From** lets you choose a range of pages to export.

To set the pages for export (Mac):

◆ Use the Setup dialog box for each of the file formats to set the number of pages to be exported as follows:
  - **All** exports all the pages into the selected file format.
  - **From** lets you choose a range of pages to export.

TIP Because the Pages option is built into the Macintosh Setup dialog box, there is a distinctive difference between the Windows and Macintosh options for some formats ③.

Exporting as Raster Images

When you export in the following formats, you convert FreeHand's vector objects into pixel-based illustrations. The TIFF, BMP, PICT, and Targa options are the most basic raster images.

To export as BMP, TIFF, Targa, and PICT files:

1. Choose one of the following formats:

   - **BMP** (bitmap) is the most basic pixel format for the Windows platform.
   - **TIFF** (Tagged Image File Format) is the preferred choice for importing into applications that can't accept FreeHand EPS files.
   - **Targa** is widely used in professional video editing.
   - **PICT** is the most basic bitmapped format for the Macintosh platform.

2. Click Setup to open the options or setup dialog box for each format ❹.

3. Choose the resolution. For most print work this is 300 dpi. For most Web work this is 72 dpi.

4. Choose an amount of Anti-aliasing to smooth the edges of the image.

5. To export an alpha channel that can be used as a mask, click Include alpha channel.

6. To make the alpha channel include the background, click Alpha includes background.

7. Set the Color Depth for how many colors are supported. Higher color depths create larger files.

8. For Targa files, choose the Compression option to make the file smaller.

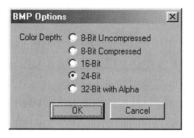

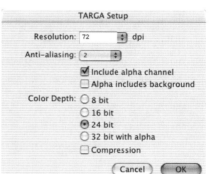

❹ The **Setup options** for exporting BMP, TIFF, Targa, and PICT files.

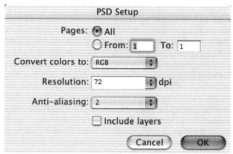

⑤ *The* **Photoshop Export** *options.*

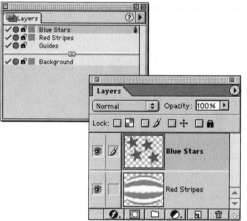

⑥ *The* **Include layers** *option for Photoshop export allows you to retain FreeHand layers in the Photoshop file.*

Exporting as PNG, GIF, and JPEG

The other three raster formats—PNG, GIF, and JPEG—are primarily used for Web graphics. Their export options are covered in Chapter 26, "Moving to the Web."

FreeHand also lets you export documents in the Adobe Photoshop format. This too converts the vector paths into raster images.

To export as Adobe Photoshop files:

1. Choose one of the following formats:
   - **Adobe Photoshop 3 EPS** saves the image as a Photoshop 3 file. Use this format if it needs to be opened in Photoshop version 3. The EPS designation means it can be imported into a page layout program.
   - **Adobe Photoshop 4/5 RGB EPS** saves the image as a file that can be opened in either Photoshop 4 or 5.
   - **Adobe Photoshop 5** saves the image in the native Photoshop 5 file format which can be opened in version 5 or newer. This format gives you additional setup options.

2. If you have chosen Adobe Photoshop 5, click the Setup button. This opens the Photoshop Export dialog box **⑤**.

3. Use the Convert colors to menu to choose one of the following:
   - **CMYK** creates a 4-channel file that is acceptable for process-color separations.
   - **RGB** creates a 3-channel file that is usually used for Web and multimedia graphics.
   - **Grayscale** creates a single-channel file that is usually used for one color separations.

4. Choose the resolution. For most print work this is 300 dpi. For most Web work this is 72 dpi.

5. Choose an amount of Anti-aliasing to smooth the edges of the image.

6. Check Include layers to convert the FreeHand layers into the equivalent Photoshop layers **⑥**.

Exporting as Vector Images

There are quite a few options for exporting as vector files. This is very helpful for placing FreeHand artwork in page-layout programs or for working with other applications.

To export as EPS files:

1. Choose one of the following formats:

   - **Generic EPS** saves vectors in an Encapsulated PostScript file without any preview. This is the smallest format but is difficult to work with in page layout programs.
   - **Macintosh EPS** (Mac) saves the EPS file with a PICT preview.
   - **MS-DOS EPS** (Mac) saves the EPS file with a TIFF preview.
   - **EPS with TIFF** preview (Win) also saves the EPS file with a TIFF preview.
   - **QuarkXPress EPS** saves the file in the best possible format for importing into QuarkXPress.
   - **DCS2 EPS** creates a pre-separated EPS that is usually used with OPI pre-press software.

2. Click the Setup button to select the other options ❼.

3. Check Include FreeHand document to add the native FreeHand document to the EPS file. This makes it possible to edit the file later using FreeHand.

4. Check Include Fonts in EPS to add the font information necessary to print the file.

5. Choose the color conversion as follows:

   - CMYK for standard process-color output and separations.
   - RGB for use in an image-editing application such as Macromedia Fireworks.
   - CMYK and RGB for print applications that can handle PostScript files such as Illustrator or Photoshop 4 or higher.

❼ *The* EPS Export *options.*

What Does It Mean to Include Fonts?

What does it mean when you include fonts in an exported EPS file?

As discussed in Chapter 19, when you open a FreeHand file that uses fonts not installed on your computer, you get a warning dialog box. This lets you know that if you don't have the original fonts in the file, the text will not display correctly unless you change the fonts.

So does that mean that if you include the fonts with an EPS, you don't get any warning? Can you work without installing those fonts?

No, no, no! Absolutely not!

All it means is that there is enough information about the font to *print* the file. But there is not enough information to *edit* the file later.

In order to edit the file you most definitely need to install the proper font.

The Include font option helps those who send their EPS files for placement in newspapers and magazines. Those publications may not have the fonts installed. They can print the file, but they can't open and edit it without the fonts installed.

8 *The* **EPS Setup** *for Illustrator 7 files lets you set the color conversion options.*

Working with Other Vector Programs

However, what if you need to send your FreeHand files to someone who uses CorelDraw or Deneba Canvas? Don't panic just because there isn't any export option for CorelDraw or Canvas. Most other vector programs allow you to open Illustrator files.

So, check with the person you're working with and find out if their version of the program can open Illustrator files. Although you may find some special features such as transparency lenses or envelopes are converted to ordinary objects, most likely you will be able to transfer most of the information to the other program.

That's one of the reasons Macromedia has included the Illustrator 1 format. Almost all vector drawing programs can open that basic file format.

Although FreeHand doesn't export in the CorelDraw format, you can *import* uncompressed CorelDraw 7 and 8 files.

You can also save FreeHand files in formats compatible with previous versions of the program. This helps you exchange files with people who do not have FreeHand MX.

To export as FreeHand files:

◆ Choose one of the following formats:

- **FreeHand 8 document** for use with FreeHand 8.
- **FreeHand 9 document** for use with Freehand 9.
- **FreeHand 10 document** for use with Freehand 10.

TIP There are no Setup options for the FreeHand file formats.

Despite a fierce competition between Freehand and Illustrator, Macromedia lets you convert FreeHand files to Illustrator files.

To export as Illustrator files:

1. Choose one of the following formats:

- **Adobe Illustrator 1.1™** for use with the oldest versions of Illustrator and Macromedia FreeHand.
- **Adobe Illustrator 88™** for use with the second version of Illustrator.
- **Adobe Illustrator® 3** for use with Illustrator 3 (Mac) or Illustrator 4 (Win).
- **Adobe Illustrator™ 5.5** for use with Illustrator 5.5.
- **Adobe Illustrator™ 7.x** for use with Illustrator 7 and higher.

2. If you choose Illustrator 7, click the Setup button to set the options as follows **8**:

- **CMYK** for standard process-color output and separations.
- **RGB** for use in an image-editing application such as Macromedia Fireworks.
- **CMYK and RGB** for print applications that handle PostScript files such as Illustrator or Photoshop 4 or higher.

FreeHand also lets you save documents as PDF (portable document format) files. This file format allows anyone who has the free Acrobat Reader application to view your files. In addition, the PDF format compresses files so they take up the smallest amount of space.

To export an Acrobat PDF:

1. Choose PDF from the Format pop-up menu.

2. Click the Setup button to open the PDF Export box ❾.

3. Set the Color Image Compression.

4. Set the Grayscale Image Compression.

TIP Choose None if the PDF file will be used for professional printing. This ensures that all the information is retained in the file.

5. Set the Compatibility menu to choose which version of Acrobat can open the file.

6. Check which options you want applied to the PDF:

   - **Compress text and graphics** reduces the file size even further.
   - **ASCII format PDF** may be required when sharing PDF files on older networks and e-mail systems.
   - **Editable text format** allows the text to be changed in the PDF.
   - **Export notes** converts any notes added in the Note text box in the Navigation panel into PDF annotations ❿.
   - **Export URLs** converts any URLs as PDF links.
   - **Embed fonts** embeds the fonts used in the file. This ensures the document appears exactly as you created it.

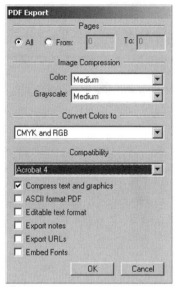

❾ *The* **PDF Export dialog box** *allows you to set the attributes of an Acrobat file.*

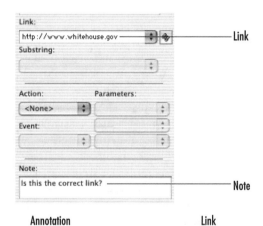

❿ *The* **PDF Export options** *can convert FreeHand notes and links (top) into Acrobat annotations and hyperlinks (bottom).*

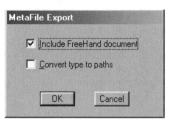

⓫ *The* MetaFile Export dialog box.

⓬ *The* Enhanced MetaFile Export dialog box.

What about Flash?

There's one more vector file format that FreeHand lets you export files in—the Macromedia Flash (SWF) format.

SWF is the vector file format that is used for Web graphics, animations, and page layout. It has become one of the most important elements of creating Web pages.

Because working with Flash files is so important, exporting in the SWF format is covered in Chapter 27.

Exporting the Other Vector Formats

The final vector formats are Windows Meta-File, and Windows Enhanced MetaFile. Quite frankly, these are very specific file formats and most FreeHand users will hardly ever need to use them.

To export MetaFile and Enhanced MetaFile (Win):

1. Choose one of the following from the format menu:
   - **MetaFile** contains 16-bit color depth.
   - **Enhanced MetaFile** contains 32-bit color depth as well as other information.
2. Click the Setup button to select the other options **⓫**.
3. Choose Include FreeHand document to be able to re-open the file in FreeHand.
4. Choose Convert type to paths to avoid the need to have the fonts for printing and editing.
5. If you are working with an Enhanced MetaFile, you can add a description of the file that can be used when searching for it **⓬**.

Adding Image Information

FreeHand also lets you add information that can be used when your artwork is part of an Extensis Portfolio image database. This makes it easier to find your artwork in large catalogs.

TIP Sadly, this option is only available on the Mac platform.

(Mac) To add Portfolio information:

1. Choose **View > Portfolio Info.** The Portfolio Info dialog box appears **13**.

2. Type the keywords in the Keywords field. Use commas to separate the different keywords.

TIP Keywords are usually descriptive labels that can categorize how the graphic might be used.

3. Type any description of the graphic in the Description field.

TIP Descriptions are usually more lengthy information about the file or its use.

4. Click OK. The Portfolio information is included as part of the file and can be read by the Portfolio application.

TIP To add a preview to your FreeHand file so it can be seen in a Portfolio database, you need to check the Preferences settings for Import/Export *(see Appendix C)*.

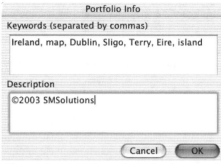

13 *Use the* **Portfolio Info dialog box** *to add keywords and descriptions used in a database.*

MOVING TO THE WEB

Designers are focusing more and more on publishing to the Web as an alternative to—or even a replacement for—traditional print publishing. As a result, Macromedia FreeHand now incorporates many features for creating Web graphics and Web pages.

For example, FreeHand lets you choose colors that are specially designed to look best when viewed on various computer monitors. It also lets you export your graphics in special formats that used by Web browsers.

Finally Macromedia has created a direct route to converting your FreeHand graphics into HTML *(HyperText Markup Language),* the *lingua franca* of the Internet.

Note: As handy as FreeHand's Web features are, they are not a substitute for programs such as Macromedia Fireworks or Macromedia Dreamweaver. Rather, FreeHand's Web features are handy for those occasions when you need to convert a print brochure into a set of Web pages, not to design an entire Web site.

Working with Web-safe Colors

In the early days of the Web, the people behind the Netscape Web browser put together a set of 216 colors that reproduced well on both Macintosh and Windows monitors with the capability to display only 256 colors. These are now called the Web-safe colors.

Most people today have monitors that display more than just 256 colors. This makes the need for the Web-safe colors almost nonexistent. However, there are some people who still insist on using only the Web-safe colors in their Web pages. FreeHand gives you two ways to pick colors from the Web-safe set.

To choose Web-safe colors:

◆ Click the Fill or Stroke color box in the Tools panel. The default listing shows the Web-safe colors ❶.

TIP The first number for the color is the hexadecimal code used to specify the color in HTML pages. The second number is the RGB value for the color.

To import Web-safe colors:

1. Use the Swatches panel menu to choose the Web Safe Color Library. The library appears containing the 216 Web colors ❷.

2. Select the colors you want in your document.

TIP Web pages take less time to display if you design them with a small number of colors.

3. Click OK. The colors you have selected appear in the Colors List ❸.

TIP The Web-safe colors are identified with both their hexadecimal codes and their RGB values. The hexadecimal codes are the tags used by the HyperText Markup Language (HTML) to designate Web colors.

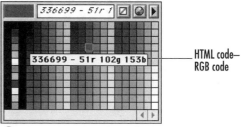

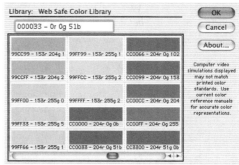

❶ The **Web-safe colors** are displayed in the Fill and Stroke color box.

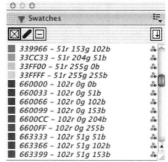

❷ The **Web Safe Color Library** lets you choose up to 216 colors that can be used for Web graphics.

❸ Web-safe colors are displayed in the Colors List with their HTML hexadecimal codes as well as their RGB values.

4 *A* **blend between Web-safe colors** *creates non-Web-safe colors between the original colors.*

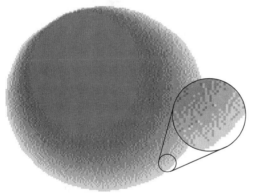

5 *With* **Dither turned on,** *the area between the original Web colors has a speckled look as the colors mix many Web-safe colors together.*

6 *When a blend is converted with* **Dither turned off,** *the intermediate steps abruptly change from one Web-safe color to another.*

Blending Web-Safe Colors

If you insist on using only Web-safe colors, your best best is not to use any blends or gradients. Both blends and gradients will create colors outside the range of the Web-safe colors.

When you convert a gradient or blend to GIF format, you need to decide how the colors in the intermediate steps are created **4**. One way is to dither those colors. Dithering is the process that makes a few colors look like more. For instance, a dither between red and yellow means that dots of red are next to dots of yellow. An even mix between the red and yellow dots appears orange. More red than yellow appears red-orange. More yellow than red appears yellow-orange.

Dithering is the best way to preserve the look of blends in Web graphics **5**. When blends or gradients are not dithered, there are abrupt changes(called *banding*) in each step of the blend **6**. This usually looks unacceptable. Dithering helps avoid banding in gradients or blends.

When colors are not dithered, they are converted to the closest Web-safe color. This may mean that a deep red turns brown or a light green turns dark.

My own personal feeling is that since so many people have monitors that can display millions of colors, it is no longer such a big deal to limit yourself to the Web-safe colors.

Blending Web-Safe Colors

Exporting as Web Graphics

FreeHand lets you export your files in three popular Web formats. This means you can convert a print logo into a Web graphic. *(For more information on exporting, see Chapter 25, "Exporting.")*

To export a file for the Web:

1. Create the artwork you want to turn into a Web graphic.

2. Choose **File** > **Export.** This opens the Export Document dialog box.

3. Choose one of the following from the Format (Mac) or Save as type (Win) menu:
   - **GIF** is used for images with flat color.
   - **JPEG** is used for photographs or images with many blends or gradients.
   - **PNG** is not often used. Choose it only if you are sure your viewers will have the proper browsers.

4. Click the Setup button. On Windows, this opens the Bitmap Export Defaults dialog box ❼. On the Mac, the options are part of the setup for each file format.

(Win) To set the Bitmap Export Defaults options:

1. Set the Resolution. For Web graphics, this is usually 72 dpi.

2. Use the Anti-aliasing pop-up menu to control how much softening of the image is applied. *(For more information on anti-aliasing, see Appendix C.)*

3. To create an alpha channel that can be used as a mask for your image, check Include alpha channel.

4. To include the background area in the alpha channel, check Alpha includes background.

5. Click the More button to open the options for each of the bitmapped formats.

❼ *(Win) The* **Bitmap Export Defaults** *dialog* **box** *allows you to set the overall options for exporting files into different Web formats.*

Naming Web Graphics

Both the Windows and Macintosh platforms give you much freedom in how to name a file. They allow a file name to contain spaces, upper-and lowercase letters, and have really long file names.

If you're like me you may have files with names like *Final copy of the Second logo.eps.*

Unfortunately many Web pages are hosted on Unix systems that have much stricter file formats. So if you save your files for the Web, you may need to limit your names to all lower case letters and no spaces. This means a name such as final_logo.gif

---

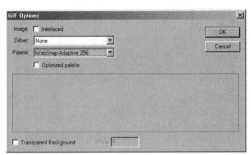

❽ *The* **GIF Options dialog box** *let you control how the image is displayed on the Web.*

GIF Palette Options

GIF images can have up to 256 colors. However, you have a great deal of choices as to which colors to include in the color palette.

- **Exact Palette** creates a color palette with only the colors used.

- **WebSnap Adaptive 256, 128, or 16** creates a color palette that is converted to the closest Web-safe color equivalent.

- **WebSafe 216** includes the standard 216 Web-safe colors.

- **64 colors, 32 colors, or 16 colors** lets you quickly select preset Web-safe color palettes.

- **Macintosh System** uses the 256 colors native to the Macintosh OS.

- **Windows System** uses the 256 colors native to the Windows OS.

- **3-3-2** uses the palette of the original FreeHand GIF Import Export Xtra.

- **Grays** uses a palette of 256 gray-scale colors.

You don't have to use all 256 colors. Fewer colors make smaller GIF files.

Once you have set the general attributes, you then need to set the options for the specific file format you have chosen. One of the most common formats for Web graphics is the GIF format. *(GIF is pronounced as "gif" and not "Jiff" because I don't like peanut butter on the Web.)*

To set the GIF export options:

1. (Win) Click More in the Bitmap Export Defaults dialog box. The GIF Options dialog box opens **❽**.

   or

   (Mac) Click More in the GIF Setup dialog box. The GIF Options dialog box opens **❽**.

2. Use the Palette pop-up menu to choose one of the palette options described in the sidebar on this page.

3. Use the Dither menu to select the amount of dithering applied to colors. None applies no dithering. High applies the most dithering.

   TIP Turn off the Dither option if you have detailed artwork, text that needs to be clearly visible, or areas of flat color.

4. For Image, select Interlaced to create an image that appears almost immediately in a rough form and then gradually becomes clearer.

5. Select Optimized Palette to automatically remove unused colors from the palette. This creates the smallest file with the least number of colors.

   TIP To create a GIF image with a transparent background, see the exercise on the following page.

Exporting as Web Graphics

FreeHand lets you create a transparency in a GIF based on the object's outlines. The Exact and WebSnap Adaptive palettes do not support transparency.

To apply a transparent background:

1. Select Transparent Background in the GIF Options dialog box. The Index color palette appears along with the Index field ❾.

TIP Each color used is represented by a small color square. The small squares with an **X** indicate unused colors.

2. Click a color swatch to define which color should be transparent.

   or

   Enter its number in the Index field.

TIP If you select Transparent Background, be sure you also choose Include alpha channel in the Bitmap Export Defaults or GIF Setup dialog boxes.

TIP If you choose a transparent background color, make sure the color is not used inside the image or that part of the image will also be transparent ❿.

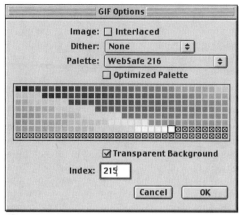

❾ *When you choose* **Transparent Background** *you can set which color is transparent from the color palette.*

❿ *The Transparent Background option (right image) lets the background of the Web page be visible without a white rectangle.*

Working with Fireworks, a Dedicated Web Graphics Program

A terrific as FreeHand is, it is actually very primitive when it comes to converting artwork into Web graphics. One of the reasons is that you can't preview what the different palettes and compression options do to your file. You have to export them, and then view them in a Web browser.

Fortunately, there is a terrific program that was created especially for producing Web graphics—Macromedia Fireworks.

Fireworks not only gives you exceptional control when you create GIF, JPEG, or PNG files; it also gives visual feedback of how the final exported file will appear on the Web.

Even better, you can simply drag FreeHand objects right into Fireworks. Of course, if you do work with Fireworks, you should get the *Fireworks MX Visual QuickStart Guide* by Sandee Cohen, *(Hey, that's me!)*, and published by Peachpit Press.

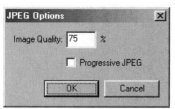

⓫ *The* **JPEG Options dialog box** *lets you control the quality of your image and how the image is displayed.*

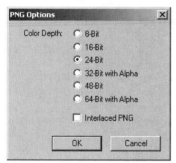

⓬ *The* **PNG Setup dialog box** *lets you control the image colors and how the image is displayed.*

Another format used on the Web is the JPEG (pronounced "Jay-peg") format. This is primarily used for photographic images or images with lots of blends or gradients.

To set the JPEG options:

1. (Win) Click the More button in the Bitmap Export Defaults. This opens the JPEG Options dialog box **⓫**.

or

(Mac) Click Setup in the Export dialog box. This opens the JPEG Setup dialog box which contains the Bitmap Export options as well as the JPEG Options.

2. Enter a percentage for Image Quality. Low quality settings create smaller files. High quality settings create larger files.

3. Click Progressive JPEG to create an effect similar to the Interlaced GIF.

The last format is the PNG (pronounced "Ping") format. This format has applications for both Web graphics and printing.

To set the PNG options:

1. (Win) Click the More button in the Bitmap Export Defaults. This opens the PNG Options dialog box **⓬**.

or

(Mac) Click Setup in the Export dialog box. This opens the PNG Setup dialog box which contains the Bitmap Export options as well as the PNG Options.

2. Choose the options for the color bit depth. Use high bit depths for print work.

3. Click Interlaced PNG to create an effect similar to the Interlaced GIF.

Exporting as Web Graphics

Adding URL Links

One of the most important features of a Web page written in HTML is its ability to include URL links. Links let the reader click on a word or phrase or an image and go to another location, either on the current Web site or on a totally different site. Links also let the reader send e-mail or download files.

To add a URL to an object:

1. Select the object that you want to apply the link to. This can be a path or text block.

2. In the Navigation panel, type the URL address in the Link field ⓭.

   or

   If you have already added the link to that document, use the Link menu to choose the link.

   or

   If you are working with multiple pages, use the Link menu to choose a link to another page ⓮.

TIP You can create invisible hotspots in your document by creating paths with no stroke and a lens fill with the opacity set to 0. This will allow you to link to a specific area of an image.

Links can also be added to selected text within a text block.

To add a URL to selected text:

1. Use the Text tool to highlight the text that you want to apply the link to.

2. Use the Link menu or field to add a URL link to the text. The selected text appears in the Substring field.

⓭ *Use the* **Link field** *of the Navigation panel to add URLs to graphics.*

⓮ **Page links** *automatically appear in the* **Link menu** *for multi-page documents.*

URL Link Choices

The three most common URL links are http, mailto, and ftp.

http: Stands for HyperText Transfer Protocol, used when you want to access a Web site. For example, **http://www.vectorbabe.com** is my Web site.

mailto: This URL is used to send e-mail. For example,you can use the link **mailto:sandee@vectorbabe.com** to send me e-mail.

ftp: This stands for File Transfer Protocol. This lets people download files. A sample URL link would be **ftp://ftp.vectorbabe.com/sandee.sit.**

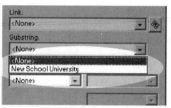

⓯ *The* **Find button** *in the Navigation panel lets you find objects that have a specific link attached.*

⓰ *The* **Substring menu** *in the Navigation panel lets you find text that has a specific link attached.*

To search for an object with a specific link:

1. In the Navigation panel, enter a URL in the Link field.

   or

   Select a URL from the Link menu.

2. Click the Find button in the Navigation panel **⓯**.

3. All objects in the current document that are linked to the URL are selected in the Document window.

The Find button only finds objects or text blocks that have the link applied to the entire object. You use the Substring menu to find selected text that has a link applied to it.

To find selected text with a specific link:

1. With the Text tool, click inside the text block. If there is a link within the block, the Substring menu becomes active.

2. Choose the Substring listing from the menu **⓰**. The text that contains the link becomes highlighted.

Once you have found or located all the objects with a specific link, you can easily change the URL information.

To update a URL for all the objects linked to it:

1. Deselect all objects in the document.

2. In the Navigation panel, select the URL you want to update from the Link menu.

3. Click the Find button to the right of the Link text box.

4. Modify the URL in the Link text box as needed. The URL is updated for all objects linked to it in the current document.

Creating HTML Pages

Billions of years ago Web pages were created by hand-coding the text and HTML instructions in word-processing applications. Then someone got the clever idea that they could convert FreeHand documents into HTML pages. Of course, this doesn't make FreeHand a substitute for professional Web-layout programs such as Macromedia Dreamweaver. But it does make it easy to convert a small brochure or print project into Web pages ❶.

To convert a document to HTML:

1. Select **File > Publish as HTML**. This opens the HTML Output dialog box ❶.

2. Choose a setting from the HTML Setting menu.

   or

   Click the Setup button to create a new one. *(See the following exercise for how to create a new HTML setup.)*

3. Check Show Output Warnings if you want to be alerted to possible problems with the export of the file to HTML.

4. Check View in browser or HTML Editor if you want the file to open immediately in a browser such as Internet Explorer or Netscape Navigator.

5. Select a browser or HTML editor from the pop-up menu.

   or

   Click the Browse button to choose a Web browser using the navigation dialog box.

6. Click Save as HTML. FreeHand creates the HTML file in the folder selected as the document root in the HTML Setup dialog box. The images are placed in a subfolder within that folder.

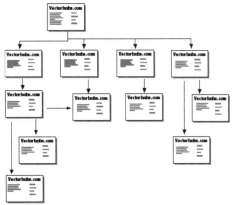

❶ *The* **multiple pages of a FreeHand document can be converted into Web pages.** *The arrows were manually added to show the links between pages.*

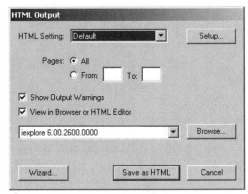

❶ *The* **HTML Output dialog box** *for creating Web pages from FreeHand files.*

① *The* **HTML Setup dialog box** *controls specific elements of the HTML conversion.*

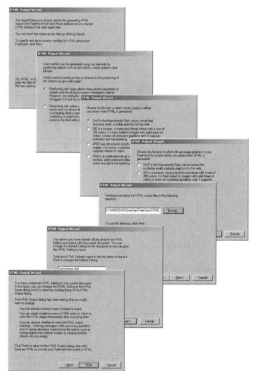

② *The* **HTML Export Output Wizard** *(Win) or the* **HTML Output Assistant** *(Mac) guides you through the process of setting up the creation of an HTML file.*

Rather than go through all the setting controls every time you create HTML pages, you can save the settings under one name.

To create an HTML setup:

1. In the HTML Output dialog box, click Setup to open the HTML Setup dialog box **①**.

2. Click the + button to create a new setup. Give it a name and click OK.

3. Use the Document root menu to choose the folder/directory in which you want to save the HTML files.

   or

   Click the Browse menu to choose a new folder.

4. Use the Layout menu to choose one of the following:

   • **Positioning with Layers** uses Cascading Style Sheets to make a very precise equivalent of the layout. However, older browsers may not be able to display Cascading Style Sheets.

   • **Positioning with Tables** uses a less precise mode to convert the layout. This option can be seen by a larger number of browsers.

5. Use the Encoding menu to choose the language for the page.

   TIP Leave this set to Western (Latin 1) unless you have a very good reason to do otherwise.

6. Choose one of the following as the Export defaults for Vector art and Images:

   • **GIF** creates GIF images.
   • **JPEG** creates JPEG files.
   • **PNG** creates PNG graphics.
   • **SWF** creates SWF (Flash) images.

7. Click OK to accept all your preferences.

   TIP Click the Assistant (Mac) or Wizard (Win) button to let FreeHand help you through the setup process with short explanations of each step **②**.

To check the HTML Output Warnings:

1. If you selected Show Output Warnings in the HTML Output dialog box *(see page 374)*, the HTML Output Warnings dialog box appears, indicating any HTML errors in your document .

2. Click either Scan Page or Scan Document. FreeHand displays a list of potential problems with the export to HTML.

3. Click each problem in the list. FreeHand selects the item so that you can decide if or how you want to change it.

TIP Some of the items listed as HTML output warnings may not have any impact on the Web page you create; experience will help you evaluate which ones need to be dealt with and which can be safely ignored.

TIP If you have checked the View in browser or the HTML Editor checkbox in the HTML Output dialog box, the file opens and you will be able to see what the exported HTML file looks like .

㉑ The **HTML Output Warnings window** *lists possible problems in the document before you create the HTML pages.*

㉒ *The HTML file can be viewed in a browser or HTML editor.*

ANIMATIONS AND ACTIONS 27

One of the most exciting developments in Web design has been the addition of Flash movies and Flash Web sites. Flash movies are much smaller in terms of file size than GIF animations. So they don't tax slow modem connections. Flash files don't even have to be movies, *per se*. Instead of playing all the frames of a movie at once, you can start and stop each frame one at a time. This makes Flash movies behave like individual Web pages.

Unfortunately, Flash doesn't have many of the sophisticated drawing tools that Macromedia FreeHand has. There's no enveloping, no perspective, no power duplicating, and none of FreeHand's special effects. That's why many Flash designers start by using FreeHand to create their artwork or lay out their projects and then bring the files into Flash.

FreeHand makes it easy to copy and paste or export into Flash. You can even add basic Flash navigational elements to move from page to page. And you can create animations by sending objects and text to layers.

This makes FreeHand, in my opinion, the best vector program to use with Flash.

Pasting into Flash

The easiest way for a designer to work with both Freehand and Flash is to copy FreeHand artwork and paste it into a Flash frame. Or, if you have the monitor space, you can drag and drop artwork from one application into another.

TIP Before pasting into Flash, set the Export preferences to convert colors to CMYK and RGB for the clipboard formats *(see Appendix C)*.

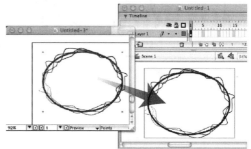

1 *You can easily* **drag and drop** *FreeHand artwork into Flash documents.*

To paste into Flash files:

1. Select the FreeHand object or objects.

2. Copy the objects.

3. Switch to make the Flash file active.

4. Paste. The FreeHand objects are imported into the Flash file.

TIP Unlinked text blocks become Flash text objects.

TIP Linked text blocks or text on paths are converted into paths.

TIP Vector-based objects become a group that can be ungrouped and edited like any other Flash element.

TIP Bitmaps become a single grouped object just like imported bitmaps. You can break apart pasted bitmaps or convert pasted bitmaps to vector graphics.

To drag and drop into Flash files:

1. Position the windows so you can see both the FreeHand and Flash files.

2. Select the FreeHand object or objects.

3. Use the Pointer tool to drag the FreeHand objects into the Flash window **1**.

4. When you see the rectangle box appear in the Flash document window, release the mouse. The FreeHand artwork is imported into the Flash file.

FreeHand features supported in Flash files

The following FreeHand features will be kept when imported into Flash.

- Basic strokes and fills. However square endcaps will be changed to round endcaps.

- Transparency lens fills remain transparent upon export. Other lens fills are changed into objects with masks.

- Gradient fills except the contour gradient.

- CMYK or RGB TIFFs and embedded images (JPEG, GIF, PNG).

- Blended paths.

- Composite paths, including text converted into paths.

- Clipping paths containing vector path image files.

- Text blocks. However, text on a path is converted to objects.

- Arrowheads.

Pasting into Flash

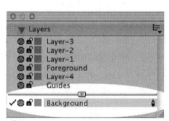

The type of objects that can be animated (from top to bottom): text, text on a path, blend, blend on a path, group of objects, and brushes.

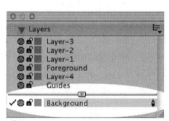

❸ *The* **non-printing layers** *hold the artwork that is seen throughout the animation.*

Creating Layer-Based Animations

As much as I enjoy creating simple Flash animations in FreeHand, I know that there is far more power and sophistication in Flash itself. However, FreeHand does have a few techniques to convert blends, text, text on a path, groups and brushes into animated sequences ❷.

To prepare artwork for animation:

1. Set text as a single line of type or attach the text to a path *(see page 292)*.

   or

   Create a blend or attach a blend to a path *(see page 260)*.

   or

   Group individual items in the order that you would like them to appear.

   or

   Brushes must be released and ungrouped as many times as necessary until each individual symbol is selected. Then the individual symbols should be grouped into one object.

2. If you want an object to appear throughout the animation, place the artwork on a non-printing background layer ❸ *(see page 172)*.

One way to create animations is to put objects on their own layers so that each layer acts like a movie frame. Although you can manually place the objects, it is easier to do it automatically.

To create an animation sequence using layers:

1. Select the artwork to be animated.

2. Choose **Xtras > Animate > Release to Layers.** The Release to Layers dialog box appears ❹.

3. Use the Animate menu to choose one of the following:

    - **Sequence** releases each object individually to separate layers.
    - **Build** creates a stacking effect by copying the objects in sequence to separate layers.
    - **Drop** copies the objects to all layers but omits one object in sequence from each layer.
    - **Trail** copies and releases objects to the number of layers you specify. Objects are copied incrementally to the specified number of layers.

4. If you have chosen Trail, use the Trail by field to specify the number of layers on which objects will be copied.

5. If desired, select Reverse direction to release the objects in reverse stacking order and animate the sequence in the opposite direction.

6. Select Use existing layers to release objects to existing layers, beginning with the current layer. Deselect Use existing layers to create new layers for the objects that are released.

7. If you have chosen Use existing layers, you can also select Send to Back to release the objects to the back of the stacking order.

8. Click OK. The objects appear on new layers ❺.

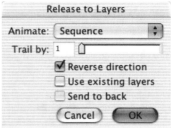

❹ *The* **Release to Layers dialog box** *gives you several choices as to how objects are animated.*

Animation Choices

The four animation choices make different movie effects.

- **Sequence** animations show one element at a time. They are used to give the effect of any object moving from one place to another.

- **Build** animations add the next element to the previous one. For instance, they can be used to give the effect of letters appearing to create readable text.

- **Drop** animation displays all the elements of the sequence and then turns off each element, in sequence, as if it was a ripple in the display.

- **Trail** animation displays the new elements in the sequence as the previous elements disappear.

Creating Layer-Based Animations

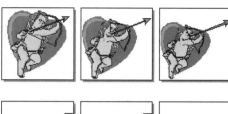

❺ *Individual pages can be used to lay out a page animation.*

❻ *The common elements for this page animation come from the master pages.*

Creating Page-Based Animations

You're not just limited to working with layers to create animations. You can use the document pages as the individual frames of an animation. The benefit of this method is that you can easily visualize the animation as you work.

To manually create a page animation:

1. Create your first frame's artwork on a page.

2. Duplicate the page and modify the artwork on that duplicate page.

3. Continue to duplicate pages and modify the artwork. Each page of the document becomes a frame of the animation **❺**. You can then export the file as an animation. *(See page 394 for the steps on how to export the file as an SWF movie.)*

To use master pages to create a page animation:

1. Create the master page or pages that contain the artwork.

2. Create as many child pages based on those master pages as you want **❻**.

3. Add individual elements to each page.

   or

   Use the Release child page command in the Document inspector panel. This releases the objects on the page from the master page symbols so they can be modified.

4. Select and modify the individual elements on each page.

Page- and Layer-Based Animations

Finally, you can create animations that use both pages and layers as the animation frames ❼. The pages act like different scenes that you jump to, while the layers act like different frames.

First book on Background layer　　　Text released to layers.

To create page- and layer-based movies:

1. Apply the elements for the first scene on the first page.

TIP To view the elements throughout the scene, place them on a non-printing layer.

2. Apply the elements for each frame to individual layers. These are the elements that change during the scene.

3. Apply the elements for the next scene to the next page.

4. Apply the elements for each frame to the individual layers. These are the elements that change during the scene.

TIP Objects on each layer are seen only on the page that is displayed. So one layer can contain frames for different scenes.

TIP You must have at least one element on a printing layer in order for any non-printing layers to be visible during the animation.

Page 2

Second book on Background layer　　　Text released to layers.

❼ *An example of how using both pages and layers can create an animation with two scenes. In this case the first scene shows the text appear over the first book. The second text shows the next book and its text.*

❽ *The* **Action tool** *in the Tools panel.*

❾ *Use the* **Action tool dialog box** *to apply actions to objects.*

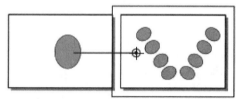

❿ *Drag the Action tool from the object to the target page.*

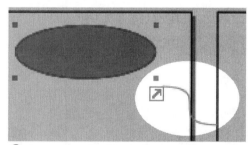

⓫ *A curved action line indicates that an action has been applied from an object to a page.*

Adding Actions

Movies don't necessarily have to move—that is, you can go through a movie by manually advancing each frame. This treats the Flash movie as if it were a set of Web pages. An *action* is a command that plays the frames of a movie. If you want you can apply actions to objects that can act as interactive buttons. The Action tool makes it easy to apply actions to objects.

To assign actions using the Action tool:

1. Double-click the Action tool in the Tools panel ❽. This opens the Action tool dialog box ❾.

2. Choose one of the actions as follows:
   - **Link to target page** creates a link that moves from one page to another.
   - **Print target page** creates a link that adds a command that prints the target page.
   - **Load target page as a movie** takes the artwork on one page and allows you to add it on top of the artwork on the current page. *(See the special sidebar exercise on pages 386–387 for how this action can be used.)*

3. Click OK to close the Action Tool dialog box.

4. Drag the Action tool from the object you want to act as the button to the destination page. A line extends from the object to the target page ❿.

5. Release the mouse button. A curved action line indicates the action is applied from the object to the page ⓫.

TIP Use objects with a fill, thick stroke, or thick text as the buttons for actions. This makes it easy for the viewer to find the active area in the button.

Adding Actions

The Action tool allows you to apply three actions. However, there are many other actions you can apply using the Navigation panel.

To assign actions using the Navigation panel:

1. Select the object or objects to which you want to assign actions.

TIP Objects must have a fill or stroke (or both) to create an area that will trigger the action.

2. In the Navigation panel, use the Action menu to select an action **⑫**. *(See the sidebar on facing page for details on the actions.)*

3. Use the Event menu to select the event that will trigger the action **⑬**.

TIP Depending on the action, you may need to set some or all of the Parameters menus **⑭**.

4. If you selected Go To and Stop/Play, Print, Load/Unload Movie, or Tell Target, use the first Parameters menu to select from the list of current document pages.

5. If you select Go To and Stop/Play or Print, use the second Parameter menu to specify which part of the document should be displayed or printed.

6. If you select Tell Target, select an action from the second Parameter pop-up menu to control playback of another movie: Go To, Play, Stop, or Print.

7. If you select Go To and Stop/Play or Print in step 6, use the third Parameter menu to specify which part of the document should be displayed or printed.

⑫ *The* Action *menu in the Navigation panel lets you assign actions to pages.*

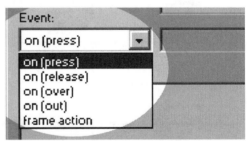

⑬ *The* Event *menu in the Navigation panel lets you control how actions are prompted.*

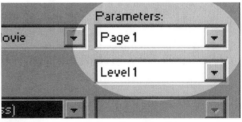

⑭ *Depending on the selected action, you may need to choose options from the* Parameters menus.

Assigning Actions

Here are the actions that can be applied to FreeHand objects.

- **Go To and Stop** creates a button that jumps to a particular frame, scene, or page in the movie. It then stops the playback. This action can also be applied using the Action tool to jump to a particular page. If you want to move to a particular frame or scene, you need to apply the action using the Navigation panel.

- **Go To and Play** creates a button that jumps to a particular frame, scene, or page in the movie. It then continues playing the movie from that point.

- **Get URL** creates a button that is used to go to the URL listed in the Link field of the Navigation panel. The URL should be applied to the object that triggers the action. The parameters allow you to specify a target window that displays the URL.

- **Play** creates a button that allows you to start a paused movie.

- **Stop** creates a button that allows you to pause a movie in progress.

- **Print** creates a button that allows you to specify a page that users can print directly through the Flash Player. Once the page has been chosen, you can also specify which layers of the page will print. This action can also be applied using the Action tool.

- **Full Screen** displays the movie in the Flash Player in full-screen mode, rather than normal mode. In the full-screen mode, the movie takes over the entire computer screen. This is particularly useful when playing movies on a local computer rather than through a Web browser.

- **Start/Stop Drag** is applied directly to the movie artwork. This action makes it possible to drag the movie clip around the page when an event happens, and stops the behavior when its opposite pair event occurs. The **on** (**press**) and **on** (**release**) events are the first set of paired opposites. The **on** (**over**) and **on** (**out**) events are the second set of paired opposites.

- **Load Movie** creates a button that loads the movie from one page onto the current movie frame. This action can also be applied using the Action tool. The Load and Unload actions are only available for FreeHand documents that have two or more pages.

- **Unload Movie** creates a button that unloads (deletes) a loaded movie from a page.

- **Tell Target** creates a button that controls the movies or movie clips that were loaded into the current movie with the Load Movie action. The parameters for this action lets you set the page that was loaded. The events are Go To and Stop, Go To and Play, Stop, Play, and Print. FreeHand allows only one level of loaded movies; thus you can assign only one movie to load at a time.

I would like to thank Ian Kelleigh for his help in describing actions. Ian is the brains behind **www.freehandsource.com**. This unofficial Web site is one of the best online resources for anyone who is learning FreeHand.

Adding Actions

Actions in Action

Rather than wade through a lot of abstract explanations of how actions work in FreeHand, here's an explanation of a small game I created. To play the game you click a button which adds the artwork of the cannon from the second page onto the first page. You can drag the cannon into the correct position. Then you use buttons to trigger or stop the cannon blasts.

I started by creating the artwork as a two-page FreeHand file . The first FreeHand page contains the buttons and instructions for the game. The second page contains the cannon and the blast clouds.

The instructions, buttons, and cannon need to be visible all the time. Those elements are put on non-printing layers positioned below the line in the FreeHand Layers panel .

Each puff of smoke for the cannon blast is placed on its own above-the-line, printing layer. The artwork for the first blast is placed at the bottom of the stacking order. The artwork for the final blast is placed at the top of the stacking order. When these layers play as part of the movie, it gives the effects of the cannon firing 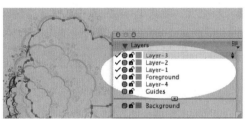.

At this point, we have all the movie elements in position. But the movie has no controls. We need to add actions to control the various elements of the movie.

The first movie action is the Load Movie command. This command adds the image of the cannon and the blast onto page one. In this case, the Action tool is used to drag from the selected button onto page two—the page that contains the movie we want to load .

Page 1

Page 2

⓯ *The cannon game starts on two pages.*

⓰ *Artwork that needs to be visible throughout the movie is placed on a non-printing layer.*

⓱ *Artwork that is visible only when certain actions happen is placed on printing layers.*

⓲ *The Action tool set to Load Movie is dragged from the button onto page two.*

⑲ *Use the Navigation panel to apply the Tell Target action set to Play to the button that triggers the cannon blast.*

⑳ *Use the Navigation panel to apply the Tell Target action set to Stop to the button that stops the cannon blast.*

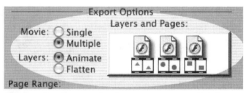

㉑ *Use the Navigation panel to apply the Start/ Stop Drag action to the background artwork of the movie so that it can be moved when loaded.*

㉒ *Set the Export Options to create multiple movies, one for each page, and to animate the layers movies.*

㉓ *Turn off the Autoplay feature under the Movie Properties to only have the cannon blast play when the button is pressed.*

The Tell Target action with Level 1 as its first parameter and Play as its second parameter was applied to the *Shoot the Cannon* button **⑲**. This creates the button that plays the smoke animation layers in the loaded movie.

The Tell Target action with Level 1 as its first parameter and Stop as its second parameter was applied to the *Stop the Blast* button **⑳**. This creates the button that stops the smoke animation layers in the loaded movie from playing.

The Start/Stop Drag action was applied to the cannon artwork. Without this action, the loaded movie would appear on the page, but we wouldn't be able to drag the artwork around the page **㉑**.

Once the actions were added to the artwork, we still needed to set the Movie Settings.

First we set the Export Options to control which elements of the pages would be animated. The Multiple setting was chosen so that the movie on page two can be loaded onto page one **㉒**. Without this setting, FreeHand would export both pages as a single movie. This would have made it impossible to load page two as a separate movie onto page one.

We also needed to select the Animate Layers option. Without this setting, the layered artwork for the cannon blast would not have played as part of the the movie.

Finally, we needed to turn off the Autoplay option **㉓** under the Movie Properties. This way the cannon would appear on the page without immediately playing the blast effect. The blast artwork would start only when the trigger button was pressed.

Actions in Action

Testing Movies

Once you create an animation, you will most likely want to see if it is running correctly. Fortunately you can test your movies within FreeHand.

To test a movie:

1. Choose **Window > Movie > Test Movie.**

   or

   Click the Test button in the Controller toolbar ㉔. FreeHand processes the movie which opens in a separate window.

   TIP The Test Movie command opens a Flash Player document window ㉕. You can then play the movie to see the animation.

   TIP The Flash Player window also has a set of movie controls at the bottom of the document window ㉖. These can be used instead of the Controller.

2. To play the movie choose **Window > Movie > Play.**

   or

   Click the Play button in the Controller.

3. To stop the movie, choose **Window > Movie > Stop.**

   or

   Click the Stop button in the Controller.

4. To move one frame at a time, choose **Window > Movie > Step Forward** or **Window > Movie > Step Backward.**

   or

   Click the Step forward or Step backward buttons in the Controller.

5. To move to the start of the movie, choose **Window > Movie > Rewind.**

   or

   Click the Rewind button in the Controller.

6. To jump to the end of the movie click the Fast Forward button in the Controller.

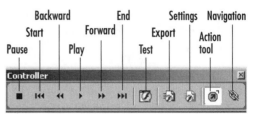

㉔ *Use the* **Controller panel** *to work with Flash movies.*

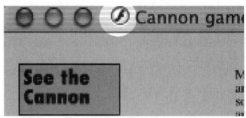

㉕ *The* **Flash Player icon** *in the test document window indicates you are previewing the SWF movie.*

㉖ *The* **movie controls** *in the Flash Player window allow you to test the movie as well as change its settings and export the movie.*

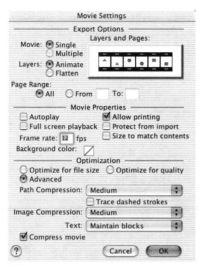

㉗ *The* **Movie Settings dialog box** *lets you control how SWF movies will be played.*

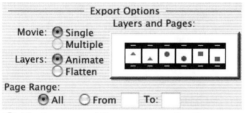

㉘ *The* **Layers and Pages area** *under Export Options in the Movie Settings dialog box.*

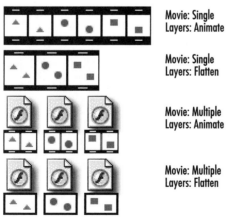

Movie: Single
Layers: Animate

Movie: Single
Layers: Flatten

Movie: Multiple
Layers: Animate

Movie: Multiple
Layers: Flatten

㉙ *The* **four Layers and Pages displays** *for the Movies and Layers options.*

Modifying the Movie Settings

The way a Flash movie plays depends on how you set the options in the Movie Settings dialog box. You may need to change these settings as you test your movie.

To modify the movie settings:

◆ Choose **Window** > **Movie** > **Movie Settings.**

or

Click the Movie Settings button in the Controller. This opens the Movie Settings dialog box.

There are three different areas in the Movie Settings dialog box **㉗**. The Layers and Pages settings under the Export Options control how the FreeHand pages and layers are animated **㉘**. These controls can dramatically change how an animation plays.

To choose the Layers and Pages settings:

1. Choose one of the two Movie options:
   - **Single** exports all the pages as a single SWF file.
   - **Multiple** exports each page as a separate SWF file. Use this option if you want to load one page as a movie onto another page.
   TIP Watch the Layers and Pages preview for an indication of how these settings affect the final movie **㉙**.
2. Choose one of the two Layers options:
   - **Animate** divides any layers on the pages into separate frames in the movie.
   - **Flatten** merges all the layers on the pages into a single frame in the movie.
   TIP The Guides layer and hidden layers are not seen in the animation.
3. Use the Page Range controls to choose which pages are included in the animation.

The second area of the Movie Settings dialog box, Movie Properties, controls how the movie plays **30**.

To set the Movie Properties controls:

1. Select Autoplay to have the movie start automatically as soon as it is opened.

2. Check Full screen playback to have the movie expand to take over the computer screen.

3. Check Allow printing to let the viewer print the movie frames.

4. Check Protect from import to keep the viewer from downloading the SWF onto their own computer. This option is used by designers and animators who don't want others to be able to manipulate their movies.

5. Check Size to match contents to automatically resize the Flash Player window to the size of the animation.

6. Enter an amount in the Frame rate field. This amount is in frames per second (fps). A normal speed is around 12 fps. Lower the number to slow down how fast the animation plays. Increase the number to speed up the animation.

7. Use the Background color well to choose a color from the swatches color palette to put behind the artwork in the animation. The default color of none allows one page to be seen on top of another.

30 *The* **Movie Properties area** *in the Movie Settings dialog box.*

Flash or SWF: What's the difference?

Strictly speaking, there are no Flash files on the Web.

A Flash file (.fla) is the native file format created by the Macromedia Flash application. You don't post those files on the Web.

What most people call Flash movies on the Web are actually Shockwave Flash files (.swf). This is the file format that FreeHand exports as Macromedia Flash (SWF).

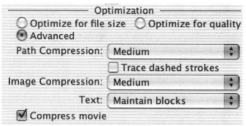

③① *The* **Optimization area** *in the Movie Settings dialog box.*

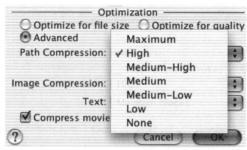

③② *The* **Path Compression and Image Compression menus** *control how the vector paths and raster images appear in the final movie.*

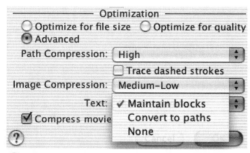

③③ *The* **Text menu** *under the Optimization options lets you control how text blocks are exported in SWF movies.*

One of the advantages of using SWF movies on the Web is that the file sizes are much smaller than other types of Web graphics. The final area of the Movie Settings dialog box, Optimization, lets you control just how small the final SWF movie will be **③①**.

To set the Optimization controls:

1. Choose one of the following to automatically set the rest of the Optimization controls:

    - **Optimize for file size** creates the smallest possible SWF movie. This may cause some elements of the movie to be distorted.
    - **Optimize for quality** creates a larger file but keeps the artwork at its best appearance.

    or

    Choose Advanced to set the individual compression controls.

2. Use the Path Compression menu to control the compression applied to vector artwork in the file **③②**.

3. Use the Image Compression menu to control the compression applied to raster images **③②**. This includes imported raster files as well as raster images created by the special effects.

4. Use the Text menu to control how text is converted **③③**:

    - **Maintain blocks** keeps the text as editable text blocks.
    - **Convert to paths** changes the editable text into path outlines.
    - **None** deletes all the text from the file.

5. Check Compress movie to further reduce the size of the movie.

Working with Flash

Just as FreeHand has a special relationship when working with Macromedia Fireworks, so also does FreeHand have a special relationship when working with Macromedia Flash. At the very least you can import SWF movies into FreeHand documents. Even better, you can use the special Launch and Edit session of Flash to modify those placed SWF files.

To import SWF movies into FreeHand:

1. Choose **File** > **Import** and navigate to select the SWF file you want to import.

2. Click to place the file at its actual size or drag to choose a specific size.

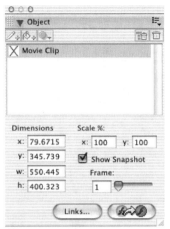

❸❹ *The Object inspector for an* **imported SWF Movie clip**.

You can control a placed SWF file using the Object panel. Although most of the controls are the same as those for other imported images, there are some special controls for SWF files **❸❹**.

To control imported SWF movies:

1. With the SWF file selected, choose Show Snapshot in the Object panel to see a representation of one of the frames in the movie **❸❺**.

   TIP If Show Snapshot is turned off, you see only the Flash logo **❸❻**.

2. Use the Frame slider to choose which frame of the movie is displayed in the snapshot.

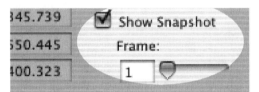

❸❺ *The* **Show Snapshot** *checkbox and* **Frame slider** *let you control the display of an imported SWF file.*

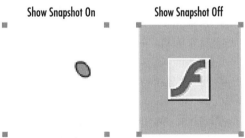

❸❻ *The* **Show Snapshot** *setting lets you see a preview of one frame of the movie. With the setting turned off, the Flash logo is displayed for the placed movie.*

37 *Click the* **Launch and Edit button** *in the Object panel to edit the original Flash file that created an SWF file.*

38 *Click the* **Done button** *to end the special Launch and Edit session in Flash.*

The SWF files imported into FreeHand are not the original Flash files. However, given the special relationship between FreeHand and Flash, you can use the Launch and Edit command to open the original Flash file which created the SWF movie. Then once you make changes to the Flash file, those changes are automatically transferred to the imported SWF file.

To edit imported SWF movies:

1. Select the imported SWF movie in the FreeHand file.

2. Click the Launch and Edit button in the Object inspector **37**.

3. If necessary, FreeHand asks you to locate the original Flash file that created the SWF. When located, the Flash application opens the Flash file.

4. Make whatever changes you want to the Flash document.

TIP The FreeHand to Flash logo at the top of the Flash document indicates you are working in a Launch and Edit session of Flash.

5. When you have finished making the changes, click the Done button at the top of the Flash window **38**. This closes the Flash file and returns you to the FreeHand document. The changes to the Flash file are automatically applied to the imported SWF file.

Working with Flash

Exporting an SWF Movie

Once you have all the movie settings to your liking, it is a simple step to export the SWF file. If you are in the Flash Player window for the Test Movie command, you can easily export the movie at the current settings.

To export an SWF file from the Flash Player:

◆ Choose **Window** > **Movie** > **Export Movie.**

or

Click the Export Movie button in the Controller.

or

Click the Export Movie button at the bottom of the Flash Player window. This opens the Export dialog box where you can name the exported file and save it to a location **39**.

TIP The Flash movie is exported using whatever settings are currently active in the Movie Settings dialog box.

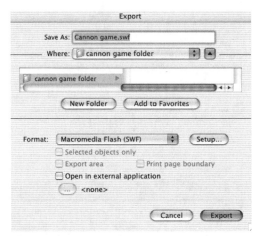

39 *The* **Export dialog box** *lets you name and export an SWF movie.*

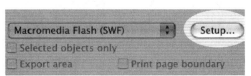

40 *Click the* **Setup button** *in the Export dialog box to open the Movie Settings dialog box.*

You can also export an SWF file directly from the FreeHand document.

To export an SWF file from the FreeHand window:

1. Choose **Edit** > **Export.** This opens the Export Document dialog box **40**.

2. Choose Macromedia Flash (SWF) from the format list.

3. Click the Setup button. This opens the Movie Settings dialog box.

4. Make any necessary changes to the Movie Settings dialog box and click OK.

5. Name the exported file and save it to a location.

PRINTING 28

When I first started using illustration programs, print was the ultimate goal. You printed to a low-end desktop printer in your own office or you sent your work to a high-end service bureau or a print shop to be printed on a professional imagesetter.

Nowadays, people turn their Free-Hand files into Web pages and never see their work in print.

But many FreeHand users want to hold a hard copy printed version of their artwork. Some of them need to print only to their own office printer. The Basic Print Options section of this chapter is for them.

The others are interested in sending their files to professional service bureaus and print shops. They need to read the basic options and then the Advanced Print Options section.

Setting the Basic Print Options

For most basic printing, there are just a few options that you need to set. For instance, you may simply want to specify the number of pages you need to print.

To set the number of copies and print range (Mac):

1. Choose **File** > **Print.** The Print dialog box appears ❶.

2. If it is not active, choose the Copies & Pages option from the menu in the printer dialog box.

3. In the Copies field, enter the number of copies you want to print.

4. In the Pages section, check All to print all the pages in your document.

   or

   Enter the range of pages. If you want to print only one page, type that page number in both the From and To fields.

5. Click OK to print the file.

TIP The Mac Print dialog box may look different if you have different printer software.

To set the number of copies and print range (Win):

1. Choose **File** > **Print.** The Print dialog box appears ❷.

2. In the Output section, enter the number of copies you want to print.

3. In the Print Range section, choose All to print all the pages in your document.

   or

   Choose Current page to print the active page in the document window.

   or

   Choose Pages and enter specific page numbers to print only certain pages.

4. Click OK to print the file.

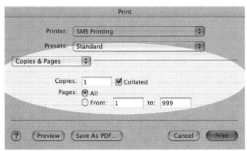

❶ *The* **Copies & Pages options of the Macintosh Print dialog box** *let you choose the page range and number of copies to be printed.*

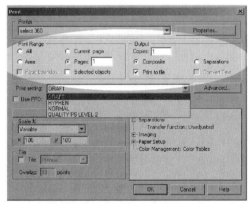

❷ *The* **Print Range** *and* **Output** *sections of the* **Windows Print dialog box** *let you choose the page range and number of copies to be printed.*

Do You Have a PostScript Printer?

Before you print your document, determine what kind of printer you will be using. If you use a non-PostScript device—if you use an ink jet printer, for instance—the Custom, Textured, and PostScript fills and strokes do not print. If you are in doubt as to the type of printer you have, check the documentation that came with the printer.

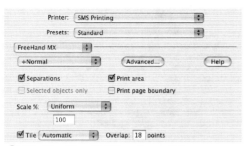

3 *The* **FreeHand MX options** *of the Macintosh Print dialog box.*

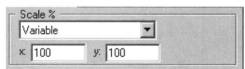

4 *The* **Scale menu options** *of the Print dialog box let you change the size of the printed file.*

5 *The* **Scale % Uniform field** *lets you control how much the file is reduced or enlarged.*

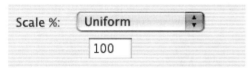

6 *The* **Scale % Variable fields** *let you enter separate amounts for the x (width) and y (height) changes.*

To scale as you print:

1. (Mac) If it is not active, choose the FreeHand MX setting from the menu in the Print dialog box **3**. This displays the basic print options.

or

(Win) All the basic print options are displayed in the Print dialog box.

2. Choose one of the following from the Scale menu **4**:

- **Uniform** scales the artwork proportionately without distorting it.
- **Variable** scales the artwork with different amounts for the **x** and **y** dimensions.
- **Fit on paper** changes the size of your illustration so that it fits on the paper.

TIP The Fit on paper option is very helpful when using the Output Area tool to print many different pages *(see page 399)*.

3. If you have chosen Uniform, enter the amount in the percentage field **5**.

4. If you have chosen Variable, enter different amounts in the **x** and **y** fields **6**.

Printing Color Separations

Most likely you will always want to print a *composite* image of your file ❼. This is an image that combines all the colors together into one image. However, if you want you can print separations. That gives you an individual print for each of the ink colors that are used to create the file ❽.

TIP You can print separations on your desktop printer to make sure you have set your document up properly for different color plates. Each piece of paper that is printed counts as a color plate in your document. Too many plates means you have probably defined too many spot colors.

To set the basic separations options:

◆ (Mac) The default setting will create a composite print. If you want to print each color plate on its own sheet of paper, choose Separations ❾.

   or

   (Win) If your illustration has color in it, you can explicitly choose either Composite or Separations ❿.

❼ *A* **Composite print** *displays a combination of all the colors.*

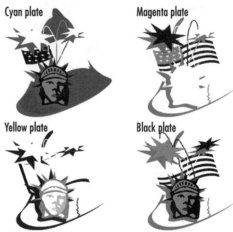

Cyan plate   Magenta plate

Yellow plate   Black plate

❽ **Separations** *print each individual color of the image.*

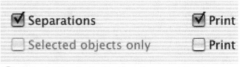

❾ *(Mac) Check the* **Separations** *option to print each individual plate of a color image.*

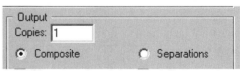

❿ *(Win) Choose the* **Composite** *or* **Separations** *options to print the plates of a color image.*

Printing Color Separations

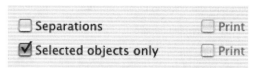

⓫ *Choose the* **Selected objects only** *to print only the objects selected on the page.*

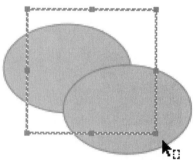 ⓬ *The* **Output Area tool** *in the Tools panel.*

⓭ *The* **Output Area handles** *let you define a specific area to print.*

⓮ *Choose the* **Area option** *of the Print dialog box to print the area defined by the Output Area tool.*

Printing Custom Selections

The basic print options allow you to print a single page or a range of pages. FreeHand also gives you the flexibility to create custom print options. For instance, you can print just the selected objects on a page.

To print selected objects:

1. Select the objects you would like to print.
2. Choose **File** > **Print** to open the Print dialog box.
3. Check Selected objects only ⓫.
4. Set any of the other options and print as usual.

In addition to printing selected items, you can also print within a selected area. This lets you print just a portion of the artwork on a page. You can also use this option to create thumbnails of many pages on a single page or print items that are positioned off a page.

To print a selected area:

1. Select the Output Area tool in the Tools panel ⓬.
2. Drag the Output Area cursor around the area that you want to print. A box with handles appears ⓭.
3. Use any of the handles to adjust the area within the box.
4. Choose **File** > **Print** to open the Print dialog box.
5. Choose the Area option to print the area defined by the Output Area handles ⓮.
6. If you have defined multiple pages as a single output area, you can choose Page boundary to indicate the page edges on the final printout.

TIP Multiple pages printed on a single page is an excellent way to present thumbnails of a multi-page project.

If your artwork is bigger than the paper in your printer and you don't want to reduce it to fit on one page, you won't be able to fit the illustration on one page. *Tiling* is a technique that lets you break up your illustration onto many pieces of paper that you can assemble to form the larger illustration.

To set the tile options:

1. In the Print dialog box, select the Tile checkbox.
2. Choose one of the following from the Tile options :
   - **Manual** lets you manually choose where the tile breaks should appear.
   - **Automatic** sets each of the tile breaks automatically.
3. If you choose Automatic, choose how much overlap you want between each page.

To manually tile an illustration:

1. In the document, move the zero point from the ruler down onto the artwork 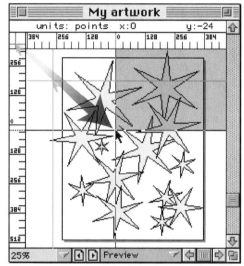.
TIP The zero point sets the artwork above and to the right of that point to print.
2. In the Print dialog box, set the Manual tile option and print that portion of the artwork.
3. Set a new zero point and print that next portion of the artwork.
4. Repeat step 3 as many times as is necessary to print the entire illustration.

⑮ *Use the* **Tile controls** *to print portions of the artwork to more than one page.*

⑯ **Drag the zero point** *from the ruler to set the position of the page for Manual tiling. (The shaded area shows the portion of the page that will print.)*

Printing Custom Selections

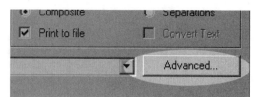

⑰ *Click the* **Advanced button** *of the Print dialog box to open the Print Setup dialog box.*

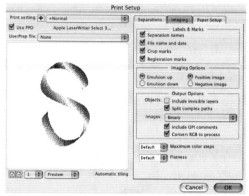

⑱ *Set the advanced print features in the* **Print Setup dialog box.**

⑲ *Use the* **Page Number menu** *to choose which pages are displayed in the Print Setup preview.*

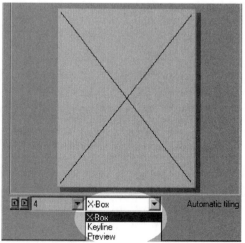

⑳ *The* **Preview menu** *lets you choose the type of preview displayed.*

Setting the Advanced Print Options

If you are printing to an office printer, the options in the Print dialog box are all you need. However, if you want to print to a high-end imagesetter, you will want to set the advanced print options in the Print Setup dialog box.

To open the Print Setup dialog box:

1. Choose **File > Print** to open the Print dialog box.

2. Click the Advanced button **⑰**. This opens the Print Setup dialog box **⑱**.

The left side of the Print Setup box shows a preview of the artwork to be printed. You can make some modifications to the artwork in this box.

To control the Print Setup preview:

1. Use the page number menu to control which pages are visible **⑲**.

2. Use the Preview menu to choose one of the following preview options **⑳**.

   - **Preview** displays the artwork with all the fills, colors, and so on.
   - **Keyline** shows just the paths that define the objects without the fills, colors, and so on.
   - **X-Box** fills the preview area with an X that indicates the page.

   TIP If your artwork is extremely detailed, you may find it faster to view the print preview in the Keyline or X-Box modes.

3. Drag with the mouse to move the artwork to different positions in the Print Preview area.

   TIP If you have moved the preview artwork, click the area just outside the print preview to restore it to the original position.

Setting the Imaging Options

When you print a file, you can add labels and marks around your artwork.

To add labels and marks:

1. In the Print Setup dialog box, click the tab for Imaging. The Labels & Marks options appear on the right side of the dialog box ❷❶.

2. Choose the Labels & Marks options as follows:

    *   **Separation names** adds the name of the color plate that is printed.
    *   **File name and date** adds the name of the file, page number, and date and time that the file is printed.
    *   **Crop marks** adds the marks that indicate the trim size of the artwork ❷❷.
    *   **Registration marks** adds registration marks and color bars that are necessary for printing multiple colors ❷❷.

The imaging options control the look and direction of the images when printed. These options are important when printing to film.

To choose the imaging options:

1. In the Print Setup dialog box, click the tab for Imaging. The Imaging Options appear on the right side of the Print Setup dialog box ❷❸.

2. Choose one of the following options for *emulsion* (chemical areas) of the film:

    *   **Emulsion up** prints the file so that the emulsion faces up.
    *   **Emulsion down** prints the file so that the emulsion faces down.

3. Choose one of the following color options.

    *   **Positive image** is used for printing to paper.
    *   **Negative image** is used for printing to film.

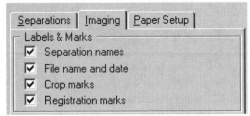

❷❶ *Check the boxes for each of the Labels & Marks to have those marks printed around the artwork.*

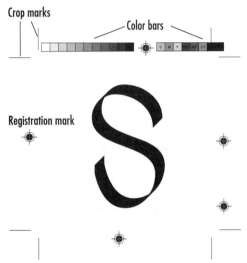

❷❷ *Artwork printed with* **Crop marks** *and* **Registration marks** *selected.*

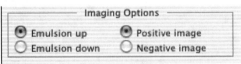

❷❸ *Choose the* **Imaging options** *to control the direction of the image and film orientation.*

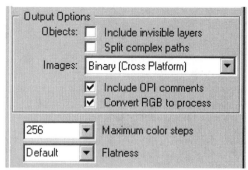

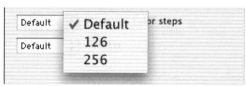

*The **Output options** control the aspects of a FreeHand file and exported images.*

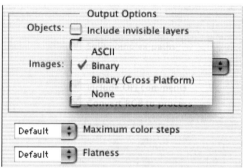

*The **Images menu** controls how linked images are sent to the printer.*

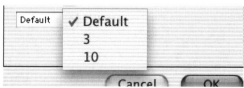

*The **Maximum color steps menu** controls how many steps are created when printing gradients and color blends.*

*The **Flatness menu** helps you avoid limitcheck errors when printing.*

FreeHand offers various options for printing to a PostScript device. These options stay with the file when it is saved or exported as an EPS file.

To set the output options:

1. In the Print Setup dialog box, click the tab for Imaging. The Output Options appear ㉔.

2. Check Include invisible layers to print objects that are on hidden layers. Otherwise those layers do not print.

3. Check Split complex paths to automatically split long paths.

TIP Modern printing software is less likely to need this option.

4. Choose one of the following from the Images menu ㉕:
   - **Binary** or **Binary (Macintosh)** is used for printing on the Macintosh platform.
   - **Binary (Cross Platform)** is used for both Macintosh and Windows.
   - **ASCII** is used only for the Windows platform or if you have trouble outputting on the Macintosh platform.
   - **None** is for when using an OPI system.

5. Check Include OPI comments if TIFF images will be replaced during prepress.

6. Check Convert RGB to process if you have RGB TIFF images in the file.

To set the maximum color steps:

- Leave this field set for Default. If you have trouble printing, use the menu to set a lower number in the Maximum color steps field ㉖.

To set the Flatness:

- Leave this field set for Default. If you get a limitcheck error when printing, enter a number from 1 to 100 in the Flatness field ㉗.

Setting the Separations Options

The Separations options control how the colors of your file print when outputting your work to separate pieces of film.

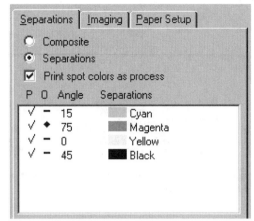

To choose the separations options:

1. In the Print Setup dialog box, click the tab for Separations ㉘.

2. If you want all the colors to print together, choose Composite.

3. To separate the colors to different plates, choose Separations.

4. Check Print spot colors as process to override the settings for spot colors.

5. To prevent a color from printing, click its checkmark in the **P** column to delete the checkmark for that color.

㉘ *The* **Separations** *controls.*

To set the overprint options:

1. In the separations options, click the **O** column. The Overprint Ink dialog box appears ㉙.

2. Choose one of the following:
   - **On** sets all instances of that color to overprint.
   - **Threshold** specifies what percentage tint of that color or higher will overprint.
   - **Off** turns off overprinting.

▥ A checkmark in the **O** column indicates an overprint. A diamond indicates an overprint at a threshold level.

㉙ *The* **Overprint Ink** *dialog box lets you turn on overprinting or set an amount at which overprinting will occur.*

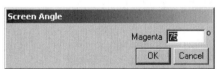

㉚ *The* **Screen Angle** *dialog box lets you set the angle at which a color's screens will be printed.*

To set the screen angle:

1. Click the Angle column for that color. The Screen Angle dialog box appears ㉚.

2. Enter the angle you want for that color and click OK.

3. Repeat for each color.

▥ Consult with your print shop before you adjust the screen angles, screen frequency, or overprinting options.

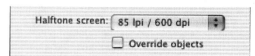

③ *The* **Halftone screen controls.**

② *The* **Halftones panel** *lets you change the halftone screen for individual objects.*

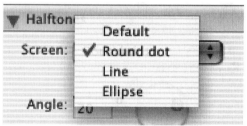

③ *The* **Screen menu** *lets you choose the shape of the Halftone screen.*

④ *The difference between a screen angle of zero degrees (left) and 45 degrees (right).*

If your artwork has any screened objects, you may want to set the halftone screen.

To set the halftone screen:

1. Open the Separations options.

2. Use the Halftone screen menu in the Separations options to choose from the list of common screens for your output device **③**.

3. To override any halftone screens set for individual objects, click Override objects.

TIP If you print to a laser printer and find banding in your blends, lower the screen frequency to around 35 lpi (lines per inch) or 40 lpi. While the screened artwork may look a little "dotty," this should reduce the banding.

In addition to setting the halftone screen for the entire illustration, you can set the halftone screen for individual objects.

To set the halftone screen for individual objects:

1. Select the object whose halftone screen you want to set.

2. Choose **Window > Panels > Halftones**. The Halftones panel appears **②**.

3. Choose the shape of the screen dot from the Screen menu **③**.

TIP The Default setting uses the shape of the screendot that's been set by the output device.

4. Enter the angle of the screen in the Angle field or rotate the wheel to set the screen angle. If no value is set, the default angle of 45 degrees is used **④**.

5. Enter the frequency (lines per inch) of the screen in the Frequency field or use the slider to set the number. If no value is set, the default of the output device is used.

The Transfer function controls the dot gain for screened images.

To set the transfer function:

◆ With the Separations tab selected in the Print Setup dialog box, select one of the following from the Transfer function menu ㉟:

- **Unadjusted** is for printing to a specially calibrated output device.
- **Normalize** is for printing to an ordinary laser printer.
- **Posterize** speeds printing but reduces the number of levels of screens.

In addition to the Trap Xtra, FreeHand has a global trapping option called spread.

To choose the spread size:

◆ Use the Spread size menu or enter an expansion amount in the Spread size field ㊱.

Saving Print Settings

FreeHand lets you save all the print options so you can easily apply them to other work.

To save print settings:

1. Set all the print options the way you want the file to print.

2. Click the + sign next to the Print settings menu ㊲. A Save dialog box appears.

3. Use the Save dialog box to name and save the file in the PrintSet directory. This adds the preset to the menu.

To apply print settings:

◆ Choose a setting from the Print Settings menu.

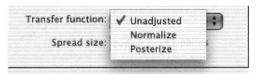

㉟ *The* **Transfer function menu** *lets you choose how halftone screens are printed.*

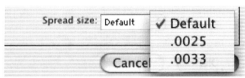

㊱ *The* **Spread size menu** *lets you apply a small amount of spread to expand the size of fills and strokes.*

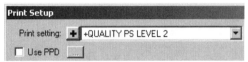

㊲ *The* **Print setting controls** *allow you to save and apply preset print options.*

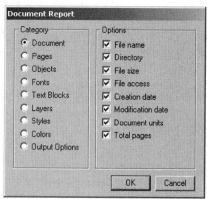

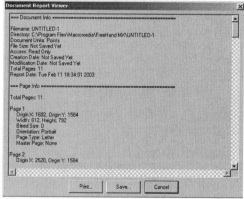

③ *The* **Document Report dialog box** *lets you select the information to be included in the document report.*

③ *The* **Document Report Viewer** *lets you read the report, save it as a text file, or print it.*

Collecting for Output

If you send out your document to be printed by someone else, it is handy to have a record of all the information about the file. FreeHand provides you with a very sophisticated report for all your documents.

To create a document report:

1. With the document open, choose **File > Report**. The Document Report dialog box appears **③**.

2. Choose the categories listed on the left side of the Document Report dialog box. Each one of these categories then displays a different set of Options. *(See the sidebar on the next page for a list of the options for each category.)*

3. Check each of the Options for each category to indicate which information you want listed.

4. Click Report (Mac) or OK (Win) to see the Document Report Viewer **③**, where you can read the complete document report.

5. Click Save to create a permanent text file of your report.

Unless you have your own high-resolution imagesetter, you must transfer your work onto a floppy disk or some type of removable media such as a CD-ROM. You then send the disk to a service bureau that will output the file. You must send certain files along with your FreeHand file. Rather than making you collect these files manually, the Collect For Output feature automates the process.

To use the Collect For Output command:

1. Choose **File > Collect For Output.** An alert box appears warning you that you should find out whether or not you have the rights to distribute fonts **40**. Click OK.

TIP Click Don't show again to stop the alert from appearing.

2. The Document Report dialog box appears *(see previous page)*. Check each of the Options for each category to indicate which information you want listed. Click OK.

3. Choose a destination for the report and files, such as a folder on the current drive or a removable cartridge. Click Save.

4. FreeHand collects all the files necessary to print the document **41**. This includes the original FreeHand file, linked graphics, the document report, fonts, the printer user prep, and printer driver (Mac).

40 *The alert box that appears as part of the Collect For Output process.*

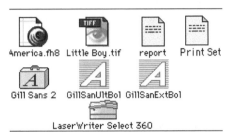

41 *The files assembled by the Collect For Output command.*

Information in each report category

Here is a list of the items in each report category.

Document:	File name, Directory, File size, File access, Creation date, Modification date, Document units, Total pages
Pages:	Page location, Dimensions, Bleed size, Orientation, Page type
Objects:	Set Note, Halftone, Place file
Fonts:	Font name, Font PS name, Font file format, Font style, Font size
Text:	Blocks Fonts used, Color used, Bounding box, Line count, Paragraph count, First line
Layers:	Foreground layers, Background layers, Visibility, Editing color, Access, Preview status
Styles:	Graphics styles, Text styles
Colors:	Named colors, Separations
Output Options:	Invisible layers, Split paths, Image date, Convert image, Max color steps, Flatness

CUSTOMIZING FREEHAND 29

Assemble a group of Macromedia FreeHand users in the same room and you're going to hear from a very diverse group of people.

For instance, those who have been working with FreeHand for many years can't stand the idea of someone changing a single keystroke.

Others who work extensively with a particular feature, such as the Xtra tools, may want them added to the Tools panel.

Others may have migrated over to FreeHand from another program such as Adobe Illustrator, CorelDraw, or QuarkXPress. They may want to make FreeHand work similarly to those programs.

Finally, someone just might want a different page size to come up each time they open a new document.

Fortunately FreeHand gives you a wealth of opportunities to customize the program.

Changing the Toolbars

Each of the toolbars comes with different themes—the main tools, Xtra tools, Xtra operations, and so on. However, you can easily customize each toolbar with whatever commands you would like.

To open the Customize Toolbars dialog box (Win):

1. Choose **Edit** > **Keyboard Shortcuts**. The Customize dialog box appears.

2. Click the Toolbars tab to open the controls for the Toolbars ❶.

To open the Customize Toolbars dialog box (Mac):

◆ Choose **Window** > **Toolbars** > **Customize**. The Customize Toolbars dialog box appears ❷.

To add an icon to a toolbar:

1. Open the toolbar that you want to customize.

2. Open the Customize Toolbars dialog box as explained in the previous exercises.

3. Open the categories on the left side of the Customize Toolbars dialog box to find the command that you want to add to a toolbar.

4. Select the command. The icon for the command is highlighted on the right side of the dialog box.

5. Drag the icon for the command onto the toolbar.

TIP In addition to the toolbars listed under the **Window** > **Toolbars** menu, you can drag icons onto the Tools panel ❸.

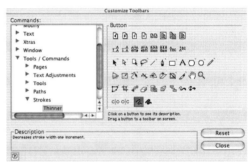

❶ *The Windows* **Customize Toolbars** *dialog box lets you add commands to the toolbars.*

❷ *The Macintosh* **Customize Toolbars** *dialog box lets you add commands to the toolbars.*

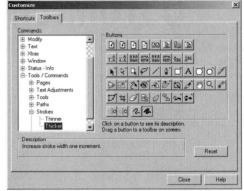

❸ *An example of how the icons to decrease or increase the stroke weight appear when added to the Tools panel.*

❹ *You can* **drag an icon off** *a toolbar.*

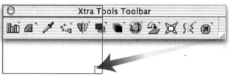

❺ *Drag the corner to* **resize a toolbar.**

To delete icons from the toolbars:

◆ With the Customize Toolbars dialog box open, drag an icon off any toolbar **❹**.

or

Hold the Cmd/Alt key and drag an icon off a toolbar at any time without opening the Customize Toolbars dialog box.

To add icons from one toolbar to another:

◆ With the Customize Toolbars dialog box open, drag an icon off one toolbar onto another.

or

Hold the Cmd/Alt key and drag an icon off one toolbar onto another without opening the Customize Toolbars dialog box.

To change the shape of toolbars:

1. Position the Pointer over the corner of a toolbar.

2. Drag the toolbar to the new shape **❺**.

TIP Toolbars cannot be reshaped while they are snapped to the edges of the screen.

Changing the Toolbars

Modifying the Keyboard Shortcuts

FreeHand lets you customize the keyboard shortcuts that are assigned to commands. This allows you to add shortcuts to commands or to change the shortcuts so they match those of other programs.

To customize keyboard shortcuts:

1. Choose **Edit** > **Keyboard Shortcuts**. The Customize Shortcuts dialog box appears ⓖ.

2. Use the categories on the left side of the dialog box to find the command that you want to customize.

3. Click the command. The current shortcut keys, if any, appear in the Current shortcut keys area.

4. Type the keyboard shortcut that you want for the command.

5. If the shortcut is assigned to another command, that command appears after the words *Currently Assigned to*. Type a new command or change the conflicting shortcut.

6. Click Assign to set the shortcut.

7. Repeat the steps to assign additional commands or click the Close button to return to the work page.

To choose one of the shortcuts for other programs:

1. Choose **Edit** > **Keyboard Shortcuts**. The Customize Shortcuts dialog box appears ⓖ.

2. Choose a program under the Keyboard shortcut setting menu. *(See the sidebar on the right for a list of these programs.)*

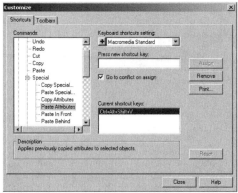

ⓖ *The* **Customize Shortcuts dialog box.**

Preset Shortcuts

The following are the preset shortcuts that are available. Where indicated, some shortcuts are available only for the Windows or Macintosh versions of FreeHand.

Authorware 4

CorelDRAW 6 (Mac)

CorelDRAW 7 (Win)

Fontographer 4.1 (Mac)

FreeHand 8

FreeHand 9

Illustrator 6 (Mac)

Illustrator 7

Macromedia Standard

PageMaker 6 (Mac)

Photoshop 4 (Mac)

QuarkXPress 3.3

QuarkXPress 4

Modifying the Keyboard Shortcuts

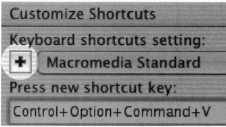

⑦ *Click the plus sign to add a custom keyboard setting.*

⑧ *The* **Keyboard Shortcuts Summary** *contains a list of all the keyboard shortcuts.*

What is the Macromedia Standard?

The set of shortcuts that is active when you first install FreeHand is called the Macromedia Standard set. This set uses slightly different shortcuts from previous versions of FreeHand. It was created for those who use applications such as Macromedia Flash or Macromedia Dreamweaver.

If you have used previous versions of Freehand, you may be more comfortable using those presets. However, if you work with other Macromedia products, you may be more comfortable working with the Macromedia Standard set.

Once you have created a set of shortcuts, you can save that set as a preset that you can choose at any time.

To save a custom preset:
1. Click the plus sign next to the Keyboard shortcut settings menu **⑦**.
2. Use the dialog box to save the preset. This lists the setting along with the other presets.

Once you have created your own shortcuts, you can apply them at any time as you work.

To apply the preset shortcuts:
1. Use the Keyboard shortcut setting pop-up menu to display the list of preset shortcuts.
2. Choose from the list of presets and then click Assign.

You can also print out a list of the keyboard shortcuts to hang next to your computer screen.

To print the keyboard shortcuts:
1. Click the Print button. The Keyboard Shortcuts Summary dialog box appears that displays all the shortcuts **⑧**.
2. Click the Print button to print the list of shortcuts.

   or

   Click the Save As button to save the list as a text file.

TIP This text file can be imported into a page layout program and formatted as desired. *(See Appendix A for a printout of all the default shortcuts that ship with FreeHand.)*

Modifying the Keyboard Shortcuts

Setting the Preferences

Preferences control the entire application. This means that any changes you make to the Preferences settings will be applied to all documents — past, present, and future. Of course, you can always change your Preferences settings at any time as you work.

To change the preferences (Mac):

1. Choose **Edit** >**Preferences** (Mac OS 9) or **FreeHand MX** >**Preferences** (Mac OS X). The Preferences dialog box appears **9**.

2. The preferences settings are divided into 11 categories on the left side of the Preferences dialog box.

3. Click the category you want to control and change the settings as needed.

To change the preferences (Win):

1. Choose **Edit** >**Preferences**. The Preferences dialog box appears **10**.

2. The preferences settings are divided into 10 categories shown as tab settings at the top of the Preferences dialog box.

3. Click the category you want to control and change the settings to suit the way you work.

TIP For a complete list of each of the preferences and how they affect working with FreeHand, see Appendix C.

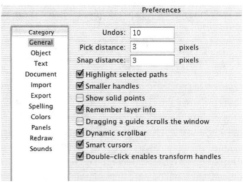

9 *The* **Macintosh Preferences settings** *with the categories controlled by a list on the left.*

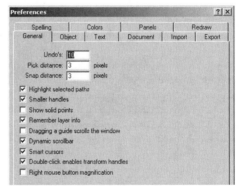

10 *The* **Windows Preferences** *settings with the categories controlled by the tabs on the top.*

KEYBOARD SHORTCUTS

Working with keyboard shortcuts is probably the fastest way to work on a computer in any application. FreeHand offers a wealth of keyboard shortcuts for almost all the menu commands as well as for many non-menu items.

As explained in Chapter 29, you can change the keyboard shortcuts to fit your own particular work habits. You may do so in order to make Freehand work similarly to another program that you are used to or to add a shortcut to a command that doesn't have a shortcut.

If you change your keyboard shortcuts, you can print a copy of those changes to use as a reference.

This appendix lists the default keyboard shortcuts in FreeHand. If you have not made any changes to your settings, you will find that this list matches how FreeHand works on your computer. If you have changed your settings, you can use the Print command in the Customize dialog box to print your own list.

Macintosh Keyboard Commands

The following are the default keyboard short-cuts. These are the abbreviations used:

Cmd = Command key
Opt = Option key
Shift = Shift key

File Menu

New	Cmd+N
Open...	Cmd+O
Close	Cmd+W
Save	Cmd+S
Save As...	Cmd+Shift+S
Import...	Cmd+R
Export...	Cmd+Shift+R
Print...	Cmd+P
Quit	Cmd+Q

Edit Menu

Undo	Cmd+Z
Redo	Cmd+Y, Cmd+Shift+Z
Cut	Cmd+X
Copy	Cmd+C
Paste	Cmd+V
Special> Paste Attributes	Cmd+Opt+Shift+V
Cut Contents	Cmd+Shift+X
Paste Inside	Cmd+Shift+V

Duplicate	Cmd+Opt+D
Clone	Cmd+Shift+D
Select> All	Cmd+A
Select> All In Document	Cmd+Shift+A
Select> None	Cmd+D
Find & Replace> Graphics	Cmd+F
Preferences...	Cmd+U

View Menu

Fit Selection	Cmd+Opt+0
Fit To Page	Cmd+Shift+W
Fit All	Cmd+0
Magnification> 50%	Cmd+5
Magnification> 100%	Cmd+1
Magnification> 200%	Cmd+2
Magnification> 400%	Cmd+4
Magnification> 800%	Cmd+8
Keyline	Cmd+K
Fast Mode	Cmd+Shift+K
Toolbars	Cmd+Opt+T
Panels	F4, Cmd+Shift+H
Page Rulers> Show	Cmd+Opt+R
Text Rulers	Cmd+/
Guides> Show	Cmd+;

Guides> Lock	Cmd+Opt+;
Guides> Snap To Guides	Cmd+Shift+;
Grid> Show	Cmd+Opt+G
Grid> Snap To Grid	Cmd+Opt+Shift+G
Snap To Point	Cmd+'

Modify Menu

Transform> Scale...	Cmd+F10
Transform> Move...	No shortcuts
Transform> Rotate...	Cmd+F13
Transform> Skew...	Cmd+F11
Transform Again	Cmd+,
Arrange> Bring To Front	Cmd+Shift+Up Arrow
Arrange> Move Forward	Cmd+Up Arrow
Arrange> Move Backward	Cmd+Down Arrow
Arrange> Send To Back	Cmd+Shift+Down Arrow
Align...> Top...	Cmd+Opt+4
Align...> Bottom...	Cmd+Opt+6
Align...> Center Horizontal...	Cmd+Opt+5
Align...> Center Vertical...	Cmd+Opt+2
Align...> Left	Cmd+Opt+1
Align...> Right	Cmd+Opt+3
Align Again	Cmd+Opt+Shift+A

Join	Cmd+J
Split	Cmd+Shift+J
Combine> Blend	Cmd+Shift+B
Combine> Join Blend To Path	Cmd+Opt+Shift+B
Unlock	Cmd+Shift+L
Group	Cmd+G
Ungroup	Cmd+Shift+G
Symbol> Edit Symbol	Cmd+E
Symbol> Convert to Symbol	F8
Convert to Image...	Cmd+Opt+Shift+Z

Text Menu

Size> Smaller	Cmd+Shift+,
Size> Larger	Cmd+Shift+.
Font Style> Bold	Cmd+B
Font Style> Italic	Cmd+I
Font Style> BoldItalic	Cmd+Opt+Shift+O
Effect> Highlight...	Cmd+Opt+Shift+H
Effect> Strikethrough...	Cmd+Opt+Shift+S
Effect> Underline...	Cmd+Opt+Shift+U
Align> Left	Cmd+Opt+Shift+L
Align> Right	Cmd+Opt+Shift+R
Align> Center	Cmd+Opt+Shift+C
Align> Justify	Cmd+Opt+Shift+J
Special Characters> Em Space	Cmd+Shift+M

Macintosh Keyboard Commands

Windows Keyboard Commands

Special Characters> En Space	Cmd+Shift+N
Special Characters> Thin Space	Cmd+Shift+T
Special Characters> Discretionary Hyphen	Cmd+-
Editor...	Cmd+Shift+E
Flow Around Selection...	Cmd+Opt+W
Flow Inside Path	Cmd+Shift+U
Attach To Path	Cmd+Shift+Y
Convert To Paths	Cmd+Shift+P

Xtras Menu

Repeat Last	Cmd+Shift+=

Window Menu

New Window	Cmd+Opt+N
Tools	Cmd+F2
Object	Control+F3
Answers	Cmd+Opt+F1
Layers	F2, Cmd+6
Swatches	Cmd+F9
Styles	Shift+F11, Cmd+3
Library	F11
Color Mixer	Shift+F9, Cmd+Shift+C
Align	Cmd+Opt+A
Movie> Test	Cmd+Return
Movie> Settings	Cmd+Shift+Return

Windows Keyboard Commands

The following are the default keyboard shortcuts. These are the abbreviations used:

Ctrl = Ctrl key
Alt = Alt key
Shift = Shift key

File Menu

New	Ctrl+N
Open...	Ctrl+O
Close	Ctrl+W
Save	Ctrl+S
Save As...	Ctrl+Shift+S
Import...	Ctrl+R
Export...	Ctrl+Shift+R
Print...	Ctrl+P
Exit	Ctrl+Q, Alt+F4

Edit Menu

Undo	Ctrl+Z
Redo	Ctrl+Y,Ctrl+Shift+Z
Cut	Ctrl+X
Copy	Ctrl+C
Paste	Ctrl+V
Special: Paste Attributes	Ctrl+Alt+Shift+V
Cut Contents	Ctrl+Shift+X
Paste Contents	Ctrl+Shift+V
Duplicate	Ctrl+Alt+D
Clone	Ctrl+Shift+D

Select: All	Ctrl+A
Select: All In Document	Ctrl+Shift+A
Select: None	Ctrl+D
Find And Replace: Text	Ctrl+Shift+F
Find And Replace: Graphics	Ctrl+F
Preferences...	Ctrl+U

View Menu

Fit Selection	Ctrl+Alt+0
Fit To Page	Ctrl+Shift+W
Fit All	Ctrl+0
Magnification: 50%	Ctrl+5
Magnification: 100%	Ctrl+1
Magnification: 200%	Ctrl+2
Magnification: 400%	Ctrl+4
Magnification: 800%	Ctrl+8
Keyline	Ctrl+K
Fast Mode	Ctrl+Shift+K
Toolbars	Ctrl+Alt+T
Panels	F4,Ctrl+Shift+H
Page Rulers: Show	Ctrl+Alt+R
Text Rulers	Ctrl+/
Guides: Show	Ctrl+;
Guides: Lock	Ctrl+Alt+;

Guides: Snap To Guides	Ctrl+Shift+;
Grid: Show	Ctrl+Alt+G
Grid: Snap To Grid	Ctrl+Alt+Shift+G
Snap To Point	Ctrl+Shift+/, Ctrl+'

Modify Menu

Transform: Scale...	Ctrl+F10
Transform Again	Ctrl+,
Arrange: Bring To Front	Ctrl+Shift+Up
Arrange: Move Forward	Ctrl+Up
Arrange: Move Backward	Ctrl+Down
Arrange: Send To Back	Ctrl+Shift+Down
Align: Top	Ctrl+Alt+4
Align: Bottom	Ctrl+Alt+6
Align: Center Horizontal	Ctrl+Alt+5
Align: Center Vertical	Ctrl+Alt+2
Align: Left	Ctrl+Alt+1
Align: Right	Ctrl+Alt+3
Align Again	Ctrl+Alt+Shift+A
Join	Ctrl+J
Split	Ctrl+Shift+J
Combine: Blend	Ctrl+Shift+B
Combine: Join Blend To Path	Ctrl+Alt+Shift+B

Windows Keyboard Commands

Lock	Ctrl+L
Unlock	Ctrl+Shift+L
Group	Ctrl+G
Ungroup	Ctrl+Shift+G
Symbol: Edit Symbol	Ctrl+E
Symbol: Convert to Symbol	F8
Convert to Image...	Ctrl+Alt+Shift+Z

Text Menu

Size: Smaller	Ctrl+Shift+,
Size: Larger	Ctrl+Shift+.
Font Style: Bold	Ctrl+B
Font Style: Italic	Ctrl+I
Font Style: BoldItalic	Ctrl+Alt+Shift+O
Effect: Highlight...	Ctrl+Alt+Shift+H
Effect: Strikethrough...	Ctrl+Alt+Shift+S
Effect: Underline...	Ctrl+Alt+Shift+U
Align: Left	Ctrl+Alt+Shift+L
Align: Right	Ctrl+Alt+Shift+R
Align: Center	Ctrl+Alt+Shift+C
Align: Justified	Ctrl+Alt+Shift+J
Special Characters: Em Space	Ctrl+Shift+M
Special Characters: En Space	Ctrl+Shift+N
Special Characters: Thin Space	Ctrl+Shift+T

Special Characters: Discretionary Hyphen	Ctrl+-
Editor...	Ctrl+Shift+E
Flow Around Selection...	Ctrl+Alt+W
Flow Inside Path	Ctrl+Shift+U
Attach To Path	Ctrl+Shift+Y
Convert To Paths	Ctrl+Shift+P

Xtras Menu

Repeat	Ctrl+Shift+=

Window Menu

New Window	Ctrl+Alt+N
Tools	Ctrl+F2
Object	Ctrl+F3
Answers	Alt+F1
Layers	F2,Ctrl+6
Swatches	Ctrl+F9
Styles	Shift+F11,Ctrl+3
Library	F11
Color Mixer	Shift+F9, Ctrl+Shift+C
Halftones	Ctrl+H
Align	Ctrl+Alt+A
Transform	Ctrl+M
Movie: Test	Ctrl+Enter
Movie: Settings	Ctrl+Shift+Enter

FILL & STROKE DISPLAYS

As shown in chapters 14 and 15, there are some fills and strokes that you can apply to objects but can't preview on screen. The Custom fills, Textured fills, and Custom strokes can't be previewed because those fills and strokes are based on the PostScript language.

However, since they do not display onscreen within Macromedia Free-Hand, it is difficult to see how to use them properly. This chapter provides a printout of those fills and strokes so that you may find it easier to work with them.

You'll also find a printout of the Pattern fills and strokes. These do appear onscreen, but as there are so many of them, I thought it would be helpful to have them printed in one place so you can see what they look like. (Remember though, that the Pattern fills and strokes may not print correctly to high-level PostScript devices such as imagesetters.)

Custom Fills

The ten Custom fills appear onscreen as a series of Cs in the artwork. The examples below show how each Custom fill prints at its default settings. The gray circles show which of the Custom fills allow background objects to show through their transparent areas.

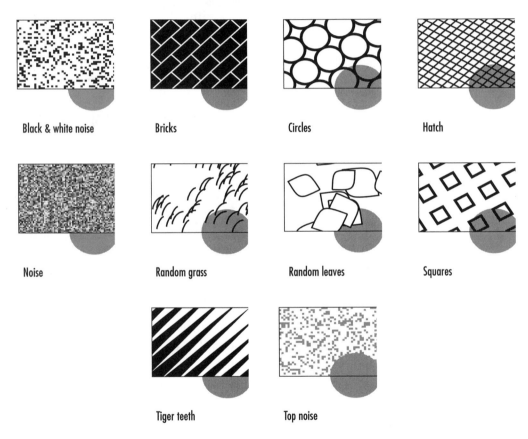

Black & white noise   Bricks   Circles   Hatch

Noise   Random grass   Random leaves   Squares

Tiger teeth   Top noise

1 *The* ten Custom fills *at their default settings.*

Textured Fills

The nine Textured fills appear onscreen as a series of Cs in the artwork. The examples below show how each Textured fill prints at its default settings. The final example shows how only the fill responds to a change in color.

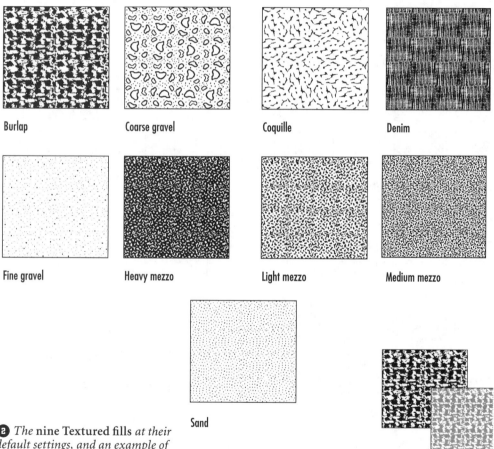

Burlap

Coarse gravel

Coquille

Denim

Fine gravel

Heavy mezzo

Light mezzo

Medium mezzo

Sand

❷ *The* **nine Textured fills** *at their default settings, and an example of a color change.*

Color change

Pattern Fills and Strokes

The Pattern fills and strokes are bitmapped
patterns that appear onscreen and print as
shown below. In addition to these default
settings, each of the patterns may be inverted
or have its pixels edited one by one.

❸ *The* 64 **Pattern fills and strokes** *at their default settings.*

Custom Strokes

The 23 Custom strokes appear onscreen as solid strokes. The examples below show how each of the fills will print at its default settings. The gray circles show how the white areas react with backgrounds. Either they will stay white or become transparent.

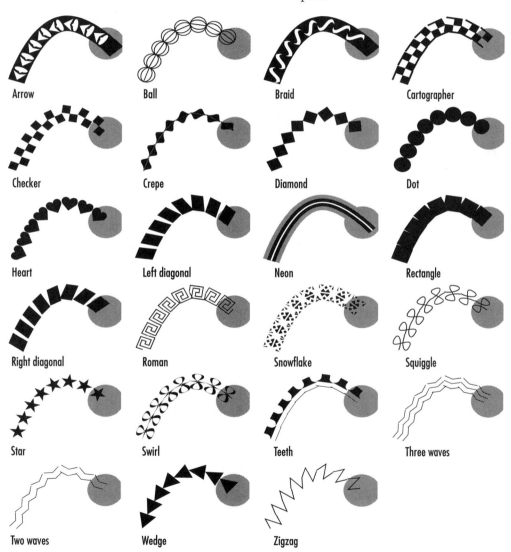

Arrow	Ball	Braid	Cartographer
Checker	Crepe	Diamond	Dot
Heart	Left diagonal	Neon	Rectangle
Right diagonal	Roman	Snowflake	Squiggle
Star	Swirl	Teeth	Three waves
Two waves	Wedge	Zigzag	

❹ *The 23* **Custom strokes** *at their default settings.*

PREFERENCES C

Just because Macromedia Free-Hand installs with certain settings doesn't mean you have to keep them the way you found them. FreeHand gives you a wealth of choices as to how your application operates.

In addition to the custom toolbars and keyboard commands covered in Chapter 29, FreeHand gives you many different preference settings for working with the program.

Some of these preferences are merely cosmetic—that is, they only affect the look and feel of how you work with the program.

Other preferences are more substantial and can change the way files are exported or copied.

Some of the preferences cover very esoteric actions. If you don't understand what a preference setting does, it's best to leave it the way it was set during installation. That default setting is almost always the way most people will need to work.

General Preferences

Undo's lets you set the number of actions that can be reversed.

Pick distance controls, in pixels, how close the cursor has to come to manipulate a point.

Snap distance controls how close the cursor has to come when snapping one object to another.

Highlight selected paths displays paths and points in the color of the layer they are on 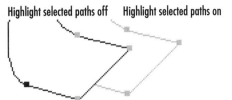.

Smaller handles changes how the control handles of points are displayed ❷.

Show solid points reverses how FreeHand displays selected and unselected points. When this option is off, selected points are hollow. When it is on, selected points are solid ❸.

Smart cursors changes how the cursors for the tools are displayed ❹.

Remember layer info means an object copied and pasted from one document to another will be pasted onto the same layer it originally had.

Dragging a guide scrolls the window means that if you drag a guide into a ruler, you move to a different section of the artwork.

Double-click enables transform handles gives you the transformation handles when you double-click on an object.

Dynamic scrollbar lets you see your artwork as you drag the scrollbars of the window.

Right mouse button magnification (Win) allows you to click-drag with the right mouse button pressed to define an area to be enlarged.

Highlight selected paths off   Highlight selected paths on

❶ *How the* **Smoother editing** *and* **Highlight preferences** *affect the display of points and paths.*

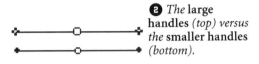

❷ *The* **large handles** *(top) versus the* **smaller handles** *(bottom).*

Show solid points off   Show solid points on

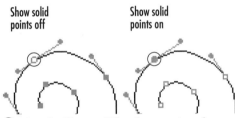

❸ *How the* **Show solid points** *setting changes the display of the selected point (circled).*

❹ *The* **Smart cursors** *on (top) versus* **Smart cursors** *turned off (bottom).*

Object Preferences

Changing object changes defaults means that if you change an object's fill or stroke, the next object has those attributes.

Groups transform as unit by default means that all items in a group transform together, but this may result in unwanted distortions.

Join non-touching paths means when you join objects that don't touch, FreeHand draws a line between the two nearest points.

Path operations consume original paths means that when you apply path operations commands, the original paths are deleted.

Opt/Alt-drag copies paths controls whether holding the Opt/Alt key while dragging or transforming creates a duplicate of the object.

Show fill for new open paths allows you to see the fill in open paths. Only those paths drawn after changing this preference display the fills.

Warn before launch and edit controls whether the External Editor automatically opens when you double-click imported files.

Edit Locked Objects allows the stroke and fill attributes of locked objects to be modified. Also text within a locked text block can be modified.

External Editor menu selects the application that opens when you double-click imported files.

Default line weights field controls the sizes, in points, in the Stroke Widths submenu.

Auto-apply style to selected objects controls how an object is used to define a new style.

Text Preferences

Always use Text Editor means that the Text Editor appears when you click with the text tool.

Track tab movement with vertical line means a line extends through the text when tab stops are placed on the ruler ❺.

Show text handles when text ruler is off lets you see the text block handles even if the text ruler is turned off ❻.

New text containers auto-expand means that if you click to create a text block, the text block will expand as you type.

Text tool reverts to pointer causes the Text tool to change to the Pointer tool when it is moved outside the text block.

Display Font Preview shows a representation of the font when you choose it in the font menus ❼.

"Smart quotes" and its pop-up menu allows you to have FreeHand substitute typographer quotes or guillemets instead of plain tick marks ❽.

Build text styles based on controls whether styles are defined by the first paragraph or the shared attributes of the text block.

Dragging a text style changes controls whether the whole text block or a single paragraph changes when you drag a style icon.

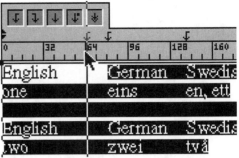

❺ *A line extends through the text to mark the tab location when* **Track tab movement with vertical line** *is turned on.*

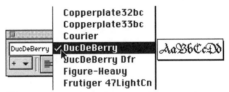

❻ *Working in a text block with the* **Show text handles when text ruler is off** *turned on.*

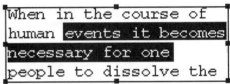

❼ *Turning on* **Display Font Preview** *lets you see a representation of the font when the cursor passes over the font name.*

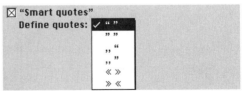

❽ *The various choices for* **Smart Quotes.**

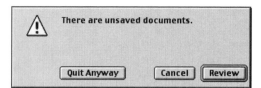

9 *The* unsaved documents *dialog box.*

Document Preferences

Restore last view when opening document prompts FreeHand to remember the last view of a document before it was closed.

Remember window size and location prompts FreeHand to remember the size and position of the window that holds the file.

Changing the view sets the active page means that as you scroll or change pages, the page that comes into view will be the active page.

Using tools sets the active page means that if you use a tool on a page, that page is active.

Always review unsaved documents upon Quit means that you will be presented with a dialog box prompting you to save each unsaved document when you quit **9**.

New document template lets you change the file that FreeHand uses for the defaults file.

Search for missing links (Mac) lets you set which folder to search through for graphics that have lost their links to the original image.

Import Preferences

Convert editable EPS when imported means that, when possible, placed EPS files are converted to objects that you can select.

Embed images and EPS upon import means that the information necessary to print those graphics is embedded directly in the FreeHand document—not linked.

Convert PICT patterns to grays (Mac) converts the bitmapped patterns from MacDraw Pro and Canvas into a gray color.

DXF import options (Mac) control how objects are converted from the DXF format when they are imported into FreeHand.

Document Preferences; Import Preferences

PDF import options control how objects are converted from the PDF format when they are imported into FreeHand.

Clipboard paste format (Win) controls which formats FreeHand imports from the clipboard.

Export Preferences

FreeHand file preview lets you choose the type of image that is used for the thumbnail preview when opening files.

Bitmap PICT previews (Mac) changes the preview of files exported to programs such as QuarkXPress or Adobe PageMaker. This means faster redraw.

Include Portfolio preview (Mac) means that a preview is created for the program Extensis Portfolio.

UserPrep file field lets you choose the file FreeHand looks for when printing.

Override Output Options when printing (Mac) lets you choose between binary and ASCII image data. Your files print faster if you choose binary.

Clipboard output/copy formats controls the information on the Clipboard when you switch to another application.

Convert Colors/EPScolor space lets you save your colors in the various formats.

Spelling Preferences

Find duplicate words controls whether the checker finds errors such as "the the."

Find capitalization errors controls whether the checker finds mistakes such as "Really? how did that happen?"

Ignore words with numbers skips words such as H_2O.

Ignore Internet and file addresses skips entries such as http://www.vectorbabe.com or Hard Disk:artwork.eps.

Ignore words in UPPERCASE skips entries such as NAACP or UNESCO.

Add words to dictionary exactly as typed means that case-sensitive words such as "FreeHand" or "QuickStart" are entered with capitalization intact.

Add words to dictionary all lowercase means the words are not case sensitive.

Dictionary lets you choose the U.S. English or British spelling dictionary.

Personal Dictionary lets you specify the location of the dictionary that you add your own custom words for spell checks.

Colors Preferences

The boxes for **Guide color or Grid color** open color pickers where you can choose the colors for guides and grid dots.

Swatches shows Container color means that when a text block is selected, the Fill color shows the color of the text block.

Swatches shows Text color means that when a text block is selected, the Fill color in the Color List shows the fill color of the text, not the block.

Auto-rename [changed] colors means that the names of colors automatically change when their CMYK or RGB values change.

Color Mixer/Tints panel uses split color well allows you to compare any changes to a color in the Color Mixer with the original color.

Color management gives you options for how colors are displayed onscreen.

Panels Preferences

Show Tool Tips shows explanations of what the icons in the toolbars mean when your cursor passes over them **10**.

Clicking on a layer name moves selected objects means you do not have to use the options pop-up on the layer panel to change the layer an object inhabits.

Label tabs lets you choose text, icons, or text and icon for the tabs of nested panels **11**.

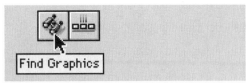

10 *Showing the* **Tool Tips.**

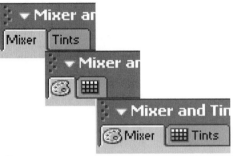

11 *The three settings for the labels for the panel tabs.*

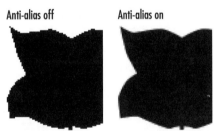

12 *The effects of the* **Anti-alias** *option.*

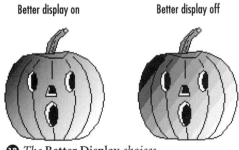

13 *The* **Better Display** *choices.*

Colors Preferences; Panels Preferences

Full-resolution preview	Low-resolution preview

⑭ *Two of the* Smart image preview resolution choices.

⑮ *The* Os *indicate that the fill overprints.*

When in the course of
human events it becomes

⑯ *An example of* Greeked text *(top) and visible text (bottom).*

⑰ *Dragging* without a preview.

⑱ *Dragging* with a preview.

Redraw Preferences

Enable Anti-aliasing adds soft edges to the display of objects onscreen **⑫**.

Better (but slower) display means that Graduated and Radial fills are displayed in smoother blends **⑬**.

Display text effects means that special effects such as Inline and Zoom are visible.

Redraw while scrolling means that you see your artwork as you scroll instead of after you finish scrolling.

Smart image preview resolution lets you choose low-, medium-, high-, or full-resolution previews of TIFF images **⑭**.

Display overprinting objects means that **Os** are displayed when an object is set to overprint **⑮**.

Image RAM cache (Win) controls the amount of RAM set aside for the import of images from other applications.

Greek type below controls the size at which text is *greeked* or displayed as a gray band **⑯**.

Preview drag field controls how many items are displayed as a preview as they are moved or transformed **⑰** – **⑱**.

TIP Press and release the Opt/Alt key as you drag to see a preview of all the items regardless of how the preferences are set.

Sounds Preferences (Mac)

FreeHand lets you hear sounds when you snap to different objects such as grids, points, and guides. The pop-up menu next to each action lets you choose the sound for that action.

None turns off the sound.

Play lets you preview the sound.

Snap sounds enabled turns on the sounds for all the choices.

Play sounds when mouse is up plays the sound whenever the cursor passes over the object, even if the mouse button is not pressed. (Very noisy!)

TIP While most changes you make to the Preferences settings take effect in your document immediately, they are not saved to your hard disk until you quit FreeHand.

INDEX

D

E

Index

Index

Index

O

Index